BACKPACKING
One Step at a Time

BACKPACKING

One Step at a Time

4th Edition

Harvey Manning

Foreword by Jim Whittaker

Cartoons by Bob Cram

Photos by Keith Gunnar

VINTAGE BOOKS

A Division of Random House • New York

Library of Congress Cataloging in Publication Data
Manning, Harvey.
    Backpacking, one step at a time.
    Includes index.
    1. Backpacking. 2. Backpacking—Equipment and
supplies. I. Title.
[GV199.6.M36 1986   796.5'1   84-40537
    ISBN 0-394-72939-0 (pbk.)

B987654

Contents

Foreword

Backpacking, camping, and mountaineering have grown tremendously in popularity since I came to REI (Recreational Equipment, Inc.) in 1955. As an outdoor equipment co-op, REI's membership and sales figures provide a reliable indicator of the increased interest and participation in the exploration of the outdoors.

My brother and I operated the guide service on Mount Rainier from 1949 to 1952. In 1951, 291 persons reached the summit. In 1983, 7,672 registered for summit climbs and over 3,600 reached the top! But as the number of climbers on the mountain increases, so do some problems associated with greater populations.

In our early era of climbing, the garbage at 10,000-foot Camp Muir amounted to so little that it was jettisoned, without qualms, into the nearest crevasse; and the single privy, precariously overhanging Cowlitz Glacier, handled every visitor. Now the guides backpack 60-pound loads of garbage down from Muir twice a week, and helicopters are dispatched to haul away the remainder, including the 50-gallon containers that support the four latrines.

The population explosion on Rainier's high rock and ice has been more than matched by increasing numbers of hikers in the meadows and valleys. These areas are much more fragile and very much in danger of being crushed by masses of backpackers and campers. The delicate ecosystems of alpine parklands, desert oases, ocean dunes, lakeshores, marshes, riverbanks, and the like are threatened everywhere. We must lessen the impact of the human animal on the trail country and wilderness. One way is by education.

People must be taught to be as unobtrusive as possible in the outdoors by adopting conscientious wilderness practices. These include: using small backpacking stoves instead of wood fires, dipping water out of lakes and streams to wash dishes and bodies rather than using soap in the lakes and streams, stopping in established campsites, staying on man-made or game trails, packing out all garbage, taking only pictures and leaving only footprints.

The alternative is to limit the number of people who walk the trails and climb the mountains, and thus deprive others of the opportunity to satisfy the basic human need to experience a wilderness environment.

I think the need to experience the outdoors exists even where it is not recognized or expressed. Throughout our nation there are "children of the cities" who have never known any valleys except avenues of paved roads lined with concrete walls, and mountains, to them, are nothing but skyscrapers of glass and steel. These people need to feel the freedom of wild places, high places, and realize all things natural—including themselves—are beautiful. They would realize they can grow and expand in an environment which, even when hostile, is fair. If we can lead them into natural valleys and mountains and teach them how to be comfortable there, then I think they will learn to enjoy, perhaps love, and surely respect, nature. With John Muir I say, "Climb the mountains and get their good tidings: Nature's peace will flow into you as sunshine into flowers, the winds will blow their freshness into you, and the storms, their energy—and cares will drop off like autumn leaves."

My climbs on Mount Everest and K-2 have left me with vivid impressions of the world's beauty. One moment I will never forget came on Everest in 1963. On May 22 we began our long descent from the basecamp established March 21, having been more than 60 days above 17,500 feet, entirely in the realm of snow, ice, and rock. Coming down the Khumbu Glacier, we left the ice at last, walking onto moraine, then down to Gorak Shep. Over twenty years later, one of my sharpest recollections of Everest is that startling vision of small green plants and that incredible odor of warm, musty earth. Several days on Rainier or any other peak rising far above the timberline give a similar sensation. I wish everyone could know that feeling.

In the 1980s and into the '90s, even greater pressures will be placed on the environment. Climbers, backpackers, skiers—the type of people who join REI—are an elite corps, you might say, in preserving natural values. No one knows better that we need the wilderness to bring people closer to their better selves, and we need places to be alone, where the wilds can bring us their good tidings. But we know full well that we also need, for survival, the raw materials of the earth. Our backpacks are aluminum, our pitons, steel, our fabrics and insulation are synthetics made from petroleum. Even as we stand alone on some rock outcrop looking at a landscape few have ever seen, we know we are part of the world of men and women, of industry and energy, of expanding demands on a fragile planet.

I have long urged REI members and others to take the lead in finding appropriate ways to use, enjoy and preserve our most precious resource—nature. I now urge you again. We are all, like it or not, on a dangerous voyage into the future. The exigencies of energy and economics will be constant companions—and not very pleasant ones. And in some quarters, sight may be lost of traditional environmental values. Not, I hope, among us who cherish the experiences of wilderness.

We realize the need humans have for experiencing our environment. I feel we have a responsibility to protect it and to set an example for new climbers, campers, and backpackers to travel carefully and considerately, to fit unobtrusively into the landscape, and to remember they are part of nature and any damage they do is—in the end—to themselves.

Jim Whittaker

Introduction to the Fourth Edition

It is said of hiking, as of shooting pool, that being expert in it is the sign of a misspent youth. However, as all children know, the blame for just about anything can be shifted to parents. For example, my father grew up in Lowell, Massachusetts, roaming Shedd Park, a vast wildland of oaks and hickories, woods violets and sweetferns. He fished for trout in Marshall's Brook, flowing from Tewksbury to the Concord River, and for kibbies and pickerel in the Concord. His headquarters was the Secret Camp, a giant glacial erratic. Banquets there featured potatoes baked in coals, apples roasted on sticks, ears of corn roasted in the husk, and whatever else farmers donated when they weren't looking. Meanwhile, across the continent, my mother was hiking the beaches of Puget Sound, exploring the inland sea by ferry and mosquito-fleet steamer and naphtha launch and rowboat and canoe, and digging clams and trolling for king salmon. All this was in my blood, or perhaps my genes, when I was introduced as a child barely walking to the World-Outside-the-City on fishing trips to streams of the Cascades and Olympics.

We were among the first Americans to exploit the new freedom—the freedom of proliferating roads and fast wheels—to pioneer a new way to the wilderness. The automobile brought within easy, inexpensive weekend reach places previously accessible to city folk only on lengthy vacations (which not many had) at considerable expense (which not many could afford). We were not long alone in the woods. The good tidings were heard. Car-campers thronged.

Decades later, when universities came to have professors of wild-land sociology, their research confirmed the expectation of common sense: the recreation of the youth and adult is determined by the recreation of the child. The *form* is not necessarily the same. The crux is the *feeling*. When forests of the car campground are lonesome and dark and quiet, the child is thrillingly scared. But when the campground becomes people-stomping and lantern-glaring and radio-blaring, the youth and adult must go deeper in the woods to be satisfactorily frightened. Thus it was that in 1937 I joined the Boy Scouts.

I was a second-generation Scout, among the earliest, because only in 1910 had Scouting formally arrived in America (though numerous troops were operating spontaneously and independently before this year of "chartering"). In 1915 Dad joined the local troop. On over-night hikes to remote Baptist Pond he learned to roll equipment and food in a blanket, tie the ends, and drape the "horse collar" across his body from one shoulder to the opposite hip, in the manner of the U.S. Army in the Spanish-American War.

My troop, north of Seattle, had plenty of room to find adventure in second-growth forests and along Puget Sound beaches. The climax of the year, though, was the summer week or two at Camp Parsons, on the shores of Hood Canal, at the foot of the Olympic Mountains. There I was trained in a unique hiking style, a synthesis of official-handbook Scouting, the local lore of wilderness mountaineering, and some special Parsons techniques, such as near-nudity and semistarvation, that permitted little boys to carry exceedingly light packs, enabling us to walk remarkably far and high. My first trip to camp, in 1938, I stood at 6,000-foot Marmot Pass in a July sunset and gazed into wilderness and for the first time *knew it was wilderness*. That night at Camp Mystery, a mile above sea level, I lay me down to try to sleep and for the first time was utterly exposed to the infinite iciness and eternal blackness of a totally wild mountain night. Never got over it.

Still on the trails these decades later, I find them much changed. There aren't as many of them, what with encroachments by subdivisions and highways and logging roads and ORVs and ATVs. And there are more of us. Indeed, in the 1960s, seemingly overnight, the trails became mobbed. To explain the abrupt transformation of the wildland scene, dismayed hikers propounded Devil Theories, charging various scapegoats with responsibility for destroying the old solitude. However, more widely accepted now is a less impassioned General Theory of Trail Demography that goes something like this:

In the 1920s and 1930s the automobile carried city folk to the wilderness edge. There we car-camping children heard the owls and felt shivers up and down our spines. But as car campgrounds grew tame we became the hiking youths and adults of the 1930s and 1940s. In the 1950s and 1960s we took along our children, who as youths and adults in the 1960s and 1970s, finding crowds in camps of childhood, moved to more pristine wilderness, on and off the trails.

Meanwhile, following our example and aided by faster cars, more and better roads, more money, and more leisure, another generation took over the car campgrounds in the 1940s and 1950s. Their children, following our example and aided by better equipment and more information, and more money and more leisure, moved to the trails in the 1960s and 1970s.

Two population waves rolled from cities to car campgrounds to trails to wilder trails. Both waves were enormously swollen by the baby boom of the 1940s and 1950s. And in the 1960s and 1970s they merged to become a single tsunami.

Though other factors have played a role, very clearly the popularity of backpacking today is largely the fault of Columbus, John Muir, Henry Ford, the Boy Scouts, the New Deal, World War II, my parents, and my wife and me and our kids. But in my confession I must also implicate Du Pont, Dick Kelty, Kraft Dinner, and geese.

If hikers today had to endure 1938 equipage and diet, few would last more than a night at Camp Mystery. Few did then.

Rainproof shelter, comfortable packs, edible foods, and warm sleeping bags have removed much anguish from wilderness travel. At a price. If wilderness could speak, it would protest bulldozers and chain saws and motorcycles—but also feet, feet, feet. And many hikers do speak up to declare themselves miserable in the equipment shops, suffering a bewilderment of riches.

Commiserating with wilderness and hikers, in 1971 Jim Whittaker, the first American to climb Mount Everest and general manager of REI, asked me to do a book that would (1) teach the "new ethic" of light-foot walking and no-trace camping and the Luddite responsibility to dismantle the Great American Energy Machine; and (2) guide hikers through the thickets of equipment, helping them assemble outfits good for them—and good for the fragile land.

A decade and a half later, here we are at the fourth edition of *Backpacking*. The book remains the same in substance and spirit, but all the equipment information has been updated, new photos have been added where appropriate, and a few more cartoons have been thrown in for clarity and fun.

A little should be said about the book's credentials. My career as a mountain bum, as noted earlier, began in the Olympics and Cascades. I spent a year of childhood in Massachusetts as well, hiking with Dad to the Secret Camp in Shedd Park, where we baked potatoes and roasted apples, once again donated by farmers when they weren't looking. Over the years I've also visited Canada's Cascades, Coast Range, Selkirks, and Rockies; Montana's Madison Range and other Rockies; Wyoming's Tetons; Oregon's Cascades and Wallowas; and California's Cascades, Whites, and High, Middle, and Low Sierra, from Desolation to Mineral King. Meanwhile, my bookmaking began as chairman of the editorial committee which in 1960 produced the first edition of *Mountaineering: The Freedom of the Hills*.

However, the unique credentials of this book derive not from my misspent youth or from any time misspent since then, but from the experience of the men and women of REI who since the founding of "The Co-op" in 1938 have hiked and climbed from Seattle to Greenland, Denali to Aconcagua, Alps to Himalayas, and in serving thousands of hikers and climbers have absorbed their experience as well.

In the old tale the farm youth grew to be the world's strongest man by lifting a newborn calf to arm's length above his head and continuing to do so every day until it was a full-grown bull. I had a comparable opportunity, my Co-op membership (card No. 1102) dating to when the retail store was a closet across the hall from The Mountaineers clubroom, recently moved there from its former location on a shelf in a gas station. The firm offered two boots (Curran & Green's Rainier and custom-made), one overnight pack (Trapper Nelson), and the hot sellers were ⁷⁄₁₆-inch manila climbing rope, 7- by 11-foot nylon life-raft sails, apple nuggets, onion flakes, and dehydrated spinach. (For clothing we went to war-surplus stores and J.C. Penney.) When the store expanded and took on paid employees, I was still able to keep pace because they were old mountain friends—Jim Whittaker, Gary Rose, and Mary Anderson—with plenty of leisure to help me select, for example, my first nonsurplus down sleeping bag. But then I neglected the regular lifting and a time came when the bull chased me out of the shop and over the fence. Whatever I know about equipment, or think I know, comes from my mentors.

The contributions of many who gave instruction for the first three editions live on herein, though their names are now regretfully consigned to the archives. For this fourth edition REI's Ken Blaker again provided the superlative services of Jim Cross as manuscript coordinator and dean of faculty, repeating his role in the third edition. Jim assembled the professors and organized the seminars and tutorials at which my education was renewed by (from the earlier faculties) Cal Magnusson, Mary Michel, Gary Rose, Suzanne Silletto, and Jerry Watt and (new this time) Mike Boshart, Bob Bury, Holly Cook, Nancy Fisher, Julie Johnson, Michael Lees, Dennis Lombard, Bob McPeters, Rich Rockseth, Terry Shively, Jane Stewart, Bill Sumner, and Lynn Walsh. Particular note must be made of the dean's efforts above and beyond recruiting the faculty and himself reviewing the manuscript. In the course of discussions on how to cope with the Great Plague currently devastating the backcountry (see Chapter 4), he undertook personal research by contracting a first-class all-out explosive case of giardiasis.

My home chancing to be in the middle of a hotbed of backpacking, a number of other shops are readily at hand, and they have been notably kind to a slow learner. During a period when I was experimenting with superlight footgear, destroying these sampan "boots" in weeks or days and my arches and Achilles' tendons only less rapidly, Swallows Nest took pity on my hobbling and gave me a pair of Asolo Superscouts, my personal on-foot introduction to a new breed of boots—lightweight yet not harmful to the health. Simultaneously I was receiving instruction in the fundamentals of bootmaking and the state of the art from Dave Page the Cobbler, who for years has marveled at how rapidly boots decompose on my feet and has striven to help me mend my ways. An Eddie Bauer shop is so close to Cougar Mountain that my wife can run there quickly to buy me a new pair of pants when the old ones become a scandal. It's always a delight to stop in Marmot Mountain Works to see 625 fill-power goose down and Early Winters for the newest in wilderness musical instruments and the latest rates on renting a llama. Other shops around Puget Sound have been helpful, whether they know it or not, despite some doubts about the anonymous customer who looks at price tags, shrieks, and flees. ("Who *was* that masked man?")

Catalogs of outfitters whose premises lie beyond a visit are thoroughly reviewed to be sure the entire nation of backpackers is marching to approximately the same drummers.

Information gained from all the above is the more important in that as a matter of principle I read no other books on the subject, on the grounds that merely *writing* one risks an exposure to the subject matter exceeding safe limits. I also avoid magazines, though Jim Cross and his professors often press an article on me. The exceptions are *Sunset* magazine, whose Northwest Editor, Jim Poth, does his research so meticulously it would be a waste not to borrow his results, and our local *Signpost*.

For information on the early years of Scouting I'm indebted to the late Harvey Simpson Manning, and on military history to Harvey Paul Manning, and on how to lead children in the wilderness, to Penelope Lou, Rebecca Jo, Claudia Anne Manning, and new recruits Julia, Jenna, Christopher, and friends. Betty Manning served as rear guard and omelette cook and mushroom tester, permitting the rest of us to enjoy new species of fungi in safety, forty-eight hours later. Other companions of peaks and bushes have requested they not be named here.

Indispensable to these past three editions have been letters from the readers. A girl described with great sensitivity her first venture on wildland trails, at the same age I was at Marmot Pass. (Many things change, but many remain the same; all is not lost.) A fellow troglodyte recalled certain memorably disgusting meals of the 1930s. (For some changes, thank golly.) Hikers from just about everywhere corrected errors, criticized opinions and prejudices, offered their own, compensated for my provincialism by describing how it is in their home provinces. Obviously a great many American childhoods, youths, and adulthoods are being profitably misspent.

Harvey Hawthorne Manning

Part I

Off and Away on the Trail

1
How to Walk

People whose memories go back a baker's dozen of presidents and a quartet of major wars remember when nearly every American was an expert walker, traveling by foot to work and school, taking morning constitutionals and evening strolls, idling away Sunday afternoons on park paths or country lanes.

Nowadays, though, in an age and nation where the definition of Homo sapiens has been amended to "featherless *wheeled* biped," few urban folk know more than the rudiments. Everyone legs it around town a little, but awkwardly. City walking is too disjointed—from stoplight to stoplight, from parking lot to supermarket—to develop rhythm. Hard sidewalks heat the feet and gelatinize cartilage and rattle the vertebrae. Walkers sweat—considered impolite in mixed company. And in three-cars-per-home suburbs the mere fact of being unwheeled—unless huffing and jiggling in jogger's skivvies—is prima facie evidence of criminal intent.

Nevertheless, any nondisabled person can quickly master the refinements, even if his longest habitual journey afoot is from subway to elevator. Mark Twain pronounced Russia a nation of geniuses, observing that tiny children there were fluent in a language so formidable that despite listening intently he couldn't understand a word. Americans similarly marvel at how adeptly their offspring skip about. Yet in every creaky adult is the nimble child—once off wheels onto feet, the body recovers old skills. No coaching is necessary, no manual instructing how to point the toes and bend the knees and what to do with arms and teeth. Such manuals have been written; the U.S. Army prepared one but abandoned it when the troops became so intent on doing what the sergeant said that they all fell down, and the sergeant too. To learn (to remember) to walk well, one simply goes walking.

The major obstacles are mental. The beginner (relearner) may be alarmed by a new awareness of heart, lungs, and muscles and imagine he is at the point of death. Also, after years of swift motion on wheels, the slow passage of the landscape may lead to a sense of futility.

The following discussion, therefore, pretty much ignores mechanics and concentrates on attitude; the intent is to help the reader overcome superstitions and enjoy an easy and pleasant transition from enslavement by machines to the freedom of the feet.

PACE

How fast a pace is too fast? Too slow? Just right?

Manuals often declare 2 miles an hour is the proper rate for such-and-such circumstances and 3 mph or 4 for others, and that 1,000 feet of elevation gain per hour is socially respectable if not quite admirable. All such pronouncements should be ignored; there are too many variations among individuals, and trails, for any rules to be meaningful. A small child may do well to toddle half a mile an hour while a troop of competitive boys are running 5 miles. Gaining 500 feet of elevation an hour may destroy an accountant wheezing after a long winter at a desk; a logger may climb 3,000 feet an hour while sucking a jawful of snoose.

Travel times given by guidebooks must be viewed with suspicion. One guide has been published by an egomaniac plainly aiming to

humiliate all who follow in his path. Another was written by two hill-hardened geologists whose legs separate just below the neck. At best a guide inevitably is hung up on the elusive "average." Average *what*? A hiker must test each book individually, comparing his own times on sample trips with those stipulated, and in this manner find a personal conversion factor.

How fast a hiker *can* go is one thing; how fast he *wants* to go is another. Some find joy whizzing through wildlands, jotting in their journals: "Made it from Bug Bog to Blister Pass in 3 hours 7 minutes flat—18½ minutes better than my previous best and possibly a new record." To each his own. Racers don't hurt anyone except competitors gnashing teeth because their best time from Bug to Blister is 3½ hours.

Most hikers, though, aren't out to set records but to enjoy the full walk, the trees and flowers and birds and waterfalls, the clouds and breezes and horizons. The most pleasurable pace gives each of these its due and thus is somewhat or considerably slower than the maximum. (Of course, when darkness is near and the goal distant, or clouds of flies gather for the kill, the rule is to say the heck with fun and *run*. Or at least stagger as rapidly as possible.)

Setting the Pace

The beginner must understand that despite superficial similarities, the walking done by the ordinary hiker and backpacker is not akin to running or jogging or "exercise walking," glanced at, somewhat askance, later in this chapter. Its goal is not to expiate sins by self-flagellation or to batter the consciousness into a mystical experience. The walker sets his pace to make the body feel good, not bad.

Legs and lungs and heart are the monitors. When legs feel leaden—slow down. When lungs seem about to burst into flame—slow down. When the heart is battering the ribs—slow down. When a chipmunk by the path dispels all awareness of legs and lungs and heart, the pace is just right.

Comfort is important not merely for its own sake but because only a tolerable pace can be sustained. The dash-and-drop tactics of novices—going at top speed until completely breathless, gasping to a halt, then resuming all-out attack—are a constant misery and over the long haul slower than a steady plod.

The first stretch of trail should be taken at a deliberate loiter; the body, slothful from sleeping bag or car, complains less if introduced gradually to the task. Speed automatically increases as muscles loosen and juices flow free and easy; often there is a sensation of "second wind," indicating the system has gotten it all together.

How Long a Walk?

The beginner, while experimenting to see how fast he can walk comfortably, must also find how far he can walk, taking into account not only mileage but elevation gain—5 miles with a rise of 5,000 feet demand more energy than 15 miles on the flat.

Each hiker must learn his own potential and adjust ambitions to match. One may cover 20 miles a day, or gain 6,000 feet with ease; another may struggle to make 5 miles or 1,500 feet, or 2 miles or 500 feet. When personal abilities are defined, future trips can be planned accordingly, keeping in mind the beauty part—that the more one walks, the farther and faster one can walk.

Some hikers love traversing great distances in a grand rush, rambling a dozen or two miles in a day to feel a wildland unity—"the One that remains while the many change and pass." Others are content with several miles a day, lingering over rocks and springs and mosses.

A related matter is how many *hours* a hiker can travel in a day, regardless of pace. Fresh from a city desk a person may not be able to stand erect, much less move, more than 4 or 5 hours; a trail-toughened veteran may pick 'em up and lay 'em down 10 or 12 consecutive hours with no pain, or 16 or 20 when seized by the mood.

Water, Food, and Salts

Water is as essential to life as air; at rest the normal adult may require 2 quarts a day, more when working hard. In desert travel 4 quarts a day is a commonly recommended ration. Except in deserts, death by dehydration is a rare threat, but not debilitation— the average body is reduced in efficiency 25 percent by losing 1½ quarts of water, and during strenuous activity in hot weather this much can be perspired in an hour.

The old Puritan formula was to suck prune pits or pebbles, on the theory that excessive drinking endangers the soul. With dry martinis maybe, but not water. Except in areas where pollution is

a problem, the hiker should sample every tempting spring and creek and even in wet country carry a loaded canteen in case the dry spells are long. To be sure, moderation is the rule: gulping too much cold water can shock the stomach; also, dumping pounds of liquid into the body may require an extended rest while the bloated tank empties into the bloodstream.

Similarly, nibbling a snowball while walking a high, hot ridge—slowly, of course, to avoid "ice cream headache"—can prevent a blazing sun from shriveling the brain.

During hard hiking, lunch should be an all-day meal, consumed in small, frequent installments to provide a steady flow of fuel without overloading the stomach. Weariness tends to kill the appetite, leading to a vicious circle of deeper weariness, less appetite. Though the thought of food may be loathsome, the tired hiker should take a bit of candy, a sip of fruit juice; the shot of quick calories often miraculously revitalizes a depleted system by almost instantly raising the level of blood sugar. (However, a sudden *excess* of sweets can in some people trigger a complex physiological reaction in which the blood-sugar level is actually lowered.)

A person's precious bodily fluids are more than a simple sugar solution. As water is lost through perspiration, both in the *sensible* form (visible, palpable sweat) and the *insensible* (vapor exhaled unseen and unfelt from pores), so too are sodium chloride and other salts

essential to the inner chemistry. A hiker may nibble constantly and chug-a-lug at every stream and still grow weaker than the work alone can explain. Worse, he may develop headache, nausea, or muscle cramps. Or he may topple to the ground with heat prostration and awake, if lucky, in a hospital. The traditional remedy has been to swallow a salt tablet or two every several hours, washed down with water, and preferably accompanied by food. However, nowadays many hot-country travelers and heavy exercisers anywhere drink synthetic sweat, packaged as Gatorade or Gookinade or the like, and thus restore not only sodium chloride but the other vital salts. These preparations are said to win football games in Florida, help climb steep trails naked to the sun, and in deserts, even to save lives, never mind that they taste like what they are. All this notwithstanding, a dissenting medical opinion is that unadulterated water and a normal diet suffice to sustain the bodily fluids: additives may do a person more harm than good. So, ask your doctor and take your chances.

UPHILL

Rambling happily along the flat is easy enough—when the trail turns upward, that's the time of testing.

Physically speaking, the secret of success is meeting steepness with slowness, constantly adjusting the pace to maintain uniform—comfortable—energy output, heeding signals from legs and lungs and heart. For very steep grades and weary hours the *rest step* combines mental discipline with robot regularity: (1) one foot advances; (2) motion halts momentarily while the forward leg rests, unweighted, knee bent, the body entirely supported by the rear leg with knee locked; (3) the rear foot advances to rest.

Occasionally as low as 7,000 feet and commonly above 9,000, oxygen shortage may cause *mountain sickness*, the symptoms including lack of appetite, nausea, and debilitation. The immediate remedy is getting more air into the lungs, using the rest step, and at each pause taking a deep breath or two, best done by forcible, total exhalation, which results automatically in full and complete inhalation. The long-term cure is to *acclimatize*, devoting several days to a reduced level of ambition, accepting that for a time every High Sierra mile, for example, will be twice as long as an ocean beach mile. Somewhere around 7,000 feet a hiker usually begins to note a stretching out of the terrain. At 9,000 feet acclimatization may take 7 to 10 days; at 12,000 feet, 15 to 20. *Warning*: If bad headache or cough develops and persists, descend to richer air; if symptoms continue, hasten to a doctor.

Deterioration of the spirit often is the major uphill hazard. Hope dwindles as the ridge crest seems as far above in afternoon as in morning. Panic may trigger a mad assault, but as each crazed dash ends in collapse, the certainty of final defeat erodes the will. Despair is deepened by boredom; one may grow terribly sick of a tree that cannot be left behind, that stands there eternally mocking the sluggish pace. The answer is to forget the impossible ridge, ignore the wicked tree, and retreat into a reverie about baking brownies over a campfire, what tactics might have won for Darius at Arbela, the plot line of a Marx Brothers movie.

At last the best energies are spent and still the path climbs and the sun falls. What now? Cry a little perhaps, but better shift gears farther down, grind out a step at a time, and sink deeper into thoughts of other times, other places.

In the extremity, think no farther ahead than some easy objective.

Decide, for example, "I will take exactly 200 steps and stop for a breather." Or, "I will go to that boulder, then decide if I can continue or must lay my bones down, nevermore to rise again."

DOWNHILL

Downhill travel is simpler than uphill, as witness a falling rock. However, though some muscles and organs can pretty much relax, on a steep and rough trail other parts of the body take their lumps.

One alternative, typical of the young, is a semi-run, letting gravity have its way; but the jolt of each hard landing may reverberate up the spine and hit the head like a club.

The other method, favored by older folk, is patient restraint; but the knees, in holding back body weight, may become as loose as a rag doll.

And it is on the downhill that blisters blossom. Before beginning a sustained drop, tender places (the fronts of the toes) should be taped, an extra pair of socks added, the boots laced double-tight. The first sensation of hot spots on soles or toes demands an instant halt for repairs (see Chapter 8).

REST STOPS

Walking is two separate and equally important actions—moving and not moving. Rest stops do not in themselves advance a party toward its destination but are an integral part of the long day's journey— and at least half the fun.

Manuals are full of rules. One expert dictates a mandatory stop every 40 minutes, lasting precisely 2 minutes. The hiker is forbidden to sit down, presumably lest he forget his sinful nature or even succeed in sucking juice from the prune pits. Rules are excellent for games, and for wars, too—resting by the clock and marching in column by the bugle are appropriate en route to battle. Civilian pedestrians, though, generally lean more toward a comfortable anarchy.

Particularly with a party of any size, a halt usually is necessary

in the first half-hour for relacing boots, shedding sweaters, adjusting packs, and stepping privately into the bushes.

Beyond that there is no formula for frequency. Many hikers like to charge from trailhead or camp an hour or two without pause to get a few quick miles under the boots for the sake of a lazy afternoon. An interval of 30–40 minutes is more typical; near the end of a tough day, 15–20 minutes. A person who must stop every 5–10 minutes should try a slower pace. But when time is plentiful, each waterfall, vista, and marmot on a boulder demands attention—after all, this is what the hike is about.

Neither is there any formula for duration. A party on a tight schedule must be content with efficiency stops of several minutes and resume walking before muscles cool and blood slows. Another party, on so loose a leash that wherever they are is exactly where they're supposed to be, may pause a half-hour to hear out a bird song all the way to the coda or watch a bumblebee creep inside every bluebell in the meadow.

In early hours, with the entire day's task yet to be done, hikers tend to rest briefly. In late hours of a slog they commonly go down like falling trees and lie inert like logs until moss grows on their boots. At any hour a standing breather lets legs and lungs and heart catch up with past overexertion—as in commencing a long uphill grind too fast—in preparation for resuming at a more respectful pace.

Morning, noon, or evening, after a very long rest hikers should go gently a bit, just as at the start of the trip, while muscles reloosen and the heart works back up to speed.

Stops are so important that they should, whenever possible, be selected carefully. That is, if a rest will be wanted sometime soon, it is well not to collapse in a swamp but to glance at the map to see what lies ahead and then totter on a few more minutes to a bubbling creek, a splendid view, a field of flowers, a patch of cool shade.

SOCIAL PROBLEMS

The complexity of walking increases geometrically with party size, as Napoleon found on the retreat from Moscow. Many problems can be eliminated by abandoning the Grand Army and traveling in small groups.

The lone hiker has no social difficulties at all, except the possibility of discovering, while talking to himself, that he's a bore. He must walk more carefully, suspecting every pebble and twig of plotting to kill him—in lonesome country they may be able to do so merely by twisting his ankle.

The etiquette of social hiking reduces to simply thinking about the other fellow. For example, a swift walker who crowds the heels ahead may lose a friend—or on a brushy trail suffer the retaliating discourtesy of willow whips released in his face without warning. By the same token, a slow walker should not frustrate friends by hogging the centerline but step graciously aside and wave them on with a smile. The dozens more rules that could be stated are adequately covered by the Golden Rule.

Strangers met on the trail deserve the same consideration—unless they are riding motorbikes, in which case the proper response is every manner of hostility short of lynching.

Marching in a crowd is far more exhausting and nerve-racking than tramping alone or with several companions. The pace of a bunch in close formation is always too slow for some, too fast for others, a pain for all. The garrulous walker is also disruptive, constantly forcing conversation; the big mouth has plenty of spare breath but the gasper may be prevented by politeness (which develops into hatred) from settling into an efficient breathing rhythm. Thus, unless individual paces are nearly identical, an experienced party generally strings out on the trail, regathering for sociability at rest stops.

However, if the route is obscure or the party green, safety takes precedence and the rule is: *Stay together*. The inconvenience is nothing compared to that of a search.

A WORD TO WOMEN (AND THEIR MALE COMPANIONS)

All but hopeless sexists, of whichever sex, admit that when it comes to hiking, a woman is just like a man—just as fast (or slow), just as strong (or weak), just as tough (or delicate), just as brave (or timidly), just as smart (or dumb). If short-legged or small, perhaps she can't hold the same pace as a long-legged man or haul the same load as a broad-shouldered man, but these are consequences of size, not sex.

However, one sexual characteristic has occasional significance, and novice hikers (both women and their male companions) should be aware of the possibility. In a few women the exertions of hiking or the effects of high altitude sometimes upset the menstrual cycle; the period may come earlier than usual and/or with an exceptionally heavy flow. Therefore, until a woman learns by experience how backpacking affects her, she must on every trip be prepared for the unexpected with a sufficient supply of tampons or napkins—plus plastic bags to carry them out of the wilderness if they cannot be *completely* burned in a wood fire.

Moreover, such accompaniments of the period as cramps, nausea, weakness, dizziness, irritability, and headache may be intensified.

Modifications of the planned schedule may be necessary, perhaps not hiking as far as intended or laying over in camp a day.

Finally, the odor of a woman's period attracts bears, aggravating danger to the party's foodstuffs, and may anger them—especially to be kept in mind when visiting grizzly country.

It should be noted that pregnancy need not deter hiking. Many a woman continues backpacking until ready for the delivery room and is off on the trails again in a matter of weeks, baby on back.

GETTING IN CONDITION

Most hikers earn their bread in sedentary occupations that tend to make them soft and sloppy and miserable. Partly this is why they go walking—to toughen the flesh and gain the smug self-satisfaction of healthy animals. However, to go directly from city to trail can be humiliating, depressing. Legs wobble, heart pounds, lungs heave— is it worth it? Why not buy a motorcycle and exploit the only part of the body in top condition after years of freeway and desk and television?

Despicable thought. Pride forces the alternative—to restore function to other parts of the body that have been allowed to atrophy or bloat. The best conditioning for the trail is the trail, and the ideal schedule is trails every week the whole year, but if a person can enjoy trails only for a limited season, he should commence with short trips on easy paths, the length and difficulty gradually increased. If trail country is far from home, strictly for vacations, city prisoners can get into shape—or better, stay in shape—through any exercises (swimming, bicycling, canoeing, handball, tennis, calisthenics, dancing the polka, pushing away from the table) that expand lungs and toughen muscles and slim guts.

Once thoroughly out of condition a hiker must be prudent. Unless the exercise—walking or any other—forces the heart to speed up and the lungs to labor, they are not being improved. Indeed, a healthy person should go at his conditioning with aerobic verve, to the point of racing heart and gasping lungs, because when pushed near limits, the body most rapidly extends its limits. However, at those limits lie (having fallen) the tennis-court cardiacs. Medical advice is the essential preliminary to any rigorous conditioning program; the prescription may well be to forget the verve, to go slow and easy on a longer but safe program.

Jogging and running, whatever their intrinsic merits, are not as good preparations for walking as walking. They use and thus condition different muscles. They require special equipment and care to avoid tendonitis, shin splints, runner's knee, crushed vertebrae, and dogbite. In fact, the booming business reported by podiatrists, plus a growing opinion that running is boring, has engendered a new fad—walking. A tidal wave of manuals telling how to point the toes and bend the knees. A parade of authors promoting books on TV talk shows. A technical jargon one can't understand without reading the books. A uniform to distinguish respectable middle-class walkers from hoboes. A nationwide epidemic of falling down.

It must be hoped the newly christened "exercise walking" or "fast walking" (distinguished from "race-walking" or "heel-and-toe," an Olympic event) survives beyond faddery. Walking is every doctor's panacea for the ills of civilized man. Without the medical risks of jogging and running it does as much to strengthen the cardiovascular system, relieve hypertension, tone muscles, improve posture and digestion, and burn calories that otherwise would turn to fat. Moreover, the medicine is as strong, though somewhat larger dosages are required—an hour's fast walk is roughly the equivalent of a half-hour jog or a quarter hour all-out run. Absent are the thousands of traumas to skeleton and heart. Further, the fast walker readily attains "runner's high," the glow of well-being caused by endorphins and hormones released in the body by hard work, and the sensation of exalted transcendence that comes with hypoxia, the lack of oxygen in the brain.

But there is also "not-so-fast walking." Granted, it lacks mortification, deprivation, expiation, and mystic vision. But it's fun. The fast walker, with the runner, looks inward to his soul, not always a pretty sight. The pleasure walker looks outward to flowers and clouds, dependably nice. And though the dogs bark, they seldom bite.

THE LIGHT FOOT

When the country was young and empty, the lonesome pioneer, fearing for his survival, built paths and roads for safety and convenience without concern for how they affected the health of the wilds. Now the country is getting older and very full, freeway promoters are not cheered but hissed, and the reflective walker fears for the survival of the wilds.

Most of the world is so traumatized by plow and wheel and house, chain saw and bulldozer and motorcycle, that a regiment of King Kongs wearing army boots couldn't walk heavy enough to make a perceptible dent. But in some of the world—the best part, hikers would say—machines are banned and a major punisher of the landscape is the human foot. One can easily slip over the line into silliness about this. After all, avalanches and floods and elk radically remodel the scene and nobody denounces *them* from a pulpit. But that's because avalanches and floods and elk *live* in the wilds; the human walker, a visitor, must be respectful and polite, must walk with a light foot.

Just as cities and highways can be very good things in their proper place, so too can trails, despite being strips of devastation, if they stay where they belong. To help maintenance crews keep them under control, hikers should not kick dirt for the sheer heck—such as by running wantonly downhill, whooping and hollering and jumping and skidding and churning. They should not cut switch-backs—shortcuts become erosion gullies. They should walk on the trail, not beside it to stay out of the rut—the parallel tracks in turn become ruts.

Off the trail the rules are more complex, require more judgment. The aim is twofold: (1) to avoid building new trails with the boots; (2) to avoid damaging plants and soils. For the sake of the first goal, in suitable terrain a party should fan out rather than travel single file, should shun incipient paths, choose rock or snow in preference to flowers and dirt. Often easier said than done. And often for the sake of the second goal it's better to follow an obvious game trail, already for, lo, these many centuries a brown track beaten through the green. Common sense tells us where feet hurt the land most—such spots as the deep but soft and easily erodable soils where meadows dip to lake or river, and barrens of steep, unstable scree where tiny plants struggle for roothold.

A considerate person who understands that his feet are small bulldozers will guide them wisely. He won't, for example, spend the evening running around a meadow playing with a Frisbee.

2
Hoisting Pack on Back

A hiker may enjoy a rich wildland life never carrying a load heavier than fits neatly in a rucksack. Especially in the Alps, where huts are closely spaced, and parts of America with an abundance of near-city trails, a person can walk miles and years and always eat supper at a table and sleep in a bed under a roof.

But the day is only half the trail world. Hoisting pack on back has great symbolic importance, signifying acceptance of the other half, the night.

Day is simple by comparison; with a commitment to night come sleeping bag and tent or tarp, cookstove and pots, suppers and breakfasts—and the pack.

Backpackers grow sentimental about the "stone" that holds all necessities and amenities—is bedroom and kitchen and wardrobe complete in one bundle—and delight in the renunciation it expresses of the appliance-cluttered house in the city, the pollution producer parked at the road, and all the frenetic complications of a society up to its neck in material possessions. To be sure, the renunciation is temporary, but the brief escapes into simplicity—and the anticipation beforehand and the memories afterward—do much to settle nervous stomachs and calm trembling hands.

However, though the veteran feels freedom in hoisting the load, the beginner, particularly the reluctant one bullied by family compulsion or social pressure, may feel naught but dread. There is, first of all, a fear of the night inbred by millennia of hiding from its jaws that bite and claws that scratch, its things that go bump, in the tightest available cave, hut, castle, house, or apartment. And second, there is a suspicion the sport might be prosecutable under the statutes covering sadomasochism.

EASING IN GRADUALLY

Very sad cases are on record of disastrous introductions to backpacking, even when the equipment was ideal and the country beautiful and the weather superb. Such as the honeymoon couple setting out for a week in the wilds, the longtime-hiker husband gently helping his never-having-hiked bride into the pack straps, and her toppling to the ground and lying there sobbing. The scene is the more poignant when the roles are reversed.

Generally it is best to learn (remember how) to walk before attempting a backpack. The promoters of exercise walking tell us that walking 2½ miles an hour while carrying a pack weighing 12 to 25 pounds gives the same cardiovascular benefits as running 7 miles an hour; these benefits, though, are not so apparent at the time they're being obtained. On afternoon strolls, unloaded, then day hikes with rucksack, the use of lungs and legs is mastered, irrational fears allayed.

Having grown familiar with wildland days and accustomed to 10 or 15 pounds, the time arrives to try the "complete home" pack of 20 pounds or so and penetrate mysteries of the night.

Wisdom and nonsense have been written about how heavy a load a human can haul. Again, each hiker must experiment to discover his capacity. A rule with more basis in reality than most is that a person of average strength can carry about one third of body weight, or 60 pounds for a 180-pound man, 40 pounds for a 120-pound woman; of course, these figures are above the comfort range—the man will be happier with 40 pounds, the woman with 25. They

also assume the body is not overweight and thus substantially burdened even without a pack. They further assume equal conditions of health; in some partnerships it's the little woman with the strong heart who carries the heavier load, the big man whose weak heart must be protected from *macho* vanity. The body-weight rule does not apply to growing children; however, the average girl at fourteen and boy at sixteen have adult capacities.

The rule perhaps has as many exceptions as applications. Tiny porters employed by expeditions often carry half or more their body weight, as do American backwoodsmen and climbers. ("It's not the stove that bothers me," says the legendary iron man to the awestruck stranger met on the trail. "It's the darn sack of flour in the oven shifting around and throwing me off my stride.") A frail person, even after attaining top condition, may stagger under a quarter or fifth of body weight.

Then, how far can the stone be toted in a day? Some may never manage more than 5 miles with 25 pounds, while others may easily do 15 miles with 60 pounds.

Finally, how heavy *must* the load be? With moderately careful planning, 20–25 pounds can be adequate for every eventuality of an overnight or 3-day trip. Some experts regularly go for a week in mild-climate, gentle country carrying only 30–35 pounds. Travelers of rough and stormy wilderness, perhaps not quite so attentive to ounces, eating somewhat better and having included gear essential for foul weather and emergencies, find 40 or 50 pounds more common for a 9-day trip—and that therefore 9 days is close to the limit for a hike in reasonable comfort, though shaving grams and gritting the teeth can extend the length to 2 weeks before having to resort to relay-packing or horses.

In summary, the beginner must test his own back, starting with modest loads and short hikes, and gradually increase the pack weight and the length and duration of trips; this cautious progress is also important when an experienced backpacker is initiating a novice. Maybe that honeymoon would be better spent day hiking and car camping, with an occasional night in a mosquitoless motel.

ORGANIZING THE PACK

In olden days the typical pack consisted of a single large bag or a tarp-wrapped bundle lashed to the frame, and the entire contents had to be dumped out whenever any article was wanted. The modern pack eliminates the bother, specifically designed as it is for efficient organization.

Still, the hiker must give some thought to stowing gear; any system will work so long as he remembers what it is. Obviously, things used only in camp, such as supper food and cooking pots, belong inside the bag, and those required on the trail or for emergencies, in the outer pockets. Aggravation can be saved by always putting each item in the same place to avoid, for example, unzipping every pocket, every time, to find the matches.

Chapters 7–15 discuss what should be carried; a preliminary word needs to be said about what shouldn't. Will that third sweater really be necessary? Will anybody be hungry enough to eat all those canned peaches? Will any possible storm be long enough to get through the unabridged *Cambridge Medieval History*?

Considered individually, each item may be small and weigh only ounces and "come in mighty handy once in a while." But a dozen superfluous articles add up to the pounds that can lengthen the final miles of the day to infinity.

When assembling gear, the hiker should give every piece of equipment a hard-eyed scrutiny. The Ten Essentials (see Chapter 15) must be exempted, but all else demands careful consideration, remembering that mile by mile, hour by hour, the stone grows.

LIVING WITH THE STONE

Walking with a pack is the same as walking without one, only more so. The pace is slower, the day's range shorter; rests are needed not only for the legs and lungs but for the aching back.

There are two basic ways to get into a pack: (1) Grab it by the shoulder straps and lift to the knee, slip one arm through a strap, swing the load onto the back, and slip in the other arm. (2) With pack on the ground, sit against it, slip on the straps, then turn onto knees and stand up. To get out of the pack, reverse. When the load is very heavy, rest spots should be chosen so the latter method can be used. In any event, the hiker must never, no matter how weary, drop the pack hard—that's how frames are broken and bag seams split.

Brief breather rests give more benefit if a boulder or log is available upon which the pack may be set while still on the back, the weight thus momentarily removed from the body.

When the pack is taken off on steep terrain it should be placed with care; nothing is more depressing than watching bed and board bound down the meadows, over a cliff, into a river.

The backpacker has options in scheduling not open to the day-hiker. For example, when the planned camp lies thousands of feet up a sun-blasted slope, the party may prefer to spend the dessicating afternoon sacked out by a river, cook supper there, and make the climb in the cool of evening. Similarly, walkers of deserts in spring-time typically take a "lunch" break of 4 to 6 hours, dozing in the shade of a cactus. In the Low Sierra in summer only mad dogs and visitors from the rainy Cascades go out on trails in the midday sun; the natives typically travel from dawn to late morning and from late afternoon to dusk; in the long interim they may be seen by suffering foreigners cooking a luncheon stew, snoozing under a Jeffrey pine, splashing in a creek that tumbles down granite slabs.

And when the moon is full and a broad trail follows a high ridge, the party may wish to sleep away the day to hike by night, seeing the world anew, answering coyotes howling all around.

By hoisting pack, the hiker accepts new chores, but gains new freedoms too.

3
Sleeping

The day's journey ends, packs are dropped, the hikers are home. If the weather is mild and night not urgently close and bugs no threat to reason, the first order of business is mixing a pot of punch, pulling off boots and slipping on camp shoes, and sprawling at ease to admire river or lake or ocean, forest or meadow, glacier moraine or desert oasis. Eventually (immediately in storm or impending darkness) the time comes to stir about on housekeeping duties, to build a bedroom and a kitchen. But gently!

Nostalgia for the Arcadia of barbarian ancestors was expressed years ago by Horace Kephart's *Camping and Woodcraft*, the classic on remodeling the landscape to suit a pioneer. The yearning persists so urgently that a bookstore may display fifty or more volumes on building log cabins, tossing salads of fern fronds and caterpillars, surviving with a fishhook and sharp stick, and other lore the frontier child learned as naturally as breathing. Woodcraft is good sport, and where forests are extensive enough to permit logging they surely can tolerate, in appropriate places, less drastic chopping and whittling. In the doing, something can be learned about times past, useful in understanding the present.

However, on most trails outside "classroom areas," woodcraft is dead. Dead because the modern equipment described in Chapters 11 and 12 makes pioneer-style engineering unnecessary. Dead because there are too many wildland visitors and too little wildland.

The goal of the new hiker is not to erect a replica of Fort Ticonderoga as an exercise in ingenuity but to camp so utterly "without a trace" that following parties must minutely inspect the site to find evidence of his stay.

Here, then, the subject of camping, to which libraries have been devoted in the past, is given a mere several pages—and these concerned less with what the beginner should do than what he should *not* do.

CHOOSING A CAMPSITE

In anthropocentric days of old, when folks were few and room for self-indulgence plentiful, camps were chosen for physical gratification and esthetic delight. Vanities though these may now be judged by wilderness Savonarolas, they still are not entirely contemptible. However, in biocentric days of new, they receive second priority. First comes the land.

For the Land's Sake

In the Golden Age the meager governmental presence in the back-country was single-mindedly devoted to dogmas of Smokey the Bear. So long as hikers stopped at the ranger station for a fire permit, didn't smoke while traveling or let campfires run away or otherwise conspire to burn down the woods, they were as free as the squirrels. About the only other subject of sermons was letting porkchop bones and whiskey bottles lie where they fell rather than burying them to keep the bears busy. Actually, Golden Agers had a sneaking fondness for the squalor of garbage dumps, which all popular camps were; it was homey. Through the generations, the kitchen middens grew—but slowly, because the backcountry population was so small.

Then came the explosions. Of population. Of garbage. Which were soon followed, to the grief of twenty-second-century archae-ologists, by an explosion of disgust, by a Great Big Cleanup Crusade that in a brief decade made the wilds tidier than they'd been since the invention of the tin can. However, resting from labors, garbage crews were dismayed to see that the land was by no means pristine. Campfires were burning green trees and silver snags and brown soil.

Boots were crushing flowers, sleeping bags flattening meadows. The
water was going bad.

So the crusade has marched on to more comprehensive objectives—preservation and restoration of primeval purity. Thus the
sent and continuing explosion of management, of regulation. Going,
going, where not already gone, is the laissez-faire of the Golden
Age, subverted by the population bomb.

As usual during crusades, there's a certain amount of turmoil in
American wildlands. Not every slob is submitting tamely to clean
living. Not every crusader has the patience of a saint. Though the
army of the faithful is united in the one true religion, it is split into
a number of sects. A substantial proportion of the old bare-dirt
camps inherited from the Golden Age are being closed for rehabil-
itation of the vegetation, hikers directed to new deep-in-the-bushes
sites, but not in every case is it agreed that the new camps are less
damaging and more pleasing than the old. The regulations in a
jurisdiction may be different from the one next door. The regulations
in a jurisdiction may be different from one year to the next. Administrators are studying human impacts, debating conflicting phi-
losophies, and experimenting with techniques of managing wildlands and hikers; in some cases they are changing their minds, in
others hardening into dogmatism. A perplexed hiker may decide to
flee to unregulated lands and fight it out with the loggers and
motorcycles.

Yet this, too, will pass. Regulations are not a burden when understood to be designed to provide visitors with the maximum practical
quality of wilderness experience while holding the impact on wil-

derness to the practical minimum, to be intended to counsel hikers on how to behave as befits an area "where the earth and its community of life are untrammeled by man, where man himself is a visitor who does not remain . . . which is protected and managed to preserve its natural conditions."

The primary means of achieving the maximum/minimum are restrictions on choice of campsites. The key tools are wilderness permits in (some) National Forests and backcountry permits in National Parks, issued at or near trailheads or by mail. Wilderness rangers (National Forests) and backcountry rangers (National Parks) who behave wisely do not so much police the regulations as host visitors.

In this time of flux a hiker must be very sure to learn the rules of the local game in advance. Arriving at the trailhead stoveless, discovering that wood fires are banned, means a lot of cold gruel. Traveling half a continent to find camping no longer permitted in Shangri-la is the cruel death of a dream. A vacation, a summer, may be shattered by the ranger announcing the whole wilderness is full up until a week from next Thursday, when the hiker is due back at his job in Chattanooga. Following are some of the regulations, and suggestions, current in this or that jurisdiction:

Avoid popular seasons, popular places. Go early and beat the rush, or late, when it's over. Go midweek. Don't go on holidays at all. Go places nobody (perhaps even you) ever heard of.

Limit party size. In some areas twelve is the legal maximum, in others less. A large family may have to get a divorce.

Limit total population. The permits do this. After managers determine the "carrying capacity" of a valley or basin—how many people it can accommodate at any one time, and in any one year, without serious damage—they limit campers, rationing the space (usually) by issuing permits on a first-come, first-served basis, offering latecomers suggestions on alternate destinations.

Beside the trail, concentrate impact. In many jurisdictions, camps are being specifically designated along major trails, and no other sites may be used. Elsewhere managers simply tell hikers to use established camps and to build fires only at existing fire rings. In both cases, a certain amount of "dustbowl" space having been accepted as inevitable to the human presence, campers are confined to the bare dirt, kept off the grass.

Off the trail, disperse impact and employ "no trace" techniques. Though in some jurisdictions no camping is permitted away from trails, in most the cross-country traveler can stay where he likes, though usually without a wood fire. To achieve the "no trace" ideal, recommendations are: camp on tough land, such as in forests, on ridge crests, on rocks, sand, gravel, even snow; do not camp on tender land, such as soft and wet meadows; do not camp near water, lest you pollute the liquid and mangle the shore; carry a collapsible container to minimize path-stomping trips to water; do no cutting, no digging; move camp frequently; if a site obviously has been used before, don't use it; upon leaving, obliterate every trace of your stay.

Preserve the experience. Even if it is legal, don't homestead a scenic shore or overlook, hogging the view. Respect the solitude of others by camping at a distance. Be quiet—the shouter intrudes on the peace of a whole valley. Use clothing and gear of subdued "earth tones" rather than circus razzle-dazzle—a gaudy tent intrudes on the isolation of folks miles and miles away.

Other ethical matters are discussed later in this chapter, in the next, and in Chapter 20. So much talk about virtue may well disgruntle veterans longing for the good old crummy laissez-faire Golden Age. Too bad about them—they shouldn't have had so many children. Perhaps when the population of America shrinks back to 120 million there won't be need for ethics anymore.

For the Hiker's Sake

Though the health of ecosystems has absolute priority, comfort and convenience still influence choice of camp; the great thing about modern equipment is that it permits a good sleep with a clear conscience.

The old woodcrafter rule was that a camp must offer wood, water, and shelter. But the new hiker carries shelter and fuel, and when need be, water, and thus can build cozy homes in spots that would have appalled Daniel Boone—a salt flat, a moraine, a glacier.

A camp with water still is better than one without. Aside from that, the main considerations are ground reasonably level (though not necessarily flat), reasonably dry (though ground sheet and/or tent floor plus sleeping pad allow sleeping in snow or a semi-marsh), and reasonably free of large rocks.

During rainy weather it is wise to avoid dips or swales that may become ponds or creeks; knolls and slopes are less likely to be flooded.

During windy weather the lee of a hillock or clump of trees may be sought; in buggy weather the wind may be preferred.

The study of microclimates—why ridges and knolls often are warmer in summer than valleys and basins, why passes frequently are cold and windy while meadows a few yards away are warm and calm, and so on—intrigues a hiker as he gains experience.

When regulations and conscience permit, a party obviously chooses a camp with a view of valley, peaks, waterfall, lake, garden, or whatever may be the local attractions.

MAKING CAMP

In the woodcrafter era preparing for night was nearly as lengthy as proving up on a 160-acre homestead. The hiker with modern equipment can do the whole job in minutes.

The only possible exception is shelter. Any tent is self-explanatory, and the typical tarp rigs illustrated in Chapter 12 are simple enough, but the techniques should be mastered in the backyard or during a car-camping trip or short hike rather than, say, at midnight on the tundra in a blizzard.

The first step in making camp, of course, is to set up tent or tarp (assuming shelter is felt necessary) on ground suitable for sleeping, perhaps removing prominent stones and logs that can't be slept around, making sure to replace them precisely later.

No regrade projects should be undertaken, no rock walls or wood tables or earthen dams built. Contrary to old custom, tent or tarp should *not* be ditched. Whenever possible, a site should be chosen with natural drainage away from the sleeping area. Otherwise, the new rule is to wait until the floods come and then scratch the very smallest channels required, carefully filling them when breaking camp.

Do not build a soft bed by cutting boughs, forbidden in most areas and anyhow unnecessary with the ground sheet/sleeping pad combination described in Chapter 11.

SANITATION

One more facility of the wildland home, the toilet, requires mention, because some hikers don't have the manners of a cat and many who do are puzzled about what to do for a sandbox.

Some backcountry camps are provided with privies and that takes care of that. Where hikers are on their own, three rules must be observed: (1) Pick a spot 300 feet or more from watercourses, whether or not water is running—go up on a hill in the woods or off amid boulders of a moraine. (2) Don't foul a site a following party may decide is a lovely place to pitch a tent or have a picnic. (3) Preserving sod if any is cut, dig a small hole, no deeper than 6–8 inches, in the "biological disposer" soil layer where active ingredients decom-

pose organic material in a few days, and fill in after, replacing sod; if the ground is too hard or rocky (a moraine) or too root-matted (a field of heather) for digging, cover the evidence with leaves or dead bark, loose dirt or gravel.

Be sure to explain all this very carefully to the children.

There remains the problem of toilet paper, which in dry climates may last out the summer, working its way to the surface or being mined by little nest-builders or big salt-seekers, then blowing in the wind, beflowering hill and dale. If the spot is not tinder-dry, a lighted match quickly eliminates most of the paper; otherwise, it should be gathered up and taken elsewhere for safe burning. An alternative increasingly favored because it also reduces the logging of forests for wood pulp is use of local vegetation; the only caution is to be wary—very sad stories are told of hikers who grabbed the wrong leaves.

COURTESY

In much-traveled areas, hikers must learn to get along with strangers. It is quite possible for dozens or scores of courteous campers to live congenially on an acre or two. However, a single thoughtless bunch can ruin the neighborhood.

A major stimulus to the popularity of backpacking is the bedlam of car-camping. See the dark and silent campground. At midnight, the new arrivals. They drive around and around, shining headlights at every site, occupied or not. At last they park—motor running and headlights on. For half an hour they perform the door-slamming ritual, then spread out and begin yelling back and forth. At 2:30 A.M. they go to bed—and an hour later are chopping wood, banging pots and pans, slamming doors, waking up the birds. Shortly they will be thrashing about the lake in motorboats or razzing the trails on motorcycles.

Backpacking does not offer total escape. For the moment forget (impossible, but try) the motorcycle invasion. See the troop of bois-terous children swarm into camp, and *hear* them—none going more than ten seconds without a shriek, whistle blast, or bugle call. The adults in charge smile benignly, drink covertly from flasks. See the packs of dogs, apparently only loosely associated with human companions, tour the scene, sniffing tents and stealing steaks. Hear the musicians, plucking guitars and singing through their noses far toward dawn. Campers who have been contemplating the solemnity and mystery of wilderness either grit teeth and begin suffering the nervous symptoms they took this trip to cure, or unrig camp and move on, seeking the peace and quiet of a snake pit or avalanche slope.

Noise is not the only pollution. Satan said, "Let there be light!" And lo, the gasoline lantern! Those who illuminate a camp invariably consider themselves benefactors and hang the lantern high so neighbors can enjoy the spillover. But the neighbors may wish to become one with the night; when philosophy is lost, they may sit in the harsh glare and make plans to buy noiseless, darkness-creating air pistols.

Certainly the sublime appeal of wilderness travel is the freedom to howl with the coyotes, to sweat and break wind, to be a natural animal unconstrained by stifling conventions. But whenever the population of a valley is considerable and a degree of crowding

unavoidable, each hiker should do his utmost not to pollute the quiet or the darkness, should strive to be more feline than simian.

In enjoying freedom, do not invade the freedoms of neighbors. Impinge not upon their rights and privileges lest they, in maddened retaliation, impinge upon yours and a lousy vacation be had by all.

4

Eating

As explorers slashing through Yucatan jungles were astounded to stumble on ruins of temples built by ancient Mayans, so do hikers now, chancing on rotting kitchenry of ancient woodcrafters, marvel at such industry for purposes beyond today's comprehension. To be fair to oldtimers, in their era meals of any kind beyond pilot bread and jam were complicated, and tasty dishes were just barely within the grasp of a talented and experienced engineer-chef. Now and then a grizzled relic still may be observed lashing poles to trees and pounding nails and bending wire and whittling twigs and piling rocks and rigging dinglesticks. His craft was hard-learned and he is loath to renounce it, to admit any beardless youth can eat well with no fuss, no muss. The new hiker ought to be patient with the old crock—he may be somebody's grandfather.

However, except on special occasions in "classroom areas," and only so the past shall not be forgotten (as history buffs dress in costume and refight the Battle of Gettysburg), the backpacker shouldn't manhandle the landscape for the sake of a dinner. Using equipment and foods described in Chapters 13 and 14, the beginner will find meals absurdly easy and quick to prepare and in a very short while he becomes an expert.

This chapter, therefore, has little to say about cooking and eating and is almost entirely concerned with lightening the pressure of the camp kitchen on tender terrain.

KITCHEN ORGANIZATION

An overnight hike requires no fancier advance organization than dumping cooking and eating utensils and food in packs—only making sure to do so. Discouraging words to be heard ten miles from the road: "But I thought *you* had the pots!"

For trips lasting several days or more, an hour of city preparation reduces time spent ransacking packs in camp. Complete meals may be packaged in poly bags (which also help keep foods dry) labeled Bean Supper, Oatmeal and Prune Breakfast, and so on. Considerable weight is saved by shucking cardboard and paper containers—but not the cooking directions! A simpler method is grouping foods at the trailhead into, say, Soup Bag, Candy Bag, and whatever. Cocoa and sugar and the like should be double-bagged to avoid sticky sweaters.

Meal preparation can be organized any number of ways. In a party of experienced hikers, typically someone rigs tent or tarp while another assembles pots and food and others start the fire (with wood or stove) and haul water—all wordlessly and automatically by in-

dividual initiative. Generally each meal should have a single boss; too many cooks kick over too many pots and in the confusion forget to stir the macaroni. Except in the presence of a master chef, the job usually is best rotated from meal to meal.

An inexperienced party, especially with a number of children, ordinarily needs a self-appointed leader or two (such as father and mother) to assign chores—preferably by mild request or suggestion and with instant cheerful acceptance. A regime of shouted commands and sullen obedience is the prelude to eventual desertion of the troops, if not armed mutiny.

FIRE

The backpacker stove (see Chapter 13) has become indispensable because that treasured symbol of the wilderness home, the wood fire, has been banned in much American backcountry, for good reason: heavily camped areas are wall-to-wall charcoal, fire pits replacing natural ground cover. In popular campsites all the easy wood was burned years ago, and gathering fuel is a pain in the neck. Where the wood is gone but fires are still allowed, idiot hatchetmen cut green trees—to no avail, since they won't burn—but in the process log parklands. In high meadows the only wood may be silver snags and logs, bleached bones of trees long dead; in a single evening a party may consume scenery that otherwise would have enchanted hikers for generations to come. Finally, it is disappointing to travel far from city smog seeking clean air and have to camp in an acrid cloud, coughing and crying from the smoke of a valleyful of fires.

Cooking With Wood

Still, the wood fire is not completely a memory. A stove is always less bother and gives more leisure for sunsets but seldom inspires philosophical reflections, and except in a tent is worthless for warming cold bones. In forests which annually yield a large crop of dead branches and windfall, in high valleys regularly receiving a fresh fuel supply from slope-pruning avalanches, on ocean beaches replenished with driftwood by each high tide—*and where campers are few*—fires are not immoral and may not yet be illegal.

Let it be noted, though, that a hiker's judgment and conscience only apply in the absence of regulations—build a fire in violation and a party risks a ticket, or worse, a sanctimonious lecture. Land managers, who in the era of empty trails didn't get agitated unless hikers burned whole forests, now have swung pretty much to the far extreme, generally condemning wood fires as the devil's work, at best viewing them as venial sins unworthy of the truly pure. Rules can be discussed with rangers but must be obeyed. And the most nostalgic of unreconstructed anarchists admit that past damage was so great that a time of overreaction, of conservative caution, is wise and proper. Eventually fire may regain some lost dominions, once the debate descends from the realm of theology to ecology.

In any case, even the hiker who always cooks on a stove should have some notion of how to start a fire in emergencies. (The life-saving value may be overrated, however—rarely can an exhausted person succeed in kindling soaking-wet wood; carrying proper clothing and a light bivouac tarp is more dependable.) As Smokey the Bear keeps warning, no technique is required when dry wood is

plentiful. In hard rain and wind the wiliest veteran may be defeated without supernatural assistance.

A few hints may help the beginner; for thousands more, consult the woodcraft literature. First gather a substantial supply of the driest wood available; in rainy weather, look under large logs and break dead underlimbs from living trees. No ax or hatchet is needed, nor should one be carried; if finger-picking fuel ("squaw wood") cannot be found, a fire should not be built and probably can't be, anyway. Some woods burn better than others; this must be learned through experience with local species.

Begin by igniting food-package paper, moss, twigs, or knife sliverings; the emergency fire starter from the Ten Essentials (or a splash of stove gas) may be employed if kindling is damp and wind disruptive. Proceed from small wood to large, never smothering the fire with excess fuel, helping as required by putting the mouth at the critical point and blowing sparks into flames, tiny flames to big. An enclosure of rocks—the traditional "fire ring"—increases efficiency by reflecting heat inward. A fire pan (Chapter 13), required in some jurisdictions, lessens damage to soil.

The kitchen fire should be small; if conscience permits, it may be enlarged later for a social or warming fire, but that's a rare indulgence nowadays. Pots are best suspended on a light metal grate (see Chapter 13), infinitely simpler and quicker than the dinglesticks and crossbars dear to the hearts of woodcrafters.

Minimizing Fire Damage

Whenever possible, an established fire ring should be used to avoid killing yet another patch of plants. If a virgin site is the only choice, virtually every trace of a fire built on bare dirt or gravel can be obliterated when breaking camp by returning fire-ring rocks to exact original positions and widely scattering ashes and leftover wood. A further step, if the fire was on living soil, is to restore a semblance of virginity and speed regrowth by mulching the spot with duff or humus.

The rules for putting out a fire are rigid and mandatory. Drown the ashes with water or snow and stir until all are cool to the touch. Drench fire-ring rocks (watch out—if very hot, they may explode) until none can possibly harbor a living ember. Make sure no underground hot spots are overlooked; a fire apparently out may creep beneath the surface in forest duff or along dead roots or buried sticks and, long after hikers are gone, erupt to the surface and sweep through grass, touch off forests.

The more talk about wood fires, the more reasons for carrying a stove.

GARBAGE

In the 1920s, reformers began replacing the drop-and-toss method of garbage disposal with "Burn Bash and Bury," a rule that sufficed in most American wildlands until mid-century. In such areas as the High Sierra, though, plant communities were destroyed at an alarming rate by pits dug to bury garbage—pits that often disinterred old garbage. And studies revealed that steel ("tin") cans do not reduce to soil components in less than 20–40 years, or in dry climates 100 or more; if gone they're not forgotten because iron salts leach into and "rust" springs, creeks, lakes, and meadows. The thinnest polyethylene takes 10–20 years to decompose, heavier plastics 50–80. Aluminum lasts 80–100 years, maybe 500; glass 1000 years, perhaps 1,000,000.

Thus a new law: PACK IT OUT.

Adherence wasn't instantly universal. For example, in the 1960s three elderly birdwatchers from Seattle were joined by an elderly birdwatcher from California for an 80-mile, 10-day walk across the Pasayten Wilderness. The Seattleites felt this section of the Cascades was so empty (then) that B, B & B continued conscionable, and anyhow nobody but a Sierra fanatic would put garbage in a nice clean pack. The fanatic didn't argue, but when companions started off after each meal to bury refuse, mildly asked if he could have it. At trip's end all the garbage plus the double-poly carrying bag were put on a scale. Total weight: *1 pound 14 ounces*. Seeing that it cost them merely ¾ ounce per man-day, the Seattle birdwatchers became fanatics too. And so, now, are all pure-hearted backpackers, everywhere.

PACK IT OUT means PACK IT ALL OUT. On the trail, stuff in pockets every gum wrapper and orange peel. In camp, if cooking on a stove, perhaps hold a discreet little paper fire to burn food packages—but don't bother on any hike up to 5 or 6 days; paper doesn't weigh that much. If a wood fire is built, paper and plastic may be burned—but not aluminum foil, some of which will oxidize but never all; inevitably the ashes glitter. Food packages of foil and paper or plastic are best given a quick burn in a hot flame, and the naked metal fished out before it starts disintegrating. Some hikers still like to scorch cans to remove food residues before stamping

The total nonburnable garbage of four elderly birdwatchers from a 10-day hike. Weight including carrying bag: 1 pound, 14 ounces. It's no strain to PACK IT OUT.

them flat for the garbage bag; others wash the cans along with the cooking pots. The final nicety is to spend a half-hour or more meticulously removing tiny bits of foil and unburned paper, orange peels, and egg shells while drowning and stirring the ashes—and meanwhile policing the camp for oddments of debris. Into the bag it all goes for hauling to the road, glorying in the name of garbage-men.

WATER

Keeping It Clean

Wildland water may be dirtied by rotting vegetation, fish, ducks, beaver, deer, coyotes, sheep, cattle, cloudbursts, or glaciers, and nothing much can be done about *them*. The most disgusting and dangerous pollution, however, is caused by humans, and there's no excuse for it. People-caused contamination can be easily eliminated from the backcountry if every traveler obeys several simple rules.

First, as discussed in the previous chapter, take care of toilet needs far from watercourses.

Second, minimize the human presence in the immediate vicinity of the water supply.

Third, rather than washing dishes in lake or creek, loosing food particles and detergent, carry buckets of water into the woods or up on a knoll and scrub and rinse there.

Fourth, don't put bodies in water unless there's lots of it, as in a big river, Great Lake, or ocean, and never where swimming is banned, and never soap up—bodies should be washed out in the woods with the pots.

Finally, when other travelers are observed polluting the water, politely ask them to stop, and if they ask why, tell them certain of the more horrifying details in the next paragraphs.

Cleaning It Up

Not since the Red Death held illimitable dominion over the domains of Prince Prospero has there been such panic as in the American backcountry the past decade. From time immemorial incautious travelers drinking where the buffalo roam and the deer and the antelope play, and also horses and sheep and dogs and humans, have on occasion performed, *con brio*, the Tenderfoot Tarantella, energized by any of a number of maladies caused by waterborne critters ranging from tiny viruses through large bacteria to gigantic amoeba and protozoa.

Giardiasis

A protozoan parasite first seen by microscope in the 18th century and subsequently identified in domestic water supplies of virtually the entire Third World, many major cities of the Second, and an amazing number of God-fearing towns in the heartland of the Amer-

ican First, was long supposed to be simply another of the myriad harmless citizens of the digestive tract. In the 1940s, however, *Giardia lamblia* was convicted as the culprit in an especially nasty intestinal disturbance, christened giardiasis. When excreted by wild or domestic animals or humans, the parasite's cysts—the dormant stage in which transfer is made from one host to the next—can survive for months, and not merely in murky soups of summer ponds but also in sparkling-clear snowmelt pools of winter. The following discussion reflects a dabbling in the massive literature, noting some of the scientific uncertainties, particularly where research to date is thin, but is based mainly on the very full, careful discussion by Dr. James A. Wilkerson in the 1985 edition of his *Medicine for Mountaineering*, for decades accepted as the standard manual for wilderness doctoring.

As the (confused and confusing) story goes in the massive literature, typically 1–3 weeks (or up to 6 months?) after ingesting the necessary number of cysts (50 or so, says one expert, while another says 10 will do the job, possibly even 1; to put this in perspective, in a single day a carrier may pass 500,000,000) the onset is announced by fever, chills, headache, vomiting, and fatigue. An acute phase of 3–4 days (or 2 weeks or more?) is characterized by explosive diarrhea, cramps, bloating, smelly burping, foul gas, anorexia, and

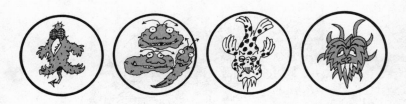

Representative inhabitants of various waters, and the maladies they cause. Left to right: *Free World—the Highland Fling; Second World—Red Revolutions; Third World—the Big Yak Attack; Mars—Canal Fever.*

weight loss. In 5 days to several months the parasite is usually entirely expelled from the body, leaving a resistance to re-infection. Often, though, a subacute misery continues indefinitely, perhaps with periodic recurrences of violence. A cure may demand a lengthy course of drugs, themselves ferocious. The acute phase is said to have so disabled victims they have had to be evacuated to a hospital by stretcher, mule, canoe, or helicopter.

Were only a handful of the horror stories true, the panic would be understandable—and so, too, the fire and brimstone loosed by hikers who come upon idiots blithely fouling wilderness waters.

The good news about giardiasis, as found by Dr. Wilkerson in his study, is that it "certainly is not the scourge it has been regarded." Less than half the individuals who drink water heavily contaminated by the parasite develop infestations; of these, only about a fourth feel any symptoms; symptoms, even if totally untreated, go away of their own accord after 7–10 days. As for the severity, an alumna of the Peace Corps in Equatorial Africa has commented, "When all we had was giardiasis, we thought we were *well.*"

Let it be noted that people who never feel any symptoms whatsoever may be carriers; by different estimates, 3–20 percent of United States citizens *are*, meaning many a victim is laid low by a healthy, smiling companion on the trail—or in the home. More than thirty species of animals have been identified as carriers; initially beavers headed the list, but new research suggests the wee timorous vole may be the worst subalpine miscreant; the question is still unsettled whether the wildland residents always were infected or whether man and his domestic animals have infected them in recent years.

The middling news is that plenty of wildland water is certain-sure safe. A person with common sense will suspect meadows roamed by farm animals, swamps busy with muskrats and beavers, and lakes ringed by horses and thrashing-full of human bodies. He will pause at a pretty brook and darkly speculate about possible atrocities being committed upstream, out of sight around the bend. Yet he is likely to feel quite confident about a wide, deep, swift river bellowing from a snow-white wilderness, a waterfall from a hanging glacier, raindrops that keep falling on the head. Many hikers stubbornly vow they will not give up burying hot faces in cold foam—not until they, personally, are struck down. They will be constantly suspicious, they say, but then, they always have been. They will consider the risk, balance it against the pleasure. They will take their chances with the protozoan, as they do with volcanoes and meteor showers.

The best news is that though *Giardia* cysts are hard to kill inside the body, and outside seem never to freeze to death, they (in company with every other aqueous malefactor) can be finally and absolutely destroyed by heating. However, whereas some sources say heating water to 158°F (70°C) for 3 minutes suffices to kill the cysts and every doubt can be dispelled by bringing the water to a rolling boil for 1 minute at sea level, 5 minutes at 10,000 feet, Dr. Wilkerson disputes the substantiation and finds 20 boiling minutes at sea level best supported by the data, and no verified data about the necessary time at higher elevations.

Still, fire is the answer, if there's enough of it. The problem occasions are when time or fuel won't allow frequent brew-ups, thirst grows as canteens go dry, and wayside water is dubious yet alluring. Before going to the alternatives, some worse news.

Hepatitis

Giardiasis is caused by a protozoan parasite. Most varieties of "tourista" come from bacterial infections caused by one or another of the innumerable strains of *Entamoeba coli* or by the parties responsible for salmonellosis, shigellosis, typhoid fever, or cholera. Far more devastating are hepatitis virus infections, for which no effective therapy is available and no vaccine, except for one type. Such infections can progress to chronic hepatitis, commonly cutting decades from the victims' lives.

Thus far, only two of the many hepatitis viruses have been isolated and characterized. One causes hepatitis A, which is most commonly transmitted via water contaminated with fecal matter. It causes mild illness (90 percent of patients don't know they're sick) and doesn't result in chronic hepatitis.

Hepatitis B, which can be transmitted by contaminated food or water but is spread primarily by body fluids, is much more dangerous, leading to a chronic type. It affects approximately 200,000,000 individuals around the world but fortunately can be prevented by a vaccine, urged for any traveler going abroad.

Non-A, non-B hepatitis has become notorious because it can be transmitted by blood transfusions and in about half of all cases comes from intravenous drug abuse. It is frequently spread by contaminated water in undeveloped countries and advances to chronic hepatitis more frequently than hepatitis B. The responsible organisms have not been isolated and thus no vaccine is available; travel to such nations as India is therefore extremely dangerous unless compulsive disinfection of water is rigorously practiced.

"So what is that to me?" shrugs the backpacker in the Canadian wilds. Well, the rate at which jets nowadays transport disease across the oceans (and helicopters into Canadian "wilds") must stir suspicion in the mind of anyone who drinks from a stream where returned trekkers have been disporting.

Chemical Purification

Boiling the water is the age-old remedy for every ill, whether caused by protozoa, bacteria, or virus. Equally dependable and frequently much more convenient is treatment with iodine. (Chlorine compounds, such as halazone, though used in most municipal water systems, are too unstable to be relied upon for wilderness purposes.) Even in moderately turbid water with organic color, at 73°F (23°C) and an iodine concentration of 8 mg/liter (8 parts per million) a contact time of 10 minutes eradicates bacteria, viruses, parasites, and parasitic cysts with a considerable margin of safety. In cold water (32°–41°F, or 0°–5°C) contact time must be increased to 20 minutes. For cloudy, heavily contaminated water, the iodine concentration should be doubled, to 16 mg/liter.

Contrary to warnings by misinformed laymen, iodine is not highly toxic. Individuals, even pregnant women, whose thyroid function is normal can consume water disinfected by 8 mg/liter of iodine for several months with no ill effects.

Tablets containing *tetraglycine hydroperiodide*, or *TGHP* (*Globaline*, *Potable-Aqua*) are convenient and readily available. A single fresh tablet dissolved in a liter of water gives the required iodine concentration of 8 mg/liter. The compound is stable in an unopened bottle but loses iodine when exposed to the air; bottles of tablets probably should be discarded a few months after being first opened. Use is very easy, demanding only that the disinfected water be visually inspected to ensure enough iodine has been released to produce a definite brown color. A single tablet, let stand 10–20 minutes, ordinarily suffices. A second tablet should be used in very cloudy water, and 20–30 minutes allowed in cold water.

Tincture of iodine, sold at pharmacies, is widely recommended but has little if any advantage over the TGHP.

The Kahn-Visscher method, utilizing a *saturated aqueous iodine solution*, described by investigators in 1975, has been denounced in inflammatory terms ("It can kill you!") because of the possibility of ingesting iodine crystals or breathing the sublimed fumes. In fact, neither risk is significant. Indeed, iodine poisoning is so rare that one hospital experienced no deaths among 327 patients who used it to attempt suicide. Iodine crystals (2–8 grams, USP grade, resublimed) are placed in a 30-cc (1-ounce) clear glass bottle with a paper-lined Bakelite cap. The bottle is filled with water and shaken vigorously for 30–60 seconds to produce a saturated solution. After the crystals have settled, one half of the solution (15 cc) is poured into 1 liter of water. If the water in the solution bottle is at 68°F (20°C), achieved by carrying it in a shirt pocket, the iodine concentration in the disinfected water is about 9 mg/liter. If 4 grams of iodine are placed in the small bottle initially, it can disinfect approximately 500 liters of water; so long as crystals are visible in the bottom of the bottle, there is enough iodine to disinfect.

For informed adults, who are aware of the relatively few and small hazards, particularly members of prolonged expeditions or urban residents of undeveloped countries, the Kahn-Visscher method is safe, convenient, and reliable. However, crystalline iodine is not sold in drugstores or backpacking shops and must be purchased from chemical supply houses; therefore TGHP tablets are usually preferred for ordinary outings.

A hiker relying on chemical purification does well to have two canteens: one always "working," and the other ready to drink.

Filtration

What the world really wants is not something to put in water to make it good but a device to take out all the bad. The ideal is a microstraining purifier that would remove everything except the water itself and add no chemicals or tastes. Inventors are striving to perfect a cheap product suitable for backpacking, and though one may be just around the corner, at this writing no trustworthy, inexpensive product is on the market. The two discussed here are accepted as having genuine value, but cost more than pennies.

Moreover, at this writing no filter has been validated as effective against viruses. Giardiasis and bacterial infection can be disarmed, but *to prevent hepatitis iodine must still be employed.*

FIRST-NEED is a nonchemical filter and hand pump, certified by the manufacturer, General Ecology, to have pores of 0.4 micron. It is classified by the federal Environmental Protection Agency (EPA) as a "purifier," a designation of some stringency, and has been adopted for field use by federal agencies. The company states that this pore size will remove *Giardia* and other cysts, tapeworms, protozoan parasites, chlorine, thousands of hydrocarbons, asbestos and fiberglass, tastes and odors, radioactive solids, dirt, and rust. The pump can push through 1 pint of water a minute. A filter can purify up to 800 pints of relatively clean water, or very much less, perhaps

only a few pints, of murky water. It can be recognized as clogged
when it won't allow water to be pumped through. Sometimes it can
be cleaned by backflushing; often it cannot and has to be replaced.
FIRST NEED weighs 12 ounces and costs $35. Replacement filters
are $25. In one test series of thirty runs, 100 percent of the *Giardia*
cysts were removed in twenty-two cases; in the other eight, enough
remained possibly to cause giardiasis. The validity of this test can
be questioned. But then, the fewer the cysts, the better the odds
against infection, so at the worst, the device is a help.

Also approved by the EPA, and used by the International Red
Cross and NATO armies, is the Swiss-made *Katadyn Pocket Water
Filter*. The ceramic filter has a pore diameter of less than 0.2 micron,
small enough to remove not only *Giardia* but all other protozoans,
as well as amoeba, bacteria, cocci, fungi, and perhaps everything
else; the EPA is studying evidence that viruses may be removed.
Independent tests have found it to be 100 percent effective, easily
cleaning a liter of water every two minutes. Its surpassing virtue is
that the filter is not a sealed unit that when clogged by silt must be
thrown away but can be taken apart in the field and simply wiped
clean. It weighs 1½ pounds and costs about $170. A filter lasts 5
or more years, unless dropped on a hard surface and fractured; a
spare, which costs $75, may be desired on expeditions. The Katadyn
sells like crazy to people traveling to lands with no safe liquid except
gin.

The future lies ahead. New wonders may be expected on the market momentarily, but as the giardiasis plague extends its dominions over the domains of America—and the hepatitis viruses follow mankind in his vacation wanderings—backpackers are less and less likely to gaze upon wild waters without a degree of fear and loathing, and more and more likely to keep the iodine handy.

KEEPING ANIMALS HONEST

Nearly all the relatively few dangers from wild animals (discussed in the following chapter) come directly from sloppy kitchens.

Any much-used camp develops a resident population of scavengers. Arriving on wings are "camp robbers"—juncos, jays, nutcrackers, and, at Sierra lakes, gulls. On four feet come wee, timorous beasties that nibble and brazen snafflehounds that gobble. There are porcupines and skunks and raccoons that methodically investigate the scene by night, oblivious to threats. And deer and mountain goats that seek salt, and packrats that devour the armpits of parkas. On ocean beaches there are clouds of crows and gulls ever on the watch for unguarded lunches. And there are bears, too.

When city folk nostalgic for the vanished frontier began visiting

surviving enclaves of wilderness, they fell in love with the animals and began feeding them. Bears, especially appreciative, decided that if little gifts were good, big ones were better. So was born the Campground Bear, gourmand of the picnic table, slasher of food coolers, smasher of car windows.

Trails continued safe for years, backcountry bears shyly content to tour camps after hikers were gone, lapping up bacon grease and fish guts, excavating garbage. Then camps grew crowded and bears impatiently started taking meals when they pleased, learning that the only human retaliation was yelling and pot banging, possibly a bit of stone throwing—which could be dealt with by a bit of teeth baring and growling.

The population explosion of the 1960s and 1970s was actually a double boom: more hikers, more bears. Where trails are still lonesome (or bear hunters numerous) the olden ways prevail; bears enjoy human foods as holiday treats but not enough to endure loud noises, racial slurs, the chance of a bullet. However, where trails are thronged with people, creating an unnatural ecosystem, camps are thronged with bears. Such notorious bear freeways as the trail from Tuolumne Meadows to Yosemite Valley have an estimated five times more bears than natural foods can sustain. There can be seen red-eyed, feverish hikers staggering from night after sleepless night; ask how things are going and madness lights eyes, tales of woe are croaked: "Seven bears in one night! Can you believe it? *Seven bears!*"

It's difficult in a Seven Bear Night to love wildlife. The defense of bears thus is left to the next chapter. The topic here is defense of groceries and sleep.

The measures necessary depend on the species and numbers and determination of invaders. Local inquiry is desirable; rangers usually know which camps are under heavy attack by what. In olden-day-type (lonesome) country, stowing food in closed pack or tight-wrapped tarp may suffice, though usually not, what with quiet burglars chewing holes in expensive gear; in such situations, better leave the food out and let the two or three mice (darling little critters, watched by flashlight) eat their fill.

But where there are a hundred mice, four squirrels, or one bear, the "sacrificial offering" technique is a snare and delusion—only the Fort Knox strategy works. Maximum defense is recommended whenever enemy strength is unknown; the night is far more restful when the commissary is secure, when no alarums will mobilize groggy militia to repulse squirrels crazed by the aroma of Cadbury bars, skunks raving for a granola fix. And bears . . .

Tom Winnett, author-publisher of the Wilderness Press trail guides to High, Middle, and Low Sierra and veteran commuter on bear freeways, teaches in *Backpacking Basics* that bears are (1) too big to crawl in rock crevices and (2) too clumsy to climb rock walls. Thus, if a crevice less than 9 inches wide and at least 4 feet deep is available, the food sack can be pushed in with a stick and be bearproof. Of course, there are still chipmunks. And one must beware of pushing the sack in so far as to be peopleproof. If a ledge is available higher on a cliff than a bear can reach, and if a person can climb there, or push the food sack up with sticks, or lower it with a rope, again only coons and mice will dine that night.

The Ultimate Winnett Weapon is the counterbalance. The technique is simple in camps equipped with "bear cables," and were these and/or "bear boxes" placed in over-beared wildlands, the population would quickly drop to natural numbers via nature's way—pregnant bears, when malnourished, spontaneously abort. But many wilderness managers consider cables and boxes contrary to the Wilderness Act and prefer 500 percent too many bears, contending that this is nature's way of reducing the backpacker population.

A counterbalance is easy to rig if a tree can be found with a branch at least 20 feet from the ground that is 4–5 inches thick at

the trunk, and at a distance of at least 8 feet from the trunk is still sturdy enough to support a heavy weight. These distances are necessary in order to suspend a food bag 12–15 feet above the ground and 5 feet below the branch and 8 feet from the trunk. Close wins no cigar—anything less in any direction and the bear cries "Gotcha!" In the real world such branches are rare. It is then necessary to suspend a light but strong rope or wire (carried for the purpose) between two high points, such as trees or rock boulders atop opposite sides of a gulch. In the real world it is not always easy to find such gulches or to climb 20 feet up a tree (two trees); though Professor Tom doesn't say so, presumably a hiker then prays for two hovering angels.

In any event, with branch found or rope/wire placed, the next step is to put all vulnerable food in two large poly bags, which are then placed in two stuff bags. Whether any food is invulnerable is dubious; bears readily open tin cans. Include with the food all cosmetics and toilet articles—soap, suntan oil, lipstick, toothpaste, bug repellent—the perfumes interest bears strangely, even anger them. Distribute the weight so that one bag is heavier. Tie pots or metal cups or jingle bells to the bags as warning devices should a troupe of bear acrobats pass by on tour.

Now tie a rock to a 50-foot length of strong nylon cord (carried for the purpose) and toss it over the branch/rope/wire. Untie the rock, tie on the heavier food bag and hoist it as high as possible. Now tie the lighter bag on the cord as high as possible—perhaps standing on a chunk of log or atop a human pyramid. Stuff all extra cord in the bag—bears know how to pull strings. Using a stick, push the light bag as high as the heavy one. If branch/rope/wire sags so that either bag is less than nine feet from the ground, return to square one.

In the real world of bear freeways, a hiker must frequently expect to be unable to perform any of the above. The concern then shifts to protecting tents, packs, and bodies that might get between a bear and his supper. Food must not be kept in or near the tent but placed at a distance. Nothing should be left in the pack; all food and toilet articles must be spread on the ground to facilitate inspection. Pack pockets must be left unzipped to avoid having them ripped open.

So, Mr. or Ms. Bear comes to take inventory. What then? If new at the business, it may be repelled by loud shouts, flashlights, banging pots, derogatory remarks about its parents. If it takes offense? *Don't argue.* It may have learned it can whup any dozen pot bangers with one paw behind its back.

What then? Salvage what the bear spurned—bears usually mess up more than they eat. Beg for handouts from passing hikers. Whine to the ranger. Write letters requesting birth control for bears by installation of cables and boxes. Seek trails where hikers—thus bears—are few.

5
Bugs and Beasts and Serpents

Man is not alone in the wilderness. Innumerable creatures large and small were there first, are there now, and will remain. A visitor must learn to live with them and respect their rights —enjoying hawks in the sky, deer in the meadows, and others that make interesting neighbors and mind their own business, doing his best to get along with the hostiles and the all-too-companionables.

A few trail-country inhabitants are an occasional danger to human life and limb. Some, notably certain insects and arachnids (or "bugs" as they are ignorantly lumped in common usage and in this book), are mainly a menace to sanity. Far more for good reason are frightened by man, the most dangerous of all predators.

The beginner doubtless has heard horror stories about encounters between man and beast, man and serpent, man and bug. However, he takes vastly greater risks of being maimed or murdered or mentally unhinged on highways leading from the cities (and in the cities) than along the trails. If hikers take the trouble to learn a little about the habits of the natives, the two can share wildlands with minimum discomfort and terror for both.

SERPENTS

"Watch out for snakes," says the guidebook, and so hikers from such poison-free lands as Ireland and Puget Sound and Alaska walk foreign trails atremble, leaping high at the sight of every lizard, and lie sleepless in bags, imagining every rustle of bushes to be the approach of evil.

Venomous snakes demand respect but not panic. An estimated 1,000–1,500 persons (in another guess, 7,000–8,000), mostly toddling kids and rambunctious teenagers, are bitten in the United States each year—a small number, really, considering that millions of rural folk daily live and work amid potentially dangerous snakes. Perhaps a quarter of the bites occur during attempts at capturing or in handling for religious purposes. About 30 people a year die— a large proportion of the fatalities tiny children. Very few hikers are bitten, and fewer still suffer serious illness, much less death.

Of the scores of snakes common in American trail country, only four carry venom. The coral snake occurs in parts of the South and Southwest and the water moccasin (cottonmouth) in wetlands of

C'MON ADAM, SNAKES CAN'T HURT YOU!

the South. The copperhead ranges rather widely through the East, and various members of the rattlesnake family are found across the nation.

Residents of snake country, though they love to scare dudes with tall tales, are quite casual about the hazard. In the memory of the oldest inhabitants of the Stehekin Valley of the North Cascades, going back eighty-odd years, no human ever has been bitten there; dogs have been, some repeatedly, but only one, a pup, is remembered as dying.

Snakes fear man, and given a chance, will flee his presence; knowing this, the hiker can reduce confrontations with elementary precautions. Be a noisy walker to give ample advance notice of your approach. Watch the path ahead to avoid stepping on a snake or coming near one sunning on a boulder (after a chill night) or cooling in a cave or streambank grass (on a hot day). Listen for the rattle that often warns that a rattlesnake is close by, scared, and thus dangerous. (However, since even a coiled snake can strike less than the length of its body, the surveillance need not be extended any great distance.) Do not plunge blindly into thickets or run through boulder fields or scramble incautiously up rocks. For peace of mind, if nothing else, perhaps wear long pants rather than shorts, possibly gaiters.

Authorities generally advise carrying a snakebite kit, but in unpracticed hands of semihysterical first-aiders, the kit can be more dangerous than the bite; the victim may have an allergic reaction to the antivenin and go into fatal shock, or the first-aider wielding the razor may slash an artery. The rule is to seek instruction before entering an area where it may be needed.

Enough, here, about timid creatures too much maligned. In many parts of our continent, including most alpine regions, poisonous snakes are totally absent; the relatively few hikers who spend a good deal of time in lands of the serpents will want to study their habits thoroughly, not only to learn to live among them without fear but also for the pleasure of getting to know fellow travelers. Colin Fletcher, in *The Complete Walker*, discusses rattlesnakes at length, crediting as his major source *Rattlesnakes: Their Habits, Life Histories, and Influence*

on Mankind by Laurence M. Klauber. Dr. James A. Wilkerson, in *Medicine for Mountaineering*, is definitive on treatment for snakebite. When new areas are visited, guidebooks should be consulted to find if venom carriers are present, and where.

BEASTS

Urbanites nourished on fairy tales and frontier lies frequently are uncomfortable in forests, fearing that every thicket conceals a beast ready to pounce. The night, they suspect, does indeed have a thousand eyes—and jaws, and fangs, and claws. Though this may be so in city parks, the wildlands of America contain few animals that threaten man; the menace is the other way around. Several creatures may be cited to suggest how little there is to fear.

Cougars and other cats do not attack man unless cornered, a distinctly avoidable situation; only the rare hiker is privileged even to hear, much less see one.

The same is true of wolves, now tragically scarce, and proven by modern research to be innocent of slanders perpetrated by Little Red Riding Hood and paranoid shepherds. What substance there is for legends of lupine viciousness comes from attacks in the madness of rabies, incidents extremely rare but lingering long in memory and expanding enormously in myth. Rabies afflicts small beasts as well as large and is not restricted to wilderness; a fellow quietly besotting himself at a Manhattan Island bar once was bitten by a rabid bat that flew in from the street. On the trail or in the city no animal that seems ill or behaves oddly should be picked up, touched, or approached; it may be dying of rabies, plague, or some other disease that can be transmitted by a bite or by infected fleas. Be sure to tell the children.

Elk and moose should be shunned in the fall rutting season, when passion-mad bulls may mistake hikers for competitors and run them out of the country. In spring and summer the cows—and any mother with young—should be given a wide berth so as not to stir maternal hostility.

Skunks? Don't frighten them! Porcupines? An inexperienced dog may require hours of painful surgery pulling quills from jaws. Coyotes? Scary-sounding under the moon, but harmless. Eagles? Occasionally they attack airplanes and nest-robbing ornithologists.

A word about the horse. First, pedestrians should always yield the right of way to equestrians, who often are unstable in the saddle and have scant control of their huge, clumsy steeds. Second, when stepping from the path, a hiker should continue making normal gestures and above all *speak* to the poor dumb beast so it will know it has met an ordinary human, not an alien monster.

Save Our Bears

The most interesting large animal the ordinary person has a reasonable chance to see on the trail is the bear; eliminate bear stories and wildness would be diminished. However, bison and Indians made good stories, too, and look what happened to them; whether bears can survive, for man's sake if not their own, remains to be determined. It can only be so if hikers want them, and help them.

The first rule, elaborated on in the previous chapter, is *never feed the animals, deliberately or otherwise.* A party may consider a bit of food a small price for an anecdote. But only if animals are kept wild and honest can they be kept alive—and the trails safe.

Second, do not fraternize. Forget Jellystone Park and Yogi and Gentle Ben and Teddy—real-life bears are not cute. Forget Smokey—bears are nothing like dogs, never become humanized, at best tolerate and usually hate people. Enjoy them—but from a distance. Stay away from cubs! Though unseen, the deadliest of the species, the mother, is near, ready to take off after photographers.

There are bears and bears. Before entering the realms of the Alaska brown and polar bears, a hiker must consult local experts, who often as not advise visiting a lawyer to draw up a last will and testament.

The novice does well to skip grizzly lands altogether; as more hikers crowd Yellowstone National Park, Glacier National Park, and wildlands of Canada and Alaska, scenes of most backpacker-*Ursus horribilis* encounters, grizzly behavior is more unpredictable,

tragedies more common. The veteran who knows the habits of bears on his home ground knows the risks and how to reduce them—the stranger may do precisely the wrong thing in exactly the wrong place. Rangers constantly study grizzly behavior and try to keep pace with changing patterns by refining rules and closing dangerous camps and trails. Heeding their warnings is mandatory but may not suffice; many warnings come only after episodes of blood and slaughter. Recommended procedures:

- Leave dogs, perfumed cosmetics, and toilet articles at home.
- Sit this one out if you're a menstruating woman.
- Avoid solitary hiking.
- Camp in a tent.
- Keep no food, garbage, or perfumery near camp.
- Keep all garments and gear free of food odors.
- Make lots of noise on the trail.

But even hikers who have obeyed all these rules have been mauled, killed, even eaten. Too much to pay for an anecdote.

Suppose the hiker shuns grizzly country. What about the black bear? To forgo its terrain is virtually to evacuate the trails. And if the black (which in other color phases may be brown, cinnamon, even white) is the smallest of the clan, it's big enough to win any hand-to-paw combat. And if it's the least belligerent, that too is only by comparison—and evidence suggests that black bears all over America are getting more irascible, more aggressive. On lonesome trails, where bears are of the old school and dodge man assiduously, the hiker may avoid surprises by making normal noises as he walks, perhaps supplemented by bells on pack or boots and occasional bursts of nervous laughter. But fewer and fewer trails are lonesome, more and more bears are incompletely wild, and as they've grown dependent on human food, they've evolved socially. Every year brings more reports of black bears throwing their weight around, "bluff-charging"—a highly effective tactic, since few hikers call the bluff. More than once, anyhow.

And so, as with the grizzly, defense strategies need revision.

When a black bear invades camp, night or day, the technique still applicable in areas of few humans is to yell and holler and bang pots and throw rocks. An inexperienced bumpkin bear will light out for the next county. But the experienced, mod, with-it bear may give a hideous toothy grin, growl, or charge. Is it bluffing? Don't ask. Shut up and run.

When the meeting is on the trail and the bear doesn't flee, that's a very, very bad sign; shouting and rock-throwing are inadvisable unless a run-for-it or climb-for-it sanctuary, tree or cliff, is at hand. Best to stand still or slowly retreat, saying a few pleasant words in a calm and friendly voice. If pursued, throw down the pack—the bear may spend enough time ripping it to shreds for a tree to be found. If caught, go limp and quiet, do not resist or scream, assume the fetal position to protect vital areas, cover the head with the arms, and pray.

Can hikers and bears share wildlands? The question is open. Remember, the bears were there first.

BUGS

Every longtime hiker has a lurid repertoire of bug stories—the air thick with flailing wings, loud with snapping jaws—infants wailing, wives weeping, strong men teetering on the brink of madness. Wil-

derness veterans who face tempest and jungle with fortitude quail at the prospect of entering the domain of the Lord of the Flies. However, formidable though the insect legions are, rarely can they totally defeat the hiker who learns their habits and employs proper defenses.

In camp a bugproof tent (see Chapter 12) provides a near-perfect haven. For tarp sleepers, as well as for anyone sitting around camp or resting on the trail, a "habitat" can be instantly rigged: a sheet of mosquito netting (or better, finer-mesh no-see-um netting) a couple of yards wide and several yards long, enough to drape over the entire upper body, weighing mere ounces and compressing to a tiny wad in pack pocket. True peace is never possible while hiking or doing chores, but the target areas can be minimized by covering up with clothing and donning a head net. Insect repellent (see Chapter 15) generally prevent bugs from drilling and biting but doesn't keep them at a respectful distance. The attentive cloud hovers close, landing on untreated clothing and glasses and flying into eyes, nostrils, and open mouth. Chemicals thus don't eliminate the harassment, which is often the worst part of the whole business.

Frequently, the only salvation lies in resolute stoicism. Those who yield to paranoia have lost the battle and are not long for the trails. It is necessary to realize that bugs *belong* on the earth, that if the Architect had intended wildlands to be perfectly comfortable for man, He would have designed them more like Disneyland.

In extremities some hikers find tranquilizers useful in gaining the proper mental composure; others prefer a shot of rum.

The Cast of Villains

By learning to enjoy "bugs" (that is, insects and arachnids and other arthropods), a person enlarges his circle of trail companions; only a very few ever are a bother. Admire the gorgeous butterfly, the spectacular dragonfly, the patient spider, the graceful water skate, the glistening beetle. Ponder the anecdote told by the zoologist G. Evelyn Hutchinson about J. B. S. Haldane. The great biologist "found himself in the company of a group of theologians. On being

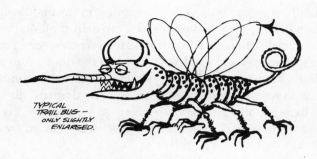

TYPICAL
TRAIL BUG —
ONLY SLIGHTLY
ENLARGED.

asked what one could conclude as to the nature of the Creator from a study of His creation, Haldane is said to have answered, 'An inordinate fondness for beetles.' " Illustrating the point in a review of a Hutchinson book, Stephen Jay Gould said, "Since Linnaeus set the modern style of formal naming in 1758, more than a million species of plants and animals have received Latin binomials. More than 80 percent of these names apply to animals; of the animals, nearly 75 percent are insects; of the insects, about 60 percent are beetles." What's good enough for the Lord ought to be good enough for man. Still, folks with a phobia about creepy-crawlies do well to sleep in floored tents.

The experienced hiker has too many problems with genuine menaces to fret about innocents, outlandish and gaudy though they may appear, and adopts the attitude, "If they don't bite, they don't count." It's a frame of mind worth cultivating, saving much squirming and yelping and gallons of repellent.

Except in fire-ant areas of the South, ants trouble only the hiker who unwarily spreads his sleeping bag atop a colony—a typical location being the remains of a rotten log—and is wakened in the night by the pricking of a myriad tiny needles.

Unless they are of the killer-bee sort, now moving northward and westward from the South, bee-type bugs (honeybees, bumblebees, yellowjackets, hornets, wasps, etc.) normally let people alone, except to briefly investigate bright-colored clothing they mistake for huge flowers; together with flies and mosquitoes, they are attracted and thoroughly confused by damsels and lads who wear perfume.

Accidentally stepping on a yellowjacket nest in the middle of a trail can be unpleasant, since a single warrior can deliver numerous stabs, but the spectacle can entertain dirty old men when several get inside a female's blouse, or dirty old women when the drama is in a man's pants. Individuals vary in their physical reactions to bee stings: some find them no worse than nettles; others puff up dramatically; in rare cases of extreme allergy the victim may go into severe, even fatal shock—the proper medication should always be carried by people who suspect they have a problem.

Midges or gnats often fill the summer evening air in the vicinity of lowland marshes and lakes.

The chigger, found mainly in the East, is a mite that lives in grass, digs into skin, and causes an itch.

Annoying these bugs may sometimes be, but none is so dreaded by hikers as the next characters in this sordid chapter.

Ticks

The tick burrows into flesh and engorges on blood. Sometimes (but rarely) it carries Rocky Mountain spotted fever, fortunately now readily cured by antibiotics. Nastiest of all, the bite of a tick infected with a certain spirochete causes *Lyme arthritis*. A few days or weeks after the bite a circular redness appears, perhaps followed by more of the same. Antibiotics quickly clear up the rash but if these are not given it may persist—succeeded some two years later by a crippling arthritis of a single joint.

The tick rarely ventures more than several feet from the ground; Typically it anchors to brush and grass along the paths of mice and deer, extends hooks, and waits for a host to come within reach; the hooks then clamp tight, and the tick climbs aboard.

Ticks are most plentiful in dry lands when grass is sprouting and leaves are budding and browsers are enjoying salads. Hiker–tick encounters mainly occur in May and June on trails leading to alpine regions of Western mountains, but they can occur anytime, almost anywhere. (The town of Lyme is in Connecticut.)

When passing through tick-thick terrain, it is wise to wear long pants treated with repellent. When the hiker is sleeping in tick country, repellent may be applied to all clothing, to sleeping bags and perhaps tent entries. In the absence of sufficient repellent, hikers may wish to pair off morning and evening to inspect completely each other's bodies. (Please, no giggling.) By this means the danger of disease (which actually is not all that common) can be largely avoided, since a tick normally explores several hours before choosing a drill site, and even if infected, cannot transmit germs for several hours more.

In the early stages of drilling, the entire tick can be gently pulled straight out (not "unscrewed"); then or later, it possibly may be induced to withdraw by touching its rear with a drop of repellent, kerosene, or gas. Once the tick is partly imbedded, the only remedy is to pull off the body, halting the creature's operations by killing it. Perhaps later the patient should visit a doctor to have the head cut out. If localized infection develops, or high fever and severe headache, chills, aching back—and/or a rash—medical treatment should be sought—in the case of these last symptoms, urgently.

Ticks can roam through clothing and sleeping bags and gear for several days and thus must be watched for after the party has ascended into high mountains or returned to the city.

Mosquitoes

Except perhaps in parts of the South, the mosquitoes of America do not transmit malaria or yellow fever, and the only region where they are potentially a mortal peril is the far North, where by one estimate an unprotected person could lose half his blood in a half hour. The needle is painless, and the itching usually minor and temporary. The central hazard is mental—the maddening whine, the constant cloud, the probing of ears, eyes, nose—moderated but not eliminated by repellent. Mosquitoes probably have stimulated the buying of more tents than rain and driven more hikers into fits and off the trails than all other causes combined.

In lowlands mosquitoes may be met in every season except winter—one or two, a few, or many, depending on the local climate. In alpine meadows and Arctic tundras they achieve the continental

climax of mind-boggling when the ground is moist from snowmelt and the air is calm and warm. As pools and humus dry, their numbers diminish; with the first frosts of fall they vanish. Through miserable experience a hiker learns the intolerable times and places and thereafter can schedule trips to notorious hellholes for the off-season.

Mosquitoes have a limited temperature range. In high mountains they ordinarily go instantly to bed with the evening chill, probably to arise at dawn, thin out during the heat of day, and return in force as the afternoon cools. In warm lowlands they may appear at dusk and work all through the night.

A wind keeps them from clustering, and thus a camp may be placed on a knoll for the breezes in preference to a sheltered nook nearby. Similarly, a dry hillock may be quieter than a lush vale a stone's-throw away.

Flies

Scores of members of the fly family infest trail country. Several may be described as representative examples of the range in size and habitat.

The tiny, silent *no-see-um*, mistaken for a speck of dust until it grabs hold, able to pass through most netting as if it weren't there, often gets off an incredibly painful chew but is felt mainly as an overall prickle and itch. No-see-ums are generally confined to low-lands, such as dank river bottoms, which they may on occasion render uninhabitable.

The chief threat is the medium-sized category, represented in Eastern forests by the *black fly*, a humpbacked devil that chews a hole in the skin and leaves a scabby welt the size of a dime, and in Western forests by the *deer fly*, which in a typical manifestation resembles the housefly. In "fly time" every square yard of a Western trail may harbor hundreds of sharp-eyed, sharp-toothed, loud-buzzing villains, and to calculate the numbers in an entire valley is to submerge sanity in a vision of infinity—an infinity of evil. Driven by heat to fiendish hyperactivity, flies attack most furiously precisely on those sweaty, gasping uphill drags when the hiker moves slowest. Now and then a kamikaze plunges into ear, nose, eye, or wide-open mouth—to feel wings and legs scrambling around in the throat, to gag and retch, is the ultimate initiation.

But all is not lost. The unbearable deer fly time usually lasts only a few weeks of summer, ending with the first heavy frosts, and the fly empire, though extending from low valleys to meadows, is usu-ally impossibly crowded only in the upper forests. Moreover, deer flies vanish in the wind and evening chill; even the cool microclimate next to a waterfall may allow a peaceful lunch when the forest world all around is pure hell. Finally, since flies patrol at random in search of a victim, the interior of a lean-to (or a tent with one closed end) has only one-quarter the number of the surrounding woods, since from three directions they bump into walls. Even an open-ended tarp cuts the population in half, and a closed tent is perfectly secure.

Deer flies ordinarily diminish or disappear in parkland and mead-ows, which apparently by family agreement are the domain of the *gollydang little brown fly*, which inflicts pain in the biting and injects a poison that causes an itchy bump, and of the *elk fly*, which ranges upward into snow and rocks but luckily occurs in dozens rather than thousands. These enormous beasts, which take such big bites that they seem to be slicing off steaks, can be slapped with relative ease—though for final destruction one may have to take a club and beat them to death.

CRIMINALS

Despite occasional raids by frontiersmen living off the land, snatching bacon from unguarded camps and jacking up cars to steal the wheels, hikers used to feel safe from crime in the hills. Largely this was because hikers used to be such a ragtag lot that when dressed up in surplus gear after World War II as the Khaki Gang they actually thought themselves rather dashing. But burglars weren't impressed. It was when hikers got rich and pretty that they got into trouble. In 1978 more than 8,000 felonies, mostly theft and vandalism, were reported in National Parks.

As tourism and backpacking brought the campground bear, so the $100 pack and $200 tent and $10 freeze-dried porkchop brought the trail thief. There are amateurs unable to resist the sleeping bag airing on a tree. And there are professional bandits, indistinguishable from other backpackers, who case a basin, spot the nobs, and when camp occupants go on a flower stroll, dart in and out, pack stuffed with $1,000 worth of geodesic tents, Gore-Tex parkas, and freeze-dried strawberries.

What to do? Above all, as with bears, don't let crime pay. Starve the crooks. Camp in secluded spots with subdued gear that doesn't scream for attention. In crowded areas, leave camp unattended as little as possible. When going off on a day jaunt, carry costly bags and parkas and the like some distance and hide them in the bushes.

The trailhead is the major danger zone, the operations area of interstate gangs including spotters who loiter around parking lots chatting with folks about where they're going, for how long, and watching who locks what in which trunk; lookouts posted down the road and up the trail with CB radios; fences in distant cities; and guns.

These gangs will go out of business at some future time when they open a hundred cars and net nothing but moldy tennis shoes, stinking T-shirts, rotten bananas, and warm root beer—or when all gear is so prominently and indelibly marked by the owner that no fence will touch it. A hiker who owns a car with mag wheels, $1,000 carburetor, and tape deck-stereo AM-FM radio should buy a second car, a battered relic with retreads and broken windows, for driving to trails. Valuables must never be left in the car, must always be carried on the trail; picklocks open doors and trunk as fast as a key, and the pro knows all the clever hiding places for cash and credit cards. If the hike is in the course of an extended highway tour, store extra gear in a nearby town; many motels provide such service.

The ultimate solution, of course, is abject poverty. Nobody ever stole from the Khaki Gang.

6
Danger!

Before this invitation to wildland pleasures continues, a word from the devil's advocate.

There is misery on the trail, and pain, and death. Questions for the new hiker: *Do you know what you're getting into?* Are you aware of the risks? Are you willing to accept those you cannot invariably avoid? If so, welcome to the wild bunch. If not, think about it.

A number of discomforts and dangers are discussed in other chapters; they will not be repeated here. Nor will an exhaustive catalog of perils be presented in the tradition of seeking to frighten the innocent out of his wits and the wilds. However, a germ of fear must be implanted, hopefully to grow to a mature respect.

BEGINNER-KILLERS

If a person brooded incessantly on all the ways there are to be maimed, he would never get out of bed—until he began worrying about burglars, earthquakes, and bedsores. Certainly no one would ever stride blithely along a trail if at each step he were watching for snakes and bears, falling trees and mountains, flash floods and lightning bolts.

76

Paraphrasing the last journal entry of Scott of the Antarctic, at the death camp on the return from the Pole, "We take risks, we know we take them. Therefore, when things come out against us, we have no cause for complaint." To live is to be insecure. But to die from ignorance is a shame.

Over the years a hiker encounters numerous hazards, common and uncommon. Encyclopedic coverage of the threats in every realm of hiking terrain from snow to deserts is given in *Outdoor Living: Problems, Solutions, Guidelines,* edited by Eugene H. Fear, as well as in his similar *Surviving the Unexpected Wilderness Emergency.* Certain perils seem to have a particular affinity for the inexperienced, and several are especially notorious among rescue experts as beginner-killers.

Weather: Hypothermia

Except in desert country, where sunstroke and dehydration are the killers, the vast majority of weather-caused fatalities—among veterans as well as novices—result from hypothermia, whereby the body loses more heat than it can generate. (Older names were "exposure" and "freezing to death.")

A hiker need only get rain-drenched and wind-blasted a few times to pay close attention to the forecast before leaving on a trip, and constantly watch the sky while in wildlands. Eventually he learns the characteristic weather patterns of home hills, develops some skill at interpreting clouds and winds, and can guess with better-than-random accuracy the prospects for coming hours.

But every summer, somewhere, a beginner sets out in morning sun so warm that only a loony would carry an extra sweater or parka. He admires the pretty billow on the horizon—too far away, surely, to be a threat. But in the afternoon the cloud arrives, and he wishes for that sweater and parka, yet still no need to worry—the car is just a couple of hours distant. Then begins rain (or snow), driven by a gale. Muscles become clumsy, thinking gets tangled. He stumbles and sprains an ankle, or misses the path and is lost in mist. Unless rescuers find him in time, the rest is silence.

A common misconception is that hypothermia is a danger only at below-freezing temperatures. The accompanying table shows that a wind of 20 miles per hour at 40°F cools the body as effectively as still air at 18°F. *Wind chill* can cause hypothermia at temperatures far above freezing.

Moisture cools somewhat by wetting the skin but mainly by reducing the insulation value of clothing; the thermal conductivity of water is 240 times greater than that of still air. Hypothermia is not confined to high ridges but can occur in low forests from *water chill*. The combination of wind and rain is particularly lethal.

Well-equipped hikers, faithfully carrying the Ten Essentials (see Chapter 15), rarely die from hypothermia; when they do, it is usually because they ignore the sky and their inner voices, and push forward rather than retreating or holing up.

WIND CHILL

Wind Speed (miles per hour)	Skin-Effective Temperature (°F)						
0 (still air) 50	40	30	20	10	0	−10	−20
10 40	28	16	4	−9	−21	−33	−46
20 32	18	4	−10	−25	−39	−53	−69
30 28	13	−2	−18	−33	−48	−63	−79
40 26	10	−6	−21	−37	−53	−69	−85

NOTE: To find the approximate effective temperature (cooking power) of wind-driven air compared to that of still air, read downward from the still-air thermometer readings of the top line to intersect the wind speed in the left column.

Lightning

Of the hundred or so Americans annually killed by lightning, most were swimming, boating, playing golf, or talking on the telephone; few were hiking. However, every year thousands of people on mountain trails are frightened half to death by the possibility of getting hit by lightning. A discussion of wildland danger would be incomplete without a glance at electricity.

In some ranges of the Rockies, and in some High Sierra summers, an afternoon opera is so regular the rangers set their clocks by it and experienced hikers arrange to be off the ridges before the overture. In other areas, the storm pattern is unpredictable. An excellent rule for novices, and for visitors to highlands whose weather habits they don't know, is to accept a doom-black horizon as the signal to run. Caught in the middle of a furor, a hiker can take substantial measures to eliminate the danger, if not the terror:

- If dense forest is near, plunge on in and relax—you're home free.
- If in open meadows, do not seek shelter from the downpour under a lone tree or in an isolated clump of trees; the number one scene of lightning fatalities is the shelter of lone trees or isolated clumps. Also in open meadows, get out of and away from your tent, which in the absence of trees may be the best available lightning rod.
- If on a ridge, get off it, or at least off the crest.
- If anywhere in the open, seek the lowest ground, any sort of depression. But stay away from lakes.
- If the flash and bang are simultaneous, meaning you're right in the middle of the action, and especially if your hair stands on end and you see the ghostly dance of Saint Elmo's fire and hear the rocks and your pack emit the "buzzing of the bees," *do not lie flat* on the ground; this places the body in maximum contact with the electrical flow. Instead, drop to your knees and bend forward, putting hands on knees, a

stance that presents the lowest vertical profile consistent with
the least ground contact.
- If you are struck and severely shocked, hope someone in your
party knows cardiopulmonary resuscitation technique.

Gravity: Falling and Being Fallen Upon

Chapter 17 discusses rough-country travel and warns against attempting cliffs and snowfields properly left to trained climbers. Such
ill-advised adventures by daring beginners fill pages and pages of
the annual reports of rescue groups. The reports also devote considerable space to falls from trails; in steep terrain the tread is often
wide and safe, yet inches away is a cliff and to stumble over the
edge is perhaps to tumble dozens or hundreds of feet.

How do hikers fall off trails? By rushing when they should be
creeping. By fainting from heat exhaustion. By not carrying a flashlight and by staying too long on sunset-colored ridges and then,
while blindly descending dark woods, missing a switchback.

Another danger of gravity is that piece by piece, year by year,
mountains are disintegrating. Far more common than spontaneous
rockfall, though, is the peril of heavily traveled trails where carefree
and careless hikers kick rocks loose to plunge onto people below.

Getting Lost

Hikers who know the techniques of finding and keeping the route,
as introduced in Chapter 16, are rarely lost longer than overnight.
Moreover, those who carry the Ten Essentials have a survival rate
of virtually 100 percent.

Even ill-trained, ill-equipped novices generally do not become
seriously lost if the party always remains together in confusing
terrain. They are, for one thing, less likely to miss the way, and if
they do, they reinforce one another physically and spiritually. It is
the lone traveler who succumbs to panic, the prelude to tragedy.

If lost, what then? Rescue experts emphasize that the problem is
not being lost but staying alive long enough to be found.

First, as soon as confused, *stop*; don't plunge onward, getting more thoroughly lost. Sit down, rest, have a bite to eat. Think calmly. Do not let fear lead to panic. If two or more persons are lost together, discuss the situation—and do not henceforth become separated! The annals abound in incidents where every member of a lost party was eventually found except the one who went for help.

Second, mark the location. Chances are the trail is not far away. Conduct short sorties in all directions, returning to the marked spot if unsuccessful.

Third, shout—and listen for answering shouts. Or blow a whistle if one is in the emergency kit—an excellent idea—as whistling can be sustained much longer than shouting. (Three blasts at a time, three of anything being the universal signal of distress.) Friends or strangers may answer, their shouts guiding the way back to the trail.

Fourth, prepare for night well in advance. Conserve strength for the cold, dark hours. In bad weather, look for the snuggest available shelter under trees or overhanging rocks. Build a fire if possible, not only for warmth but because searchers may see the flame or smoke.

The hiker lacking considerable experience in cross-country navigation should, if first efforts fail, concentrate not on finding the way but on letting rescuers *find him*. Above all, this means staying in one place. The hard cases are those who go and go as long as legs work, leaving the area being combed by the rescue party, eluding searchers as if playing hide-and-seek—at last dying alone, from injury, hypothermia, starvation, or a combination.

GOING FOR HELP

Most provinces of North American trail country are served by rescue systems coordinating land administrators, regional and local police, military and naval forces, news media, helicopters, and unpaid volunteers from outdoor clubs, Explorer Scouts, and/or units of the Mountain Rescue Association.

Though the average hiker ordinarily is never asked to join a rescue (for which only experienced and trained wildlanders are wanted), he must always be prepared to undertake the very important task of summoning experts. Thus, before setting out on any trail, he must know how to activate the local system—usually by contacting the nearest ranger or policeman.

When a member of the party has been lost, injured, or become ill, what's to be done? It depends. How large is the party?

A lone hiker, disabled, can at most shout and wait and pray. Something for soloists to think about. (In empty country a broken leg or inflamed appendix can be fatal.)

In a two-man group the victim—perhaps unconscious or delirious and requiring constant attention—must be left alone by his companion seeking help. Something for two-pal, girl-boy, and daddy-son parties to think about. (In rough terrain, walk as if in a minefield.)

With three in the party the victim can be constantly tended while a messenger runs for the ranger. With four, two messengers can go, thus eliminating the chance of a single one becoming lost or hurt and compounding the problem.

Before leaving the scene of the accident (or illness or loss), the messenger should gather (preferably write down) data the rescuers will want: nature and location of the accident, extent of injuries, number of people on the scene and their resources of equipment and experience, names of party members and phone numbers of next of kin.

Wherever they exist, hikers should scrupulously observe sign-in/sign-out regulations, which in effect make the rangers backup members of the party who will automatically come looking if the return is delayed. Where such procedures don't exist, often rangers or law officers regularly check trailheads. Their task would be eased if every car had a note taped to the windshield saying where the party is and when it expects to return, but this would also ease the task of burglars. Nevertheless, a note with the names and addresses of party members, and a whom-to-notify phone number, doesn't aid thieves and does help authorities solve mysteries. On any trip in an area lacking sign-in/sign-out provisions, the schedule and route should be left with relatives or friends so rescuers can be alerted if the party is late getting back. Such precautions have sustained the life of more than one walker lying helpless, alone, but not without hope.

RESPECT

Probably no longtime rough-country wanderer can look back on his travels without wondering how he survived. He recalls the time he tripped on a root and his pack flew over his head and he teetered on the trail edge looking straight down at a boiling river. And the time he was strolling along a ridge under a fantastic cloud and suddenly hail pelted and rocks buzzed and lightning blinded. And the time he waded into a meltwater flood and in an instant the torrent threw him against a boulder 100 feet downstream. And the time he swam to the middle of a cold mountain tarn and found his legs and arms going limp from hypothermia and only while sinking for good was able to crawl ashore. And the time he was walking a broad trail through forest and a mild breeze arose and with that final delicate push a huge snag killed in a fire fifty years ago crashed to the ground right in his path. And the night of the big storm when he huddled in his tent while torrents pressed down the roof—and the next morning he crawled out to find that a few feet from his bed the meadows were obliterated under tons of boulders and gravel.

And so on and so on, over the campfires the tales are told, the memories renewed. At last one veteran asks old companions of the hills, "How did we ever *make* it this far?" And they all laugh nervously, for they all should have died many times when they were young and raw and fearless. And maybe they are silent a moment, remembering the companions who didn't make it. Including those who missed this campfire only by months or days—because veterans, too, sometimes die.

All well and good for the surviving veterans—they have buried friends and now know that fear is healthy, and when scared, say so loudly and proudly, having ceased years ago to fret about being called "chicken." They quote the maxim from the Alps, "When a climber (hiker) is injured, he apologizes to his friends. When a climber (hiker) is killed, his friends apologize for him."

But the beginners? They may be driven by social pressure to run when they know it would be wiser to walk, to continue toward the planned objective when they know it is time to retreat. Or they may be dumb slaves of internal compulsions—a fear of not measuring up to manhood (common among boys), of not meeting a husband's expectations (the bride syndrome), of becoming old (the middle-aged athlete syndrome).

A hiker, no matter how inexperienced, almost always realizes when he is in great danger. He *knows* when the terrain is so steep that a fall could be mortal. He *knows* when the wind is so ominous that a bad storm is building.

Beginners die on the trails because they do not have the guts to be cowards. They have been led to believe that man has conquered the earth and that to quail when confronted by the naked force of amoral, uncaring nature is to break faith with the pioneers, to deviate from the American Way.

Hiking tends to build humility. And respect. Qualities that not only improve the soul but enhance chances to walk wildlands for years with only an occasional disaster.

Part II

Equipment: Into the Thickets of the Catalogs

7
Assembling the Outfit

In that dimming past when backpackers were so few they weren't called that, or anything else, choosing equipment was simple. For the feet there were boots, and a boot was a boot was a boot, unless it was a tennis shoe. For the nights the question wasn't the comparative efficiencies of sleeping-bag insulations but whether to make do with an army blanket, this perhaps also serving—rolled up around food and spare clothes, slung over one shoulder and tied at the opposite hip—as the pack.

Equipment wasn't worth talking about, except to cuss at. The sport (so it was classified, to distinguish it from what holy men did in stony deserts, eating beetles and scorpions, whipping their flesh raw and rubbing salt in the wounds) consisted by definition of shivering when it was cold, getting wet when it rained, eating strictly from hunger, and gradually bending the vertebrae out of shape.

Today the backpacker travels dry and sleeps warm in all but major convulsions of nature, quickly prepares gourmet meals, and carries a load lighter and easier-riding than elders believed awaited on the Golden Shore. Yet luxury, too, has its ills. Backpackers, generally, are from the most environmentally well-educated level of society and feel wretched about their hoggish superconsumption, are worried by portents in the balance of payments and prime rate, uneasy about moral decay and eternal damnation. Nevertheless, so spoiled have they become that rather than taking satisfaction in staying dry 95 percent of the time, they pout about the 5 percent wet, and when yesterday's miracle garment disappoints, they fling it aside and dash to the shop for today's marvel.

In the shop the veteran watches the novices fondle boots brutal enough to give Attila the Hun a laughing fit or suave enough for the dancing at Prince Charming's ball, gape saucer-eyed at the array of packs so comfortable the wonder is the owners ever could bear to take them off to go to bed, salivate on the floor of the food department, and exit the shop towing a train of shopping carts, equipped for an expedition to the Karakoram or a flight to Mars.

The veteran smiles wryly, doesn't sneer. The reason he stops in every month to buy the latest parka is that when he stays away as long as half a year he feels on a revisit as disoriented as Buck Rogers awakening in the twenty-fifth century. He has friends, creaky Old Crocks, companions of his youth, who are worse off. Having blinked and thus fallen hopelessly behind the stampede of progress, they are so intimidated by the shop they won't buy anything new but

socks; stubbornly defend their medieval torture racks because they fear humiliation by the internal-frame pack; and at great expense have their aged boots rebuilt because they suspect the new models are secretly running shoes.

Though not necessarily better than the old, in obedience to the laws of thermodynamics the new is invariably more complicated. Explaining equipment to customers—novices or veterans—requires a steadily higher competence in expository skills. Because clerks' time is limited, buyers need the assistance of minutely descriptive catalogs. Because these are costly and thus written partly in the shorthand of a vocabulary that didn't exist two decades ago, they have engendered a whole new species of publication, exemplified by this book, devoted to deciphering the catalogs.

GETTING ORGANIZED

The average person walks 65,000 miles in a lifetime. Very likely every reader of these pages has done his/her share on trails, if only strolling in city parks. However, the most difficult case will be assumed—that of a person who has always lived amid concrete and plastic and now by a supernatural flash has decided to go hiking and is so ignorant as hardly to know the flowers from the birds.

The transition from sidewalks to trails can be organized in the following steps.

First, Decide What You Want to Do, and Where and When

If day hikes on broad paths are the maximum ambition, that's one thing. If the goal is roaring wilderness on week-long backpacks, that's another.

Will most trips be in lowland forests or in high mountains? On ocean beaches or in deserts? Cold and wet country, or hot and dry, or hot and wet? Entirely in summer or partly on the fringes of winter?

Each sort of hiking, each hiking area, and each season requires more or less special tailoring of the basic outfit.

Second, Define Your Style

Four decades ago Dave Brower edited and the Sierra Club published *Going Light With Backpack and Burro*. Years earlier, Boy Scouts routinely set out for week-long adventures in the Olympic Mountains with 20-pound packs. Earlier still, John Muir rambled for weeks in

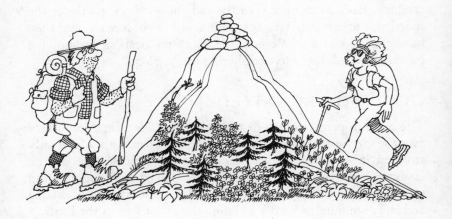

the High Sierra with no pack at all. *Lightpacking*, then, is no recent revelation; it is older than Stonehenge. There are, however, two principal sects.

The high-church majority might describe its practices as *state-of-the-art packing;* the chapelites, theirs, as *good-enough packing.* Establishmentarians, being reasonable people, ask why anyone would lunch on overripe salami hash when the menu lists ptarmigan tetrazzini; in the dissenting congregation, they are called *fancy-packers.* The low-churchers carry sufficient gear and food to sustain life and stave off mystic experiences; they are likened by their opposites to refugees from advancing glaciers and called *Neanderthal packers.*

The two do not mix well on the trail. The Neanderthal, who accepts semisimultaneous sensations of too cold, too hot, too wet, too dry as man's fate, is driven to gibbering by a fancy-packer forever tinkering with layers, intricately rigging tent-womb, fine-tuning his tech. As for tech-man, observing his companion wearing the same greasy, stinking wool shirt all week, day and night, in the heat rolling up sleeves and unbuttoning the front, in the chill rolling down and buttoning up, sleeping under stars or a flimsy tarp, he will begin to hallucinate woolly mammoths and saber-toothed tigers.

Before committing to the high or the low or the middling, a newcomer should observe the alternatives in action: see the state of the art, which among other miracles nowadays enables winter ascents of the Eigerwand, where the summer mortality rate used to be close to total; see the Neanderthals, the soul of poverty, yet so comfortable and content so much of the time; see, too, the fanatic sectarians, the *minimum packers*, whose pride is to walk the fine line on the farthermost edge of survival. Then go shopping.

Third, Set Up a Budget

The myth is that all recreational backpackers of long ago were poor. In fact, the Boy Scouts shivering in army blankets and sucking prune pits were only too aware that elsewhere on the planet was eiderdown, that somewhere over the rainbow wealthy explorers were feasting on bully beef and powdered eggs and dried spinach.

However, it is true that during the Great Depression all hikers (aside from patrons of Abercrombie & Fitch, a firm that on request would engage native porters) were misers and that subsequently they were confirmed in their thrift by the cornucopia of World War II surplus.

Emerging in this period, the equipment purveyors, later to become backpacking shops, catered to cheapskates. They employed advanced materials and designs to fabricate equipment immensely superior to that of yesteryear, yet rigorously excluded superfluous niceties because their customers, seeing the better and the cheaper side by side, typically would ogle the one, buy the other.

In the 1950s, something new: Americans commenced routinely flying to the Alps to scramble, Africa to photograph, Chile to ski. In large numbers they took to buying sleeping bags and packs with never a glance at the price. The restless inventors found throngs beating paths to the doors of their basement workshops. Merchants opened establishments with carpets on the floor and chamber music on the hi-fi. The 1960s witnessed twin phenomena—the spiraling of backpacking from idiosyncrasy to mass enthusiasm and the revolution in wildland expectations fueled by the rising tide of national wealth. Novices given a choice between two identical products spurned the less expensive (what's wrong with it—last year's model?) for the costlier one. Old cheapskates, astonished to find they too could afford to walk in the Lake District and trek in Nepal, went a little crazy and bought Gore-Tex earmuffs and gold-plated Sierra Club cups.

Wildland merchandising of the 1980s is as remote from the 1930s as a jet-powered movie theater is from a DC-3. A substantial segment of the industry focuses exclusively on the topmost several percent of the market, the most profitable and the most fun, where quality and ingenuity and forefrontery are everything, fashion and flash and wit something, and priciness nothing. Free of drudging economics, experiments can be imaginative to the verge of weird, contributing invaluably to the advancement of the art.

As for the shops originally founded by and for cheapskates, they'd have gone the way of the Model A Ford had they not changed with

the times, jettisoned the lower end of their price offerings, left in the lurch the unregenerate misers, and extended the upper end to compete for the custom of rich old ex-cheapskates. Nevertheless, these shops have kept faith with their origins by conducting extensive research to support a policy of good value at reasonable price.

Combined, these top-of-the-line and broad-range shops may be said to serve the backpacker more fully, and with more value and intelligence and humor than he has any right to expect. It only might be wished there still were places specifically for the cheapskates and Neanderthals and misers and young indigents. But then, the Model A is gone, and even the VW beetle has retreated to the Third World to join the DC-3.

Having picked his terrain, his style, the backpacker must choose an economic niche. In the neighborhood of the $500 sleeping bag and freeze-dried hummingbird hearts, *la dolce vita*? An army blanket and a cheese sandwich? John Muir would've snorted, called it too much.

Fourth, Seek Advice

Backpacking shops and the backpacking departments of more generalized stores are now so ubiquitous that most people can readily visit one to try on a boot and shoulder a pack and crawl in a bag and ask a clerk's advice. Many shops publish catalogs, indispensable guides to the latest miracle inventions and staggering prices; even if a person doesn't wish to buy by mail order, reading prepares for in-shop visits.

Magazines keep abreast of the state of the art and provide addresses of shops that issue catalogs and of family enterprises that handcraft things of beauty in the basement. Publications of national circulation come and go; the current roster can be found in the displays of backpacking shops. Those of regional circulation, as well as journals of climbing and hiking clubs, are useful for close views of individual trail provinces and expert commentary on equipment locally appropriate. Some newspapers run backpacking columns.

Then there are books. How many backpacking manuals a person can read without permanent impairment of literary taste is a question, even though so far as content goes, most of the dozens published in the past decade or so are fair to superb and only a few are penitentiary offenses. Reading (or scanning) more than just a single manual can save a beginner from being led deviously into eccentricity. A novice of the Appalachians does well to listen to an Appalachian veteran wise in the perils of 100 percent humidity and black flies and lurking moonshiners. And to learn the technique of the midday nap and crossing a river on an air mattress, consult the veteran of the Low Sierra and other deserts. For rain you're already in the right book.

By joining an outdoor club, a beginner can be tutored in locally favored gear. With common sources of supply has come, in recent years, substantial continent-wide and earth-wide uniformity, but there remain regional and national differences. As a further benefit, if the club has an environmental conscience, the beginner can instantly start doing his share to preserve trail country.

A novice with a trail-wise friend quite naturally and simply receives counsel and absorbs quirks.

One should not be bashful about striking up conversations with strangers met in wildlands; often they will be delighted to lecture at length on their equipment—and lecture, and lecture, and lecture.

Fifth, Prepare a Checklist

Starting with the general checklist at the end of this chapter, and advice from anywhere and everywhere, prepare a personal list of needed gear.

Sixth, Draw Up a Schedule of Purchases

But before spending a nickel, ransack the closet, basement, attic, and kitchen. Unless the immediate goal is to join the ranks of the beautiful people in the catalogs, much clothing too shoddy for city wear (old trousers, shirts, sweaters) or acquired for other outdoor activities (shorts, windbreakers) serves for hiking. A decent enough camp kitchen can be improvised from home utensils and tin cans. Work shoes may suffice for the first hikers, or sneakers for any and all short hikes.

Don't buy anything until it's needed for the next trip. Such as, if planning a series of day trips before trying a backpack, delay purchasing a pack and sleeping bag until the last minute and use the time to examine options.

Some articles can be rented from some backpacking shops—another way to postpone decisions, as well as to experiment with various styles of boots, packs, tents, snowshoes, and so on.

Buy inexpensive items for stopgaps while carefully considering large cash outlays. For example, make do with a tarp that costs several dollars while studying the intricacies of tents.

However, avoid false economy in major purchases. Don't pay $40 for a pack that looks sharp in the drugstore but falls apart on the first hike; instead, spend $100 for one that will last years. And don't waste $25 on a "down" sleeping bag that spits chicken feathers every time a cock crows.

The schedule of purchases obviously depends on financial resources. With no trouble at all and in a matter of minutes, a big spender can run through $2,000 acquiring a complete, first-class outfit. However, by scrounging around the house and charity-operated thrift shops, buying secondhand equipment and cheap fill-ins, renting and borrowing, a rough-and-ready basic outfit can be put together for not much more than $200; the ideal outfit can be assembled piece by piece, as the budget allows, in succeeding hiking seasons. Families have more of a financial problem, but that's not news.

WHERE TO BUY

In the Golden Age, the 1930s, places to buy trail gear were as few as the items available, and hikers resembled fishermen, loggers, sour-doughs, or Boy Scouts, and mostly that's what they were.

For a brief period after World War II, when surplus stores flourished on every corner of America, the trails seemed to have been

conquered by a vaudeville version of the Mountain Troops, the legendary Khaki Gang. There were army boots and army pants, army sleeping bags and army tents, army canteens and parkas and sweaters and mess kits and field rations. And from the South Pacific there were jungle hammocks, camouflaged ponchos, and bug juice so potent it shriveled the skin. And for combined operations, navy life-raft sails and air force goggles. From the standpoint of the backpacker, that was the only war ever worth having.

Mountain shops, the early ones founded by climbers unable to get needed ice axes and dehydrated spinach from regular sporting-goods stores, grew in numbers until by the 1970s few cities near mountains or trails lacked one or several. However, increasingly their climber customers were outnumbered by pedestrians using no hands. Where they got the name "backpacker" is uncertain—perhaps in the Sierra, to distinguish them from the burros. The neologism was resisted in the Pacific Northwest. There, unless folks hired a packer and horses for a "pack trip," they simply "went hiking." If overnight, obviously they carried packs, and where else than on backs? "Backpack" seemed as redundant as "footsock" or "headhat." But the term prevailed and the sport has overwhelmed mountain shops, which thus have been rechristened "backpacking shops," under which are included the backpacking departments of more comprehensive stores.

These specialty shops are logical headquarters for the beginner, even though not all are staffed exclusively by experienced mountain bums, as once was the case. That's why this book was published—to provide genuine bum advice.

Further, as noted earlier, the shops have succumbed to the tyranny of the majority, expressed in the first law of merchandising: "What people don't buy, you can't afford to stock." Where once shops catered to tightwads and indigents who proudly strutted around the glaciers in 50-cent war-surplus parkas, now their inventories appeal to well-heeled hikers who flit from fashion to fashion and don't always know what's good for them. Difficult to believe but true, today it's virtually impossible to find a mountain/backpacking shop that still sells dehydrated spinach.

As for other retailers, department stores lacking specialty departments may carry such things as sleeping bags and tents of good quality at bargain prices—if the hiker knows gear well enough to recognize a bargain. Fast-in/fast-out emporiums often advertise hiking gear at fantastic prices. The canny hiker may find real steals—loss leaders or genuine military surplus.

Many small trail items are sold by supermarkets, drugstores, hardware stores, etc.

Thrift shops run by Salvation Army, Goodwill Industries, St. Vincent de Paul, local churches and charities, offer outstanding buys in used clothing and kitchenware and the like. The beginner on a lean budget should tour the thrift shops immediately after ransacking the basement and before starting heavy spending. Even this late in the inflation spiral a person can obtain wool pants, shirt, and cap for less than $5. Parents with fast-growing kids should spend a lot of time at thrift shops. So should conservationists-environmentalists striving to "waste not, want not, despoil not."

The garage sales in the neighborhood ought to be assiduously attended. Pots and pans and sweaters abound, for nickels and dimes.

Anyone with access to basic sewing equipment can take measurements of costly gear in a shop, purchase materials (which are sold by some shops), and make reasonable copies at a fraction the expense. Families have been known to hold assembly-line "bees" that turned out whole neighborhoods of tents and put parkas on regiments of children. Similarly, Scout troops have outfitted members with packs decent enough and very cheap. A wealth of money-saving do-it-yourselfery is in the book *Make It and Take It* by Russ Mohney.

As a portent, perhaps, the once-popular kits vanished from the market in the late 1970s, but returned in the mid-1980s when the originator, Frostline, was rejuvenated, its catalog offering kits with all materials and full instructions for making a wide variety of backpacking gear. (Write Frostline, 2501 Frostline Avenue, Grand Junction, Colorado 81505.)

Hikers near factories may find stunning bargains in "seconds" (items with minor flaws), overruns (in excess of what could be sold to retailers), returns, damaged goods, or seasonal merchandise. Much is sold only at factory outlets, but some is scattered around the nation and appears at department stores on budget floors and in end-of-month sales and warehouse clearances.

Increasingly common are exchange shops featuring used gear; bring what you can't use, trade for what you can.

Warning: Putting price tags on backpacking equipment is like keeping track of the earth's population—memorize a figure, blink your eyes, and it's gone up, up, and away. And as long as the population rises, so will prices. Hikers recently coming upon the first edition of this book, published in 1972, have been disabled by convulsions of laughter, then sobs. One is reminded of Germany in 1923, when workers were paid twice a day so their wages could be raised fast enough to buy potatoes. Nevertheless, in the following chapters prices are noted for many articles. These are *not* exact and are intended merely to suggest the approximate range; they were advertised by one retailer or another at the time of writing.

BASIC EQUIPMENT CHECKLIST

As noted above, the beginner should prepare a checklist of equipment to be purchased or otherwise assembled. The list, regularly revised to reflect experience, has continuing utility, perhaps being posted in whatever corner of the house serves as the "hiking center" and consulted when the person is getting ready for trips to make sure nothing has been forgotten.

No hiker, not even a raw beginner, can be satisfied by someone else's checklist, no matter if it was drawn up by a forty-year veteran of thousands of miles of trails. Each person must do his own, based on conditions in his regular hiking terrain and on his personal idiosyncrasies.

The following list is limited to basics and does not include the myriad nice little items like binoculars, candles, pliers, reading material, playing cards, and the hundred other things individuals may come to consider indispensable for safety or pleasure.

For short afternoon walks in summer sunshine on broad trails, no equipment is really necessary—nor any clothing where local authorities are tolerant and the climate benign, as in Hawaii.

For full-day hikes the items listed below for "Day Trips" are generally essential; those in parentheses may be essential in some areas, under some conditions. (See Chapter 15 for a discussion of the Ten Essentials.)

For backpacking, additional gear is listed under "Add for Overnight" and a few more things under "Add for Special Situations."

Except among the broad-backed, elephant-legged bullies who carry double-bitted axes and watermelons, the motto of the age is *light-packing*. Many shops assist customers by recommending basic outfits from their stock and giving itemized weights.

REI, for example, has three checklists—for cold, cool, and warm weather. For a day trip with a low temperature of O°F, the total weight of recommended equipment is 23 pounds 15 ounces, and that includes 2 pounds of food and a quart of water; for overnight, add 7 pounds 11 ounces. For a day trip with a low of 30°F, total weight is 13 pounds 2 ounces; for overnight, add 6 pounds 3 ounces. For a day trip with a low of 45°F, the weight is 11 pounds 7 ounces; for overnight, add 4 pounds 14 ounces. Adding another day's food and a few incidentals, a person can do a warm weekend backpack carrying 20 pounds; a cool weekend, 23 pounds; a winter freezeout, 35 pounds. The possibilities are underlined by the further refinements of *ultralight backpacking*, whose adherents take pride in doing 3- to 5-day summer trips never carrying more than 20–30 pounds.

Marmot Mountain Works stresses the efficiency of the "new generation of backpacking equipment" by comparing two layering composites, one employing traditional low-tech clothing, the other, the new high-tech. A trip is assumed with temperatures ranging from 50°F in day to 0°F at night, rain and snow showers, wind on the heights. The situation can be met with a traditional outfit of down parka, storm parka, coated raingear, wool underwear, wool sweater, trousers, and wool shirt weighing 10 pounds 10 ounces. But it can be met equally well with Gore-Tex-and-down parka, all-weather parka and pants, polypropylene underwear, and pile sweater weighing 5 pounds 10 ounces—5 pounds less. Half a watermelon.

DAY TRIP

	Chapter		Chapter
Trail shoes or hiking boots	8	Purification tablets	4
Socks	8	Food	14
Underwear	9	(Sunglasses)	15
(Short pants)	9	(Sun cream)	15
Long pants	9	(Insect repellent)	15
Shirts and sweaters	9	Knife	15
(Rain jacket)	9	Matches	13
(Parka)	9	First-aid kit	15
Headwear	9	Toilet kit	15
(Mittens)	9	Flashlight	15
Rucksack	10	Map and compass	15
(Child carrier)	10	(Whistle)	15
		Water bottle	13

ADD FOR OVERNIGHT

	Chapter		Chapter
External- or internal-frame pack	10	Cooking pots	13
Sleeping bag	11	(Collapsible water carrier)	13
Sleeping pad or mattress	11	Eating tools	13
Ground sheet	11	Garbage bag	4
Tent or tarp	12	Food containers	13
Stove and fuel	13	(Bear wire and cord)	4
(Grate)	13	Repair kit	15

ADD FOR SPECIAL SITUATIONS

	Chapter		*Chapter*
Gaiters	8	Ice ax	17
Poncho	9	Hiking rope	17
Rain pants	9	Snowshoes	19
Insulated clothing	9	Cross-country skis	19

8
Boots

Everybody ought to go barefoot now and then. A dawn meadow delightful to the eye is equally so to the naked sole chilled by dewdrops sparkling on the grass. A stream is most intensely felt by toes probing swift water for a fingerlike grip on pebbles. Glacier-polished granite, squishy black muck, powdery volcanic ash freshly blown from Mount St. Helens, beach sand, pine needles, snow, all excite the sensual foot.

Anthropologists say that for most of his span mankind has been as free of foot clothing as apekind, and even today in some lands the inhabitants, given shoes and glass beads, string them together in necklaces. Other travelers, though, report being puzzled by automobile tracks on aboriginal paths, the mystery later explained by meeting local folks wearing sections of wornout tires strapped to their feet. No matter how callused, skin never truly enjoys prolonged contact with hard, sharp, hot, or cold earth and will exploit anything handy as a buffer—woven grass, chunks of bark, slabs of wood, animal skins, castoff Firestones and Michelins.

Over the eons mankind's savagery yielded to barbarism, then civilization, and primitive sandals were adapted in myriad ways to street, ballroom, bedroom, and trail. By the 1930s the wildlands of most of America were dominated by a boot that in its pure form was made for loggers, but when modified, also served hunters, fishermen, prospectors, trappers, hikers, and climbers. Entirely leather, except for fittings and the caulks or hobnails pounded into the leather sole, with an upper 8–10 inches high, in design an unembellished shell relying on socks for warmth and cushioning, the "logger" or "work boot" was the basic model sold everywhere, from custom bootmakers to the work-clothes department of J. C. Penney.

Among recreational wildlanders the beginning of the end for the logger boot was World War II, when the Mountain Troops brought home from the Alps the European climbing boot, a complex construction of thick slabs of leather reinforced with steel, padded and hinged to permit walking, lined for warmth, heavily soled with rubber lugs. For a quarter century this awesome creation dominated not only the Great North Walls, the glaciers and felsenmeers, but the meadows and trails and even the groves of academe, where it was considered as sexy as a Mercedes or a Tiger tank.

The "Eigerboot" did not go unchallenged. Many a climber carried the Frankenstein monsters on his back along the approach trail, there wearing the tennis shoes intended primarily for high-angle rock climbing. Many a hiker took a look at the price tag and went

to Penney's for a pair of work boots. As wildland recreation grew in popularity, bootmakers found a profitable market for scaled-down Eigerboots—lighter and less expensive and more than adequate for trails and meadows. The less savage boots were approved by the environmentally aware, increasingly concerned by the unnecessary damage to fragile ecosystems by overarmored feet. Finally, as tastes grew suaver and the bicycle began to be viewed as sexier than a Porsche, on campuses only the engineers still wore Eigerboots, the liberal arts students having regressed to sandals.

Then came running. Suburbs, where to be afoot once was to invite suspicious stares from police prowl cars and to be moving at a rapid pace was to set the siren whining and red light flashing, were suddenly thudding from dawn to dusk with joggers. As the costume was perfected and the chic widely envied, people dressed like runners to walk the dog, buy groceries, sit in bars drinking white wine. They flaunted their footgear; a shoe that was "lean and light and racy" implied the wearer was, too. Given the economic stimulus, manufacturers responded in the late 1970s with a burst of creative engineering, striving for running shoes that cushioned feet and spine from relentless thuds and supported foot and ankle from twists and turns and strains and sprains while weighing the absolute minimum.

When canny hikers commenced wearing their running shoes on trails, manufacturers were quick to see a new market. The materials and designs of "running-shoe tech" were adapted for the hiking boot, this new current of technology paralleling and at points synthesizing with the effort to scale down the Eigerboot.

The end is not yet. Certain experiments have failed outright, some miracle cures for ills of the wildland's feet have been denounced as quackery. Yet fresh ideas bubble up and are sent out for testing. New words are coined, a whole new language invented. Catalogs meant to instruct may, instead, bewilder.

So may books. The beginner might best skip the next section of this chapter, a high-tech jungle, and proceed to the following one, essentially nontech. Better yet, he might throw himself on the mercy of a boot supplier and beg the staff to make the choice. Most hikers throughout most of their careers find this the simplest way to buy boots. However, sooner or later a person may become curious about the insides and outsides of his footgarb. Especially if his feet hurt. Then it's time to try to decipher the secret code.

THE INS AND OUTS OF BOOT CONSTRUCTION

All boots are composed of three parts: the upper, the middle (insoles, midsoles); and the lower (outsole). Materials used in the upper will be discussed first, then the structure of the upper. The argument will proceed downward through the boot toward the hard, sharp, hot, cold, or wet earth.

Upper: Leather

Early on in his ascent from the primordial soup, and long before jungles and steppes were strewn with wrecked trucks and castoff tires, barefoot man in many parts of the hard, sharp, hot, cold, or wet world settled on animal skins as the best buffers for the human skin.

No material has yet been found to match leather's combination of flexibility, breathability, waterproofability, durability, and comfort—a "second skin." Moreover, though it is true that when a finite number of cows were asked to cover feet proliferating by the googols the price of leather rose as rapidly as that of freeze-dried shrimp, the effect on the final cost of a pair of boots has been relatively minor because boots are not so much material-intensive as labor-intensive.

Leather may be bragged up in the catalogs as "shoulder leather" or "Russia leather" or "Swiss Grade AA"; the man on the trail is unlikely to have any way of knowing if these are superior to Mexican bat wings or Persian mouse skin or a PG rating and must assume that if he's paying a pretty price, he's getting a pretty good leather.

Tanning

Since the hide would rot quickly without treatment, it is put through as many as nineteen mechanical and chemical operations while being cured, or tanned, into leather.

In *chrome tanning*, or *dry tanning*, the most common process in America and most of Europe for making the leather in city shoes and also boots, the hide is tanned with soluble chromium salts, giving a hard finish with a dry look. The pores of the leather are then, most commonly, wax-filled to maintain suppleness and water-repellency or, in a few cases, silicone-filled for the sake, it is hoped, of something approaching waterproofness.

In *oil tanning* and *vegetable tanning*, favored by a few manufacturers, the hide is tanned either with oils or vegetable material (bark tannins) from plants and wood, giving a soft, supple finish that has a wet, oily look.

The advantages of the methods—and of the self-explanatory *combination tanning* and *double tanning*—are as debatable as how many devils can dance in a frying pan. Excellent leathers are produced by all, and a hiker has little reason other than idle curiosity to learn anything about the subject—except as it may determine proper boot maintenance, discussed later in this chapter.

How Is It Sliced?

As worn by the animal, the hide varies in thickness from one part of the body to another. In preparation for boot (or other) use, the hide may be sliced in as many as half a dozen layers of different thickness, or *gauge*. Thin-gauge leather is characteristic of light-duty boots, heavy-gauge of heavy-duty.

Leather made from a layer including the outer surface of the hide (*grain side*) is called *top grain*. This is the best slice for boot uppers, the toughest and most water-resistant. The inner surface of the hide is called the *flesh side*.

Any slice not including the outside of the cow is called a *split*. Splits traditionally have been considered good for insoles and mid-soles but inferior for heavy-duty uppers, being very stretchable and impossible to waterproof. When used for an upper, split leather is called *suede*, a poor choice for slogging wet trails but excellent for dry paths, especially hot ones, because it is lightweight, porous, and easy-breathing. The reputation of splits may be under revision. In European experiments they are being backed with polyurethane to yield a low-cost, low-weight substitute for top-grain leather.

Which Side Outside?

The cow wears its skin with the grain side outside, the flesh side inside. Hikers, when they appropriate the hide for their feet, may do the same, or may not.

In a boot upper, top-grain leather with the grain side outside, the "right" way, is called *smooth* or *smooth-finish* or *smooth-out* leather. Partisans say this tougher and more water-repellent surface is the proper one with which to confront the wilderness. Critics say the tough outer layer is quite thin, readily breached in rough travel; once penetrated, it allows water to pour through the soft underlayer.

A top-grain leather with the flesh side outside is called *rough-out* or *flesh-out* or *reversed* or *reverse-tanned* or *rough-tanned* leather. (The term "suedelike," sometimes encountered, is misleading; to be sure, flesh-out leather looks the same as suede, but the latter is a split.) Partisans say that to preserve its water-repellency, the tough outer layer of hide is best kept from contact with the wilderness and that the flesh side, though it scuffs and abrades easily, is never weakened structurally and wears away only bit by bit.

Experts argue back and forth. They agree, though, that the quality of a hide is more significant than whether it is used rough-out or smooth-out; first-rate boots are made both ways. The important distinction is whether a leather is top-grain or split.

Natural or Prettified?

A bootmaker using a quality hide is frequently so proud of it that he retains as much as possible of the original appearance. In such *full-grain* or *natural* leather no buffing has been done to smooth the surface and thus conceal healed scratches or small pits caused by tick and fly bites. The natural look is not only considered the most beautiful by connoisseurs but maintains the full inherent strength, durability, and breathability. The color of boots made from full-grain leather is usually not uniform throughout due to variations from hide to hide.

A *corrected-grain* leather is not necessarily inferior in strength and may be of excellent quality. However, the manufacturer has chosen to hide blemishes to obtain a uniform appearance. For example, in a *pebble-grained* leather the surface has been stippled by tiny gouges.

A smooth- or rough-out leather is usually *dyed* only very lightly (or not at all) to retain the natural look. Most suedes and some other leathers are dyed black, gray, green, blue, red, brown, or whatever. The dye doesn't harm the leather and may appeal more to stylish walkers than the color of a cow.

Upper: Vegetable Fabrics

In the era of the logger boot with iron-studded sole, climbers customarily carried for use on slabby rock or thin holds a pair of tennis shoes, the most famous brand being Keds, the same brand traditionally supplied kids in June, when school let out for the summer. The upper was cotton canvas, and though toes inevitably peeked through by September and attempts to keep the treasured sneakers over the winter were frustrated by Mother's objection to the stench, and they eventually found their way into the furnace, come June and freedom and there'd be another pair.

Remarkably, in the reaction against leather, it was not America that remembered Keds. For hot weather the French army supplied troops with an exact copy except for the color (khaki) and the sole (lugs).

Korea and Taiwan and Hong Kong went farther, glued cotton canvas to synthetic rubber, and produced a "Keds boot" that is marketed under names that make it seem to have sprung from American mountains. Light, cheap, and pretty, with luck a pair will last from June to September, or at least until the Fourth of July.

Upper: Synthetic Fabrics Combined With Leather

American bootmakers, recognizing the brief life of canvas and the impossibility of attaching it firmly to rubber, turned to synthetic fabrics, combining them with leather to obtain lightness while retaining durability.

Typically, the panels of the upper are nylon (ballistics nylon, nylon pack cloth, Duro Mesh nylon, or Cordura), much more abrasion-resistant than canvas, much lighter and cooler than leather, and with the capacity to be sewn to leather. The fabric may be coated to make it temporarily water-repellent. The areas of heavy wear, too great for the fabric to withstand, are leather, a top-grain or a suede depending on the intent of the boot.

Upper: Plastic

The plastic boot has long since become the standard on downhill ski slopes, giving a far more rigid connection between foot and ski than is possible with leather. More recently it has replaced the old Eigerboot for really hard-nosed climbing, so firmly attaching foot to crampons that a person can front-point up icicles, and so warm and dry that the toes are safe from frostbite in Antarctic blizzards.

The less expensive of the plastics appeal to climbers whose noses aren't particularly hard but who enjoy cozy feet.

Koflach, a leader in plastique, has recently introduced hiking and hunting boots with all the advantages of warmth and dryness yet surprisingly flexible because the plastic is molded in the forefoot.

Upper: In Quest of Waterproofness

The rule of thumb in the day of the logger was that during a person's first year with new boots he could slog snowfields and wade creeks and never wet his socks, and that from the second year on he could grease night and morning and never have dry tootsies after crossing a field of wet grass. Adopting a philosophical attitude, people shrugged, saying that being 95 percent water on their inside it was silly to fuss about 1 percent more on the outside. Nevertheless, wet feet get cold, shrivel, blister. The vision of ever-dry toes was a Grail pursued through the wildlands and the years.

In the late 1970s the notion arose that if Gore-Tex was good for parkas and gaiters and whatnot, it also ought to be good for boots. Enthusiasts led a stampede, predicting that in the near future "leather would be reduced to a trim."

In the early models the Gore-Tex was laminated to nylon and the seams were sealed—very briefly. Moreover, connective stitching couldn't "grab" the Gore-Tex fabric, which separated from the nylon. Further, the Gore-Tex membrane, so vulnerable to dirt, sweat, and filth in a parka, simply gave up the ghost when plunged into mud.

The manufacturer then produced a special boot membrane twice as thick and four times as tough as the normal. To avoid problems with bad grabbing and poor sealing, bootmakers adopted the *dropped sock*, or *sock liner*, the Gore-Tex membrane and its backing fabric suspended from the top of the upper to "hang" inside, enveloping the foot, guarding it from the outside wet. The Gore-Tex also was protected from exterior nastiness.

In the judgment of an overwhelming majority of hikers who have tried it from the Cascades to the Brooks Range to Nepal, of cobblers and retailers and other footwear professionals, Gore-Tex does not work in a boot—it has never kept a single foot dry that wouldn't have stayed just as dry inside plain nylon, cotton canvas, or suede leather. Many believe that Gore-Tex is still used in boots only because hikers who have swallowed the advertising hook, line, and fishing rod demand it and, if denied, will go elsewhere, just as in a supermarket the fans of the Saturday morning TV cartoons insist on Captain Winky's Fortified Purple Candy Flakes. The shops therefore meet the request. However, clerks will be glad to steer skeptics to the oatmeal.

Nevertheless, the manufacturer claims Gore-Tex will perform beautifully if bootmakers will use it right, and so bootmakers are trying new expedients. Not every professional believes the final verdict is in.

Meanwhile, Gore-Tex does no harm in a boot and so little is involved that the manufacturing cost isn't significantly increased, though the selling price may include a substantial glamor factor.

Upper: Construction

Regardless of the materials used, the methods of constructing a boot upper follow certain general principles and fall within a certain range of standard alternatives.

The Upper in General

One school of experts holds that the best way to build a boot upper is from a *single piece* of leather, thus keeping seams—lines of potential weakness and leakage—to a minimum. Another school defends *sectional* construction (from two or three pieces), saying that (1) the upper can more easily be made to conform to the foot, (2) smaller pieces of prime leather can be utilized or leather can be combined with other materials for lightness and thus the expense is less for the same quality, and (3) seam leakage isn't that much of a problem anyhow. Neutrals don't get very sweaty about the matter, admitting that most climbing boots have one-piece uppers, most hiking boots sectional, and that perhaps this means something, but insisting that either method will work fine for either purpose. Certainly, a lot of stitching on an upper by no means indicates a bad boot.

A *double-stitched* upper has two lines of stitching at every point, thus reducing chances of all stitches being cut at once. Triple-stitching gives that much more insurance.

The *shell boot* has pretty well gone to join the dinosaurs, and all modern boots except the skimpiest have some lining, reinforcing, and padding. The more there is, the more the foot protection, insulation, comfort—and weight and sweat and expense.

The *lining* may be complete, partial, or nonexistent. Usually of pigskin, calfskin, or some other soft, supple leather, the lining lets the foot glide smoothly in and out, and minimizes chafing.

Most boots have *padding* in the ankle area; some are padded elsewhere, perhaps throughout, though rarely to the toe. The padding material, inserted between the outer wall and the liner, may be foam, rubber, or felt. (To be avoided for ordinary hiking is the *insulated* boot designed for extreme cold.)

Reinforcing at heel and toe is discussed below. There may also be *side reinforcements* of leatherboard or other material above the ball of the foot and from the ball back toward the heel. Reinforcements where needed for foot support and protection, designed whenever possible for softness and flexibility, are characteristic of the best boots. Cheaper boots may give protection and support with stiff materials but are uncomfortable and difficult to break in. The Eigerboot, heavily reinforced, had a *hinged instep*, a small cutout from the leather of the upper to allow the boot to flex.

The Upper Part of the Upper

The logger boot had an overall height of about 9 inches measured from the top to the junction of upper and sole, extending far enough up the calf to prevent mud, snow, and creeks from slopping down inside. (More popular in much of the West was the "rattlesnake boot" or "ranger boot" coming almost to the knee.) Few 9-inch boots remain on the market, and most hikers are content with 7½ or 5½ inches or, in low-cut walking and trail shoes, even 4½ inches, which is barely enough to support and protect the ankle. For fending off mud, snow, and creeks, the *gaiter*, discussed later in this chapter, is preferred to an upward extension of the upper, where excess leather increases the difficulty of getting in and out of boots.

Many boots have a gap-closing device at the top to prevent water, snow, or pebbles from slipping down inside. Most common is an elastic fabric, perhaps padded, that fits snugly against the leg. Among the names for the device are *scree shield*, *scree collar*, *scree gaiter*, *snow protector*, and *cuff*. Half or less of all hikers find this feature effective; the others feel it doesn't work at all (though few think it detrimental) and prefer to do the job, when necessary, with a gaiter.

The collar may include a roll of foam padding to comfort the Achilles tendon. With some boots the tendon is further pampered by cutting the leather of the upper low in back and adding a soft panel of garment leather.

The Back of the Upper (Heel Counter)

All but the lightest boots have long had a *heel counter*, or *heel cup*, a piece of leather, rigid fiber, thermoplastic, or molded nylon inserted inside. Cupping the heel, the counter helps anchor the foot to the boot sole, thus minimizing the vertical motion of heel lift. It also gives additional protection to the heel.

A discovery of running-shoe tech is that side-to-side stability of the foot is best ensured by a stiff heel counter, which holds the lower ankle and keeps it from sliding and potentially twisting. It is said that with a good counter even low-cut shoes feel stable, and without one even calf-high boots don't properly support the ankle.

A *heel cup* (sometimes called *outside heel counter*) is an extra piece of leather stitched to the boot exterior to guard against abrasion.

The Toe

Boots in the American pioneer tradition have a completely *soft* toe, which is easy on the foot—until it runs into or is fallen upon by a rock. So frequent are foot-rock encounters that toes on nearly all modern hiking and climbing boots are more or less *hard*, ranging from being slightly stiffened by a piece of plastic inside to total bombproofing by counters of leather, leatherboard, molded nylon, or plastic. The result may be described as a *toe counter* or *guard*, *hard toe*, *box toe*, or, in a running shoe, *external toe protector*. Some boots have a *toe cap*, serving the same purpose as a heel cap.

The moccasin toe still has fans. Because the structure is soft (and difficult to make hard), the hiker's toes are cozy. Moccasin toes and high-top uppers generally go together on boots of the old, old design still beloved to woodsmen who mainly tramp soft forest duffs or paddle about in canoes.

Tongue and Closure

In the tongue-and-closure area the boot designer has three concerns: (1) preventing water from seeping or pouring through the gap, (2) providing the foot expeditious entry and exit, since donning and doffing wet or frozen boots can be an excruciating test of muscle and will, and (3) being kind to delicate flesh. In the upward progression from easy, dry trails to rough, sopping terrain, increasing

Tongue and closure. Left: *Leather-synthetic hiking boot with gusseted tongue.* Right: *Leather hiking boot with overlapping split tongue.*

attention must be paid to the tongue and closure. The expedients adopted by designers are countless; they all, however, represent one of two basic approaches.

The *gusseted tongue* bars water by placing an unbroken barrier between foot and wet world. On simple boots the barrier may be nothing more than a small strip of soft leather attaching the tongue to the boot upper, the tongue being described as *sewn in*; the barrier strip, and sewing, may extend to the top or only part of the way. On more complex boots the barrier is a considerable mass of flexible leather that opens out in a *bellows* to let the foot in and out, and folds neatly when laced. In a variation, the boot has two tongues, a soft inner one for comfort and an outer gusseted tongue.

The *split tongue* permits the boot to be opened very wide so the foot can gain easy ingress when the leather is frozen rock-hard; it keeps out water (though perhaps never so absolutely as a gusseted tongue) by creating, with the help of laces, devious passageways that discourage inward-creeping moisture. Many a split-tongue design has two tongues, a soft inner (often partly sewn in) and an outer which actually is the boot upper, split down the middle. The most elementary example of the split tongue is on city oxfords and light-duty trail shoes, where the halves of the upper are drawn together over the inner tongue by laces. On heavier-duty boots the split halves of the upper overlap. A few boots have a third tongue outside the split tongue for more complete baffling of water.

Having thus cast light into the swampy darkness of the tongue situation, it is now necessary to murk it up again by saying that there are many combinations of gusseting and splitting, resulting in a variety of hybrid designs.

On light-duty trail shoes the tongue proper may be a single thickness of leather. On heavier-duty boots that require tight lacing, the inner tongue is *padded* to cushion the foot against pressures of laces; it may also be *contoured* or *hinged* for easy flexing.

Lacing

Completing the closure is the lacing, which may be by eyelets, D rings (also called swivel eyelets), hooks, or a combination.

Lacing systems. Left: *Leather heavy-hiking boot with swivel eyelets and hooks.* Center: *Leather-synthetic hiking boot with grommets and hooks.* Right: *Cotton-canvas trail shoe with all-eyelet lacing.*

A very few boots, including light trail shoes as well as some traditional American designs, have *all-eyelet* lacing, with eyelets formed by grommets set directly into the upper. The advantage is that grommets virtually never fail until the boot is ancient, and even then the holes seldom enlarge or split out, since before this can happen, the metal pieces must break loose. The disadvantage is that lacing is tedious.

More common are boots having *eyelets partway up, then yielding to hooks*—the latter much quicker to lace and unlace. An alternative to the grommet-type eyelet set in the upper is the *swivel eyelet*, a D ring attached to a clip riveted to the upper; this combines easy lacing with maximum water-repellency and insulation. *Speed lacing* employs closed hooks; a single quick pull tightens the laces from bottom to top.

Incidentally, most hikers do not realize that hooks, rings, clips, and grommets can quickly be replaced in any shoe-repair shop and many backpacking shops. There is no need to accept the loss of metal fixtures fatalistically and go about with half a lacing system, the boot flopping on and off the foot.

As for *laces*, leather retains a few adherents but stretches when wet and thus loosens. Nylon is more popular nowadays for its greater durability; soft-woven, unwaxed laces hold knots best.

A tip about lacing: The beginning walker, or any walker at the start of the season, may find his tender shin abraded by the top of the boot, especially the knot. The remedy is to lace to the top, then lace back downward two or three rows and tie the knot there. This gives support the full height of the boot but removes the knot from the tender spot, as well as from the knot-loosening activity of the ankle; it also reinforces the heel and helps keep the entire lace system secure.

Another tip: If toes feel cramped, lace the lower area of the boot loose, then tie a knot and lace the upper area tight. Or in a different situation, such as downhill walking, lace tight down low, especially at the toes, tie a knot, and lace loose up high. In summary: experiment.

One final tip: If lacing stiff boots tight enough is difficult, try the *cargo knot*. Bring laces to the middle of the boot, wrap them over each other, and thus, when cinching, reverse the normal direction of pull and gain a mechanical advantage.

Insole-Midsole

The function of the upper, with heel counter, toe cap, and scree guard and all, is to rebuff boulders, exclude dirt and water, and keep the ankle from twisting. The role of the sole—insole, midsole, and outsole—is to cushion the foot against the thud of hard places, the punctures of sharp things, and the treachery of slithery spots.

Insole

The insole or inner sole immediately touches the foot bottom. In older boots meant for heavy duty it is a soft leather—*calfskin*, glove-tanned, or *garment-tanned*—with a thin layer of some species of slippery nylon for low-friction foot entry. In light-duty boots, really walking shoes, there may be nothing more elaborate than a slice of jute or a sandwich of polyurethane and tight-woven cotton.

Midsole

Extreme lightweights intended for soft paths and feathery-stepping pedestrians often lack a midsole altogether, and on bumpy ground each pebble bruises the foot unless the hiker has the agility to pirouette.

Surviving in many heavier models are midsoles inherited from the logger and the Eiger, composed of leather, reconstituted leather (a cemented composition of ground-up scraps), rubber, neoprene, or wood, with perhaps a filler of cork or foam for cushioning.

The newer boots are described as having the hearts of running shoes, combining lightness, strength, and cushioning. The material may be *EVA* (ethyl vinyl acetate), a foamy plastic that compresses and then springs back to the original shape; a *blown rubber* (or *expanded rubber*), which does the same and lasts longer; or some other good

Leather heavy-hiking boot sliced in half front to back to show interior details of insoles and midsoles. This boot has a half-length steel shank, hard toe and heel counter, and padded upper. Construction is by Norwegian welting. Unlike the newer "running-shoe" boots, it lacks a heel wedge.

stuff. Typically there is both a midsole and, to absorb heel shock, a *heel wedge* or *cushion plug wedge*. Inasmuch as a customer can't slice open boots in the shop to study the vitals for omens, one has to take the advertising claims on faith.

In the past only the most rudimentary boots lacked a *shank* to support the arch, protect the instep, and hold the foot straight, the materials ranging from tempered spring steel to plastic to reconstituted leather to laminated wood to stiffened nylon; the length, from full to half. Heavy-duty boots retain the shank, and so do some lighter boots, though scaled down—if not utterly replaced—by running-shoe tech, whose midsoles and footbeds are claimed to give more consistent protective stiffening than steel. Asolo boots are notable for this, the Asoflex midsoles so graded to the size of the boot that a women's size 5 flexes as appropriately as a men's size 12.

Outsole

Until World War II just about every American hiker and climber gained traction on trail, footlog, meadow, and snow with nailed soles. For the hiker there were hobs, rosebuds, and slivers, plus needle-sharp logger's caulks (pronounced "corks") in the instep. For the scrambler and climber there were Swiss edge-nails favored by a scattering of oldtimers—but for the masses (all couple of thousand or so) there was the tricouni nail, or "trike."

Then the Mountain Troops came home from Italy wearing the "Bramani," a legendary boot that weighed a ton, sold for nickels and dimes at surplus stores, and was fitted not with an iron-studded bottom but with rubber lugs—the invention, in 1935, of Vitale Bramani. A passionate debate began throughout North America. Trikes were attacked as "heat sinks," conducting the heat of the foot out of the boot. They were defended as infinitely superior to lugs on hard snow, footlogs, heather, steep grass—indeed, in virtually every terrain except rock and well-maintained trails.

Here and there may still be found a mountain shop whose cobwebby back room has tricounis to please those ancient pedestrians

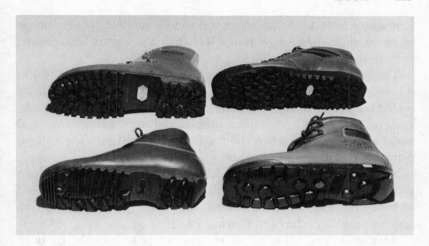

Four examples of common rubber-lug outsoles. Dozens are on the market from a number of manufacturers.

who stubbornly prophesy a return of the Iron Age. And maybe they're right, but the debate waned in the early 1960s, and since then the lug has held almost universal dominion on American, as well as European, trails and peaks.

These ancient pedestrians recall the familiar signs on doorways of fire lookout cabins and ranger stations, TAKE OFF BOOTS, and on forest-frontier saloons, NO CORKS ON DANCE FLOOR. They remember how warmly housekeepers welcomed the gentility of rubber lugs. They were startled when, in the 1970s, preservationist friars began preaching against black fangs chewing up fragile soils, ripping tender plants, digging erosion gullies, condemning them as being as vicious as bulldozers and trailbikes. Said the "tenny-runner freaks," hikers with heavy boots can't feel the earth through their armor and thus wound it, while those wearing light shoes must walk softly for feet's sake and in consequence also spare the land.

At outdoor rock concerts where minds were blown and throats cut, the lawns suffered remarkably little damage despite trammeling by thousands of feet, many under the loosest control; subalpine meadows walked by mere scores of flower children were devastated.

One study concluded that bare feet do one-seventh the plant damage of street shoes—and how much less than the lugs of Eigerboots, even in the slimmer versions?

The response of the backcountry community was twofold. First, hikers learned the rules of walking with a light foot: stay on maintained trails where they exist, and do not cut switchbacks; off trails, stick to hard rocks and resilient forests and expendable snow, and avoid soft meadows; when the fragile and the delicate are walked, place boots with care not to stomp, not to erode.

Second, the extreme ascetics abjured boots altogether, at least those with lugs. Compelled to walk more respectfully, they rejoiced in their kindness to the wilderness. However, particularly in steep and wet country, they fell down a lot.

Accused of providing no alternative except to hurt the Earth or the body, manufacturers developed a new generation of outsoles, a broad spectrum—some for level or gentle trails in the dry season when a firm enough grip on the ground is given by unassisted gravity; others for steep trails or mud or snow, where lack of a dependable connection between boot and earth may lead to bruising and bleeding and screaming and fracturing.

Lug materials range from the very hard and durable (high-carbon neoprene), which resists the buffeting of granite and schist and gneiss, to the soft (gum rubber), which mates intimately with sandstone and moss while respecting the feelings of lichen and heather, to the spongy (crepe, superb for pavement, and foam, which blunts the thrust of sharp rocks yet is very light).

Lug patterns range from the all-over pimples (not really lugs at all) of *crepe* to a *ripple* or *dimple* or *rib* that has nearly as much surface contact as crepe and deeper penetration of the ground, for better traction; to a *shallow lug* that has less traction on hard surfaces than the ripple but gets farther down in the mud and grass to grip something solid; to a *deep lug* that reaches even deeper; to a *needlepoint*; to close-spaced *low-impact lugs*; to innumerable other interesting patterns.

Vibram (*Vito Bram*ani) offers a dozen neoprene compounds hard and soft, in patterns deep and shallow. Galibier, Pirelli, and other companies contribute their share.

As in the case of insole and midsole, the material and design of the outsole are married to other boot components to achieve a unified purpose, dependably reflected by the gross weight. The hiker can trust a lightweight boot to permit him to tread the land gently, a heavier one to let him run about the talus, banging the boulders.

Attaching Sole to Upper

The leading cause of boot death is the final and incurable separation of outsole from upper. Despite a research effort as dedicated as that against giardiasis, bootmakers have not as yet conquered the disease. Every method of attachment has its pluses and minuses.

In *vulcanizing*, a preformed rubber outsole is bonded by heat and pressure to the upper—not very well or for very long, but very cheaply.

Cementing is the next least expensive method. The outsole is cemented directly to the midsole/upper or the upper. As the technique has been refined, it has increasingly gained favor for light-duty boots.

With the somewhat similar *injection molding*, molten neoprene is applied under pressure, replacing cementing or welting (see below).

With the *inside-stitching* method, also called *Littleway construction* (or *Littleway welt*), the upper is folded under and sandwiched between insole and midsole, the outsole is glued to the lower midsole, and the layers are fastened together by a double row of lockstitching, concealed within the boot and thus protected from moisture and abrasion. (A boot so made can be recognized by the absence of exterior stitches.) Advantages of Littleway are that the sole can be closely cropped to be nearly flush with the upper, the boots are narrower, lighter, and more waterproof than outside-stitched ones, and they are less expensive to build and repair. The better trail shoes, most hiking boots, and a few climbing boots are of Littleway construction.

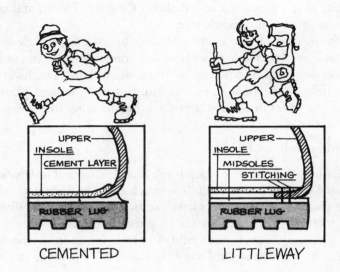

CEMENTED   LITTLEWAY

The term "welting," though sometimes applied to Littleway, ordinarily is reserved for *outside-stitched* (or *welted*) boots, of which two types are common.

With the *Norwegian welt* (or *European welt*), one line of stitching angles inward, securing insole to upper, and a second (sometimes a third) line is vertical, securing midsole to the outward-turned upper. (A Norwegian-welted boot can be recognized by the two or three lines of stitching visible on the ledge atop the sole, though the inward-slanting line may be difficult to see.) Its main advantage is that because the last remains in the boot until construction is complete, the insole conforms around it without distortion, assuring a good fit; this is the only way Europeans know how to make a boot. Disadvantages are the expense of manufacture and the vulnerability of the outside stitching to wear and leakage. As the Eigerboot has declined, so has the Norwegian welt.

With the *Goodyear welt* (also called *U.S. welt* or *true welt*), which is found on most men's street shoes and on many American-made boots, the upper is stitched directly to a raised rib on the insole and

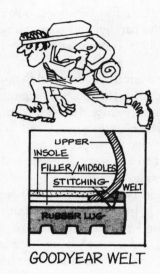

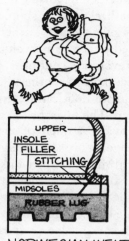

GOODYEAR WELT   NORWEGIAN WELT

to a narrow piece of leather (called the *welt*, just to complicate
terminology) that goes completely around the boot exterior at the
junction of sole and upper. The welt is then stitched to the midsole.
(A Goodyear-welted boot can be recognized by the single line of
stitching on the ledge atop the sole.) The main advantage of this
method is that it permits rapid machine production. However, newer
methods make better and cheaper boots so the Goodyear welt seems
on the way out as well.

Not to be confused with the Norwegian or Goodyear welt is the
rubber storm welt (or *welt gasket*), which has become common in recent
years. After the upper and outsole are assembled, a rubber ring is
glued to the junction, helping waterproof this most permeable zone
of the boot.

VARIETIES OF BOOTS

Neither the old American logger (work, woodsman) boot nor the
old European Eigerboot is absolutely defunct; both may be found

in one odd merchandising nook or another. They are gone, however, from the backpacking shop, where the parallel and converging evolutions of a lighter leather boot and a running-shoe boot have combined to create a revolution.

The revolution continues, thesis and antithesis interacting toward a future unknown synthesis, and the catalog that this year announces the Ultimate Boot can be expected to introduce the New Ultimate next year. The hiker needn't wait. The syntheses produced to date have provided a range of choices that are far wider than those of a decade ago, more accurately tailored to a variety of needs and desires, and much simpler to select among.

A person's first consideration should be a negative: *Don't buy too much boot*. The U.S. Army Research Institute of Environmental Medicine has determined that carrying 1 pound on the feet requires as much energy as 6 pounds on the back; switch from Eigerboots to running shoes and you can afford to pack a watermelon for lunch.

The second should be a positive: *Buy enough boot*. As the thrifty and the environmentally sensitive recapitulated the history of footgear backward through time toward Keds and sandals, a sorry number began pulling up lame, Achilles tendons sore, bones bruised, arches fallen, hubris humbled.

What *is* enough? Two factors rule: the terrain to be walked and the load. In lands of dry trails (say, the High Sierra in midsummer) or soft forest duff (say, Ozark ridges), sandals may nearly do; lands of rain and snow and brush and moraines all jumbled up (say, the British Columbia Coast Range) may dent General Patton tanks. The second factor is of equal importance. If the feet must support only the 120 pounds of a small person with day-hike rucksack, they can skip nimbly about to dodge danger and need only modest protection. But if a 200-pound body and 60-pound pack are above, there'd better be a lot of substance below, guarding the blundering feet of the tottering tyrannosaur.

In olden days the *weight* of a boot was a fair indicator of what it was designed for: Heavy weight meant heavy use, light weight, light use. *Complexity* was a close companion—the more parts, the more weight. Now, however, some features may be added to reduce weight. Indeed, the most striking benefit of new tech is that in every category boots today weigh less than a decade ago.

Cost used to accompany weight and reflect sturdiness and durability. For a number of reasons this is no longer invariably true; some footgear of modest price plugs along for several years, while some very expensive products survive only a single beautiful summer.

A person's *style* must be considered. Devotees of the running-shoe boot have described it as "feeling sharp, responsive, and precise, like a racing car or finely tuned pair of slalom skis." The hiker whose tastes lean toward Volkswagen and snowshoes and who never learned to dance may prefer a solid slab of cowskin between toes and boulders.

While refining the designs of boots in the past decade, manufacturers and retailers have also improved the definitions of boot categories, immensely easing the task of choosing the boot that will have to suffice until the Ultimate comes along.

Note: In the following paragraphs when boot weight is given, the reference is to an average men's size; in the average women's sizes, weights are a bit less.

Camp Shoes

The most concentrated impact of the human foot is where it spends the most time—camp. Even those hikers who formerly felt that loosening their boot laces or packing along a dry pair of socks was sufficiently pampering to their trail-sore feet have now taken to carrying camp shoes, for the sake of the flowers.

The camp shoe must be very light, isn't expected to provide traction, and need only be waterproof enough to keep out dew and mist. Few backpacking shops stock anything suitable. A *sports shoe* (new moniker of the old tennis shoe), weighing 1 pound the pair and costing $20, is about as much weight and money as a backpacker can afford. Bedroom slippers can be found that are lighter and cheaper and perfectly adequate, especially if a poly bag is slipped over them and held at the ankle by a rubber band.

Walking Shoes

As runners slow down, on doctor's orders or hints from leg bones, and fulfill aerobic goals by the "fast walking" described in Chapter 1, they often feel compelled to change uniforms. Since these people walk, as once they ran, on level, hard surfaces, a low-cut oxford with a cushion sole of foam or crepe and the innards of the running shoe serves the purpose. Some models have a shallow lug or a ripple to permit fast walking on slippery grass.

The walking shoe is sleek enough to be worn on a city sidewalk, in an office, or to a fine restaurant and is a boon to the worker whose job requires pounding miles of hard floors or pavement while maintaining a neat appearance. Another sales stimulus is that in the mid-1980s the running-shoe look, which supplanted the European-climbing-boot look, seemed itself to be yielding on campus to the preppy look of white shirts and ties and traditional leather shoes. The price—$50 and up—argues against messing them up on a muddy

Examples of footwear suitable as camp shoes. Left: *Down booties, for softness and warmth, with waterproof sole.* Right: *Thong sandals, to let the toes expand and cool off, with a sole that permits walking on sharp stones.*

Left: *A walking shoe presentable on a city street and giving the foot enough protection on many paths.* Right: *A lightweight, inexpensive, limited-use trail shoe.*

trail, but an old, scuffed pair can be worn in wildlands with the out-at-elbows blazer.

Trail Shoes, Light and Cheap

Models of footwear in this category are lithe, between 1½ and 2½ pounds, and nicely affordable, $25 to $35. However, they are called "shoes" rather than boots, no matter how clever the resemblance, because they are not designed for hard and steady use. Worn for the occasional afternoon stroll, a pair may last several years and be a splendid bargain at, say, a cost of $10 a year. Expected to serve for a daily ramble around the woodlot, a new pair may be needed every month, for a year's cost of $300—except that along about the third pair the rambler is likely to switch to $100 boots.

Let it be noted that some of this bunch, hustled together on sampans in Hong Kong harbor, do well to last a day, which, if a fool were to so persist, might give an annual footwear cost of $9,000. Of course, at a reputable shop one may ask for his money back. Beware of pushcarts.

The uppers are cotton canvas or nylon or Cordura, reinforced—or not—at wear points with suede leather or rubber. A few models have elementary toe caps and heel counters. Some are oxford-high, others extend above the ankle as far as the old Keds. Midsoles are minimal to absent, though a few go so far as to have a little steel shank. The outsole typically is a shallow lug, "low impact," often of a gum rubber that could scarcely harm a flower or defend a foot against a broken beer bottle. The outsole is bonded to the upper by vulcanization, which with some materials fails utterly and almost immediately.

The ethical shop advertises this category for "day hikes and city strolls," says only that such shoes do very well indeed for the occasional trail, and asks: Why buy a 1,000-mile boot when you plan to walk only 100 miles a year?

Trail Shoes, Light and Not So Cheap

Another name is *approach shoe*, as the running shoe was rechristened when transported to the scene where oldtime Eigerbooters used to wear their rock-climbing tennis shoes. The litheness is only a bit less than the sampan products, about 1⅔–2⅔ pounds. The price isn't terribly formidable either, from $40 to $85. They are classified as "shoes" partly because of the low-cut top, distinctly unbootlike in looks, and partly because many models are not meant to live forever but rather to give a few weeks of ecstasy and then expire. Some, though, log 1,000 miles and beg for more. The buyer should be sure to ask about longevity at the shop; certain brands have established certain reputations.

Durability, where it exists, is not the reason these shoes are so often seen on wildland trails. They are popular because they feel good from the first minute, never need a break-in, and are light and maneuverable, magnificent for trail-dancers, the folks who weave easily through rush-hour traffic on freeways and mobs of skiers on tow hills. They are not so suitable for stumblers and lurchers, particularly on rough ground where the hiker must place the foot

Examples of lightweight trail shoes, or approach shoes, not so inexpensive but quite durable and very versatile.

carefully, inasmuch as the ankle bone is connected to the leg bone, ultimately, to the head bone, all breakable.

The uppers are nylon reinforced with split leather; the ankle is supported by the stiff heel counter of a running shoe, from which also derive the EVA-or-relative guts. The outsole is a shallow lug or some ingenuity beyond Vitale Bramani. It is attached to the upper in some cases by vulcanizing or, most often, by cementing, a process that has advanced to a stage where failures are rare.

Hiking Boots, Leather-Synthetic Combinations

It is here that some prophets predict the coming birth of the Ultimate Boot. Also called *light hikers*, the offerings range from 1¾ to 3 pounds, $40 to $140, overlapping the weights and prices of trail shoes. They earn the name "boots" by withstanding terrain of some rudeness, giving as much protection as the average foot will ever need. In this or the following category the typical backpacker will find his main boot, supplemented though it may be by shoes of this kind or that for special situations.

Thanks to the substitution of nylon (Cordura or other) panels for portions of the upper that in the past were leather, a thinning of the sole lugs, and exploitation of running-shoe tech, these boots are pounds lighter than the "light hikers" of yesteryear. They share with trail shoes the blessing of feeling good from the first minute.

Examples of leather-synthetic hiking boots, or light hikers, with and without Gore-Tex.

The category suffers from an unfortunate confusion. Because it was here that Gore-Tex was introduced to boots, a person is liable to suppose all models are Gore-Tex boots and judge them on the basis of whether or not he's a believer. Some of these boots *do* have Gore-Tex, which adds something to the cost and—as discussed earlier—nothing to the water-repellency. But many have panels of just plain nylon and make no claims about keeping creeks and snowmelt and rain out of the socks. (A splash of silicone on the panels may help for an hour or so.)

None of these boots, Gore-Tex or any other, are water-repellent. However, all of them, once wet, dry far faster than all-leather boots. And in dry, hot weather they all freely exhale sweat, with or without help from a miracle.

Uppers are one or another variety of nylon, coated or not (a coating will keep out heavy dews the first several days on the trail), combined with suede or top-grain leather. The top extends above the ankle, bootlike. Toes are hard-guarded and the heel is snug in a counter. Inside are footbeds, EVA wedges and midsoles, and often a Gore-Tex sock. The outsole, usually attached to midsole and upper by Littleway, is low-impact, whether a shallow lug or "flathead pyramidal" or other geometry.

A classic example is the Asolo Superscout, leather and nylon and no Gore-Tex, 3 pounds, $100. Support and protection are ample for any wildland trail except miles of rockslides (the bottoms of the feet get sore) or snow (the feet quickly get very wet and soon very cold). For such terrain a person needs the "real thing."

Hiking Boots, Leather

The real thing, often labeled *standard hiker* or *medium hiker*, weighs 3¼–4 pounds and costs $90–$150, and for backpackers in hostile country it may be the only thing. By slicing off the battering rams and armor plate of the panzers and adopting the subtlety of the long-distance runner, manufacturers have produced an all-leather boot with many virtues of the leather-synthetic combination and others exclusively its own.

Uppers are top-grain leather, extending over the ankle. The toe is hard, the heel counter and midsoles and insoles and shanks are fully state-of-the-art, typically somewhat sturdier than in the average leather-synthetic combination. The outsole is one or another pattern of lug, typically rather heavier-duty than in the combinations. Norwegian or Goodyear welting lingers in a few models; most are Littleway. A welt gasket impedes the passage of water through the boot's most vulnerable zone, as well as protecting the welt from abrasion.

Examples of leather hiking boots, or standard hikers, with and without Gore-Tex.

An example of the breed is a model that weighs 3¼ pounds and costs $100, virtually the same as the Asolo Superscout. It could cost a few dollars less by eliminating the Gore-Tex sock. The reason the boot is more water-resistant than the Superscout is the leather, which is not interrupted by nylon panels that let the sweat breathe out yet allow the creeks to flow in. The reason the boot is more suitable for tough terrain is, again, the leather, not so instant-snuggly as the pliable synthetics yet much more able to fight back against hard rocks. A hiker who owns both boots is likely to wear the combination in country mainly soft and dry and warm, the all-leather in the hard and wet and cold.

Heavy Hikers

Another name is the *medium climbing boot,* indicating that crampons can be attached and that the foot is given sufficient authority to kick steps up mountains of hard snow.

Construction is generally the same as in the medium hiker, except there's more of it, and the welting typically is Norwegian or Goodyear. Even here, though, the new tech has brought benefits; where

Climbing boots. Left: *Example of a traditional all-leather boot, sometimes called a "heavy hiker." Right: A plastic boot, excellent on glaciers and icy rock, the outer shell a rigid plastic, completely waterproof, the inner bootie soft and cuddly and warm.*

models in this category once weighed up to 8 pounds, now they are in the vicinity of 5 pounds, which by the rule of the U.S. Army researchers saves enough weight on the feet to make way for the watermelon in the pack. Whereas the old Eiger, when last seen, was rocketing beyond $200, these mediums range from $100 to $140.

Though no trail hiker should be much interested in any climbing boot, those who habitually strike off over talus and felsenmeer, glacier and moraine, slide alder and vine maple and torrents, do well to put an extra pound of armor on each foot.

Climbing Boots, Plastic

The successor to the Eigerboot is a chemical miracle that appears fit, given a computer and a booster, to fly to Mars. The *ultra mountaineering* species is a double boot, the inner removable, the outer shells molded of nylon and plastic, utterly rigid, extremely strong, totally waterproof, and thanks to the cushioning in the inner boot, comfortable and cozy even while the outside of the outer boot is encumbered by crampons stabbing at walls of glacier ice as blizzards howl. In addition, the boots are, for all their imposing dimensions, quite light, under 6 pounds the pair, and the cost, on the sky side of $200—very reasonable for a trip to Mars.

Women's Boots

The female foot tends to be smaller, and even when not, narrower than the male. The European shoe-size system doesn't differentiate between sexes; the American system has a size-and-a-half offset— a man's 6 is a woman's 7½. But this equation is not exact because women's sizes are made on narrower lasts. A woman with wide feet thus may be happier in a man's size, and a man with narrow feet in a woman's size.

Though many models are offered in sizes for both sexes, usually the construction is the same in both and throughout the range from large to small. However, as size diminishes, the boot components become crowded, have less space to move around and loosen up.

Thus in any model the size 5 is much stiffer than the size 10, the problem compounded by the smaller person having less weight to throw around to loosen things up. For that reason some models are specifically designated "women's boots," using lighter construction for equivalent support.

Children's Boots

Children outgrow boots at a pace so ruinous that parents often shoe their offspring in any sort of herring boxes without topses on the theory kids can stand anything. In fact, little feet are as tender as big feet, and kind parents will buy the same caliber of footgear for every member of the family.

The bright side of the picture is that children's shoes or boots are usually outgrown long before they are worn out; a single pair may serve many hikers in turn, either within a multi-offspring family or passed around a circle of friends.

Manufacturers are devoting more attention to the young hiker. Models are available that are identical to those for adults, weighing little over 1 pound and costing around $20.

Boots for the Wet and the Cold

The birder who slops around in swamps and tidal marshes, up to the shins all day in water and muck, and the flower people who roam mushy tundra of the subarctic, and the penitents who mush through winter snow on webs probably don't want plain leather or any newfangled chemical miracles that pretend to breathe. Content to accept and retain such sweat as their feet may manage to generate in the wet and cold, they turn to the old chemical miracle of *rubber*, absolutely watertight, perhaps combined with a soft inner boot, felt or whatever, for comfort and warmth. They may be interested in silicone-impregnated leather that claims to be waterproof (and is for a few hours), or Thinsulate insulation in double-wall boots, or double boots, or a battery-powered electrical heating system said to be perfectly safe from dangers of electrocution in the swamps.

This is not properly the province of the backpacking the world has come to know and love. Yet the person who upon reflection realizes that on certain sorts of trips his feet are soaked minutes from the trailhead and remain wet all day or week, ought to take a serious look at the *wet boot* (duck hunters and birders), the *cold boot* (snowshoers), and the *wet-cold boot* (hikers of Pacific Northwest mountain meadows in summer).

BUYING BOOTS

The best way to buy, of course, is to visit a shop, browse around, consult the staff, and try on boots, many boots. The trying on cannot be overemphasized because boots are manufactured for that anatomical rarity, the "average" foot; actually, if people went around with faces veiled and feet bare, they would recognize each other as readily by individual peculiarities of feet as they do now by those of faces.

After the in-shop trial of an hour or less comes the in-house trial of several days. If that proves satisfactory, the out-of-doors breaking in can begin; if not, back to the shop for an exchange—usually for full credit if the boots are "like new."

In selecting the proper *length*, it is important that the toes do not extend all the way to the front of the boot; if they do, they will bump, especially in downhill travel, and soon become sore and blistered; also, the toenail will be jammed into the cuticle, causing pain and perhaps loss of the nail. As an approximate rule of thumb, with the boot unlaced and the toe pushed to the front (touching but not jamming), a person should be able to slide one finger down behind the heel. If the finger is snug, the fit borders on too tight; if two fingers can be inserted, the fit borders on too loose. When the boot is laced tight a person should not be able to push the toes against the front (stand on the slope of the shoe-shop stool to test toe room).

Variations in feet are such that a boot that fits well from the ball of the foot forward may not fit rearward to the heel (the instep area);

length of the arch (from ball to heel) can be more critical than length of the total foot.

In selecting the proper *width* for the ankle area, a visual inspection should be made to ensure that there is, when laced tight, a gap of at least ¼–⅜ inch between the tongue and hooks; otherwise, the tongue will run against the hook posts and allow no space for tightening.

The width elsewhere must be judged by feel. The boot should be comfortably snug, allowing toes to move, yet holding the ball of the foot firmly to the sole, and permitting little if any lateral movement, or "slop." Some slight up-and-down motion ("lift") of the heel is nearly unavoidable and does no harm in itself; however, with improperly adjusted socks the foot may rub back and forth and blister. Boots stretch in use, becoming somewhat wider (though not longer), and thus the width in the shop should be a bit on the tight side.

When trying on boots, wear two pairs of socks, one light and the other medium (so say some experts), or a single pair of heavy socks (so say others). Remember the stretch that will come with use; if a hiker plans to wear two pairs of heavy socks on the trail and does so in the shop, within a year he will have to wear three pairs.

Fitting Boots to Odd Feet

Many hikers, perhaps a majority, cannot find any boot that fits well precisely as it comes off the shelf. These are the people with narrow heels or flat arches or long skinny feet or short fat feet.

For those with wide bridges or toes and narrow heels, the only hope may be handmade boots; an extra pair of socks may hold the heel securely and keep it from going up and down at each step, but more often than not the solution creates a new problem—constriction of the toes.

Other foot peculiarities may also require custom boots, but various simpler alternatives suffice for most situations. For example, hikers with narrow heels may use a *heel cushion*, or *lift*. Another common device is the *tongue pad*. All hikers adjust the number and

weight of socks at various times on the trail as their feet swell or shrink. It is good to keep in mind that a leather boot can be stretched slightly at critical points by any shoe-repair shop.

Removable insoles may be added to those built in, providing extra cushioning when wanted, then removed to accommodate more socks or to speed drying. They may also remedy the fitting problems of people with narrow feet and the pain problems of those with sore feet. The thinnest and least elaborate, composed of one sort of foam or another bonded to one sort or another of durable, water-wicking, slippery synthetic, cost $6–$9 a pair. Full-size insoles of EVA or the like so intimately conform to the sole as to form veritable *footbeds* and are so well made they last a long time, as they should at $13–$16 a pair. The magic trade name is *Sorthobane*, called the nearest thing in synthetics to human flesh, absorbing 95 percent of impact and retaining shape indefinitely but totally lacking nerve endings. However, at 4–6 ounces the pair, these insoles equal a couple of cantaloupes on the back.

Two types of hikers ought to consider *arch supports*. One is the person whose feet went flat early in life, in good time to be rejected for military service; especially when wearing lightweight footgear, his foot bones may need help to avoid being crushed by the heavy body pounding down upon them. The other is the chap who after wearing a size 10½ C since adolescence abruptly finds at a certain age he can't squeeze into anything smaller than a 12 EE, and meanwhile is feeling pain below the ankle; it could be that after 100,000 trail miles his arches are falling and the flattening feet are having growing pains. Removable, padded arch supports may support the bones enough. If not, a foot doctor should be consulted, perhaps to obtain a custom pair.

Breaking in Boots

The most praised characteristic of the new generation of lightweight footwear is that they accept the foot without a minute's resistance.

All-leather boots may still require a brief period of adjustment while the leather conforms to the foot. People with very average, very tough feet needn't give it a second thought if they've chosen the correct model and size. The breaking in takes place the first few miles of the first hike—no pain, no blisters. A person with a history of tense relationships with footwear or a novice hiker is well advised to try new purchases on short walks before committing to a long trip.

Keep in mind that if a boot doesn't feel basically right in the store and during the preliminary still-returnable-for-full-credit testing time

in the living room, it will never feel good on the trail, and little trust should be put in the corrective action of breaking in. If boot and foot are fundamentally at odds, never the twain shall be happy, and the boot is going to win all the arguments.

Ordering Boots by Mail

Many American hikers and climbers cannot conveniently visit a boot supplier and must order by mail. Fortunately, a number of shops are skilled in selecting boots for distant feet.

The first thing the purchaser by mail must realize is the futility of trying to find an exact equivalence between his street-shoe size (or the size of his current boot, if any) and the proper size in the desired style and brand. The boots stocked by backpacking shops are made on several continents, in half a dozen nations. They are made on the American last and on the very dissimilar European last, British last, and Italian last. Also, every manufacturer has his own sizing system, and no two are precisely the same.

Suppliers rather uniformly give the following instructions for ordering by mail:

1. Send street-shoe size and width. These don't tell what boot size is right but provide a starting point.
2. Do not order by boot size unless you have previously tried on the *exact* style and brand of boot you are ordering, in which case give the size, style, and brand.
3. Using your larger foot (nobody has feet exactly the same size), put on the socks you intend to wear in the boots. Stand (with weight evenly distributed on both feet) on a piece of cardboard or stiff paper and trace a heavy line around the foot, making very sure to *hold the pencil absolutely vertical at all times*. (Some suppliers recommend tracings of both feet.)
4. Cut out the foot tracing, write your name on it, and enclose it with your order.

Suppliers generally add that a first choice of model should be stated plus one or two acceptable alternatives. Most boots come from distant points, and stock of any given size or style may become depleted in periods of heavy purchasing, with no chance of quick replenishment.

When the boots arrive, they should be checked carefully for proper fit, following the methods described above. Wear them *around the house* until satisfied; if not, return them. If the boots prove unsatisfactory after a hike or two, they will still be accepted as trade-ins by shops that deal in used boots.

BEING KIND TO BOOTS

The weight of the walker (and pack) and the delicacy of step have much to say about a boot's longevity; the 200-pounder who carries a cast-iron stove and attacks the trail like a linebacker sacking the quarterback wears out a shelf of boots while those of a 95-pounder with a 10-pound rucksack and ballerina toes still look new.

What a boot chiefly wants for a lengthy life, though, is to be clean, dry, and never too hot. In a box on the shelf of the shop it may retain youth for years. How long on the trail? In rain or snow?

On desert rocks? Moldering in the car trunk? In the basement, next to the furnace?

Fussy hikers follow programs of boot care so precise and comprehensive they scarcely have time to comb their hair, press their pants, floss their teeth, and do their pushups. Their boots outlive those of the slob hikers who have all they can do to keep their whiskers cut short enough to let the soup through. However, the sad and disillusioning truth is that a boot worn in wildlands two dozen weekends plus two vacation weeks a year, alternately soaked and dried, frozen and baked, caked with mud and abraded by rock and sand, cannot be expected to achieve middle age. In such conditions a boot that in milder use and kinder climate will last a decade may fall apart the second or third summer, no matter how devoted the care.

On the trail little can be done for the boot. It's going to get wet, it's going to dry out, and the wetting-drying cycle, with alternate swelling and shrinking of certain materials, particularly leather, eventually pulls the skin and bones apart. One thing the hiker can do, however, is to *avoid cooking the boot*.

The campfires are going out all over the wildland world and with them the traditional method of cooking boots—"drying them" by the flames and/or "warming up the old toe bones." Still,

though, hikers are wont after a wet spell to lay their boots in the glare of the sun on a rock hot enough to fricassee a chicken. To be sure, the cow is long dead. However, leather is still a skin and will suffer from any heat the living beast would have found uncomfortable. The test is simple. While sitting by a campfire or drying boots in the sun, touch them. If the fingers recoil, the leather is cooking. Other boot components are also vulnerable. Cemented soles come loose if exposed to excessive heat, which softens the cement. Some foam midsoles shrink premanently.

Boots may be cooked equally well on the drive home, placed too close to the car heater, or at home, stored by a furnace or hot-air vent or left to dry atop a radiator.

Mud, too, is lethal. If after a hike dirty boots are tossed in a corner, the mud dries and in so doing dries out the leather and the cement holding the boot together, especially around the sole, where the mud is usually caked. The leather hardens, the cement fails, and the end is nigh. Dry filth also is destructive, the tiny sharp-crystalled grains of volcanic ash or ground-up granite infiltrating pores of the leather and rasping away at stitches.

For any and every boot, care should begin at trail's end, using a whiskbroom kept in the car to brush off mud. Leather boots should be washed at home with a stiff brush and cool water, the interior sprayed with disinfectant or fungus preventive (Innerguard) to stop mold and then stuffed with crumpled newspapers or paper towels, which absorb moisture exhaled by wet leather, help the shape, and stop deep wrinkles from setting in. After a day or two, change newspapers. Every few months the insides should be washed to eliminate sweat residues, which are as damaging as dirt; removable insoles should be taken out and washed and dried separately. When boots are dry, they should be treated as discussed in the next section.

Note: A person who goes hiking in wet country on a regular, tight schedule may never be able to dry boots, and so never be able to treat them decently. Professional hikers—writers or photographers for guidebooks and magazine articles—often buy two or even three pairs of the identical boot in order always to have one pair drying, one soaking up conditioning compound, and one ready to wear.

Conditioning and Waterproofing the Boot

For a leatherless boot or shoe, the whisking and slow-drying are pretty much the end of the story. Nylon panels may be painted with silicone to provide short-term water-repellency. Gore-Tex stipulates special handling; believers ought to follow label instructions.

Leather must be treated to continue the process that began when the cowhide was tanned, and which must be done through the life of the boot. The cow can no longer circulate juices and oils through the skin, so the hiker must assume the responsibility. If he doesn't, the leather dries, hardens, stiffens, cracks, separates from the sole, and the rest is silence.

The treatment that does the conditioning—and is essential to that end—also does what the hiker likes to think is the waterproofing. Every edition of this book has offered different and contradictory advice, as does every expert witness, whether catalog of backpacking shop or manufacturer, magazine article, or guru. For this edition, however, the REI Quality Control Department has provided results obtained from a series of laboratory and field tests, and upon this rock we build. The news is not good; the high tech of the 1980s sings the same sad song as the low tech of the 1930s.

Suede Leather

When the leather hardens after a wetting-drying, it may be treated with a liquid silicone compound. Nothing remotely approaching waterproofing is to be expected, though if the silicone were applied every few minutes on the trail, it would repel some water.

Oil-Tanned or Vegetable-Tanned Leather

After the post-trip slow-drying, the boots should be strenuously massaged with Hubberds Shoe Grease, mink oil, or the like and set aside at room temperature to soak up the compound overnight. When the boots have had a long, rough, wet journey, a second and third application are advisable.

The treatment is for conditioning. The water-repelling effect is minor. In REI lab tests where boots were treated with the above compounds according to label instructions and then immersed in water over the toe but below the lace openings, all the boots were wet inside, substantially or completely, within 1 hour—and this while sitting quietly in a tank. Four applications gave much better results—in the tank.

Chrome-Tanned, Wax-Filled Leather

This, the most common boot leather, is conditioned by replacing the waxes with which the pores were filled after tanning. This results in better water-repellency than that possible with oil-tanned leather. Ultra Seal, Sno-Seal, and Bee Seal Plus, all waxes containing some silicone, earned good marks in the REI lab tests. Treated boots remained dry for 8 hours or longer after a single application, compared to the 1 hour for oil-tanned boots after a single application.

Chrome-Tanned, Silicone-Filled Leather

Conditioning is done with any liquid silicone such as Dow Corning Silicone or Timberland Silicone. In the REI laboratory the leather kept water out longer than others, seeming to substantiate claims it is superior for "dry hiker" boots.

Welts and Seams

In every test, repellency was greatly enhanced by painting welts and seams with Seam Guard, Welt Seal, or the like, in addition to whatever compound was applied to the rest of the boot.

So Much for the Laboratory: Now, Into the Field

The tank tests suggested that perhaps with further refinement of technique boots might be kept dry indefinitely, at least in the laboratory. There remained the real world. Two of the three compounds that performed best in the tank, Ultra Seal and Sno-Seal, were selected for field testing. Ultra Seal was found to be the easiest to apply, and was readily absorbed to yield a dry look, while Sno-Seal remained gooey-tacky. The third compound that did well in the lab, Bee Seal Plus, was midway between in ease of application. As for water-repellency, the two were very close in results, leading to an overall conclusion that these three preparations are as good as there are for chrome-tanned, wax-filled leather. (The others tested in the lab—Biwell, several mink oils, Tana Sno-Seal, Leather Line, Shoe Saver, Super Dry, and Leather Dri—were less effective.)

But how good is good? In the field trips the same pair of boots was worn on a series of hikes from winter to summer, then treated conscientiously after each, the left boot with one preparation, the right with the other. On five out of seven occasions involving wet snow or muddy trails, wet brush, or rain, both boots were soaked to the socks; the two exceptions were while walking *atop* hard snow. On four occasions in mud-wet, brush-wet grass, both boots were wetted inside, considerably or totally. However, both boots remained dry inside not only on two dry-trail tests but on four trips in wet snow where other boots in the party, treated with other compounds, were completely saturated.

In the 1980s the REI Quality Control Department confirmed what hikers of the 1930s knew. When boots are being flexed over and over again on the trail, when rain or dew or snow is ceaselessly washing the leather, when mud and brush are scrubbing the pores, no grease or oil is guaranteed to keep oil-tanned leather water-repellent, nor silicone the silicone-filled leather, nor wax-silicone the wax-filled leather. The best that can be said is that the hiker who lathers on a good enough compound fairly regularly may under some circumstances sometimes stay drier than other folks. In any event, his leather will last longer.

SOCKS AND GAITERS

Socks

Socks provide insulation, padding, and skin comfort—they do, that is, if they are the proper socks, in the proper amount, for any given foot in any particular situation.

Hikers who wear knickers usually prefer knee-high knicker socks. For others, the socks should be high enough to extend an inch or two above the boot to prevent them from creeping down in and bunching up.

As for size, the general rule is: size 8 sock for men's shoe size 3–4 and women's 4–5; 9 sock, men's 5–6 and women's 6–7; 10 sock, men's 6½–8 and women's 7½–9; 11 sock, men's 8½–10 and women's 9½–11; 12 sock, men's 10–11½; 13 sock, men's 12–13. If two or three pairs are to be worn, the outer pair might well be a size larger.

As for material, ordinarily socks should be mostly of wool, which insulates, absorbs sweat, and is warm when wet. However, owing to the lack of stretch and low abrasion resistance, all-wool socks develop holes quickly; durability is greatly increased by reinforcement of heels and toes with nylon or the addition of some nylon throughout. For most hikers, this is all they need or want to know about socks.

Nevertheless, the catalogs are replete with refinements and subtleties worth the consideration of the hiker whose feet have a tendency to whine and whimper.

Hot-country hikers like all-cotton socks—when wet, they stay wet, but in deserts that's good. A wool-cotton mix costs less than all-wool and has some of the nice feel of all-cotton.

An inner sock of polypropylene, soft and light, passes moisture out to the wool, the fiber being unable to absorb water. A trilayered sock—polypro inside, wool on the outside, nylon in the middle—combines the advantages of all three materials.

Wick-dry inner socks—70 percent olefin, 30 percent nylon—are said to wick the sweat right up through the top of the boot, keeping the feet dry in hot weather.

Silk inner socks have a luxurious feel and are very kind to hot spots. Nylon inner socks last longer.

Spandex, a stretchy fiber, is combined with wool for support socks; with cotton and polyester for tube socks, which are excellent for hot feet.

Chamois socks are advertised as "the ultimate."

A technique for the cold and the wet, as in snow slogging, is the "plastic sock." A person dons in order: (1) a light cotton sock for comfort; (2) a plastic bag that retains sweat, causing "dishpan feet," but warm, but warm; (3) a wool sock or socks, protected by the plastic bag from wetting by sweat and thus retaining full insulation; (4) a second plastic bag to protect the wool from wetting by outside water; (5) the boot. *Important note:* When exercise ceases, the sweat-wet inner socks grow cold and so do the feet; a change to dry socks is essential—to avoid possible frostbite.

The sock combination depends on the boots being worn—and on personal preference. One common choice is two pairs of medium weight, predominantly wool, nylon-reinforced socks. Another is one pair of heavy socks and one light or medium weight. And so on. Some hikers always wear three pairs. Some wear a single pair, perhaps filling out the boot with insoles.

Even for day trips, a person ought to carry an extra pair of socks in the rucksack; during the hike water literally may be squeezed from the foot, which shrinks enough to slide around in the boot. Many hikers, when beginning a long descent, stop to add socks to tighten the fit and avoid downhill blisters. Contrarily, the feet may swell on a hike and feel crowded; it is then proper to remove socks or substitute lighter ones.

On overnight and longer trips the hiker should have at least two extra pairs in the pack to adjust padding, to change into, and to replace those that wear out. (On the other hand, a climber once wore only one pair of socks, and the same pair, for forty-five straight days on Yukon glaciers. Eventually, seeing his extras weren't needed, he threw them away to save weight.)

The choice of socks is a matter of personal taste, developed by learning to know one's feet. The only general rule is to have enough to meet any changing situation.

When socks get wet the normal instinct is to dry them by a campfire; the wilderness thus is littered with charred wool. If enough time is available, and care is taken, socks can be dried by a fire, but it's a lousy way to spend an evening. Many hikers dry socks by wearing them to bed—not recommended if they are soaking wet. One alternative is to spread them on bushes in the sun, if any. Another is to tie them to the outside of the pack while traveling.

Hikers with tough feet often say the heck with it and wear the socks wet. Hikers with tender feet cannot be so casual and must carry an abundance of spares; wet socks are especially productive of blisters.

Care should be taken to avoid wrinkling and bunching of socks in the boots, since lumps make blisters. For the same reason, socks with holes should be discarded.

Gaiters

No matter how tightly constructed the boot, no matter how carefully treated with waterproofing compounds, there is always the gap at the top. When a hiker wades a creek, the stream may pour directly in. When he travels in snow, crystals creep inside and melt. When he walks through wet grass or brush, moisture soaks the top of the socks, which then wick water down to the feet.

The built-in snow or scree guard described earlier may close the gap adequately—but probably not. For extra protection the gaiter is available in several designs of differing materials and weight.

The long gaiter, 16 to 18 inches, extending from the laced area of the boots to the upper calf, is for deep, soft snow.

The short gaiter, 6½ to 9 inches, also called an *anklet*, suffices for the average hiker, assuming he worries that much about wet feet.

Gaiters with uppers of Gore-Tex (see Chapter 9) stay dry and keep trousers and socks dry.

A *gaiter sock* has a gaiter attached to the top of a wool sock; it can be folded down on dry trail, pulled up when traveling in the wet.

BEING KIND TO FEET

The hiker blessed with tough feet can break just about all the rules of boot selection and sock use and never suffer more than an occasional blister. Less fortunate souls can follow all the rules meticulously and spend their outdoor lives hobbling in pain. A brief experience of trails tells a person which category he fits into, and those who find themselves afflicted with tender feet must pay close attention to the rules at all times and devote special effort to getting their feet, along with the rest of the body, in condition for lengthy hikes by first taking a number of shorter walks.

If boots are chosen properly for the kind of travel planned and the proper mix of insoles and socks, sore feet and blisters should be a rarity.

Unfortunately, people do make mistakes, such as using a running shoe for a boulder-hopping, snow-plugging brushfight. Also they become careless, especially when tired. And finally, a beginner, or any hiker early in the season, may go through a period of developing calluses in the appropriate places—a blister being nature's way of saying here is where the foot needs a callus.

The most important rule in foot care is not to neglect warning signals. If a hot spot develops, stop instantly. Straighten crooked socks, switch socks from left foot to right, dump out pebbles, or perhaps pound down a nail that has punched through the insole. If the trouble stems from the foot sliding around in the boot, tighten laces or add another pair of socks.

Some hikers, having learned precisely where they always blister, treat the threatened spots before the hike, applying bits of adhesive tape or the products noted below. Before commencing a long down-hill—say, a trail that loses a vertical mile of elevation in a half-dozen walking miles—an excellent preparation is to tape the fronts of all the toes, put on an extra pair of socks or an extra insole, to leave absolutely no empty space in the boot for the foot to slop around in, and to lace the boots virtually to the point of cutting off circulation. The hiker will then be free of complaints from the feet, able to exclusively hear the moaning knees.

Another preventive measure especially favored by hot-country travelers (a desert in summer sun can fry eggs—and soles) is stopping periodically to wash or air the feet and apply talcum powder or medicated foot powder.

One more: Clip toenails short before a hike.

And another: If boots have been in the closet long, don them before leaving home so that on the drive to the trailhead they warm up, are moisturized by perspiration, and thus loosen a bit.

Should all adjustments and care fail (or be neglected) and sore spots develop, a tough-footed traveler is often content with the ministrations of a roll of adhesive tape. However, the person prone to weaknesses of the skin does well to carry a *blister kit*, purchased under that name or assembled from components. Dr. Scholl's Moleskin, a thin sheet of adhesive-backed felt, can be cut to size for placement over hot spots, but should not be put on formed blisters. Spenco 2nd Skin, a fluid-saturated plastic sheet, can be used on both hot spots and blisters. Dr. Scholl's Molefoam, an adhesive-backed latex foam covered by Moleskin, and the similar Spenco Stick-On-Padding, cushion tender spots on foot or ankle, such as the bones, the ball of the foot, and the Achilles tendon; they can also be applied to the boot interior to cover troublesome rivets or seams. A hiker with an odd toe or two that can't get along with neighbors will enjoy a packet of lamb's wool, inserting some in the friction zone between toes or wrapping it entirely around the maverick.

Frequently a hiker stops on the trail to treat a hot spot and finds that it has already progressed to a blister. If small, it can be covered with a Band-Aid and adhesive tape or Moleskin or 2nd Skin. If large and filled with fluid, insert a needle (sterilized in a match flame) at the base, drain the fluid by pressing gently, apply antiseptic, Band-Aid and tape, Moleskin or 2nd Skin, and over all this, perhaps Molefoam or Stick-On-Padding.

Never "tough it out" on the trail to avoid delaying companions. The party will not appreciate the thoughtfulness if afterward it is immoblized in camp with an invalid. Blistered hikers have had to be evacuated by helicopter or packhorse—sometimes even requiring medical care when the blisters have become infected.

Tramping long trails—picking up boots and laying them down thousands of times a day—is brutal for citified feet. It is therefore very nice indeed to have dry socks for wearing around camp within boots laced loose and sloppy—or better, camp shoes, which are also kind to flowers.

At the end of a hard day nothing is more delightful than to plunge hot feet in a cold river, hold them there to the point of numbness,

then screech and howl at the withdrawal. A further advantage is that the feet are cleaned in the process, not a bad idea every few days. Of course, this luxury can be indulged in only in an ocean or a river so large that foot pollution is tolerable. Lacking that, a bucket of water may be carried up on a wooded knoll, where the dishes are washed.

Awaiting the hiker in the car must be a pair of loose, light shoes or moccasins, plus clean, soft socks. No matter how deep an affection is developed for boots, trusty companions of the trail, the feet go into delirium when at last they escape.

9
Clothing

There is a certain American wildland where the summer
weather is so kindly, so steady, that even experienced backpackers,
having checked the forecast, commonly go on days-long hikes to
elevations of 10,000 feet and above sans tent, sans tarp, sans parka
and sweater and long pants, sans mittens and hat. Inexperienced
backpackers observe them, emulate and surpass them, climbing to
the meadows clothed scarcely to what used to be considered de-
cency, carrying feather-light loads innocent of essentials for emergencies. And lo, once in every so many summers a cold storm veers
from the usual track and sweeps this gentle wilderness—no surprise
to the experienced travelers, who have heeded the forecast and come
equipped with tents and parkas and long underwear, or to the rangers, who, on hearing the forecast, load their ponies with sweaters
and mufflers and thermoses of hot soup and gallop to the highlands
to rescue the nude throngs lying in the icicled flowers dying of
hypothermia.

There is another American wildland where the summer weather
fluctuates whimsically from benign to vicious and defies science to
predict what it will do from one hour to the next. The rangers here,
awakening to a Sunday dawn of brilliant summer sunshine, groan

to think of the crowds erupting from nearby cities, speeding to the trailheads, not one person in three properly clothed for the mist and rain and sleet, driven by a gale from the poles, the rangers morbidly expect by afternoon, trapping the shivering masses miles from the nearest hot soup.

In the early days of American backpacking for pleasure—as distinguished from backpacking to seek furs and gold and to locate passes for wagon trains—the extremes of adaptation to the elements were (1) flinging through wildlands light and easy and half-naked (the mode of John Muir and troops of Boy Scouts) and (2) staggering under a burden of clothing sufficient to rebuff blizzards, hurricanes, and meteor showers, employing garments designed by and for trappers and prospectors and loggers and cowboys.

Eventually, seeking a middle course, reflective hikers put away mackinaws and bearskin overcoats for lightweight shirts and sweaters that cumulatively weighed far less and because of insulation by entrapment of dead air were much warmer. Moreover, since the number of garments could be varied to adjust the thermostat, *layering* enabled a single basic outfit to fit every situation: afternoon stroll, all-day hike, overnight, weeklong expedition, in forest or desert or snowfield, in summer or winter.

Layering worked very well when virtually the only fabrics were wool and cotton. It works immensely better employing the array

of new materials, providing clothing of decreased weight and increased comfort—warmer, drier, and "with a good hand," meaning it feels nice on the skin.

A convenient way to describe the layers is to classify clothing in four categories, by the principal function:

The *underwear layer* maintains a pleasant microclimate next to the skin; it is always chosen for skin comfort, occasionally for warmth, often to wick moisture from the skin, and sometimes for all three reasons.

(Before defining the other layers, a word about the three means of heat transfer: *conduction* from molecule to molecule is halted or slowed by establishing dead-air spaces between molecules and/or by "fixing" the air to the surface of myriad microfilaments; *convection* via air motion is stopped or impeded by a tight fabric; *radiation* by light waves invisible to the human eye is prevented by shiny or light-colored surfaces, which reflect waves back to their source.)

The *clothing layer* absorbs moisture from the body and helps retain body heat; it is chosen for warmth, breathability, and freedom of action. Shirts and pants, socks and hats and mittens, are the typical components.

The *insulation layer* provides additional warmth when the basic clothing needs help; sweaters and jackets and parkas are the common garments.

Finally, the *shell layer* protects against wind, rain, snow, and sun.

Once upon a time the entire encyclopedia of layering could be written with a page or two each on underwear, shirt, sweater, parka, hat, and miscellany. Nowadays, though, each family has many genera, and each genus, many species—there are almost as many hats as beetles. The section "Layering" later in this chapter undertakes a taxonomy. First, however, the elements must be grappled with, and these, too, have proliferated enormously since that dawn of philosophy when they numbered but four: earth, water, air, and fire.

MATERIALS

In the beginning there were *natural protein fibers* from animals (wool, silk, camel hair, dog hair, sliced leather), and *natural cellulose fibers* from plants (cotton, linen, burlap, sisal, kapok, fireweed silk, shredded cedar bark). Out of the test tube in the 1920s and 1930s emerged *artificial cellulose fibers* (rayon, plaited cellophane) made from wood pulp. The early 1940s brought *artificial noncellulonic fibers*, made from petroleum, coal, and natural gas.

Of the last, *nylon* quickly became famous, the first and perhaps still the most glamorous of the chemical superstars. Because Du Pont neglected to register the name as a trademark, it is not capitalized and is the generic term for dozens of compounds boiled up out of polymers. Hundreds of fabrics are made out of the dozens of distinct fibers in the nylon genus.

Contemporary in origin, *polyester* was tacky stuff in its youth, early becoming infamous for "leisure suits." As the laboratories labored onward, it earned respect, especially when capitalized into the likes of Fortrel or Dacron, the latter expanding to a subgenus in its own right, comprising nearly a hundred species, including Hollofil and Quallofil, discussed later in this chapter and in Chapter 11.

There are more, notably *polypropylene*, the new sensation of the underwear scene, by no means lacking ability to perform on other stages; the *neoprene* rubber that never oozed from a tree; the *vinyl (PVC)* of raingear; acrylic, olefin, and who knows what tomorrow.

Wool

Wool's tightly curled fibers trap air very efficiently, giving warmth. Interestingly, the new-tech Thinsulate (discussed later), which goes about its business not by trapping air but by impeding its movement, has fibers larger than those of wool. Though they were hundreds of thousands of years getting there, the old-tech sheep evidently knew what they were doing.

Wool's other prominent attribute is its ability to continue trapping air and giving warmth when soaking wet. Fully saturated, having absorbed 30 percent of its own weight in water, it retains half its insulation value, the other half being lost to the conductivity of the water.

The faults of wool are that it tears easily, so outer garments take a ripping from brush and rocks; it resists abrasion poorly, so sock

heels and toes and shirt elbows wear through; it feels scratchy. These are eliminated by the admixture of other fibers, such as nylon, resulting in a fabric that is tougher and softer than pure wool and that retains wool's quality of not puckering or pilling, as do many chemical fabrics. A final complaint is that many people are allergic to wool and must keep it away from the skin or, in extreme cases, off the body altogether.

Silk

The silkworm doesn't build threads compartmented cell by cell but extrudes a structureless secretion in a continuous filament with the highest weight/strength ratio of any natural fiber—in fact, with a tensile strength greater than that of steel. It shares with wool the abilities to trap air for excellent insulation and to absorb up to 30 percent of its weight in moisture and still give warmth and be comfortable.

Warm, and warm when wet, and for equal strength lighter than wool, cotton, and many synthetics, silk is furthermore nature's luxury fiber, which is to say it looks good and has a supple hand (feels good). Its smoothness, softness, and elasticity—the fiber will stretch up to 20 percent over its original length before breaking,

and then spring back—give silk particular appeal in underwear, described by one catalog as "the next best thing to nothing at all," an interesting recommendation; the sour retort of a skeptic is that silk underwear is more fun in cities than on trails, and indoors than out. Nevertheless, the establishment of friendly relations between the silkworms of China and the backpacking shops of America has given new prominence to a fiber prized for 5,000 years.

Silk requires special care—it may be damaged by certain acid and alkaline substances, weakened by sunlight, perspiration, strong soaps, and high ironing temperatures.

Cotton

When dry, cotton cloth insulates well against both heat and cold, and when tightly woven rebuffs the wind. It drinks liquids greedily, which can be good or bad. Next to the flesh it absorbs sweat, which is appreciated in warm weather. Once wet, though, insulation ceases; should the temperature drop, garments freeze hard as a rock. Water-repelling compounds (Rain Chek, Scotchgard) are soaked up as avidly as water.

Cotton is soft against the skin, non-itchy, and easy to wash, though prone to mildewing and rotting if not kept clean and dry during storage. The fiber is readily manufactured into any number of different cloths for pretty shirts and sweaters and fancy pants.

In backpacking garmentry it is most often used in combination with various synthetics, as discussed below.

Nylon

"Better things for better living through chemistry," promised the radio announcer of the 1930s, delivering the Du Pont commercial. And lo, came World War II, remembered by many a sexagenarian less for the military campaigns than for the black market, in which the top three currencies were Camel cigarettes, Hershey chocolate bars (with almonds)—and nylon stockings. With peace the back-country blossomed in life-raft sails, ski hills were terrorized by the "black flash" parka. And so it went. Today, take away a hiker's nylon and what have you got? Scarcely enough to preserve modesty.

Nylon is easy to manufacture and treat and thus comparatively inexpensive, stronger than cotton for equivalent weights, abrasion-resistant, and durable. It dries quickly and usually wears out for other reasons long before rotting. It is weakened by ultraviolet radiation and stretches when wet, matters of some significance for tents but not clothing. Owing to the slipperiness of the filaments, cut edges of nylon fabric fray readily.

When only wind protection is wanted, the fabric is untreated. Fending off rain is more complicated. Because the synthetic threads are impenetrable by liquids (and that's why pure nylon feels clammy when wet), compounds must be "painted on" to fill interstices between threads. In the factory this is done with machinery and heat, the usual compound polyurethane, applied in up to five layers, depending on the degree of water-resistance wanted. A light coating constrains the cloth's stretch and thus makes it more liable to rip. A heavy coating actually increases fabric strength, the added layer being stronger than the nylon. In a typical five-layer (tent) treatment the outer layer is thinned with silicone for flexibility; ultimately it peels or abrades off, but without drastically reducing water-repellency—four layers remain. The bending and twisting of normal use eventually separate fabric and coating, but not for a very long

time. Machine washing often causes the coating to peel from the fabric; hand washing is therefore recommended for coated nylon.

When the coating wears thin and water flows through freely, a garment needn't be discarded; a pot of *Polycote* and a brush can restore the repellency—or add it to a fabric that has never had it before.

Seams used to be the leaky spots and a hiker may still find a need to paint them periodically with *Seamlock* or the like. However, many seams are now microwelded with heat in addition to or instead of sewing, and also are backed with seam-seal tape.

Some of the nylon fabrics common in clothing, sleeping bags, packs, tents, and boots are:

Ripstop. The distinctive feature is that about every ¼ inch in both warp (lengthwise strands) and fill (crosswise strands) the threads are doubled, forming reinforcing squares that stop rips from spreading. For comparable weights the fabric is stronger than others and for a time was the fad sensation of the outdoor scene. It continues to be popular for many purposes, such as tents, while fading away in others. One objection is that adding a light coating for water-repellency prevents stretching and nullifies the ripstop feature; for this reason ripstop parkas are usually uncoated, for wind protection only. One complaint has been that the fabric is unesthetic. Another, that it feels and sounds "synthetic." But new Japanese versions have a much softer and quieter hand.

Taffeta has the same tear-resistance as ripstop and equal (medium) abrasion-resistance. It may weigh a bit more—or less. A chief reason it has taken over much of ripstop's former domain is the softness and quietness of the plain-weave fabric.

Taslan yarn is "air-bulked,"—spun in a stream of swift air, giving a rough texture that has stylish "surface interest." It is also strong and abrasion-resistant.

Nylsilk. Abrasion resistance and tear strength are low but the cloth is lightweight and tight-weave, made soft and silky by calendering. Nice for sleeping bags and high fashion.

Antron. Medium abrasion resistance, low tear strength. Woven from a "trilobal" yarn that refracts light, giving a cool sheen. A common brand is Luscious.

Cambrelle is a light, knitted fabric, inexpensive and durable, used in boot linings. It's soft on the foot and wicks perspiration.

Pack cloth. Mainly used for packs, of course, but also some boots and other garments. Small, dense fibers make a smooth fabric that can be successfully coated for waterproof gaiters, overmitts, and packs. Cost is low and many colors are available, due to the easy dying.

Cordura In the 1960s, seeking a stronger cord for reinforcing automobile tires, Du Pont found that by blowing air through nylon filaments they could be spun into a strong and durable fabric, christened Cordura. Rough-looking and tougher in fact—several times more tearproof, burstproof, and abrasion-resistant than pack cloth— Cordura is used for packs, boots, and reinforcements on gaiters, mitts, and the seats of britches. The rough texture makes it more difficult to waterproof than pack cloth, but water-repellency can be obtained.

The Cordura of packs and the like is 500 or 1,000 denier (a unit of measure for textile fibers), too thick for garments. However, 330-denier Cordura has become available and been put to use in certain of the mixtures discussed below.

Ballistics cloth, developed by Du Pont for the military's bulletproof vests and helmets, is a 1,050-denier, high-tenacity nylon, very tough and abrasion-resistant and with a smooth finish. Current uses are for backpacks and soft-sided luggage.

Magnum cloth is similar but lighter—a 430-denier nylon in a basket weave with the same smooth finish. It is primarily employed in medium-priced luggage for the mass market.

Polyester

Though strong, durable, and inexpensive, virtuous in many other synthetic ways, and once proclaimed to be the chemist's replacement of wool, polyester seems to achieve its highest potential when extensively manipulated.

It is blended with cotton for pants and shirts, as well as with other fibers (see below). It is processed into several forms of *fiberfill*, such as the Dacrons that are transformed into Hollofil, Quallofil, and PolarGuard, insulations dominant in clothing and sleeping bags. In its Hollofil and Fortrel manifestations, it is knitted into pile. It is employed in Thinsulate, Kodolite, and Tex-O-Lite, and *needlepunch*, a way of chopping the fibers, stacking them, and punching them with needles into a smooth, nonwoven carrier fabric, a thin, flexible layer filled with tiny air pockets, not requiring quilting to hold in place. In summary, when a manufacturer needs a utility synthetic, polyester is likely to get the call.

Polypropylene

First bubbled out of an Italian chemist's pot of petroleum in the 1940s, polypropylene in the 1960s found uses in carpets, upholstery, ropes, and diapers. In 1969 the Norwegians succeeded in spinning fibers fine enough for textiles, and by the 1980s another revolution shook the wildlands—"polypro" rioting in the catalogs.

The selling point is that it is totally hydrophobic—absolutely will not absorb water and therefore wicks it, both visible sweat and insensible or vaporous perspiration, away from the flesh to the outer garments (or outer air). It does this six times faster than wool, preventing the heat loss that occurs when sweat evaporates next to the skin. Unable to absorb water, it necessarily dries rapidly, cannot remain wet and clammy, as does cotton. In summary, though poly-pro is not bragged up as an insulator, it gives warmth by reducing evaporative cooling when the body is overheating in hard work, and by not staying wet to do conductive cooling when the body is resting, both of these particularly important considerations in cold weather.

Being light, stretchy, and not itchy, and altogether feeling fine, polypro has come to dominate the next-to-skin area, though it hasn't been quick to expand into outerwear.

The objections are that it pills, annoying to hikers who try to look their best in their underwear; except at low temperatures it cannot be machine-washed or dried without risk of melting; unless frequently washed it stinks like an old gymnasium, driving tenters out into the storm. Moreover, because of the inherent difficulties of manufacture, it is overpriced.

Mixing polypro with other fibers eliminates some problems, such as the resistance to dying. A two-layer fabric with polypro inside and cotton or wool outside combines the virtues of each and min-imizes faults.

A recent new item is *polypro duck cloth*, resembling canvas, for luggage and rucksacks.

Lesser Chemicals

Acrylic is the generic name for the numerous fibers polymerized from acrylonitrile. Alone it has been used as filler in cheap sleeping bags and for underwear. The blends include Dunova, 40 percent wool and 60 percent acrylic, and Thermolactyl, a mix of acrylic and polyvinyl chloride (PVC).

Other chemicals strewn through these pages include *polyolefin*, another group of hydrocarbons, one of which is the raw material of Thinsulate, and *polyethylene*, the oil well's substitute for wood pulp's cellophane. Polyethylene was so early on the wildland scene, used for bottles and tarps even before garments, it is usually called simply poly, necessitating a lengthier short name for the later polypro.

If there is residual skepticism about polypro, it's nothing personal but simply that there were marvels before, all the way back to celluloid and rayon, and the pots bubble on around the world, a thousand hundred chemists lusting for wealth, fame, bright lights, dancing girls or boys.

Mixtures

Weavers, as creative as chemists, combine fibers to create new ones that may display attributes of all their constituents. Previously mentioned have been the admixtures of other fibers with wool and polypro, and the ubiquity of polyester. Other mixes have attained such independence under their given names that nobody asks to know their parents.

60/40 cloth is a "nonintimate" blend, 60 percent cotton threads running vertically and 40 percent nylon threads running horizontally. The fabric has a very good hand and a greater strength-to-weight ratio than 65/35.

65/35 cloth is an "intimate" blend, each thread in either direction having polyester (65 percent) in the core for strength and cotton (35 percent) wrapped on the outside for comfort. The fabric has a nice hand, is very durable and resistant to wind and abrasion.

Both fabrics breathe freely, and both, because of the cotton, accept water-repelling compounds (Zepel, DWR). However, since the treatment makes the fabric somewhat stiff, some choose not to use such compounds, settling for garments that bar the wind but not the rain. In any event, the treatments lose effectiveness after several cleanings (dry cleaning is essential for 60/40; that or machine washing for 65/35) and must be reapplied.

Quarpel, developed by the U.S. Army and used by the military in weather-protection garments worldwide, is a 60/40 cloth permeated with a unique formula (Zepel being one ingredient) that impregnates each fiber, providing superior water-repellency for far longer than that obtained by conventional treatments—even after nineteen washings, three times more than in a garment's usual lifetime. Being neither coated nor laminated, Quarpel has a very soft hand and is very breathable, exceedingly comfortable in itself and ideal for insulated garments.

Technicloth, a Zepel-treated 60/40 cloth, aims in the same direction.

80/20 cloth, consisting of 80 percent polyester and 20 percent cotton, is lightweight, breathable, wind and abrasion-resistant, and less expensive.

Stormshed is a tight-woven 65/35 cloth treated on the backside with Dow/Corning silicone, which, while retaining the fine hand, provides a very water-repellent yet breathable fabric. Tests have proven it to be "stormproof," a term used to describe materials that can repel a steady spray, admitting no more than 2½ grams of water in 5 minutes. Stormshed meets the test for 1 hour. ("Squall proof" might be an apter term; in the Pacific Northwest storms frequently last longer than 5 minutes, or even 1 hour.)

For those lengthier storms, when the breathing out of perspiration becomes a trivial concern against the pouring in of the saturated exterior world, the closest practical approach to total waterproofing may be sought.

The most used coating compound is *polyurethane*, light, flexible, and inexpensive. One or two layers applied to garments of nylon or cotton give repellency while retaining the fabric's flexibility; four or five coats bring waterproofness but yield a stiff garment. The owner can renew the coating at home with Polycote or the like.

Vinyl-coated cotton with welded seams is heavy, bulky, and costly but strong and durable. The vinyl outside absolutely halts penetration by storms, and the cotton inside feels nice. *Vinyl* used alone is thin, light, and cheap. But it stiffens and cracks in cold weather and has a life expectancy on the trail measured in hours, if not minutes.

Neoprene-coated cotton, "rubberized cloth," is strong, watertight, and cheap. However, it rapidly crumbles and cracks when exposed to sunlight.

Polyester/nylon laminate with welded seams is used in garments by Macbean and by Peter Storm (No Sweat, formerly Bukflex). The outside layer of nonwoven polyester coated with polyurethane repels rain; the inside layer of light, absorbent nylon prevents clamminess. Comfortable, durable, expensive.

Tri-blends mix several fibers, typically polyester and nylon for strength, elasticity, and resistance to wind and water, and cotton for softness and breathability.

One example is *Trinyl*, an intimate blend of 50 percent polyester, 25 percent cotton, and 25 percent nylon. The fabric has low abrasion resistance and tear strength but is soft and pretty, popular for sleeping-bag linings and fashion outdoor wear.

Another is *Super Blend*, 42 percent polyester, 35 percent nylon, and 23 percent cotton, yielding a soft, supple cloth, treated to be water-repellent.

Stretch cloth is a tri-blend with a component that is highly elastic, providing body-fitting comfort and allure. One combination, used in trousers, is wool, polyester, and *Spandex*. Another, common in sports bras and briefs, and in necks and cuffs of turtleneck sweaters, is cotton, polyester, and *Lycra*.

The advent of 330-denier Cordura has brought that stiff and scratchy species of nylon into bodywear fabrics. *Cyclone*, 60 percent Cordura and 40 percent nylon, is advertised as "the world's toughest outerwear fabric." *DuraBlend*, Cordura blended with polyester and cotton, claims "the strength and durability of Cordura and the soft, comfortable feel of cotton and the easy care of polyester."

Fiberpile: Pile and Fleece (Bunting)

The Norwegian climate, responsible for polypro underwear, also stimulated the invention of pile, which was extensively field-tested by fishermen in Arctic waters before it was introduced on American trails.

Fiberpile (the more inclusive term) is not a single material but a category in which synthetic fibers of various kinds are manipulated in various ways to create myriads of fine loops that trap air with extreme efficiency, giving the same insulation as wool for half the weight. In wet weather the superiority is the greater because the synthetics absorb little or no water. The material feels dry, wicks moisture from the body, when drenched can be wrung out and walked dry from body heat alone, and is machine-washable in cold or warm water.

The fans declare fiberpile has made wool sweaters obsolete and is likely to put insulated parkas on the run; combined with an outer wind shell, it prevents heat loss by conduction as well as convection, and when laminated with Gore-Tex, is water-repellent. About the only concession by enthusiasts is that it's bulky and doesn't stuff as neatly as down; of course, neither does polyester.

Three fiberpiles presently dominate the market, but others are striving for a niche, and the market is too young to be considered more than momentarily static.

Solid-fiber polyester pile (Patagonia is the best-known brand) is the warmest and the bulkiest. It is made by implanting 2- to 3-inch strands of polyester, called *sliver*, in a knitted polyester backing. Removed from the knitting machine, the backing/sliver fabric is heated on the sliver side to make the fibers stand up—to be sheared, heated, then sheared and heated again. With repetition the fibers grow fluffier but more prone to pilling; the sliver gets so curly it can slide through the pores in the backing. To close the pores a coating is painted on—the more coating, the more the wind-resistance but the less the breathability.

Hollow-fiber Dacron 808 Hollofil pile (Borglite) is said to be 5 percent warmer than solid polyester, 40 percent warmer than nylon (below), but to date it has not managed to muscle in on the Big Three.

At a certain time a certain fiberpile came to be distinguished as a subgenus *fleece* or *bunting*, the definition made on the basis of the thickness of the original strands: thicker fabrics are piles, thinner ("upgraded sweatshirts," in a competitor's sneer) are fleeces. Fleece is made from long polyester filaments knit in a flat sheet, one side smooth, the other a mass of large, loose loops. The loops are broken, then tucked back into the fabric, clogging the backing pores to prevent pilling without recourse to a plastic coating. Thus the fabric is soft and fuzzy, a fleece fit to cuddle Baby Bunting. The tucking increases wind-resistance. However, being lighter and less bulky than pile, fleece is not as warm.

Nylon pile (Helly Hansen, a pioneer, is the best known) is made much the same way as fleece, but the fibers are lock-stitched to the backing. Pilling is minimized, and no coating is required. The fabric is soft and stretchy and pleasant, lighter than fleece for equal warmth, and is the least wind-resistant and most expensive of the Big Three.

Polypropylene fleece, costlier still, must be scrupulously guarded from heat; a campfire spark will melt an instant hole. It is very warm—30 percent lighter than polyester for equal results, they say—and is the champion wicker. It also dries faster than any other fiberpile on the market. The problem is, it hardly *is* on the market, and rarely can be found for sale.

Acrylic/polyester pile is rumored to be lurking, waiting for a chance to jump into a catalog or two, and perhaps other piles are as well.

Breathables

In 1969, employees of W. L. Gore Co. playing with gobs of polytetrafluoroethylene (PTFE for short, better known as Teflon) discovered that when it is pulled rapidly in opposite directions while in a plastic state, tiny holes open in the material and adjacent molecules align in the direction of pull. Proceeding from laboratory taffy-pulls to serious inventing, in 1975 they produced Gore-Tex, 82 percent air, with 9 billion holes per square inch, yet very stong even when rolled in sheets merely .001 inch thick. The magic of the stuff derives from another boggling number—the pores are just .2 micron (.000008 inch) in diameter. Because in liquid water (rain) the molecules cluster in aggregates 20,000 times larger than that, the moisture can't pass through but rather beads on the surface. However, the "excited" molecules of gaseous water (perspiration) stay in groups small enough to slip through. The rain stays out (and so does the wind) and the perspiration breathes out, while permitting body heat to stay in.

According to U.S. Army standards, a fabric must resist a water-entry pressure of 25 pounds per square inch (psi) to be considered reasonably water-repellent. (Nothing is waterproof if enough pressure is applied.) Army tests show Gore-Tex resisting 65–80 psi, compared to 2 for untreated 60/40 cloth, 120 for Super K-Kote fabric (nylon coated with polyurethane), and 160 for vinyl-coated cotton.

Breathability is less amenable to testing or definition, as the variables of temperature and humidity and metabolism and work are so numerous, but an accepted standard for comfort for a person at rest is a breathing (water-transmission) rate of 350–600 grams of water per square meter of cloth per 24 hours (measured under laboratory conditions). A rate of 2,000–3,000 grams prevents condensation of perspiration in most hiking. (In hard work at high temperatures, no fabric can breathe fast enough.) According to the W. L. Gore Co., the laboratory rate for Gore-Tex laminated to 1.5-ounce nylon is 2,800 compared to 5 for vinyl-coated cotton, 10 for Super K-Kote, and 5,200 for untreated 60/40 cloth.

As the figures show, other fabrics keep rain out or let perspiration out, but don't do both. Gore-Tex is—or was when introduced—unique. Further, it's inert (as witness the use of PTFE for vascular grafts), nonflammable, and weather-durable, though not eternal; the Gore warranty is for three years only, a disappointment to customers misled by ads and neglecting to read the fine print on the label.

Strong though the material is, a thin membrane is too fragile to be used alone and is always laminated to other fabrics, resulting in a variety of materials. A Gore-Tex laminate may be lined with nylon taffeta, taslan, cotton poplin, or pile. Or it may be sandwiched between a knit liner inside and another fabric outside.

The long-awaited ticket to the Promised Land? Despite continuing improvements in the basic membrane and thousands of people-years of trail use, a minority of suspicious veterans who've watched many a wonder flash across the sky still whisper "Sweat-Tex." (When it comes to tents they do more than whisper, and at boots they openly laugh.) Certainly the promotion is far in excess of the reality. Dazzled hikers expect never again to be wet, imagine the miracle will part the Red Sea. The rate of returns owing to over-expectation is a steady nag on retailers—and a factor in what many observers consider the excessive price of the product.

Nevertheless, the expert consensus is that in clothing (and sleeping bags and bivy sacks) Gore-Tex really works in all but rather extreme conditions of heat/humidity/work—if given proper maintenance. It is *not* for the sloppy and scruffy. If body oils, sunburn cream, insect repellent, or plain crud contaminates the membrane, the dirty spots let rain in; the corrective treatment is sponging with rubbing alcohol. General accumulation of grime leads to overall leakage; the material should be kept clean by regular washing with powdered detergent in cold or sometimes warm water, double-rinsing to remove soap (Revive, a brand formulated for use with Gore-Tex, doesn't leave potentially damaging residues); dry cleaning is forbidden. Leaks may also be caused by trauma to the membrane; the treatment is to dip the garment in a tub of water, find the break, then dabble on seam sealer.

Gore-Tex could scarcely be expected to hold a permanent monopoly. A competitor took PTFE and made Klimate, but it lasted briefly. Other laminates are hovering on the brink of the market or girding up loins for the patent courts.

The strongest challenger to date is *Entrant*, from Toray in Japan, not a laminate but a 40-micron-thick coating of polyurethane closely bonded to the inside of a fabric (in fact, penetrating about one third of its thickness), forming a honeycomb with pores less than 2 microns in diameter—smaller than raindrops, refusing them entry; bigger than sweat vapor, permitting them exit. The outside of the fabric is given water-repellent treatment for a supplementary barrier. The base may be cotton, 60/40 cloth, woven nylon, or (for shoes) heavy-duty nylon.

Entrant is softer than PTFE laminates like Gore-Tex, drapes well and feels nice, is supple and noncrinkly, the owner having no sensation of wearing a cardboard box. Being elastic, it withstands rough handling far better than fragile PTFE. Being much quieter, it lets a person walk a trail without spooking the birds. Being much less expensive than Gore-Tex, garments of comparable quality cost 30 percent less.

But—does it work?

Comparisons are inexact, each sponsor favoring the measuring method that puts his product in the best light. The Entrant test method shows Entrant 15 percent more breathable than two-ply PTFE laminate, 31 percent more than three-ply. That's not surprising, but the laminator method also has Entrant the winner, by 4 and 24 percent.

Water-repellency is a closer contest. The laminator opts for the Mullen method, a test of the fabric's resistance to hydraulic pressure in the laboratory; Mullen gives the decision to PTFE, though not by much. Entrant employs the Bundesmann method, which simulates actual rainfall; Bundesmann has Entrant flinging laminates clear out of the ring, whether two-ply or three-ply, whether off the rack or after three washings.

Tests by the REI Quality Control Department are not so decisive, calling it pretty much a draw in both respects. One might therefore suppose that Entrant's lower cost, longer life, and pleasanter feel would easily topple Gore-Tex from the throne. In fact, it is the challenger that—so far, at least—can't even buy a ticket to the fight. Possibly it needs a new advertising agency. Or a Great Depression.

Vapor Barrier

Ponder, if you will, the attempts of the human body to maintain an ambience resembling the primordial seas. Man's remembering skin likes the relative humidity of the air immediately next to it to be about 70–95 percent, and to maintain that level respires, during rest, about 1 pint of water a day in *insensible perspiration* (gaseous water, invisible vapor). But in cold weather the air cannot be brought to the desired humidity. The body keeps pumping out vapor and still the skin dries; a person isn't sweating yet mysteriously develops a fierce thirst. If, in addition, hard work is being performed, producing excess heat, the body tries to cool itself by pouring out *sensible perspiration* (liquid water, sweat); if this is "breathed out" in accordance with the dogma of the established religion, heat is conducted away from the body by the water at a terrific rate, twenty times faster than by air; as a further complication, the insulating materials of garments are wetted.

For years the catalogs of Jack Stephenson, which vividly picture his equipment, have dissented from the establishment's stress on breathability and sought to reinstate the primordial on the trail. *Pleasure Packing*, by Robert S. Wood, goes deeply into the thermodynamics. More recently, Yves Chouinard, the renowned California iceman, has installed the vapor-barrier liner in his Patagonia catalog, and so has Marmot Mountain Works in theirs.

The Primordials concede breathability to be a reasonable guiding principle in ordinary hiking, as in ordinary life. However, the extraordinary conditions of hard labor in extreme cold and/or at high altitude are best met by erecting a vapor barrier, as follows:

1. The person dons a wicking undergarment, such as polypro underwear, as a concession to the fact that wearing a swamp next to the skin fells weird; the wick carries moisture to collar, cuffs, and waist for release to the outer atmosphere.
2. Over this he dons an impervious vapor-barrier shirt, either a large poly bag or a coated ripstop nylon.

3. He dons a sweater, parka, or whatever is being worn for insulation.

Forget "breathing." Insensible perspiration ceases because humidity within the barrier quickly rises to a cozy primordial 100 percent. Sweat can't get out to wet the insulating garments, can't conduct heat from the body. It is claimed the shirt adds 25 percent to the insulating value of the total clothing assembly—besides preventing the assembly from inside wetting.

The scientific facts of the matter are incontestable. However, the ordinary hiker, and even the climber, have such an aversion to the unavoidable slipperiness that one of America's largest outdoor outfitters faithfully stocks and strongly recommends vapor-barrier shirts—and sells ten a year.

If the shirt is neglected, the all-out vapor-barrier liner (VBL) system has about as many adherents as dried spinach. Let it be noted that dried spinach, though it may have the look of a low-grade controlled substance, cooks up deliciously. So, too, anyone who mountaineers in winter and/or at high altitude ought to investigate the Patagonia or Marmot or other system of shirt, pants, and socks, weighing merely ½ pound or so.

For VBL in socks, sleeping bags, and tents, see Chapters 8, 11, and 12.

Radiant Heat Barrier

When two surfaces of differing temperatures are opposed, the warmer transmits heat to the cooler by long-wave radiation, in the infrared end of the spectrum. The day-warmed ground radiates to the night sky; the sleeper in the meadow, to the stars; the human body and its calorie-burning furnace, to any part of the near environment that is below 98.6°F.

Just as clouds make a warmer night by reflecting the "black light" back to the ground, and a tent or tarp or overhanging branches of a tree make a warmer sleep, so a *heat shield*, or *radiant heat barrier*, helps a hiker keep warm. Several products are on the market.

Silver Lining is a nexus of two metallic membranes separated and stabilized by mesh, the entire layer only 0.001 inch thick.

Tex-O-Lite (3M) consists of two layers of aluminized polyethylene film separated and stabilized by nylon netting, tightly quilted into a sandwich 0.02 inch thick.

Solarsilk is a vacuum-plated material said by its maker, Kelty, to be as warm as Tex-O-Lite and to breathe better.

To date heat shields are used mainly in sleeping bags, but they are establishing a niche in tents and garments.

Insulation: Loft

A long time ago folks in cold country who couldn't afford six sweaters but were chilly with only two began stuffing the space between with straw, moss, lichen, leaves, or dog hair. From this expedient evolved double-wall garments filled with wool, cotton, or kapok. Finally arrived (actually, very early among goose-raising peasantry) down—and then polyester—and climbers on Himalayan peaks began surviving nights in the open without carrying sleeping bags. Because they were wearing them.

Just as the "climbing-boot" look became the campus rage, the "quilted look" grew so fashionable it was celebrated in a *New Yorker* cartoon. Not merely expeditionary mountaineers were quilted but

little old rose gardeners; Yves St. Laurent offered a Quilted cocktail dress in basic black.

However, insulated garments did not easily penetrate the American wilderness, entering as they did on a scene dominated by veterans of the Great Depression and the war-surplus bonanza. The brush apes in stinking wool shirts and khaki sweaters and Mountain Troop mook parkas recoiled in mixed horror and mirth as—in the chill of a mountain twilight—companions guiltily dug in packs and donned the new garments. Campfire conversation turned to which Great North Face or unclimbed *Achtausender* they were readying themselves for, and whether they had their letterhead printed up yet. And so passed year after year of chilly mountain twilights, and the joke grew old and the brush apes too, and one by one they went quilted, confessing that they often enough, given the invitation, would have joined Sam McGee in his furnace.

The attributes of down and polyester are discussed in Chapter 11, "Sleeping Bags." For clothing the cases may be repeated in summary here:

For down: Warmer when dry, thus better in dry cold or when fully protected by tent, stuff bag, and rain jacket, with occasional opportunity for airing in the sun. Softer, breathes easier, feels nicer. Stuffs tiny. The initial cost is higher, but life is longer: so, cheaper in the long run.

For polyester: Nearly as warm when dry, loses little warmth when wet, can be dried by wringing out and wearing. Nonallergenic. Doesn't mildew readily. Better for hikers who lack rain jackets, sleep under tarps, travel wetlands where the sun rarely shines, and for those who slog a lot in snow, much of which gets inside garments and tents, and for expeditioners who spend so much time in tents, exhaling a pint of water a night, that down delofts in a week and cannot be relofted until the end of the Arctic blackness. (Chapter 11 describes the intramural quarrel between two polyesters, Quallofil and PolarGuard. For a time the latter dominated clothing, but seems now to have lost out there, though it is still winning in sleeping bags.)

For silk: Raw silk extruded into filament batts, in the *Sun Silk* patented process, is marginally heavier than down, about as warm when dry, is warmer when wet and dries faster, and costs about a third less—but is not so compressible.

Insulation: Microfilaments

An unlikely nest of heresy, 3M (the home of Scotch tape), first challenged the dogma of lofting, whereby fibers surround tiny dungeons of trapped air. The company's chemists spun polyolefin microfilaments having twenty times the surface area of down or polyester per unit weight and propounded the theory that by "binding" air to their surfaces, the microfibers hold air as still as if in prison. A blend of 65/35 cloth and polyester (for bulk), the resulting *Thinsulate* is claimed to insulate with a thickness of ½ inch as well as 1 inch of lofty down.

That 3M had what strikes the industry as a good idea is suggested by the hot pursuit: Du Pont with *Sontique*, which is made entirely of polyester, as are Eastman Kodak's *Kodolite* and Toray's *Sunstate Teijens Eizac*.

Lofters counter the warmth without bulk argument by objections that densely packed microfilaments weigh 30–40 percent more than down of comparable warmth and that the product doesn't stuff well and therefore takes up twice the space of down in the pack.

LAYERING

The adaptations that permitted the naked ape to follow retreating glaciers northward and even jump over the margin to ice floes and igloos, and the regressions that gave fame to the Riviera and Southern California beaches and Gypsy Rose Lee, are two of the more familiar examples of layering, where things are put on the body, and taken off, as the weather and pit orchestra suggest. Lacking any interest in anthropology or burlesque, the hiker will nevertheless instinctively layer his or her body, using one or none on the beach and progressively more to answer the chilling of wind and rain and snow and the burning of sun.

The human body is most comfortable when heat production is balanced by heat loss. Twenty-six centuries ago Lao-tzu wrote, as quoted by REI's chief engineer of product development, "Movement overcomes cold. Stillness overcomes heat." This is one half of the equation. The other is choosing the correct layers for the circumstances of place and time.

To determine the efficiency of garments, singly and in combination—and also of sleeping bags (see Chapter 11)—the REI Quality Control Department employs a variable-temperature freezer, big enough to hold a mannequin filled with water and given a constant heat input equivalent to that of an average human body at rest. The freezer temperature is varied up and down to find the setting at which heat loss through the clothing balances heat input to the mannequin, its temperature stabilizing at 98.6°F. This setting is the temperature at which an "average" person at rest would be comfortable. However, to take into account activity level, body metabolism, and environment, the garment ratings are given not as single temperatures but as *comfort ranges*. (Moderate activity, such as walking, produces more body heat and thus lowers the bottom limit of comfort about 30°F from the comfort temperature at rest.)

The accompanying table of a sampling of test results merits study. The absolute comparisons are revealing; for example, a wool sweater and a pile jacket weigh virtually the same, but the first is comfortable down to 35°F, the second, to 15°F. The value of layering is plainly demonstrated by the fact that a person using the correct combination of this particular group of garments can be comfortable over a range of 120°.

PARKA WARMTH

Parka Type	Insulating Material *	Thickness (inches)	Weight (ounces)	Minimum Comfort Rating (°F)†
Expedition down	GD	2.75	52	−40
Alaskan down	GD	2.75	62	−40
Gore-Tex and down	GD	1.75	42	−10
Down	GD	0.9	32	0
Down	GD	1.5	34	0
Light down and nylon	GD	1.5	19	0
Gore-Tex and down	GD	1.3	28	5
Light down and poplin	GD	1.5	23	5
Thinsulate	GD	0.55	34	15
Thinsulate	T	0.75	33	15
Thinsulate	T	0.62	40	15
Gore-Tex and pile	T	0.5	28	20
Pile and Thinsulate	BP	0.25	34	20
Pile and Thinsulate	BP/T	0.25	32	20
Pile jacket	BP/T	0.38	18	25
Gore-Tex and pile	PP	0.20	30	25
Pile jacket	BP	0.38	21	25
Shell bunting jacket	PP	0.20	24	25
Fleece jacket	BP	0.19	19	30
Pile jacket	NP	0.31	17	30
Bunting jacket	BP	0.19	19	30

* BP—bunting pile (fleece); GD—goose down; NP—nylon pile; PP—polyester pile; T—Thinsulate.

† "Comfort Rating": Temperature at which a person engaged in light activity feels comfortable. The rating assumes that the head and lower torso are equally protected. It must be kept in mind that the rating in the field is affected by wind, rain, personal metabolism, level of fatigue, and food intake. These data, obtained in 1983 tests by the REI Quality Control Department, are indicative and suggestive rather than comprehensive and definitive. Materials and designs change from year to year, vary from manufacturer to manufacturer. The future is constantly upon us.

Before proceeding to the four layers, skin side to outside, a few reminders: to layer effectively, the entire body must be taken into account; sweaters can't compensate for heat loss from bare legs, and pants can't keep the head warm. Hiking is not done in a prone position in a freezer but in a steeply up and down, wet and windy, cold and hot world where the climate fluctuates by the minute; enough clothing for morning may not be sufficient by afternoon and dangerously inadequate at nightfall. Finally, *you are not an average person.* Nobody is, and never less so than when weary, wet, cold, and dispirited; *learn your own comfort range.*

Note: Garment weights given in the following pages are for the average men's size; weights are somewhat less in average women's sizes and more in tall-person sizes. For most garments, all sizes are the same price.

Underwear Layer

In most summer hiking, with the weather ranging from moderate to hot, underwear is chosen solely for comfort—to let air flow freely over the skin, cooling and drying, and to prevent dampness by absorbing perspiration. Whatever feels good in town is fine on the trail. Cotton underwear is the most popular, but any loose, absorbent garment will serve, whether wool, silk, or synthetic. The same is true in cool weather if the perspiration rate is low. Consequently, the ordinary backpacker moves from civilization to wilderness without changing underwear and marvels at the space given the subject in catalogs—until, on viewing the vivid colors and striking patterns and how the garments flatter a flatterable body, he understands they perhaps are meant less to please the skin of the wearer than the eye of the beholder.

The body's needs are radically different during vigorous exercise—and thus heavy perspiration—in cold weather, a situation by no means restricted to high mountaineers, winter mountaineers, and skiers but common enough among ordinary backpackers hauling heavy loads up steep trails in strong winds, under dense clouds, frequent in the summer of many a high wildland.

Underwear may, then, be asked to supplement the warmth of outer layers, and for that wool is best, followed by silk. The crucially important role of underwear at such times, however, is to get rid of the perspiration so it won't wet the insulating layers, bringing on the threat of hypothermia. The best means is a thin, snug garment that doesn't absorb sweat as do cotton, silk, and wool but wicks it outward, utilizing the "push" of body heat. Here is where polypropylene has earned its reputation.

For hiking and running, and bicycling, the lightest polypro is generally preferred, wicking most efficiently and having the feel of "a second skin." A long-sleeved shirt, crew neck or turtleneck, weighs 4–5 ounces and costs $14–$17; long bottoms are the same.

For downhill skiing, climbing, and other sports where vigorous action and extended rests alternate, the medium weight is better. A shirt weighs 6–7 ounces and costs about $22.

For winter climbing and sailing, kayaking, ice fishing, and the

Underwear, here doubling (partially) as outerwear. Polypropylene is the favorite for most such circumstances.

Clothing sufficient for a pleasant-day, several-hour walk not far from road or camp: shorts, light cotton shirt, and wool sweater in case of chilly moments.

like, there is "expedition" weight, several times thicker than standard with both insulating and wicking properties. A zippered turtleneck weighs some 12 ounces and costs $28, long bottoms weigh 9 ounces and cost $25.

For more warmth there are two-layer fabrics—Duofold and other brands. Shirts of polypro inside and wool or wool-acrylic outside weigh 7–10 ounces, bottoms, 7–9 ounces, cost about $20 each.

Another two-layer fabric, lacking polypro, is better-suited to relatively sedentary life in extreme cold. The inner 50 percent is cotton, the outer, 40 percent wool and 10 percent nylon. Shirt and bottom weigh some 20 ounces together and cost $28.

Silk underwear, combining the comfort of cotton and the warmth of wool, is worth comparing. Shirts—T, turtleneck, V neck, or crew neck—weigh 2½–4½ ounces and cost $15–$22. Long bottoms weigh 4 ounces and cost $20.

Since all the bottoms noted here are long, most hikers buy only a shirt, to wick the sweat off backs, and hike mainly in shorts. However, two-layer bottoms can add nearly as much warmth as trousers with much less weight. Canny travelers are known to carry two-layer bottoms for donning under shorts in bad weather, or under rain pants in the cold wet of brush or on the ocean beach in winter.

Clothing Layer

Shirt and pants, hat and socks, perhaps mittens or gloves, are the garments that in most of a hiker's trail life directly confront the elements and are his sole—and only necessary—protection against sunburn and wind chill. Aside from considerations of modesty, this layer is expected to provide warmth by insulation; fend off excessive sunrays and breezes; absorb perspiration and transport it to the outer air; and let the limbs swing free.

Shirts

Earlier editions of this book insisted that for any hike beyond a stroll a person should carry, if not always wear, a medium-weight wool shirt with full collar and tails below the belt line. Many an ancient hiker and a few young ones remain true to the wisdom of the ages, but the old dependable has been largely replaced by chemical combinations of underwear and jackets. Still, a few shops continue to offer a light shirt, 12 ounces, 85 percent wool and 15 percent nylon, for around $20. Ski-lodge shirts range in price to several times that. On the other hand, so enormous was the shirt production of the past that excellent ones can be picked up for a pittance at thrift shops and garage sales.

Polypro shirts are actually prettied-up underwear meant for runners and their ilk.

One catalog examined for this chapter offered ten different cotton shirts. Fabrics: chamois, light chamois, flannel, pinwale corduroy, Rugby jersey, 60/40 cloth. Styles: turtleneck, T neck, oxford, quartermaster. Colors: the rainbow. Weights: 6 ounces to 1 pound 2 ounces. Prices: $12 to $36. Other catalogs were found to have as many and more, and from one to the next there was remarkably little duplication, suggesting that backpackers are presented with a choice of possibly a hundred alternatives, assuming they visit only "their" shops and never stop off at J.C. Penney. One must conclude that the up-to-date hiker has abandoned the hair (wool) shirt for comfortable cotton, preferring to obtain warmth from other garments. So be it.

Pants

More miles are walked by more people on more trails in *shorts* than all other bottomwear combined. It's not a garment demanding a lot of thought. Running shorts of polypro-lined nylon weigh a couple ounces, cost a dozen dollars, not counting the *sports briefs* often considered mandatory supplements. Other popular styles are the cargo, trail, Bavarian, Bermuda, Sierra, Rugby, Rock, and Gurkha. Cutoffs are cheap and seem permanently in.

Though shorts are associated with sunshine, hikers in monsoon country often take off trousers when the rains come, to keep them dry in the pack, and travel in shorts. They may do the same when plunging into wet brush or fording a river. Congenital hypothermics, icicles for bones, may continue in shorts but don long-legged underwear beneath. Boy Scouts of the 1930s customarily wore pajama bottoms under shorts, rolled up in forest, rolled down in hot sun or bright snow to prevent crippling sunburn.

Knickers, mainly worn by climbers and cross-country skiers, don't bind at the knee, as trousers may, and ventilate almost as well as shorts when bottom strap and buckle are opened and knicker socks rolled down. A herringbone stretch model, 60 percent wool and 40 percent polyester/Spandex, warm without itch, hip-hugging, weighs 1 pound 5 ounces, costs $45. In 85 percent wool and 15 percent nylon, warm and strong, weight and price are about the same.

Almost without exception a hiker must have in the pack *trousers* or the equivalent—for cool nights, sudden storms, emergency bivouacs, to prevent sunburn, if the pajama solution is rejected, and to fend off biting bugs so beautiful evenings will not have to be spent cowering in the tent. A beginner can't go wrong wearing on the trail whatever old slacks chance to be around the house or in the local thrift shop. About the only thing to keep in mind is that they should be cut full to allow easy action, not binding hips or knees.

As with shirts, the conventional wisdom used to be that trousers had to be wool, and many hikers still think so. Trouser counterparts of the knickers noted above weigh a bit more and cost a bit less. A high-quality, hard-finish whipcord may run $100. An excellent buy is Army surplus, under $20. At thrift shops this sum will pay for several pairs of men's suit pants too crummy for cities but fit for miles of trails.

As with shirts, the contemporary hiker likes cotton trousers best—shocking as this is to the ancients, who remember when cotton pants were the mark of the tenderfoot on a potential death march. How-

Hikers dressed for a day hike in cool weather: knickers and wool shirt, trousers and wool sweater. Storm clothing is in rucksacks.

ever, today's add-on garments let a person enjoy the comfort of
cotton without risking hypothermia. Blue jeans were a fashion on
the trail years before they waggled so ubiquitously on the TV.
Cotton work pants, equally good if not *à la mode*, go at J.C. Penney
for $20 or less. Chinos are a bit more. Trail pants, mountain pants,
bush pants, outback pants, veldt pants, pampas pants, tundra pants,
trek pants, and whatever, of cotton/nylon or cotton/polyester, can
run several times that. Among the continuing leaders are cargo
pants, with six pockets, two on the thighs, weighing 1 pound 3
ounces, costing $22. DuraBlend rock pants are exceedingly sturdy
while cotton-comfortable, 12 ounces and $24 the pair.

Inasmuch as people very wisely tend to wear on the trail what
they have around the house, sweat pants are increasingly common
in wildlands, liked because they can be slipped on or off over boots
and shorts without undressing or unbooting, a quick response to
the brew-up of a wind or the emergence of the sun. Polypro and
cotton/polypro sweats are about 12 ounces, $30.

Head and Hands

This subcategory would be called "Extremities" except for the fact
that the feet are discussed in Chapter 8. Here are the other three
outposts of the heat-transfer system.

The most critical portion of the body for regulation of the thermostat is the area of the head and neck. The brain receives 20 percent
of the body's blood supply, 25 percent of its oxygen, and the head,
having little fatty insulation, may account for up to half the body's
total heat loss. If head and neck are cold, the whole body will shiver,
and if they are warm, one may feel quite comfortable even with
bare legs on a frosty night. It is wisely said, "If your feet are cold,
put on a hat."

Similarly, in scorching sun an overheated head can lead to dizzy
misery, even heat stroke.

Finally, in hard rain, if head and neck can be kept dry, one does
not feel totally drenched and blinded and lost in the swamp.

It is perfectly all right to choose headwear for style or personality

A sampling of headwear for various situations and personalities. Top: *Glacier hat, up-downer (modified Sherlock Holmes), and crusher.* Center: *Stocking cap, K-2 cap, and balaclava.* Bottom: *Sou'wester rain hat, beret, and handkerchief hat.*

as long as the choice gives the necessary protection. At least one climber has attained the summit of Mt. Rainier wearing an opera hat and causing a sensation, but he had a stocking cap in his pack.

For *warmth*, the long-standing trail favorite is the simple pull-on *stocking cap* or *watch cap*, wool with nylon reinforcement or polypro lining or without, weighing too few ounces to note (true of all headgear herein), selling for the low price of $5, half that if there's a knitter in the house. Warmer because it covers the face is the *balaclava* or *toque*, made of silk, polypro, or polypro/wool at about $8. Still warmer is the Hollofil II–filled *K-2 expedition cap*, with earflaps and bill, $20. The *beret*, perched jauntily atop the head or pulled down over the ears, is quite good; the British green beret has a sinister commando look, the French beret a boulevardier air. The *Tupacamaru* is handwoven of llama/alpaca wool by Incas. Any headwear not extending to the neck may be supplemented by a *scarf*; wrapped around neck and head babushka-style, it's superb in hard rain driven by high wind.

For *rain*, the *sou'wester* is occasionally seen. The high-crowned, broad-brimmed *Akubra Bushman* is worn by a distinguished few. The *umbrella* is as ubiquitous in Europe as walkers and no longer thought so eccentric on American trails. The *crusher (mountain hat, glacier hat, Aussie tennis hat)*, worn by guides because tourists expect it, guards the head against sun and—with Gore-Tex—rain, all for $12. For warmth and rain protection there are Gore-Tex pile hats, $22, and Gore-Tex/Thinsulate ones, $20.

For *sun* protection on deserts and scorched hills one may wear a *handkerchief hat*, a bandanna knotted at the corners to fit the head, periodically dipped in streams or rubbed with snow for quick cooling. The bandanna may also be worn to protect the neck, an excruciating place for a sunburn. The Bushman, with or without rattlesnake band, and crusher, *Aussie bush hat*, and *Panama* keep away the sun, as does a *baseball cap*, essential for driving RV, pickup truck, or motor home.

In normal hiking the hands rarely need more protection than sticking them in pockets. However, an experience or two of blue skin and numb fingers suggests the utility of *mittens* or *gloves*, which are, of course, mandatory if much time is spent in wintry conditions. In olden days everyone was abundantly supplied with mittens (and socks) at Christmas, knitting being a principal function of the olden-style grandmother. Sentimentalists can still buy grandmother-type mittens, all wool, for $6. However, for the same price there are polypro/wool gloves, which is what the new-style grandmothers wear when they go jogging in January.

Climbers, skiers, and winter mountaineers are the market for the gloves-mittens-overmitts of polypro, Gore-Tex, Thinsulate, pile, 60/40 cloth, and other chemical fabrics.

Insulation Layer

The distinctions between layers are not clear-cut and absolute, and in defining the major role of each, its subsidiary contributions cannot be ignored. The innermost layer, intended primarily for comfort and wicking, and the outermost layer, charged with repelling the weather, can scarcely avoid contributing some warmth as well, and perhaps a great deal. Garments that straddle boundaries, such as sweaters, may as logically be classified as basic clothing instead of, as here, "insulation." Some garments combine insulation and shell and are actually two layers in one, seemingly a contradiction in terms but not really upon close examination.

The layer under present consideration is plainly definable, functioning (1) to provide warmth when basic clothing is insufficient, (2) to let sweat and excess heat pass through and (3) to permit the hiker to move without the sensation of being an overweight polar bear.

For most backpackers most of the time insulation is best provided by more than one garment, so that warmth can be regulated by adding or removing components one by one. When all the insulation is in a single garment, such as a mackinaw or a shell/insulation combination garment, the choices are between too cold and too hot, a Scylla and Charybdis where on the one hand is hypothermia, and on the other, overheating that sweat-soaks the insulation, leading to hypothermia.

Wool Sweaters

Cotton sweaters are for patio and street and après trail in car or restaurant, not the wildland.

Polypropylene sweaters are the newest embodiment of that wunderkind chemical.

Rumors that the wool sweater died when the pile jacket was born are greatly exaggerated. To understand the survival, compare two garments of roughly equal weight: a best-selling wool sweater (85 percent Ragg wool, 15 percent nylon) and a popular pile jacket. The latter's comfort-range, down to 15°F, compared with the former's only to 35°F, might seem to end the debate. But the latter is 0.5 inches thick, twice the sweater, half as easy to stuff in a pack, and costs about three times more than the sweater's $20. Layer the sweater with a 12-ounce, $20 wool shirt, and for a total of $40 and less than 2 pounds a hiker has a comfort range well below freezing, and no thanks (well, only 15 percent thanks) to the chemists.

For sensational bargains, visit thrift shops where $3 will buy a sweater that would be $75 new and was never worn twice.

As observed previously in this book, thrift is not the preoccupation of American wildlanders it once was. The catalogs exhibit handsomely patterned pullovers and zips, vests and shawls, of Shetland wool, mountain wool, or cashmere, in styles designated as Fisherman, Nordic, Kensington, Radcliffe, Cardigan, Gloucester, Londonderry, Wales, Australia, Patagonia, Kamchatka, Katmandu, Walla Walla, West Seattle. However, just because it's pretty doesn't mean it's a bad sweater. Stylish garments weigh ½–1½ pounds, cost $20–$50, and are just as warm as those that are ugly.

Fiberpile Sweaters and Jackets (and Pants)

Discussion of "shelled" fiberpile (a weather-resisting layer combined with the insulation) is deferred to the section "Shell Layer" in this chapter. Insulation-only garments abound in the shops—in polyester pile, nylon pile, fleece, polypropylene bunting, and others. They come in various styles and a wide range of prices. A few representative examples illustrate the choice.

Jackets (with zipper) and *sweaters* (pullover), with stand-up collar and pockets, weigh ¾–1½ pounds, the warmth corresponding, and the price, $40–$70. The lighter garments are fleece; the heavier, polyester pile. Off the backpacking scale toward the Himalayan is a jacket of polypro bunting, weighing 1¾ pounds and costing $58.

Vests (no sleeves) run 12–18 ounces and cost $30 or so.

Pants, made to be pulled over boots and provided with a fly, are

Lightweight pile sweater, jacket style.

cumbersome on trails, but excellent for camp (5–17 ounces, $7–$30). For the polypro bunting, 1½ pounds, $50.

Heat Shield/Insulated Garments

Representative of the genus are three offerings of a leader in adapting spaceship technology to the wildlands of earth. In these the barrier is Silver Lining.

First is a jacket with zipper and snap front, no insulation but a shell of ripstop nylon lined with a sparkling-shiny shield. "Better than a sweater," they say, weighing a mere 8 ounces, costing $60. Use it alone on cold, still mountain evenings under the stars, or layer it with polypro, fleece, or Gore-Tex.

A vest that "makes others look and feel chubby" combines the barrier with Thinsulate (12 ounces, $50).

"You needn't look like the Michelin tire man" to be warm in a "sleek jacket," barrier plus Thinsulate (1 pound 8 ounces, $80).

Insulated Garments

As with the fiberpile/shell combination, the unions of down, polyester fiberfill, or Thinsulate with Gore-Tex or Entrant are deferred to the "Shell Layer" section.

A complication in terminology is that any insulating material requires a containing fabric, and this is called a shell. And indeed it does resist a certain amount of breeziness and mistiness. However, it is not expected to stand alone against the stormy winds that blow and the deluges that flow. Warmth is its business, and when the game gets rough, it asks the supplement of a separate shell whose business *is* the wind and rain.

Though there are insulated socks, booties, underwear, pants,

Representative insulated garments, jacket style. The filler may be either down or polyester. Most have detachable hoods. Left to right: *Sweater, parka, vest, Gore-Tex jacket.*

mitts, dickeys, coveralls, and face masks, these are for backpacking far colder than the ordinary. The two garments of most general interest are the *vest*, sleeveless, covering the trunk only, combining warmth with maximum freedom of movement, and the *parka*, extending down to the hips and having a hood, often detachable. (Features of the parka will be discussed under "Shell Layer.") The choice should be dictated by a person's individual physical characteristics and preferences—metabolism, the kind of terrain and time of year he likes to hike in. It is not unusual to see in a single camp the members of the party variously attired, at one and the same time—in parka with hood drawn tight around the face, in vest, in old wool shirt full of holes and not yet buttoned against the evening chill.

The experts' recommendation for a first purchase in insulation beyond the sweater is a goose-down vest weighing ¾ pound, stuffable in a pack pocket, costing $30, and adding 10°F of warmth. Few backpackers ever need more in this zone of their layer system.

A step up in warmth and niceties (stand-up collar, pockets) is another goose-down vest, weighing 1½ pounds and costing $55.

A Quallofil vest with a Quarpel shell weighs 1¼ pounds and costs $46.

Weighing in at little more than a pound, costing only $70, yet comfort-rated 5°–45°F, is a non-elaborate yet very functional goose-down vest.

Two Quallofil parkas suggest the opportunities there. One, rated 0°–45°F, has a Quarpel shell, weighs 2 pounds, and costs $100. The other, rated-10°–40°F, poly/cotton shell, weighs 3 pounds, and costs $80. Why, with the two side by side in the same shop, does the warmer cost less? The point is made that buying from a catalog is no substitute for being in the shop, one garment in each hand, personally feeling the differences.

A Thinsulate parka, with a shell of 65/35 cloth, weighs 2¼ pounds and costs $90.

Shell Layer

The experts emphatically counsel that the most important single garment in a hiker's layering is the shell, the outer rampart against wind, rain, snow, and sun. Tests by the REI Quality Control Department show that in still air a wind shell adds 10°–25° F to the warmth of any garment, whether polypro top, Ragg sweater, cotton chamois shirt, or polyester pile jacket. In a hard blow where wind chill is a factor, the increase may be 50°F or more—the difference between life and death.

The only truly all-purpose shell is a house, and the hiker, unable to carry his about on his back snail-like, must identify his chief threats and prepare his defenses accordingly. Outfitters offer four options:

1. Windproof, not waterproof, breathable garments. Made of uncoated nylon, cotton, or combination materials, these are meant for the hiker who doesn't plan on rain.
2. Windproof, waterproof, not breathable garments. These are of polyurethane-coated nylon, intended for the hiker who foresees more rain than sweat.
3. Windproof, waterproof (water-repellent), breathable garments. Made of Gore-Tex or Entrant, these are for the hiker who will not be perspiring heavily, who will be in a climate where there is significant humidity differential between the inside and outside of the garment and where the outer surface is not covered completely and continuously by a layer of water. They are for those who realize that anyone working hard in the rain is bound to get wet no matter what he's wearing and so they won't be running back to the shop every other week whining about betrayal.
4. Windproof, waterproof (*sic*), breathable, warm garments. These are made of Gore-Tex or Entrant, with fiberpile, down, polyester, fiberfill, or Thinsulate. They are meant for the hiker who wants it all, wants it now, and has all the money and all the faith.

The four options of materials entail four subsections. First, though, the choice of garments discussed in the subsections must be explained.

The *poncho* is a tarp that can be worn while walking. A *jacket* has a zipper or snap front, a collar but usually no hood, and comes down only to the waist. *Pants*, *chaps*, *overalls*, and *bibs* cover the legs plus varying amounts of the torso. However, when people say "shell" they mostly mean parka, and a generic description is therefore in order.

The basic parka is defined by a *hood*, integral or detachable, and a *skirt* descending well below the waist. Most models are *front-opening* ("jacket-style") with a *zipper* backed up (lest there be fatal failure) by *snaps*, the line covered by a *storm flap* to prevent heat loss. The *pullover* ("anorak") used to be purely a climber's choice, but with a half-front zipper has gained backpacker friends. *Drawstrings* may be supplied not only to pull the hood close around the face but to cinch

The shell layer: Representative jacket-style parkas.

the waist and/or skirt bottom. *Pockets* range from none or two in ultralights to four outside for cargo and hand-warming and one inside for valuables. *Velcro* (sticky tape) may be used for pocket closures, cuffs, and storm flap. There may be a single *layer* throughout or a double layer over the shoulders; or the parka can be fully lined throughout, either for warmth or to provide a smooth inner surface for ease in drawing it over undergarments. *Vents* or even zippers may be supplied under the arms for ventilation. With or without a hood, a *stand-up collar* keeps the wind off the back of the neck. In the higher price range *seams* are factory-sealed and taped; in the lowest they may require regular treatment by paint-on *Seamlock*. Light-duty parkas may be narrowly cut to save weight; heavy-duty parkas must be full cut to be used over insulating garments and still permit free motion. This is an absolute bare-bones description of the garment independently invented in Lapland, Tierra del Fuego, and Great Slave Lake in the Alps, Karakoram, and Andes, and that has been to the North Pole and the South Pole and the world's highest summits. Catalogs have infinitely more to say about the innumerable manifestations on which so much loving care has been lavished by manufacturers.

The following pages will discuss the several sorts of shell garments, mainly parkas. To help focus on this crucial apparel, a table is included here comparing the minimum comfort ratings of the offerings in a typical recent catalog of a representative large backpacking shop. Similar articles are to be found in the stock of any outdoor supplier catering for trails and peaks.

Windproof, Not Waterproof, Breathable

This is the parka primeval, the response to the stimulus of wintry tundras and windy glaciers and stormy crags, where wind is fearsome, precipitation is most likely to be snow too cold to stick, and the mist is blowing too fast to find the pores in the fabric.

This is the parka for only a relatively few hikers—those who ascend to the cold and windy, but not too wet, heights. Should the rains come in any quantity, the fabric quickly soaks through unless a rain shell is added or a tent is crawled into; better in such cases

COMFORT RANGES OF GARMENT LAYERS*

Garment	Material	Weight (ounces)	Thickness (inches)	Comfort Range (°F)
Thin polypro top	Polypropylene	6	0.07	40 to 70
Thin wool top	Wool	8	0.08	40 to 70
Two-layer top	Polypro/wool	8.5	0.09	35 to 65
Ragg sweater	Wool	19	0.25	35 to 65
Fleece sweater	Polyester	19	0.20	30 to 60
Pile jacket	Polyester	21	0.50	15 to 50
Polyester-filled parka	Quallofil	21	1.0	−10 to 30
Gore-Tex parka	Gore-Tex	22	0.95	40 to 70

In Combination

Thin polypro top				40 to 70
Polypro top and Gore-Tex parka				25 to 55
Polypro top and pile jacket				10 to 40
Polypro top, polyester-pile jacket, and Gore-Tex parka				−5 to 25
Polypro top and polyester-filled parka				−20 to 25
Polypro top, polyester-pile jacket, and polyester-filled parka				−40 to 10
Polypro top, polyester-pile jacket, polyester-filled parka, and Gore-Tex parka				−50 to −10

* Tests were conducted by the REI Quality Control Department, assuming (1) an "average" person, not exceptionally thin or stocky or unduly fatigued and with normal metabolism, (2) a uniform amount of insulation over the entire body, and (3) dry garments (wet insulation is 9°–50°F less warm).

---

to put the parka in the pack to keep it dry and put it on again only when the rain quits and the cold dry winds blow.

Several choices, in some cases with companion pants, are available.

Wind jackets and wind pants (referred to jointly as *wind suits*) add many degrees of warmth for very little weight. A nylon set, the pants with full-length side zippers for donning and doffing over boots, weighs 1 pound and costs $38—half that for either separately. A set with polypro inside and nylon outside weighs 2 pounds and costs $155.

Three parkas embody the accumulated wisdom of the ages as

expressed through the medium of contemporary materials. A "wilderness parka" of 60/40 cloth outside and easy-sliding nylon inside, weighs 1½ pounds and costs $62. A "mountain parka," the 60/40 shell lined for warmth with 85/15 wool/nylon, weighs 2 pounds and costs $70. A "timberline parka" consisting of Quarpel outside and nylon inside, weighs 1½ pounds and costs $90.

The overwhelming majority of hikers will never want any item from this category. Those who spend a moderate amount of time in the zone of cold wind and little rain might want a wind jacket (8 ounces, $19) plus a rain shell from the next category. High mountaineers who definitely do want a wind parka must think of rain protection, either a separate rain shell or a modern miracle.

Windproof, Waterproof, Not Breathable

The centuries have witnessed a continuing quest for some means of going out in the rain without getting wet. Fishermen soaked jackets and pants in fish oil; their "oilskins" were slippery and stinky, though tolerable to fishermen and, apparently, fisherwomen. Tar

was the recourse of jolly seamen ("tars"). Charles Macintosh (1766–1843) cemented rubber and cloth in the garment that carried his name through London fogs with Scotland Yard and over the misty moor with Richard Hannay.

These and other impermeable fabrics, which are truly waterproof and not merely water-repellent, prevent the passage of water in both directions, keeping rain out and perspiration in. Objection to the latter is surely frivolous when rain is descending (or blowing sideways) at the rate of inches per day; better to stew in one's own warm juices than be drowned in the sky's cold soup. The *foul-weather gear* of the winter sailor appeals as well to winter walkers of ocean beaches; a set of bib overalls and jacket, a laminate of vinyl and nylon, stiff and awkward yet absolutely rainproof, weighs 2–3 pounds and costs $25–$35.

The closest approach to a portable house is a polyurethane-coated nylon poncho with corner grommets for double duty as a tarp. One

The waterproof poncho, a portable tarp, is mainly worn while puttering around camp in the rain, but sometimes also during downpours on the trail.

example weighs 12 ounces and costs $25; another weighs 1 pound (large enough to cover the pack) and costs $28. A poncho is splendid for standing around in camp or doing chores in a downpour. In strenuous hiking it becomes an ambulatory sauna. In any but the simplest maneuvers it fouls on brush, pack, cooking pots, feet, and other hikers. Dogs flee from it, whimpering. In a high wind it flaps and flies—unless pegged firmly to the earth—and is anything but windproof.

The best choice for a backpacker—a *minimum shell* for the average hiker that is both waterproof *and* windproof—is a rain jacket of polyurethane-coated nylon taffeta. One example weighs 11 ounces and costs $35; another, considerably more durable, a two-ply taffeta, weighs 14 ounces and costs $46. With this, why bother about a separate wind shell? Because if worn too long the impervious material lets the clothing and insulation layers get wet from perspiration. It can be argued that when the rain continues *that* long the hiker ought to crawl in a tent or go home, but that is sometimes easier said than done. In any event, rain shell *plus* wind shell may weigh together as little as 1¼ pounds and cost $54. The novice ought to compare this sum to prices in categories to follow.

Wanted less often are rain pants or rain chaps.

Windproof, Waterproof, Breathable

When the rain pounds hard enough and long enough it penetrates any fabric with pores; a pity, but a scientific certainty. The "push" of the body's heat pump cannot force perspiration out through a fabric whose exterior wall is flooded or into an already saturated exterior atmosphere; sad, but a fact. Given the most meticulous care, a breathable garment fails some of the time for all hikers, nearly all of the time for some. Disillusioning. So is the expiration of the warranty a quarter of the way through the life expectancy of a garment so costly.

The low-budget hiker will seek his shell in the two preceding subsections, not here. Yet a random survey of the catalogs finds, for every shell lacking Gore-Tex, a half dozen with it. Some shops carry no shells of the nonmiracle breed and feature, if not Gore-Tex, then Entrant.

What, then, is the significance of the bitter testimony of hikers who tried Gore-Tex parkas (and boots and hats, and dogs and cats) and wail "Never again!"? What will the catalog scene be a decade hence? What newer miracles will emerge? (Such as the garment that stayed in fashion on the Pacific Northwest coast for some ten eons, a cape of plaited cedar bark?)

The summary judgment of professionals in the shops and experienced hikers on the trails is that though Gore-Tex is not everything the aggressive marketing would crack it up to be, if garments are cared for as the manufacturer stipulates and if expectations are not irrationally high, it's the best thing mankind has yet seen (with the possible exception of Entrant). Further, the manufacturer is constantly upgrading the miracle. The Gore-Tex of today should not be judged by the Gore-Tex of yesterday, and the Gore-Tex of tomorrow may live up to the claims made by irrepressible copywriters.

Some of the breathables are not an impossible stretch in price above the "minimum shell" noted earlier and give the beginner a relatively painless way to experiment. Convinced, he may then ride the escalator to the upper floors.

The economy breathable is Entrant, available in a full-scale parka for 1¼ pounds, $70. If the material stands the test of time, this might someday become the "minimum shell."

The rest of the story is all Gore-Tex. Jacket-style parkas begin in a simple yet well-made model at 14 ounces, $90. As more pockets, drawstrings, and underarm zippers are added, a second layer of laminate and liners of polypro or other is included, and the outer fabric becomes 330-denier Cordura, the weight climbs to 2 pounds, and the price, to $200.

An anorak appealing to lightpacking nonclimbers because it has a 12-inch front zipper to make it easier to pull over the head weighs a mere pound but costs no mere $120.

The true believer finds Gore-Tex rain pants indispensable for taking a shower. With full side zippers they range from 8 to 12 ounces in weight and $50 to $80 in price. Bib overalls (bibs), which cover the waist and much of the chest, are for winter mountaineers who wallow a lot in soft snow; an example weighs 1¾ pounds, costs $140.

Windproof, Waterproof, Breathable, Warm

This final group seems to flaunt the layering principle and to regress to the mackinaw, and indeed, if the miracle fails, what have you got? However, combining in a single package the shell and insulation, and the two types of shell, is convenient in certain provinces of the wild world.

The trail peasantry may wish to examine economy models, such as an Entrant/Thinsulate parka that weighs 1¾ pounds and costs $90, or a Gore-Tex/fleece jacket weighing 1 pound 14 ounces, also sold for $90.

Gore-Tex teams up with Thinsulate in a parka comfort-rated 5°–45°F; weighing 2 pounds 14 ounces, it sells for $160. A similar model but with richer refinements costs $200.

Advertised as Ne Plus Ultra is a union of a Silver Lining heat shield, Thinsulate, and Gore-Tex; this weighs 2 pounds 3 ounces and costs $195.

Also sold is a one-layer shell that comprises a goose-down sweater and Gore-Tex shell, together weighing 2 pounds 15 ounces. It can be unzipped into two garments, each of which can be worn separately. Comfort-rated -10°–55°F, it costs $190.

A goose-down/Gore-Tex parka, comfort-rated -20°–40°F, weighs 2 pounds 11 ounces and costs $210.

At most shops this is the top of the sky. At others there are flights beyond. Marmot Mountain Works, for example, has a Warm II down parka with a Gore-Tex shell. It is "40 percent warmer than a non-Gore-Tex parka of equivalent loft in a wind of 30 miles per hour," the goose down possessing 625 fill power. It is light, weighing 1 pound 6 ounces (with the hood), and costs $258.

Above the beyond soars Marmot's Too Warm parka. Weighing 1 pound 10 ounces and costing $318, it is unsurpassable for the final thousand feet of Everest or a Chicago winter.

10
Packs

Lumping together all the human-powered transport devices ever used on the world's trails as "packs" would be as informative as calling all the passengers on the Ark "animals." The pussycat and the elephant are—in the larger scheme of phyllum, class, and order—rather closely related, but which would a person put his howdah on? And which would he want in his easy chair? A person must choose his animal—and his pack—for a specific purpose in mind.

For afternoon strolls the issue can be dodged. Candy bar and apple in pockets, cup on belt, sweater around waist, camera over shoulder—off and away the happy hiker strides, chuckling at the lumps on the backs of strangers met on the way.

For a long day, though—or a short one if much lunch or children's clothing or camera or birding gear is brought along or mushrooms or pretty rocks or driftwood are gathered on the way—stuffing the pockets and draping the body and encumbering the hands interfere with free-and-easy walking. Further, at any distance from civilization the hiker must have with him the Ten Essentials (see Chapter 15). Consequently, since any weight greater than several pounds is most comfortably carried on the back, a person committed to the trails needs some sort of pack. The preferred species for day use is the *rucksack*, essentially a scaled down version of the overnighter. It is therefore, though often the first pack purchased, treated last in this chapter.

The overnight pack that until recently was the unchallenged king of the mountain has an *external frame* wedded to shoulders and back and supporting the packbag. Though this design now has company on the summit, it will always be the simplest to use, the least expensive, and for much trail country, the most comfortable.

With breathtaking speed the *soft pack* has evolved into the *internal-frame* pack, going from the idiosyncrasy of a cultist few to sales parity with the external-frame pack and garnering praise for its surpassing intimacy, the intricacy and higher cost considered a fair price to pay for bliss.

On the principle of age before beauty, the external-frame pack will be accorded respectful priority in this chapter. Much of what is said about it also applies to the internal-frame pack, which will have to wait another edition to take over first place.

EXTERNAL-FRAME PACK

Man is really not well designed to walk on his hind legs at all, and placing a heavy weight atop the precariously erect skeleton definitely

goes against nature. Yet for a very long time man has been doing so and the history of packing would in itself make a book—the basket or pot carried on the head, the pole balanced on the shoulder by a load at either end, the blanket roll slung over one shoulder and tied on the opposite hip—these are only a few of the ways man has turned himself into a donkey (another poor beast never intended to carry burdens).

Over the centuries and the miles, many a suffering soul has mused on alternatives. Among the designs that evolved in America before World War II were the "dish rack" and the Ome Daiber "string pack"; the most widely acclaimed was the Trapper Nelson, with a wood frame somewhat contoured to the body in the horizontal though not the vertical, a canvas back, and a canvas bag attached to the frame by steel wires connecting eyelet screws in the frame to grommets in the bag. The Trapper, good enough to go to Minya Konka in 1932, then the highest summit attained by Americans, lives on, as do other relics, but mainly in the basements of broken-down sentimentalists.

Let not the past be dismissed lightly. When the OPEC nations and the North Sea and the Arctic run out of oil, mulching and crop rotation may return again, and winter underwear and passenger

trains, and backpacks made by weaving willow shoots and twisting cedar bark, as described in the woodcrafter literature. Boy Scout troops will look up copies of Russ Mohney's book *Make It and Take It* and hold work parties to equip themselves with wooden packs made in a few hours for a few dollars. The wickerwork Pack Basket, called the original backpack, may have a new life, and hikers whose aesthetic discrimination has been overwhelmed by high tech may learn to appreciate the low-tech Segan pack of laminated ash and mahogany, leather, wool felt, and canvas duck—scarcely a dram of petroleum in the whole lot.

The 1930s Bergan pack, with a tubular steel frame, seems to have started the trend to metal, especially when the U.S. Army adaptation flooded American trails in the great age of World War II surplus. Frames of tubular aluminum began to appear, lighter than steel but still not compromising much with the human back, and with a tendency to fall apart when sneezed at, as they frequently were. Then Kelty and other pioneers inaugurated modern times.

This book's first edition, in 1972, marveling at the restless creativity of manufacturers, wondered if they had not gone as far as was practical to go and whether the next historical task would be to sort out the throng of Kelty-like packs, reduce the offerings on

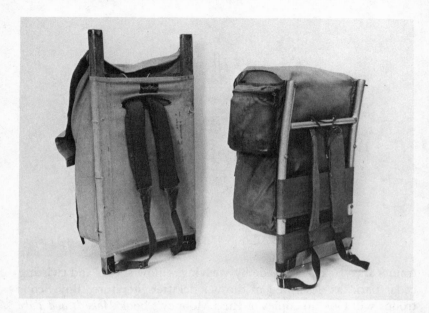

Nostalgia. Left: *The most famous of the old wood-frame packs, the Trapper Nelson.* Right: *An early aluminum-frame pack, Dick Kelty's first model.*

the market, and simplify the labors of catalogers and handbook writers—and hikers, too. Little was it suspected that in a brief decade a prodigy of invention, engineering, and merchandising as imposing as the Roman Empire would—well, not fall or even decline very much, but be forced to share its domain with the invader. Still, the external-frame pack is in some respects healthier than ever. The weaker models have been pruned; the freakier experiments, abandoned. Borrowings from the competitor have been adroitly exploited, perhaps pointing to an emerging new species of cross-breeds. Finally, novices who were sweet-talked into buying the highest available tech, and veterans captivated by the new lovelies, have learned that what's good for some people some of the time isn't necessarily the greatest for all of the people all of the time—or for some of the people any of the time. In various provinces of the wildland empire the invader is being hurled back.

The External Pack Frame

The Skeleton

The dominant external frame is the *aluminum S-ladder*. However, other materials compete, and other letters of the alphabet, too.

The usual frame material is high-strength *aluminum alloy tubes*, either "aircraft" quality or the cheaper but adequately sturdy "furniture" grade. Some frames (Kelty, for example) are quite rigid. Others (JanSport, for example) are of thinner tubing with thicker walls, strong but flexing with the body. Both approaches work fine. Experiments with *molded plastic* have resulted in frames (Coleman Peak I, for example, using polypropylene) strong enough but requiring the owner to get used to the sensation of carrying wet spaghetti.

The most common frame patterns are the *H*, or *ladder*, in which the outside members are separate, and the *upright*, or *inverted U*, which is formed from a single tube. Other patterns are the *hourglass* and the *X*, the latter so designed that the pack can be rolled up for transport. To keep weight close to the body's center of gravity, in the vertical dimension the frame is contoured to the back with either a moderate or an exaggerated bend, a sort of *flattened S* approximating the profile of the upper torso; on some, the lower portion sweeps sharply forward to bring weight more directly over the body axis.

Three to five horizontal *crossbars* (in a U design the outside member itself makes one of the crossbars) are curved to fit back contours. They give rigidity yet permit enough flexibility to absorb shocks. Most models can be lengthened at the top with a *frame extension* for very tall loads. Some frames have a *V-truss reinforcement* between the upper sides, particularly good for added strength when the extension is used.

The most frequently used method of joining metal members is *welding* (heliarc, tungsten arc), generally considered the strongest. *Brazed* frames are inexpensive and quite sturdy if carefully made. A number of designs dispense with permanent joints in favor of plastic or metal *couplings* (or *bolts* or *screws*), in theory not as rigid as welding but in practice just as satisfactory and offering advantages

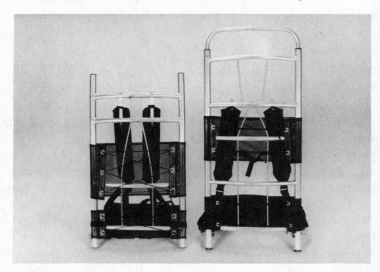

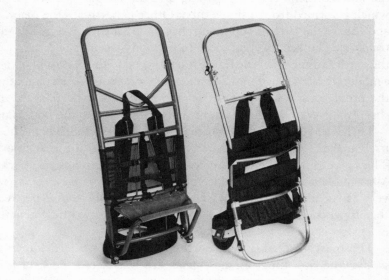

Representative external packframes. Top left: *Basic economy ladder.* Top right: *More sophisticated and versatile ladder, with extension frame.* Bottom left: *A "freighter" for extremely heavy and/or awkward loads.* Bottom right: *A U frame with couplings.*

of adjustability. Indeed, some manufacturers deny that rigidity equals strength; their coupled-together frames flex considerably, resisting stress dynamically. Care in construction matters more than the method; welds can break and couplings slip; of course, the more parts to a frame, the more the cost.

Some frames are *adjustable*, either by using couplings that let the crossbars be moved or by telescoping the outside members; frame length and packbag position can be varied to suit bodies of different dimensions and loads of different weights. Manufacturers whose frames are nonadjustable ordinarily compensate by offering two to four sizes.

Though the S-ladder has prevailed, there have been challenges to its supremacy. A brief sensation was the *hipwrap (hiploader, hip-hugger, wraparound)*, derived from a nineteenth-century patent by Henry Merriam that languished in obscurity before the concept was refined to two padded arms jutting forward from the frame bottom, tightly hugging the hips when the hip belt is snugged. Among the converts were iron men who swore there was nothing like it for carrying 100-pound loads, and women whose upper torsos were too narrow to cope with ordinary frames. The latter generally have found peace, at last, with the internal-frame pack; the former are so minute a minority nobody much cares if they're happy or not.

The Bal-Pak was invented by a fellow whose back was a wreck; it is a sort of birdcage that arches over the shoulders, carrying half the load in back and half in front.

The Modular-Pak breaks into components which serve as tent poles, camp seat or toilet, stretcher, or ladder. In a similar design, two pack frames and a companion wheel can be bolted together into a cart for hauling a moose or gold nuggets out of the wilds.

Hip Belt

The key component of the external-frame pack that was developed in the period from the 1950s to the 1970s, the central element of the system suspending the pack skeleton from the body, is the hip belt, hailed as the most revolutionary step in recorded history toward transforming suffering humans into happy asses.

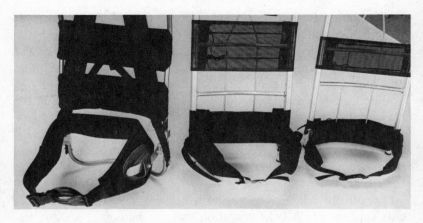

Representative hip belts, more and less elaborate.

Olden-day packs (Trapper Nelson) were "shoulder carry"; the frame was suspended solely from the shoulders, and when these sagged, the whimpering hiker leaned forward to shift weight directly onto the back. In the final extremity, he cupped his hands under the frame horns and lifted—until his arms went dead.

Dick Kelty, while advancing from old materials and patterns toward something new, didn't immediately renounce the recourse to hands—his first models had lower horns for that specific purpose. He saw the light only when a friend who was trying a pack caught his attention by yelling, "Hey, Dick—look—*no hands*!" The friend had stuck the horns in the back pockets of his pants. And so ended the Dark Ages.

The design pioneered by Kelty, Camp Trails, and others lets shoulders and back do a decent share of the work but employs the hip belt to place much of the weight on the hips—60–75 percent claim the theoreticians, perhaps 30–50 percent say skeptics. Certainly, the percentage varies from one model to another and with different adjustments of belt and shoulder straps. The load is carried high, in a vertical line parallel to the body axis; the weight is transmitted through the frame to the hip belt, from there to the strong muscles of the hip area, and thence to the sturdy legs. With this "hip-carry" system, the strain on the shoulders and back is lessened, and the hiker walks upright rather than in the old Trapper Nelson crouch.

The original simple belt—two webbing straps about 2 inches wide buckling in front of the waist—has evolved into a *padded hip belt* (*wraparound* or *full-circle belt*) 4–5 inches wide, extending all around the body, bolstered by either a hard or soft foam that spreads the weight more evenly. The latest advance is the Kelty *Ultra-Fit*, with a two-ply foam of different densities and the belt's attachment points moved inward from the lower corners of the frame to shorten the "lever-arm effect" and wrap better on small waists.

A *quick-release buckle* is convenient at rest stops and, more important, serves as an important safety device. The belt must be completely unbuckled before fording streams, walking logs, or engaging in similar maneuvers that may go wrong and require the pack to be jettisoned in a hurry. Lacking the quick-release, a hiker may not want to fiddle with the belt, decide to take a chance, and if he trips and falls off the log, there he goes, bouncing down the river tied to his stone.

No dogma goes unchallenged. There are burly, broad-shouldered hikers so strong-backed they don't need the hip belt, despise its confinement, and never use it, thus converting modern hip-carry packs to old-style shoulder-carriers. However, most hikers fully exploit the belt by keeping it tight; if a pack is properly adjusted to put weight on hips, a thumb can easily be slid between shoulder strap and shoulder.

Shoulder and Other Straps

Shoulders haven't been put on full retirement yet—they still carry a quarter to a half or more of the weight. In portions bearing on the body, the *shoulder straps* are 2–3 inches wide with built-in foam padding, tapered or, better, contoured to the body curves, the padding extending far enough down so the nylon webbing of the lower straps doesn't bite tender underarms.

Pioneered by the internal-frame pack, a *sternum strap* has been

SUNDAY

MONDAY

adopted on some external-frame models for better stability, and *lateral web strips*, for adjustments to the back contour.

The pack skeleton is suspended from the shoulders by one of two methods: shoulder-level crossbar or yoke. The original standard method was a *shoulder-level crossbar*, perhaps adjustable up or down, perhaps with two or more sets of attachment points so the straps can be moved closer together or farther apart to suit shoulder width. Strap length may be adjusted by a single pair of buckles or by two pairs.

The *yoke*, almost universal in the internal-frame packs and taken over by a number of externals, has the straps curve over the shoulders, cross in back, and fasten to the frame bottom. Another strap connects shoulder-pad tops to a shoulder-level crossbar. The strap anchor position is adjustable by use of a spacer. The overall effect is to pull the upper frame closer to the body and, so it is said, provide greater stability with less constriction of shoulders and upper torso, and put more weight on the shoulders.

Backband

Over the years the pack skeleton has been kept away from the body in many ways (upper and lower backband, full-length panel) using many materials (canvas, cords, padded or unpadded webbing). In the method currently dominant, the padded hip belt forms the lower bearing surface and above that is a single backband, usually of nylon mesh, in some models adjustable up or down. Knotted cords or turn-buckles maintain tension in the band, which must be kept taut to prevent crossbars from pressing the flesh.

The Bag

Once cotton or cotton-canvas, even leather, the bag fabric is now nylon, one variety or other (for definitions see Chapter 9). *Pack cloth* is lighter and limper than siblings and can be coated for water-repellency. *Cordura* is more abrasion-resistant but becomes so awkwardly stiff when coated that the treatment is eliminated or confined to the pack bottom. *Ballistics cloth* and *magnum cloth* are similar. A *ripstop nylon*, very light and strong, is used in ultralight packs.

Treated or not, any pack dropped in a lake or carried in a Pacific Northwest summer rain will let water in. Though a poncho or sheet of polyethylene can be pressed into service, in wet climates an impermeable *rain cover*, shaped and sized to exactly fit the full pack, and with strings for tying tightly, is indispensable. A cover weighs just ounces, stuffs neatly in a pack outer pocket, and can be rigged in a trice.

A bag may have a *reinforced bottom*, perhaps double-layer or heavy-coated for waterproofness when set down in a puddle. It may have *breathable cloth* or *mesh* next to the hiker's back to reduce sweating.

Accessory patches (or *lash points*), formerly always leather but now often heavy nylon, are commonly provided for tying ice axes, tent poles, skis, or bulky gear to the exterior.

The more *zippers* on a bag, the more important it is they be rugged and dependable, with large, easy-to-operate pulls and *rain flaps* to shed water.

Over the years bags have been connected to frames by any number of methods, none any longer giving much of a contest to the *clevis pin*, a stud that goes through a grommet in the bag, then through a hole in the frame, and is held in place by a split lock or key wire. By a mysterious process nobody ever has been able to explain, the

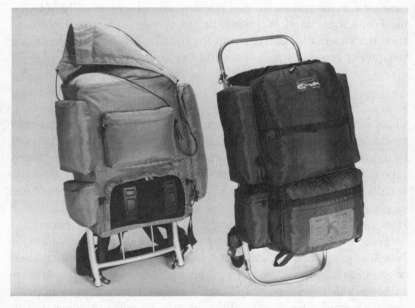

Representative bags for external packframes. Both are two-thirds length, with space below for attachment of sleeping bag. Other models have a sleeping-bag compartment. On the left is a top-opener with hold-open frame and storm flap; the right, a panel-opener with compression straps.

wires have a way of untwisting themselves, letting the pin fall out; the wise hiker always has spare pins and rings in his repair kit.

The most popular bag, sizewise, extends *two thirds of the frame length*; sleeping bag and pad are carried outside, strapped to the bottom—though some models have an integral bottom compartment, in addition to the main upper one, for the sleeping bag, giving it extra protection against rain and brush and providing additional room for clothing and whatnot. Hikers whose method of planning gear and food is to throw stuff in until there seems enough prefer the *expedition bag*, extending the *full length of the frame*, despite the fact that every article wanted is, when wanted, at the bottom.

The most popular bag, accesswise, is the *top-opener*, usually with a metal *hold-open frame* to provide an ever open top, though on cheaper models a loose top is closed by drawstrings. Over the top in either case goes a *storm flap* tied to the lower bag by straps and buckles or cords and toggles; tent or tarp may be carried under the flap.

A *panel-opener* eliminates the exasperation at having everything always being at the bottom. Lay the bag down, zip-zip-zip across the top and down both sides (two zippers), and all worldly possessions are in plain view. When the bag is overstuffed, the zippers jam, eventually fail, and the wails of the hiker's misery bring the coyotes to join in the sorrow. *Compression straps* that cinch across the back of the bag take strain from zippers.

Any bag, or frame, usually has provision—by lash points on the bag or add-on extension of the frame—for equipment that can't be crammed inside, perhaps a duffle bag holding food and miscellany.

Outside *pockets*, zippered with one or two slides, range from none to nine. Some are built-in; on other models the pockets are add-on/detachable.

Stuff Bag

For reasons elaborated in Chapter 11, where the "warm when wet" claim made for polyester is disputed and the "flat when wet" charge against down is admitted, the sleeping bag must always be carried in a stuff bag—or two. In regions where the climate is frequently drippy and often drenchy, it is best to stuff the sleeping bag in an absolutely waterproof *polyethylene* stuff bag, and this in a *waterproof nylon* stuff bag, with a drawstring closure and a weather flap to cover the opening. A *compressor* stuff bag has cinch straps to squeeze the bundle to a tiny size when carrying space is limited.

Because sleeping bag and pad are light in comparison with dense food and stoves and camera, carrying them at the bottom of the pack helps keep the weight high on the body. If the bag style has a carrying compartment, life is simpler. If not, the stuff bag is attached to the pack frame by two straps, *not one* (that way lies sloppiness and disaster, a tenacious branch snagging the bag, ripping it loose, and casting it down the cliff or into the creek). The straps, with buckles, 36–40 inches long (or longer if tarp, poncho, or whatever is also to be carried here), are wrapped *around* the two lower horizontal frame bars and *outside* the two vertical center bars. Elastic shock cords are not recommended; they may catch on brush or rocks and pull away from the pack, possibly letting the stuff bag escape and certainly throwing the hiker off balance.

Sizes and Weights and Prices

The hiker who opts for the external frame pack has it easy, *that* decision made. If he visits a backpacker shop known to be reputable and sees dozens of packs on display, closing eyes and picking at random will likely as not do the job well enough. If the shop stocks only a single model, the management surely made the choice knowing it would satisfy virtually every human back. Generally speaking, these are extremely forgiving packs. Still, there are aspects the most casual shopper will want to note.

What is the most back-easing *frame-style*? Who knows? Bodies are infinitely varied and so are opinions. A person with an "average" body (whatever that is) probably mates as well with one standard design as another. Those with deviant bodies (short torsos, narrow shoulders, thinly covered bones) may wish to experiment with the intricate models; they do well to seek the counsel of experienced hikers of similar build or a backpacking-shop clerk who seems to know what he or she is talking about. (Note the "she": having a different skeletal structure than men, women may require a different frame design and can be led astray buying a pack solely on the advice of men.)

More critical than style is *frame* (or *pack*) *size*, and here it must be stressed that a person's height is less relevant than the length of his or her torso. As discussed below, ideally the novice should spend an hour or two in a shop, marching up and down the aisles wearing various packs—loaded, or nothing is learned. If a shop with a rental service is handy, much more instructive is taking several packs out on the trail before purchase. Adjustable models should be tested with crossbars, backbands, and shoulder straps in a number of positions. Nonadjustable models usually come in two to four sizes; more than one should be tried.

A family on the trail for an overnight or longer hike. Father, son, and daughter carry various representative external packframe-bags in sizes large to small. Mother hauls the baby, her gear on the other backs.

Every *bag size* on the market is adequate for a weekend, or for a week if outfit and commissary are planned precisely. However, a lot of bags are too skimpy for 10-day trips in rough and stormy wildernesses, which demand considerable bad-weather and emergency gear. The little tiny bags that look so chic in the shop may be dandy for travels in benign meadowlands but are infernal nuisances in a trackless alder bottom, where the gear lashed and draped all over the outside tangles constantly with bushes.

A pack is useless in itself, providing neither shelter, calories, nor entertainment, so *weight* is a consideration. However, packs all weigh about the same, between 3 and 5 pounds, 4 the average. Those on the low side (the range drops to 2 pounds) require extra careful handling; those on the high side (the range rises to 6 pounds) may be sturdy or accessory-cluttered beyond any normal requirement.

Doubtless a majority of novices select the first pack largely on the basis of *price*. At any shop of sound reputation the rule is you pretty much get what you pay for. Due to economies of scale, a best-selling pack costs less than a slow mover of equal value; generally, though, price reflects (1) quality of materials and care of manufacture, factors that determine durability, and (2) the number of special conveniences, each of which adds expense. The novice must ask, "How much durability and convenience do I really need? And how much can I afford?" The hiker whose rambles are limited to trails in Appalachian forests or High Sierra meadows needs less pack than the masochist plunging into British Columbia jungles or slogging Yukon glaciers.

For the Deserving Poor

With all due respect to your friendly neighborhood handy-dandy super-thrift discount drugs and surplus, packs sold there must be viewed with suspicion. Simply to look at the $5 "Scout-type" pack sends shooting pains up and down the spine. One approaches a $10 "cruiser-style" pack in fear and trembling. "Backpack paralysis" is not a joke but a recognized medical problem, also called "rucksack palsy," particularly common among growing boys and girls saddled with cheap and cruel packs. However, crippling is unlikely on short trips. Never forget, through all the Dark Ages, packs no better were carried by generations of hikers and few are actually in traction. On the bottom rung of the price ladder, though, a youth (or parent) would do better to buy Mohney's book and make a pack in the basement workshop.

The sampan factories of Asia, where the worker is paid a bowl of rice and the tail of a fish a day, produce Kelty lookalikes at half the price or less and very lightweight (because of the very few materials). Mass merchandisers advertise these the first day of spring. For the money they aren't bad packs if kept lightly loaded (under 30 pounds), treated tenderly, used infrequently, and always accompanied by a repair kit of wire and cord.

For the Thrifty Working Class

Once upon a time the strata of pack society were distinct and widely separated. Way down there was the Trapper Nelson. Way up there was the Kelty. Lonesome in the middle, lacking many niceties of the latter but a quantum leap above the former was the REI Cruiser, considered good enough in 1963 for Jim Whittaker to carry to the summit of Everest, still the highest mountain climbed by Americans.

However, with passing years has come a leveling—upward. Costs of material, energy, and labor have so swollen the irreducible expense of constructing any pack whatsoever as to pretty well squeeze out "economy" models. Let not another factor be overlooked: The farther the Trapper recedes toward the Pyramids, the higher rise the expectations of hikers, the fewer are content to be peasants.

Sum it up as inflation—of everything—people, hopes, prices. Even the REI Cruiser, which began life in the 1950s under $20 and for years was the runaway best seller, during the 1980s (in a fancier incarnation, to be sure) topped $80. To cite America's other largest supplier, Eastern Mountain Sports (EMS) packs begin at $85. That's the bottom line.

Before climbing the imaginary step to the next class, mention must be made of a unique pack for special purposes, the Camp Trails Freighter, an unadorned frame (no bag), heavy-duty, rein-

forced with V-truss, with many lash points, designed for heavy, odd-shaped loads, such as outboard motor, half a moose, crate of watermelons.

For the Suffering Middle Class

The bulk of external-frame sales lies in the $100–$150 range, and if that dazes a Rip Van Winkle who laid aside his $10 Trapper in the 1950s to take a nap, let it be said that Rip finds, after recovering from future shock, that the new packs are not only better for the body than the old homelies but, in terms of constant dollars, scarcely more costly.

Dozens of manufacturers are active, and their entries run in the scores—though many fewer than before the internal-frame pack barged in. Kelty, of course, is synonymous with quality; "kelty" has entered the vocabulary of many languages as the generic term for any American tourist with a backpack. While honor is due a pioneer, justice owes mention of a host of other manufacturers offering superb packs. Wrangling over which is best is folly; all are splendid, each in its own special way, for its own special people.

A fair rule is that if a pack has been around a few years, it has met the test of the trails with at least passing marks.

The average hiker, if he continues long enough, eventually buys the very best pack he can afford, correctly judging that over the long run—with careful choice, a lifetime—the price of contentment will be cheap. Having made a choice, he may become a fanatic loyalist, exalting his mate above every competitor. Or he may go through life flirting with every pretty face, even dumping externals for internals, or golly-knows-what's looming on the technological horizon.

For Small Adults—and Children

Hikers shorter than 5 feet, or somewhat taller but with unusual torsos, may be unable to fit a standard model. The internal-frame pack is probably their best choice, as it may be for growing children, due to the great number of variable adjustments.

Worth comparing to the internal-frame pack, though, is the Kelty Stretch-Pack, with adjustable, telescoping frame. The 4-C fits those between 4 and 5 feet tall, costs $75; the 5-D, for 5–6 feet, is $92.

Camp Trails has the Skipper ($40) and Compact II ($62), with pin-spacer kits for varying shoulder-strap placements.

The EMS Monadnock Jr., built exactly "like the grown-ups' packs," fits people under 4 feet 8 inches, costs $50.

For a child under a certain age (rather, below a certain height), no external-frame pack is small enough and, probably, under a certain height, no internal-frame either. Nevertheless, any child being raised as a backpacker, either because the parents think it's good for him or because they can't afford baby-sitters, should be introduced to load-carrying almost as soon as he ceases being a load to be carried. Besides, at this age the kid often demands a pack, especially if an elder sibling has one; too late the young fool learns it's not a toy. The first expedient may be a rucksack from the parents' free and simple past; straps can be shortened to keep the bag from dragging. If such is not available, there are tiny rucksacks, weighing less than ½ pound, costing less than $10, that hold a sweater and a teddy bear and a box of animal crackers.

For Carrying Children

Best for the early months is a "soft" carrier, such as the Snugli, a frameless "sack with straps" ingeniously adaptable for slinging in front (so the babe can nurse or wave its hands in Mommy's face, or so Mommy can carry a rucksack on her back) or in back (so the babe can tangle Mommy's hair, or so Mommy can take pictures of the flowers). The corduroy fabric is machine-washable; tucks and darts permit expansion to accommodate growth. Weight is 1½ pounds, price about $50.

When the child becomes a real lump, 20 pounds or so, it's time to switch to a carrier with a lightweight aluminum frame. An example is the Gerry Kiddie Pack. The tot rides on the adult's back, facing forward so as not to feel lonesome. Space under the seat holds baby-type gear or even a sleeping bag. The frame sits on the ground as a stable stand. Weight is 1¼ pounds, price about $30.

At the awkward age when the child is a crushing burden (30 wiggling, squirming pounds weigh more than 60 that ride quietly), yet toddles too slowly for the family to cover many miles, recourse may be made to a regular pack, left empty and the Gerry lashed on.

Fitting and Using the External-Frame Pack

A person buying a pack unaided by an experienced clerk or friend should proceed as follows: load about 20 pounds in the bag to prevent it from "floating." Don the pack. If the suspension is from the crossbar, adjust shoulder straps so the crossbar is level with the top of the shoulders. Fasten the hip belt around the upper, curved part of the hip bone. While doing this, hunch shoulders; upon unhunching, pack weight should have settled on the hips. The pack is a good fit if, with hip belt in proper position, shoulder straps run almost horizontal from crossbar over the shoulders. If they angle sharply downward, the frame is too short; if sharply upward, too long. (Ignore a minor angle.) If trying all sizes and adjustments of one model fails, try another. Hikers with "average" backs may quickly find a perfect fit. Others may have to give up on the external-frame packs and move on to the internal-frame ones.

With a yoke suspension the fit is proper when, with hip belt in place, there is no space under the straps where they cross the shoulders. Fitting a hipwrap frame is more complex than an S, requiring consideration not only of the vertical distances but the width between hip bars.

Once on the trail, experiment with adjustable components (shoulder straps, backbands, hip belt) to find the most comfortable fit.

Any pack frame, no matter how sturdy, can be broken; never drop a loaded pack, especially on rocks—always lower it gently. Keep the pack away from fire or excessive heat. In camp, remove all food to disinterest animals, both mouse-type nibblers and bear-type slashers.

Carry a repair kit of spare clevis pins and locking wires (or whatever is suited to the particular packframe-bag) and nylon cord for emergency lashings in the rare case of the frame failing at a joint or the bag ripping.

In loading the bag, locate heavy items close to the back and up high. Keep metal objects away from the back; they may rub against the frame and wear holes in the bag. In wet climates place all gear in waterproof nylon or poly bags so that if water finds an entry it doesn't soak the entire contents; be especially sure to put wet clothing in poly bags before stowing inside.

INTERNAL-FRAME PACK

By the early 1970s the Kelty revolution had achieved packs widely deemed to be as near perfection as lay within the grasp of human ingenuity. However, the iron law of historical dialectics is that one revolution leads to another, and so it was that in the 1970s the

Two representative internal-frame packs, backside and bodyside. Both are "Ferrari class" models. Those at the "entry level" are much less complicated, though still a million miles from the Trapper.

barricades were again in the streets, illuminated by the rocket's red glare—which is to say, the prose in catalogs and magazines.

The genesis was the growth of the rucksack into a size large enough to hold the groceries and ironmongery of multiday mountaineering and skiing trips while retaining the close-to-body fit essential for climbing icicles and swinging turns in powder snow. The term "expedition rucksack" was applied, but the clientele for that sort of thing was, to manufacturers, depressingly small. *Soft pack* gained favor, in part because a famous early example was the Jensen "monocoque," totally frameless, gaining rigidity through being loaded in precisely the right manner. Unfortunately, the right manner was tricky, and an improperly loaded monocoque flopped around like a sack of potatoes, demanding frequent halts to rearrange gear and fiddle with straps. Moreover, above 35 pounds the pack became resistant to any amount of fussing.

Nevertheless, climbers and ski mountaineers, as well as hikers wont to leave trails to bull through brush, hop-skip around moraines and talus, and kick steps up and glissade down steep snow, were happy to fiddle and fuss. The contoured, body-hugging fit put the center of gravity low and snugly against the back, giving a stability and balance impossible with external-frame packs that totter high above the shoulders. Never as a skier leaned into a turn did the surly stone lurch off to maintain inertia. Never as a hiker got on hands and knees to crawl under a blowdown did pack-frame tentacles intertwine with branches. Further, the new packs were versatile, performing well in a broad spectrum of terrains, in every season of the year.

To accentuate the positive and eliminate the negative was the aim of the innovators who added an *internal frame* while retaining the general soft-pack configuration, though it no longer was completely soft. Gregory and Lowe were notable pioneers, the latter introducing a parallel frame in 1967. Ruth is credited with the X frame, the other of the two basic designs. The resulting packs could cope with any weight a hiker could and were so comfortable it was said, "You don't carry the pack, you *wear* it." Persons who had never been able to find an external-frame pack that didn't torture their bones pronounced themselves in ecstasy. The same equipment critics who praised running-shoe boots as the equivalent of slalom skis declared, "Carrying a Gregory is like driving a Ferrari."

By the mid-1980s, the internal-frame pack was so far from being revolutionary it was nearing the imperial throne. Backpacking shops now find beginners as often choosing an internal-frame pack as an external-frame one, and experienced hikers favoring the new species by three to one. The catalog of one major outfitter has four pages devoted to internal-frame packs, and a single page to the external—which has been expelled altogether from some shops.

The external frame is in no danger of extinction, however. Though many of the internal-frames have solved the ventilation problem and thus do not cause acute cases of sweaty back, the externals can never be matched in this regard. They are also more convenient, since the internals still require considerable care in stowing gear. Comparative durability? One Gregory model has 260 pieces! Though the construction is meticulous ("Everything is splendid!" summarized a breathless reviewer), that's a lot of points of possible failure. As a result of the complexity, an internal-frame pack costs $10 to $40 more than external-frames of comparable capability. If poverty ever should return to the trail country, the internals would be the first to suffer. Even in the ongoing age of universal riches, many a commentator suspects the sudden surge of internal-frames is due considerably to the hype of "tech-weenie" salespeople, who steer customers to the new and cool, regardless of suitability.

Structural Features

The materials and many details of the internal-frame pack are shared with the external and have already been discussed. Only those features that are different and distinctive will be treated here.

The *frame* is, of course, by definition, inside the pack rather than out. At the time of purchase the stays are bent to custom-fit the person's spine. The lightest of the two pioneering designs consists of *two vertical* aluminum stays. The X is not quite so close to the back, a disadvantage for cross-country travelers and climbers but well-liked by trail trippers for the coolness on the back. Newer on the scene is a *single vertical* stay that contours along the spine, permitting some of the lightest-weight, largest-volume packs. Other innovative approaches are being tried on various models.

The *hip belt* is shaped as the body is—narrower at the top for a snug fit around the waist. Belts, and shoulder straps as well, come in several sizes for a custom fit. The employment of newer materials stiffens the belt to prevent it from rolling and better distributes weight, eliminating pressure points.

A *lumbar pad*, a sheet of foam with a plastic stiffener, protects the body from the stays and improves posture, making for a more upright stance.

The *shoulder harness* consists of contoured shoulder straps attached to a leather *yoke*. Different sizes and widths of straps are supplied for different torso sizes and shoulder dimensions. The yoke is easily adjusted to conform to the length of an individual's torso and to prevent lateral movement. Set in different positions, the yoke provides three separate means of suspending the load—shoulder-carry, hip-carry, very nearly 100 percent in either case, or a combination— a versatility impossible with most external-frame packs.

The *hip-stabilizer strap*, the *sternum strap*, the *torso-adjustment strap*, and the *shoulder-stabilizer strap* provide eight adjustment points, two per strap, to suit any body.

The *bag* may be a single-compartment "garbage can," or it may have two or more compartments, perhaps including a sleeping-bag bottom compartment with an internal-compression system to reduce the bag's stowed bulk. The design may be top-opening or panel-opening. The *back panel*, within which lies the frame, is anatomically contoured and foam-padded to cushion the load and give body and shape to the stays. *Pockets* may be built-in or detachable.

All-around compression straps compact the load, very nice for the climber shuffling along a 2-inch ledge or the hiker burrowing through a slide-alder jungle. *Side-compression straps* narrow the pack profile, for the 1-inch ledges.

Fitting and Using the Internal-Frame Pack

Most models are available in long, regular, and short torso lengths. One of these, combined with the proper sizing of belt and shoulder straps, will neatly fit virtually every adult and a great many children; thanks to the adjustments, the pack can "grow" with a person over a much longer period than the adjustable external-frame packs.

The fitting of an internal generally follows the procedures earlier described for an external—but is far more complicated. First, the correct size of pack must be determined, then the proper shoulder straps and waist belt. The frame must be bent to the shape of the buyer's back, and the shoulder harness, and yoke, and the array of stabilizer straps fiddled with. In early trials on the trail perhaps readjustments will be wanted. The hiker must take pains to learn his pack's system in order to be able to fine-tune for changing circumstances.

The trouble is well worth it, and not really as great as might appear. Ordinarily, packs are supplied with complete in-depth directions, to be carefully studied during the fitting process (don't expect to accomplish the job in a few minutes—an hour may be only the beginning) and consulted on the trail. An extra pair of hands is close to essential, and a salesperson may not be able to stay with it on a busy day; bring a friend.

Having said so much, a bit of backwatering is called for. "Entry-level" internal frames, such as the REI Lodestar, are quite straightforward, easily mastered, unlike the "high-end tech freaks," such as the Gregory packs—whose purchasers, let it be noted, revel in each intricacy.

Everything said about using the external applies to the internal. There is likely to be more adjusting in the course of a day or a trip. The loading of the bag is more crucial; care is needed to locate heavy items up high and close to the back—but not so that sharp edges reach through to jab the body. Several stuff sacks, poly or nylon, in various sizes help arrange proper load distribution, as well as a handy organization of the goods.

Sizes and Weights and Prices

If the big names are Gregory and Lowe, there are fanatic disciples of the infinitely adjustable Synergy, the imaginative Marmot, the custom-made Schonhofen Ultimate, and other sleek beauties. Such well-known makers of external frames as Kelty and JanSport have entered the internal-frame game. Among the larger backpacking shops, EMS offers nineteen models, and the REI catalog has pages of them.

An outfitter may categorize offerings to suggest the range of use. One supplier (now defunct, sadly) classified its packs as Basic, Trail, Super Trail, Trekker, and at the top of the line burst into French with Trois Jour. EMS uses the terms Expedition, Backpacking, Tour-Trek, and Midsize (for women, smaller men, larger children).

With or without such appellations, the intent of a pack can be discerned by noting its *volume capacity*, which reflects its designed *weight capacity*, since the manufacturers expect the hiker will be carrying materials of a certain average density, not marshmallows or gold ingots.

A cautionary note: Volume capacity is measured in different manners by different manufacturers; figures given for one line of packs may not be comparable to those for another.

A second cautionary note: Volume figures for the internals cannot be compared to those supplied for externals; the latter species has the sleeping bag and pad outside the measured bag volume; the former has everything inside, including the frame.

Nevertheless, the customer will quickly see that most models have a capacity of 4,000–5,400 cubic inches, spacious enough for most backpackers. Those rated down to 2,700 cubic inches are plainly meant for short trips in mild climates (and under that, for children), and those up to 6,500, for backpackers who go on weeklong adventures in rotten climates and need greater space for food and parkas and ponchos and long underwear. The volumes given do not include the possible addition of detachable pockets, available for some models, or the use of the lash points to tie on a pair of skis or circus tent or watermelon.

The weight of the pack and the amount of weight it can carry are in rather exact proportion to the bag volume. The "35-pound limit" was exceeded long ago. All the new models (in their larger sizes) handle heavy loads as well as the typical external-frame pack, though the latter remains the choice when packing home half a moose or carrying a cookstove with a sack of flour in the oven. The price of a pack reflects not only the capacity but also the refinements—how many of those 260 pieces it shares with the Gregory.

A survey of representative catalogs shows packs weighing from 2⅔ pounds or so for small people to 5¾ for those long walks in bad weather.

In the *economy zone* ($80–$115), a half-dozen packs were found, their prices comparing favorably to those of external-frames. A dozen models lay in the *middle class* ($140–$180). In the *Ferrari class* (up to $225) were a half-dozen more. There are, of course, a great many other catalogs, innumerable other packs, including super-Ferraris, and so intense is the excitement in the marketplace there are certain to be countless more each year.

Travel Packs

Among the virtues bragged up for the early soft packs and the subsequent internal-frames was a greater resistance to the assaults of professional baggage manglers in airports and train stations. An additional touch of ingenuity produced a subspecies of pack ideal for the hiker-traveler who hops a jet to Wales to go walking in quest of King Arthur and Merlin and his roots in general, doesn't wish to fuss with suitcases along the way, yet also wants not to be conspicuous on London streets, wearing a pack and being mistaken for a Saxon or Angle or Jute.

A model suitable for day hiking from one bed-and-breakfast to the next is, in one configuration, a soft suitcase made of Cordura tough enough for baggage compartments, which turned inside out becomes a soft pack with a capacity of 1,400 cubic inches. Weighing under 2 pounds, it costs $60.

More versatile are Wilderness Experience's Wilderness Traveler

Example of a travel pack. Left: *In luggage configuration.* Right: *In carrying configuration.*

and REI's Travel Pack, which are similar in design. A foldaway-in-a-pocket panel, when pulled from the pocket, zips all around the pack exterior to cover up the shoulder straps, making a suitcase with a carrying handle at the pack top. The front-opening zip-around panel serves well both in traveling and hiking, as do the three outside pockets. With the cover-up panel stuffed in its pocket and the shoulder straps exposed, the suitcase becomes an internal-frame pack with a capacity of 4,500 cubic inches, weighing 4 pounds, costing $125. Many a hiker, upon returning from Cymry, is so attached to the pack as to wear it in home wildlands for weekend and longer hikes.

Features found on this model or that are compression straps,

Representative rucksacks. Left: *Two-compartment teardrop, a day pack for light loads.* Center: *Day pack for medium loads.* Right: *Pack for heavy day loads, also usable for overnight hikes.*

lockable zippers to thwart thieving baggage manglers, detachable shoulder straps, and detachable pockets.

The top of the line is the Kelty Katmandu, with *TLS suspension* and a capacity of 4,850 cubic inches. At $200, it is just the thing for Nepal.

RUCKSACKS

Hikers who ease into the sport by day-walking before venturing overnight nevertheless need some sort of pack and do well to start with a comparatively inexpensive rucksack while studying multiday options. In the larger versions the rucksack may serve decently for one-night hikes, and in any size has continuing utility for explorations from a basecamp. To avoid an extra item of gear, it may do double duty as a stuff bag for the sleeping bag or for segregating food inside the pack.

The materials (this and that variety of nylon—though at least one supplier is experimenting with a polypropylene pack cloth resembling cotton duck) and features (hip belt, zippers, pockets, shoulder straps) are much the same as in frame packs. In fact, some rucksacks have simple internal frames. The spiffier models, precursors of the internal-frame pack, are for climbers and ski-mountaineers and have attachment points for ropes, ice axes, crampons, skis, and bags of nuts and bolts. The hiker needn't be humbled—the points serve for strapping on sleeping bag, tent, fishing pole, six-pack, and watermelon—yet probaby he shouldn't spend the money for a sack so much tougher than needed for trails.

Rucksacks weigh from ¾ to 3 pounds, cost anywhere from $20 or less to $75 or more, and have capacities ranging from several hundred to a couple of thousand cubic inches. An eyeball inspection quickly separates those suitable for trips of various lengths.

Born and raised in the Alps, the early rucksacks were simply the bags the peasants had been lugging around for centuries, shaped like eggs when stuffed full and therefore going by that name. As time went by, outside pockets were added, and a *belly band* to keep the egg from beating a tattoo on the spine. Eventually the shape was changed to a *teardrop*, tapered to be larger at the bottom to put weight more directly on hips. The load hangs directly from the shoulders, painlessly enough if the weight is under 15 pounds. As with all rucksacks, the gear must be stowed thoughtfully to prevent sharp edges from stabbing the back; clothing or a sheet of foam can provide padding. Such a pack weighs ½–1¼ pounds and sells for $20–$30.

The hiker who can't spend a day on the trail without three flower books and two cameras, spare clothing for a child, a nine-course lunch, or a watermelon may decide to forget rucksacks and carry the overnighter Kelty or Gregory or whatever. In any event, he must avoid the little rucksack that when stuffed bloats out not to an egg or even a basketball but to a cannonball that will besiege the spine and by day's end break through and lay waste the kidneys, intestines, liver, and lights. A better choice is one of the larger models, weighing 1½–2½ pounds and costing $40–$85; these are tolerable for up to 30 pounds, thus serving one-night as well as day trips—or, in a benign enough climate, several nights.

The past lives. In 1979 Trudy and Jack Turner carry groceries to their home deep in Canadian wildwoods using home-made wooden packs of two different styles, both ancient. And the price is right.

A representative example may be cited, costing about $50, designed for the hiker not the climber (though very usable by the latter). The bag is of sturdy Cordura, the upper areas merely water-repellent, the bottom, double-weight and coated for waterproofness. The front-opening panel gives easy access, has two heavy-duty zippers, and two compression straps to reduce strain on the zippers and hold the panel together should both zippers fail. The interior could easily take a sleeping bag and sweater and watermelon and three cans of beans and a package of weenies. The three very large outside pockets, two of them two-zippered, have enough room for the Ten Essentials and a camera and parka and spare socks and three cucumbers and a package of cookies. Leather attachment points on the top provide for carrying a tent or tarp. Shoulder straps are padded, the belly band not. In summary, the pack could be pressed into overnight duty; for day hikes it could serve for years and never dent a vertebra.

Once scorned by hikers as a freak affected by modish skiers, the *fanny pack (waistpack, belt bag)* has been reevaluated. All the weight rides on the hips and, with properly sized and padded belt, very comfortably. Moreover, when the capacity (500–1,000 cubic inches and above) is insufficient, a larger rucksack worn in combination rests on the fanny pack, putting most of its weight, too, on the hips. The selling point (at prices of $10 and up) especially appealing to birders and photographers is that the pack needn't be removed to get at the contents—loosen the hip belt, slide to the front, unzip, and bring out camera or binoculars while still pursuing the deer or dipper; if it's a long chase, bring out a candy bar and a banana.

11

Sleeping Bags

Many a backpacker with still a few miles in his legs remembers how poignant the sunsets of yesteryear were—not as symbols of the death of day, but as reminders that soon the hour would come to leave the campfire and begin the night-long ordeal. To be sure, there were rumors of better equipment owned by the immensely wealthy, but the ordinary hiker carried a rectangular wool or kapok sleeping bag that weighed a large part of a ton and never kept out the chill of a summer night in alpine meadows. At that he felt luckier than pals who couldn't afford a bag and wrapped up in blankets. Boy Scout troops of the 1930s often ended by morning as a circle of bodies tightly coiled around a fire.

The World War II surplus bonanza introduced a whole generation of low-income Americans to the down sleeping bag, formerly the raiment of princes and magnates and climbers, and to the revelation that night need not be miserable.

Reactionary veterans scorn what has happened since. They feel today's youth is robbed of the full wilderness experience, that man ought to shiver at night for the good of his soul. But as has been said, "The past is a foreign country: they do things differently there." The backpacker now accepts as inalienable his right to sleep warm, and with modern bags there's no reason he shouldn't, most of the time, if he chooses right.

In the 1970s the experimenters were so restless, their plethora of theory so densely argued at such great length in very small print, that choosing the garment in which a third of a hiker's wildland life is spent was as agonizing as buying boots and packs. The 1980s are no less innovative, but where formerly suppliers burned with missionary zeal, now they seem content to offer the facts. Bags are simply categorized by intended *use* (Spare bedroom? Car camping? Backpacking in summer? Spring to fall? Winter?) and *price* (Is it no object? Is it the bottom line?). All other matters—weight, warmth, special fancy features—follow appropriately.

The main body of this chapter is devoted to the principles of selecting a bag. However, it is first necessary to review the fundamentals of a bag—the insulation and the structure.

INSULATION MADE SIMPLE

A sleeping bag is an article of clothing that retains body-generated heat by trapping innumerable tiny pockets of dead air. Not the components of the bag themselves but rather the air (a poor conductor and thus a good insulator) provides a barrier between the hot body and the cold, cold world. The warmth of a bag is determined by its structure, means of closure, the covers and liners that

may be added, but mainly by the kind and amount of insulating material.

Over the years many materials have been employed. Before World War II, wool and kapok (the silky covering of the seeds of the tropical silk-cotton, or kapok, tree) were standard for Scouts, down for wealthy mountain climbers. (Eiderdown, gathered from Arctic nests of the wild eider duck, was reputed to be the finest, for all that it concerned the common man; the total world supply was, and is, perhaps 100 pounds a year, barely sufficient for Arctic explorers.)

Preparing for campaigns in Alaska, Scandinavia, and the Alps, the U.S. Army contracted for tens or hundreds of thousands of bags, stripping the down and feathers from every goose, duck, and loose turkey in nations of the antifascist alliance. As war surplus, these bags—some down, some feathers, some down-feathers—met the needs of climbers, backpackers, and car campers for years.

When the surplus was exhausted, Americans were as loath to return to wool and kapok as to the Great Depression, yet down was no less costly than before, nor was the supply any greater, goose ranching being ill-adapted to techniques of mass production. Other insulations were sought. The U.S. Army tried taking a curling iron to chicken feathers. Polyurethane foam was a brief curiosity. Prior to the opening day of hunting season, sporting-goods stores offered bags stuffed with chopped-up newspapers, one-night bags that next morning could be used to cook breakfast. The Handy-Dandy Super-

Surplus Bargain Basement and Thrifty Drugs advertised bags filled with acetate or acrylic or even "down" (suspected of being stripped from the nation's street pigeons). A new entry is microfibers. Another is old-fashioned silk, made into batts by a patented process and said to compete with down in warmth and cost, though it's heavier and bulkier. Supplementary features—the heat shield and vapor barrier—add warmth.

Nevertheless, the story of insulation really has only two chapters: the same old down of yesteryear; and polyester, the latter by now advanced into middle age.

Polyester

Since issuing from the test tube in the 1940s, polyester has lived through a number of generations, the generic primal ooze spawning a succession of registered trademarks.

The uncapitalized *generic polyester* is a solid-core fiber—or rather, a number of such fibers of widely varying quality and no consistency at all. Backpacking shops use "generic" for their least expensive bags; to assure the buyer they've done their best to obtain reasonably good stuff, they usually give it a capitalized (but not federally registered) house label, such as Polysoft or Polyloft.

Lowest priced of the registered trademarks is Du Pont's *Hollofil 808*, a hollow fiber that traps more air than one with a solid core. The typical use is for inexpensive bags not meant to be carried far, if at all.

Hollofil II is the same except for the addition of a silicone agent to make the fibers softer, slicker, and more drapable and to give better fluffing for warmth and compactibility for stuffing. It is mostly employed in backpacking bags for mild climates.

The top of the Du Pont line is *Quallofil*, made of Dacron 113, itself a registered trademark. The core of the fiber is pierced by not one but four tubular holes, trapping much more air and yielding a downlike feel.

Originally produced by Celanese until that firm dropped it, *PolarGuard* is now made by 3M. Unlike the short-crimped Du Pont fibers, some 2 inches long, it is a continuous filament. Assembled in matts, the filaments are intertwined to prevent the shifting and clumping that would form cold spots. The batts are silicone-treated for softness, loftiness, and compressibility.

Quallofil vs. PolarGuard

Du Pont claims that for equal warmth, PolarGuard bags are 15 percent heavier than those with Quallofil and 40 percent less compactible; since the two cost about the same, they say their product ought to be the clear winner for cold-weather bags.

Bag manufacturers employ all the Du Pont fibers in quantity and appreciate the virtues of Quallofil. However, for reasons discussed below, they find PolarGuard easier to use. Because it requires less extra weight of stabilization, it has the advantage at the upper end of the warmth scale, the bags for the coldest weather.

The evolution of the products continues; some polyester-filled backpacking and expedition bags utilize Quallofil, some PolarGuard. What the 1990s will bring is anybody's guess.

Down

Down, the fluff growing next to the skin of waterfowl, traps air more efficiently than any other readily available lightweight substance, yet allows body moisture to breathe out; compacts in a small bundle for carrying, yet is extremely resilient, quickly expanding when released; and withstands thousands of compression-and-expansion cycles before getting too bent and broken to rise to the occasion.

The reigning champion is the *goose*, eaten (along with duck) by most of the world the way America eats chicken and turkey, though not Kentucky-fried. The best down is from a large, mature domestic fowl raised in a cold climate, the plucking done in early winter when the down is thickest and sturdiest. With the demand going up at a rate of 50 percent a year during the 1970s, merchants went beyond such traditional sources as Germany, Poland, and Mennonite communities in Canada. The People's Republic of China became the

supplier of 60–85 percent of the world's down, a scandal concealed for years by "washing" the down through middleman nations.

The demand still unsatisfied, merchants combed the planet for geese of any kind, anywhere. Taiwanese fowl that never had known a shiver were disrobed. Though the selling of down gives peasants a tidy side income, they raise the birds mainly for eating and prefer them young and tender, despite the fact that the down has not then reached its prime. By the end of the 1970s, sleeping bags and clothing were being filled with tropical-climate and young-bird down that in the 1950s never would have gotten off the farm. Many suppliers started refusing to sell their best down by itself and began mixing it with wilted quills, otherwise unsalable; the loft (see below) of the typical top-grade down of the 1980s is about a quarter less than that of the 1960s.

The insulating value of down is determined to about 60 percent by *fill power*, or *loft*, the ability to fluff up and trap air, and to about 40 percent by *recovery power*, the ability to spring out to full expansion after being crushed. Both are measurable, but are done differently by different manufacturers. Until uniform industry (or federal) standards are adopted, figures given will be useful in comparing the bags of any one supplier but possibly misleading in comparing bags of different suppliers. The best goose down in most shops is described as having a loft of 500–550 cubic inches (as measured in a

cylinder to determine how much space 1 ounce of down can expand to fill). Some shops sneer at "550 down" and advertise 625 or better.

Everything said above about geese also applies to *ducks*. Only under a microscope, with difficulty, can duck down be distinguished from goose down. In Canada a distinction is usually not made and both are mixed in "waterfowl down"; eventually this may become the rule everywhere.

If a goose and a duck were raised side by side to the same age, the goose down would be superior to that of the duck, mainly because the goose, and thus its plumes, would be larger. However, a good duck is better than a bad goose. The quality difference in their downs as marketed is often minimal, or even in favor of the duck. Top-grade duck down lofts from 480 to 520 inches, but is available to 550. Everything else being equal, a duck bag may be ever so slightly less warm than a goose bag. Or may not.

Polyester vs. Down

"Down has been relegated to the comforter business!" cried the Polyites.

"Plastic is strictly for children not yet housebroken!" rejoined the Downers.

At the end of a decade and more of this exchange, some backpacking shops were mustered under one banner, others under the opposition, stocking this or that filler exclusively. The larger shops, however, took the mugwump position and employed a variety of materials for a variety of climates and budgets. They pointed to the advantages and disadvantages.

The Case for Polyester

1. Unlike down, which once soaking wet doesn't dry for days, the fiber absorbs less than 1 percent of water by weight. Crawl into a wet bag at night and by morning it will be dry from body heat alone.
2. Unlike down, which clumps up, flattens out, and loses much loft in humid conditions and 80 percent when saturated, even if drenched the fiber loses only about 5 percent of its loft. Wring out a sopping bag, shake it vigorously, snuggle in, and be warm.
3. No matter how carefully protected from storms, down accumulates moisture from the body and the air, and over a period of a week or less collapses.
4. Unlike down, which flattens to zero loft under the sleeper, the fiber resists compression and gives a certain amount of bottom insulation.
5. Unlike down, the fiber is nonallergenic and can be washed regularly and easily to get rid of dust, and is therefore the forced choice of people who sneeze at feathers and dust. Unlike down, it also resists mildew.
6. The best polyester costs $3–$5 a pound, compared with $30 and up for a pound of decent down.
7. Though admittedly still bulky, the polyester of the new breeds is more compressible than that of the old.
8. In conclusion: Compare two completely soaked bags, one of polyester and one of down. The polyester loses 10 percent in warmth, gains 60 percent in weight, and drip-dries in less than a day. The down loses 90 percent in warmth, gains 128 percent in weight, and takes perhaps days to dry. (In such debates, don't expect consistency of statistics.)

The Case for Down

In answer to (7), no poly yet boiled out of a chemist's cauldron stuffs anywhere near so neatly as down; all polys occupy inordinate amounts of space in the pack.

In answer to (6), the cost of the filler is a small part of the total cost of a bag. A zipper costs the same wherever, and so does a yard of nylon.

In further answer to (6), first cost and final cost are not the same. Down has proven that with proper care it can last years and years. Poly has been found to lose up to half its loft in 2–3 years. Over a period of time the down cost per year is far lower.

In answer to (4), so what? Everybody nowadays uses a sleeping pad, and the trend in bags is toward reducing or even eliminating bottom insulation—a good pad does the job so much better.

In answer to (1), (2), and (8), "warm when wet" is hogwash. A wet bag is a shivery bag, period. What sort of ninny lets his bag *get* wet? Everybody carries the bag in a waterproof stuff bag, or jolly well should. Just about everybody sleeps in a waterproof tent. Okay, so tarp sleepers should use poly. Or get a tent.

As for (3), draping the bag in the sun every two or three days prevents down from collapsing; a person who backpacks where the sun never shines probably should opt for poly, or ask himself what he's doing there at all. Granted, in humid-steamy forests (eastern America from spring to fall) and Arctic cold, down fails to exhale moisture taken up from the body and there may never be an opportunity to dry the bag. Poly may have a place here, in what amounts to 1–2 percent of backpacking use.

In peroration for down: The most truculent Polyites concede their material has only 70–75 percent the insulation value of down. For equal warmth, a poly bag must be about 2 pounds heavier.

The Case for the People

Both fillers are excellent. In various situations one may be more excellent than the other. A novice uncertain how long he will engage in backpacking is best advised to start with a moderately priced polyester bag. In several years it probably will need to be replaced, and he may then decide to invest, for the long run, in down.

However, the hiker who finds difficulty keeping his bag dry, owing to traveling in hostile climates or sleeping under a tarp or being just plain sloppy, may wish to stay with polyester.

Microfibers

The theory of microfibers (see Chapter 9) is that by impeding air flow with surface friction they "deaden" it as effectively as lofting fibers do by entrapment. The fibers of Thinsulate (3M) and Sontique (Du Pont) are so micro they have twenty times more surface area per unit weight than ordinary synthetics and twenty times greater surface friction. Thus, though very thin, with negligible loft, they are nearly twice as warm per inch of thickness as competitors, including down.

The microfibers are finding a place in clothing, where the amount of material used is quite small. Sleeping bags need much more— and to date not many have tried to employ microfibers because they weigh 30–40 percent more than an amount of down equally warm. Further, the fibers are so dense and stiff that even with vigorous use of boulders and baseball bats a bag cannot be "stuffed" to a size less than double that of a down bag.

Heat Shield

Insulation, whether air-trapping or flow-impeding, slows the *conduction* of heat from the body to outer space. A heat shield reduces the *radiation* of body heat by reflecting much of it back to the source.

Of several early entries, Tex-O-Lite (3M) has been preeminent. It consists of two layers of aluminized polyethylene film separated and stabilized by nylon netting, tightly quilted into a sandwich 0.02 inch thick. Sewn into a bag—or into a removable liner or cover— it adds some 10°F of warmth with virtually no added bulk or weight.

Tex-O-Lite is also a vapor barrier (see below)—a partial one because the sandwich is needle-punched to permit some breathing, realizing some of the added warmth of a vapor barrier without the dreaded swampiness.

Skeptics murmur that any layer added to a bag traps more air; if Tex-O-Lite truly works, it may be due not to space-age spooky tech but to simple old air entrapment.

Critics who accept the heat shield nevertheless object to Tex-O-Lite as a poor breather that radically narrows comfort range. At 0°F the bag may be cozy—and at 30°, sweltering.

Kelty has come along with Solarsilk, a vacuum-plated material said to add as much warmth and to breathe much better. The status is in flux. For the present a backpacker who thinks a heat shield might be up his alley perhaps would do best to use one in a separate bag cover that can be removed in the middle of the night or left home all summer.

Vapor Barrier

By slowing the rate of insensible perspiration and the consequent evaporative cooling, a vapor barrier (see Chapter 9) increases the warmth of clothing or a bag.

The leading prophet of the concept, Jack Stephenson, calls the *partial* vapor barrier of Tex-O-Lite a fraud. Since the 1960s he has used in his Warmlite tents, garments, and bags a heat shield (a concept of which he has also been an early prophet) that is also a *complete* vapor barrier.

Winter mountaineers have been very largely converted. The ordinary backpacker can best experiment with the device by using a vapor-barrier liner slipped inside the bag at −20°F, slipped out at 30° or even 10°, and left home in summer.

ANATOMY OF THE SLEEPING BAG

A bag's warmth is determined by the insulation (discussed above), how it is contained in the bag, and how the bag is structured.

The Inside

For a decade and longer the catalogs raged with a wall-poster–like debate over picky intricacies of the interior of a sleeping bag, about which the layman could learn nothing without a sharp knife. Now, silence. The technology has stabilized, designers have agreed on how the bag guts ought to be arranged, and catalogs have moved on to more interesting matters, such as underwear.

A backpacker does best to judge bags by the exterior and by the reputation of the supplier. Still, a few words are owed to history, even if it's all over. This past passion focused on how to manipulate the insulation to hold it in place and prevent cold spots. The methods are different for down and polyester.

Baffling the Down

Down stuffed between an outer and inner shell would lump up, leaving large expanses of no insulation. In striving to "baffle" the down—that is, keep it from migrating—a designer aims to use the least weight of compartmenting fabric to gain the most freedom for the down to loft.

Feather-light summer bags, as well as bargain-basement bags, may be *sewn-through*, a simple and cheap way to connect the inner and outer shell and compartment the down; insulation along the stitching lines is zero.

Backpacker bags of the mainstream employ the offset compartmenting that has been determined to provide maximum loft for minimum panel weight and thereby the greatest warmth per pound of total bag weight. If a supplier so much as bothers to mention it, the description may be *slant tube*, *slant box*, *slant wall*, or *parallelogram*.

All quality bags have a *sideblock baffle (channel block, cross block baffle)*—a continuous baffle down the side of the bag opposite the zipper—to prevent down from migrating around the circumference.

Many bags have a *bottom box*, an around-the-bag baffle that keeps filler in place at the foot so the toe won't chill.

Stabilizing the Polyester

Low-cost bags using generic polyester or Hollofil may be *sewn-through*, to save money at the expense of warmth. If a cover is added to insulate the stitching lines, the weight is of minor concern since few of these bags are carried far, if at all.

Quallofil, though the fiber lengths are feather-short, is not truly a "blown" material resembling down and for a sleeping bag must be *backed* with a layer of Remay or similar fabric to hold it in place. The more Quallofil in a bag (for colder weather), the more stabilizing fabric—weight without warmth.

Once backed, Quallofil sheets can be *edge-stabilized*—stitched to the shell along the edges. However, PolarGuard batts are stable as is and don't require backing. Therefore, the more filler used, the more useless weight inherent in the use of Quallofil, the greater the cold-weather efficiency of PolarGuard.

The Outside

A hiker can eye the outside of a bag, fondle it, even crawl into it, since the palpable exterior of the inner shell, where the body goes, is considered a part of the outside even though, from one viewpoint, it is inside.

Shape

Other things being equal, the smaller the bag, the warmer, since there are fewer interior air spaces to be heated and more of the insulation is near the body rather than off in distant corners. The configuration of the upper opening, where the sleeper extends some portion of his face or head out of the bag, is also significant; the brain receives 20 percent of the body's blood supply and thus the head area can radiate a great deal of heat.

The warmest design, and the choice of nearly all backpackers, is the *mummy* bag, contoured to the body and closed at the top by a

drawstring that completely shuts off breezeways, leaving exposed, when desired, merely the sleeper's nose and mouth.

A few true mummies linger, the very lightest of down bags, but the contemporary standard for backpackers is the *modified* or *stream-lined mummy*, broader in the shoulder, roomier at the toe, pretty well eliminating nightmares of ancient Egypt.

As baby-boom backpackers age to thirty and beyond they tend to expand, some to the point they find even the modified mummy tight. They once had no option except the car camper's rectangle (below), because manufacturers felt unable to produce a spacious bag light and warm enough for the trails that was also reasonably priced. However, utilization of new materials, such as Quallofil (a considerable amount of insulation at much lower price than down) and the Solarsilk heat shield (much warmth at next to no weight) has enabled a Boeing-like new generation—the *wide-body barrels*. Where the standard girth of a modified mummy is around 60 inches, these are 68. They are wider in chest and hips, have a no-hood drawstring-closed top, and a full-length and around-the-bottom zipper, permitting two of the bags to be zipped together in a double.

Roomiest and heaviest, and rarely seen on the trail, are *rectangular* bags, usually with no top closure, allowing heat to escape and breezes to enter, an advantage at low elevations in warm climates. A *modified* or *tapered rectangle* saves weight by tapering in at the foot and may have a drawstring closure for sealing off the outer chill. Formerly it was often seen on the trail, but likely will be replaced there by the barrel.

The Shell—Outer and Inner

Backpacker bags have *outer shells* of nylon—strong, easy-breathing, wind-resistant, and effective at preventing filler from escaping. Car-camping bags often use cotton, cheaper and less vulnerable to camp-fire sparks and heavier for the same strength.

The nylon (see Chapter 9) is usually *high-count* (strong, light, downproof, quick-drying); *Luscious* (lighter); *Nylsilk* (feels nice); *Trinyl* (cottonlike); *taffeta* (light and durable); or *ripstop* (reinforcing threads to control tearing). Fabrics may be combined, such as taffeta on the ground side, where the hard wear comes, and Nylsilk on the sky side, in order not to weigh heavily on the lofting down.

Inner shells may be taffeta for durability; Trinyl, because it is not synthetic-slippery, gives cottony comfort; or Nylsilk or Luscious, because they *are* slippery, letting a person twist and turn without the bag following.

The Opening and Closing

The means of ingress and egress affects the warmth of a bag as much as the insulation, compartmenting, and shape and the comfort and convenience even more so.

Head of the Bag

A living, breathing body exhales so much moisture in the breath that even on the coldest nights the sleeper should keep his nose outside the bag to avoid swamping the interior. In extreme cold he may need to protect the nose from freezing by breathing through a "snorkel," such as a sweater.

Rectangular bags are ordinarily wide open at the top; if the night grows cold in the middle watches, a sleeper can slither down in and wrap a sweater around his head.

Barrel bags, and some modified rectangles, have a drawstring to reduce the size of the top opening, even to nose-size.

A mummy bag does it more neatly, the head cut taller in back, so that when the drawstring is tightened the back fabric is pulled down over the head, leaving a face hole, or nose hole. In addition to this hood-forming string, some bags have another at the neck, to let the bag be snugged there, leaving the shoulders free. Some designs have a *floating hood* that turns with the head in the manner of the owl; others have an extra measure of insulation in a *filled collar*, or *muff*, to keep the shoulders cozy.

Zippers

Very light bags dispense with zippers altogether (the more zipper, the more weight and cost and things to go wrong in the night) and are donned and doffed like body stockings.

Most bags have a *side* zipper, on either side (*left-opening* or *right-opening*). Choice mainly matters when two bags are to be zipped together, in which case one of each is required.

Mummy bags often have *half-length* zippers some 36–40 inches long, extending about halfway down from the top; as a general rule the less zipper, the less of a cold spot and thus the warmer the bag.

Other mummies, most rectangulars, and all barrels have a *full-length* (70-inch or so) zipper. Some have a zipper running the *full length and across the foot* for complete temperature control in warm weather, or *full-length zippers on both sides*.

Hikers who travel mainly in warm climates prefer a lot of zipper to avoid night-long stewing in their own juices. Cold-country hikers generally want much less zipper: when a full-length zipper fails (which occasionally happens even with the best) the sleeper is faced with either a shivering night or a massive hand-sewing job by flashlight; when a short zipper fails, the comparatively small opening can be adequately closed with several safety pins or by clutching the fabric with the hands.

Two bags with full-length zippers can be joined—if the zippers are compatible—to make a double bag. Many couples like to have this option, either for the theoretical warmth of snuggling or simply for a meaningful relationship. Another advantage is that a small child can be accommodated, saving the weight of an extra bag. However, some couples (old marrieds) declare that in cold windy weather so much heat is lost through the top that a double bag is like no bag at all, and that sleeping with a squirming, kicking infant is no sleep at all.

The best zippers are *nylon*, which, unlike metal, doesn't conduct heat, freeze, or rip the shell when snagged, and of *tooth* design rather than the cheaper, lighter, riskier *coil*. The highest-quality bags have *oversized*, or *heavy-duty*, zippers for greater dependability and a *zipper stiffener*, a webbing the full length of the zipper to prevent snagging.

A *two-way (two-slide)* zipper adds expense but is convenient in letting the bag be opened from either top or bottom; the feet may thus be ventilated without chilling the shoulders.

In the best bags the zipper, in itself a line of zero insulation, is covered by a *draft tube*, wider and longer than the zipper, to prevent heat loss.

SELECTING A SLEEPING BAG: THE CONSIDERATIONS

A sleeping bag cannot be pulled off the shelf at random like a box of corn flakes. It's an intimate garment and must be closely fitted to the individual—to the body size and shape, to personal sensibilities.

Length and Width

Bags come in three lengths: *short*, for people up to 5 feet 4 inches; *regular*, to 6 feet; and *long*, to 6 feet 6 inches. (Longer persons can improvise a bag extension: drawing the hood string reasonably tight around the neck and wearing a detachable parka hood.)

Though for reasons of warmth, weight, and expense a person should buy the shortest bag into which the body fits comfortably, the inner length of a person's bag should be some 4 inches longer than his height. When in doubt, better a too-long bag than cramped knees and neck.

The original mummies turned with the sleeper along with the underwear, not a bad arrangement and one to which backpackers grew accustomed. Modified mummies are cut generously enough for the sleeper to roll over inside without rolling the bag; aside from this being what most people prefer, having grown used to it at home in bed, keeping top on top and bottom on bottom is very important in those bags, increasingly common, with expensive high-loft insulation on the top and either less of it or a cheaper insulation on the bottom, relying there on the sleeping pad.

Where mummies reach their maximum width, and before rectangles commence, there are the barrels, essentially modified mummies modified a bit more in the girth dimension. A person should not be vain about bag width. Select in the privacy of the dressing room and rely upon the discretion of the clerk.

Test for size in the shop. Crawl in, make sure elbows, shoulders, knees, and feet can move without compressing the insulation and thus creating cold spots. Don't insist on room to roam around, though—that's a waste of money and weight and a large interior is harder for the body to heat up. Draw the hood closed to be sure the air hole is near your mouth. If the management won't let you crawl in its bags, stalk off in a huff to another shop. A person wouldn't be expected to spend $100 for a dress or jacket without trying it on. (Needless to say, the management has a right to expect prospective customers to be reasonably clean.)

Weight and Cost

Down bags for backpackers range from about 2 pounds to 5, polyester bags from about 4 pounds to 7; those on the lower end of the scale for mild temperatures, on the upper, for extreme cold. The average hiker finds the bag he wants at around 2½ or 3 pounds for down, 4½ or 5 for polyester. If a bag is to be carried long distances, weight matters a lot and the hiker may wish to sacrifice warmth. If the bag is for short backpacks an extra pound or three is insignificant.

A hiker with all the money in the free world will never check the bag price until happy with the warmth and weight and convenience. On the other hand, a semi-indigent may be content to shiver once in a while, like his old pappy used to do as a tad. Still, a person should buy the best bag he can afford; with proper care a quality bag can outlast a series of make-do substitutes and be more economical in the long run and more comfortable in the short. A first-class (down) bag is good for ten years or a lifetime, whichever runs out soonest.

Warmth of the Bag

Suppliers give the customer one or two or perhaps three mathematical indices of the warmth of their bags, often adding a non-mathematical, summary-judgment fourth that permits a person to ignore the first three.

Most manufacturers and retailers traditionally have stressed the *bag loft*. This is different from the *down loft* measured, as previously mentioned, in a cylinder. Under conditions of standard temperature and humidity, the bag is spread out, closed and fully fluffed, with no weight inside or on top, and the inches then counted from bottom to top—the *total loft*. Because the bottom half of a bag is squashed

by the sleeper, and because bottom warmth is more a function of the sleeping pad than the bag, some suppliers give only the *top loft*, the loft of the upper half.

Measuring methods vary, leaving room for mercantile maneuvering and customer misunderstanding. Loft figures may nevertheless be useful in comparing bags—if not necessarily from one shop to the next, in any single shop, though not if the shop stocks bags of several manufacturers and uncritically adopts the loft measurements they give.

The amount of loft is determined mainly by the *amount of filler*, almost always faithfully specified by a supplier. However, the figures are so difficult to interpret they are best ignored except by the scholar.

The emergence of the heat shield (see above) has made the ancient rule that loft = warmth less than axiomatic. However, this new component of the sleeping system (see below) is a factor in the next mathematical index.

A few suppliers scientifically determine the *comfort ratings* of their bags by means of laboratory tests. (For a description of the method used by the REI Quality Control Department, see Chapter 9.) Ratings so determined have proven highly accurate. At the stipulated minimum temperature a person should be quite comfortable—the

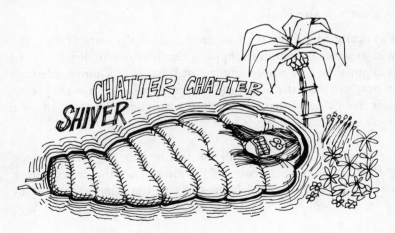

"average" person that is, in still air, with good bottom insulation, and with a dry bag and dry clothing. In the absence of any of these conditions the comfort temperature must be raised.

Individual metabolisms vary enormously in their ability to produce heat. Generally a beginning backpacker already knows if he/she is a cold person or a warm person; a cold sleeper may shiver on a tropic night in a bag designed for the South Pole, while a warm sleeper wrapped in an old horse blanket may snore up a storm on an icecap. A person who sleeps cold should add 5°–10°F to the rating; a bag rated at 25°F may be comfortable for a cold person only to 30°–35°F. A warm sleeper can subtract 5°–10°F.

The bottom line at most shops, whether or not they give comfort ratings, is the *season* and/or *situation of use*. A *three-season* or *backpacking* bag does not pretend it can cope with a North Dakota gazebo in January but promises to handle alpine meadows once the blizzards quit and before they resume. A *summer* or *camping* bag is forthrightly modest. The only backpackers who should consider a *four-season* or *expedition* bag are those who mush around in snow a lot—or whose inner furnaces burn so low that summer is a season they hear about and never feel.

Warmth of the Body

Physically fit people with much muscle sleep warmer than those who are out of shape and sloppy, a terrible blow to jiggly folks who thought they had one advantage, at least, over skinny athletes. Fit or not, whatever the metabolic efficiency, there are ways to get more heat from a bag—that is, to help it retain body heat and to get the body to generate more:

- Sleep in a tent. In still air the interior of a closed tent (or bivvy sack) is about 10°F warmer than the exterior; in a wind the differential is greater (see the wind-chill table in Chapter 6).

- At the least, shelter from the wind behind a clump of trees, a big boulder, a hillock.
- Sleep on a pad, more important on the bottom side of a sleeper than the bag.
- Eat a supper high in fats; during night-long digestion these generate much heat.
- Before going to bed, have a snack and drink lots of water.
- Go to bed warm—by means of a campfire or ten fast laps around the tent.
- Take a bottle of hot water into the bag.
- Sleep on your side in fetal position.
- Sleep close to another person.
- Take along a shaggy dog.
- Two shaggy dogs.

Of course, the best way to keep a body warm is to put clothes on it. This was universally recognized in cold climates prior to central heating; preparing for bed on a New England winter night as late as the 1930s, a person might well don more night-clothing than he'd worn in the day. A myth that long held currency among backpackers was that nude was the warmest way to sleep. However, common sense has prevailed, and the hikers who carry cleverly layered clothing for daytime have seen the foolishness of putting it all aside at night. Certainly, at any temperature lower than balmy, the sleeper should wear a hat; the stocking cap is best, clinging to the head. As the thermometer drops, pants and shirt may be added, and a pair of socks. Then sweaters, more socks, mittens, insulated parka. Another shaggy dog.

Climbers and long-distance backpackers, who must watch every pound, exploit daytime layering garments to the fullest and get by with a much lighter sleeping bag. Further, hikers who go out occasionally but not often in winter may not wish to burden themselves with a bag rated to −10°F when day clothing worn as night clothing can let them do well enough with a +10°F bag.

SELECTING A SLEEPING BAG:
THE CHOICES

The following pages briefly delineate the salient features of representative bags. The key word is "representative"—these are a few points on a continuum of hundreds of bags. Thousands.

Note: The weights and prices given are for "regular" bags. Both are lower for "short" sizes; higher for "long."

Recreational (Indoor) Bag

Far and away the greatest number of bags on the market, offered for sale in department stores, sporting-goods stores, drugstores, and garage sales, fall in this category, which is not found in backpacking shops, intended as it is for car camping, boating, and slumber parties.

The fill is usually generic polyester, the shape rectangular, the weight 4–6 pounds, the comfort rating 40°–50°F, and the price about $30.

Camping (Summer) Bag

Meant for outdoor use—car camping in summer in lowlands—these bags can be credibly backpacked. The price is right, the comfort not bad, and the weight couldn't strain a back.

A classy example is a rectangular bag filled with Hollofil 808, weight just under 6 pounds, comfort rating 35°F, price $50.

Others use generic polyester, weigh less, cost less, and comfort a person only to 45°F.

There's a different way to go. A summer-only down bag can be had for 2 pounds, a feather on the back, and $150, a heavy blow to the checkbook.

A new way is a very light, inexpensive bag—2¾ pounds, $106—rated to 40°F, made possible by the use of Quallofil and a Silverlite Solarsilk heat shield.

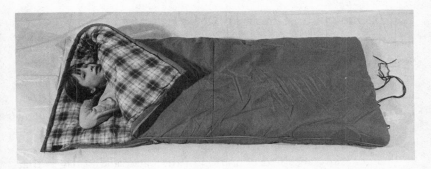

Representative "summer" sleeping bag, rectangular. A "recreational" bag looks the same but costs less, lacking the warmer insulation.

Representative "backpacking" (three-season) sleeping bag, modified mummy.

Representative "backpacking" (three-season) sleeping bag, wide-body barrel.

Backpacking (Three-Season) Bag

Though only about one in seven bags manufactured is in this category, here lie the hearts of the inventors and here their creative spirits run free. The dream is to develop One Grand Bag in which every pure hiker will be happy to rest until the trumpets sound. However, the options in filler and design are so many that the goal is elusive, designers forever juggling to find good compromises between warmth and weight and cost.

The generally accepted definition of the backpacking bag is that it fits readily into a pack (is easily stuffable), weighs under 6 pounds, and is comfort-rated to 30°F or lower. The shape is sometimes mummy, mainly modified mummy, sometimes wide-body barrel.

The examples fall into several subcategories, defined by the insulation and by this or that fancy, such as heat shield and Gore-Tex. A hiker can't consider them intelligently without referring back to the fundamentals discussed earlier in this chapter.

Polyester

A smaller backpacking shop typically offers a very few bags, chosen because among them they meet every reasonable need well enough. Assuming it's a thoughtful shop, the novice can buy what his trips require without bewilderment.

The larger shops try for finer tuning of warmth-price to person, but to eliminate the confusion problem, they often group similar bags. An example is the REI Matrix series, composed of three related bags. The Lite has a generic filler ("Polysoft"), weighs 4¼ pounds, has a comfort range to 30°F, and is priced under $70. A step up is the Matrix, combining Polysoft and PolarGuard for good loft at low cost; weight 4⅜ pounds, comfort range to 25°F, price $80. The top of this line is the Plus; PolarGuard, 4¼ pounds, 20°F, $100.

Other suppliers have similar groupings, as well as singletons, similar to the above or different in this or that aspect. A few representatives:

- PolarGuard, 4½ pounds, 20°F, $95
- PolarGuard, 6¼ pounds, 5°F, $110
- Quallofil, 4¼ pounds, 10°F, $130
- Polarguard, 5¼ pounds, 10°F, $140

Goose Down

The rising cost of down, combined with the growing dependence on the sleeping pad, has led bag makers to put, usually, 60 percent of a bag's down on top, 40 percent on the bottom. (The cutting edge of technology may be to put more and more above, less and less below.)

For the same warmth as polyester, down bags are lower in weight, higher in price:

- 3½ pounds, 20°F, $115
- 3⅛ pounds, 20°F, $150
- 2 pounds, 30°F, $175
- 2 pounds, 20°F, $200
- 2¾ pounds, 15°F, $235

The absence of a direct correlation between weights, warmths, and prices is what may ultimately lead a backpacker to become a philosopher.

Combinations

A few bags combine insulations—down on top for the loft, polyester on the bottom for the lower cost and greater resistance to body flattening. One example has duck down on top, PolarGuard below, for a bag weight of 3½ pounds, comfort range down to 20°F, price $130—a nice balance of lightness, warmth, and economy.

Heat Shield

The heat shield (see above) is claimed by some proponents to add 25°F to the comfort range of a bag; elsewhere, 10°F is more modestly stated. Science has yet to catch up with advertising here. Old miracles and new are running off and on the stage like dancers in the finale of a Broadway show. Several examples are cited below, with no assurance they are still on the market:

1. A Quallofil bag weighing 3¼ pounds, with Tex-O-Lite barrier, comfort-rated to 25°F, $135
2. A down bag weighing 2¾ pounds, costing $235, comfort-rated to 15°F, said by the maker to extend its comfort down to − 10°F by the addition of a Tex-O-Lite barrier that adds less than 1 pound to the weight and only $55 to the price
3. A PolarGuard bag with an Orcoterm heat barrier weighs 3¾ pounds, rated to 5°F, $150

Gore-Tex

See Chapter 9 for a complete discussion. Gore-Tex is intended to keep people dry, not warm, yet any material interposed between the sleeper and the Milky Way, whether space-new or shaggy-dog-old, is bound to add warmth.

To suggest the effect, one supplier has a down bag that weighs 2 pounds, is comfort-rated to 30°F, and costs $175. With Gore-Tex added for the rain-repellency, the bag is comfortable down to 25°F at an additional cost of $55.

Two Halves That Make a Whole—for Two

Many a hiker has learned that many a wildland night he is perfectly comfortable laying his body on sleeping pad, zipping his bag wide open, and using it as a blanket. Marmot Mountain Works got around to innovating from the obvious, and likely will be imitated.

Marmot has a Grouse semirectangular bag filled with goose down that weighs under 2 pounds, is rated to 30°–35°F with a Luscious shell (20°–25°F in the Gore-Tex version), and costs $180 (Gore-Tex, $230). When this bag is spread wide open and zipped to a Marmot doubling sheet (Luscious nylon, 9 ounces, $40) that rests on the sleeping pad, the result is a bag that sleeps two for a total weight of 2½ pounds. Kelty and others offer much the same combinations.

Expedition (Four-Season) Bag

Everybody loves this category—the shops because the prices are so wild, the designers because price is no object, the customers because the bags evoke the romance of weeklong gales at the South Col. A few representatives:

- PolarGuard, 7 pounds, −15°F, $130
- PolarGuard with Tex-O-Lite, 4¾ pounds, 0°, $160
- Down (goose), 3¾ pounds, 5°F, $180
- Down, 4¼ pounds, −20°F, $200
- Down, 4¾ pounds, −20°F, $220
- Down, 4¼ pounds, −15°F, $295
- Down, 5¾ pounds, −40°F, $270
- Down with Gore-Tex shell, 3 pounds, −10°F, $470
- Down with Gore-Tex ripstop shell, 4¼ pounds, −30°F, $535

Example of a couplet, where a bottom case holds a pair of Therma-a-Rest mattresses zipped together and a single rectangular bag is spread over the two sleepers and zipped to the bottom.

The cost differentials almost force a hiker to go back to school for a master's degree, to understand the whys and wherefores. In any event, the body that doesn't sleep warm in the last two can only be helped by cremation.

Liners and Covers (the Sleeping System)

In the 1950s Gerry Gunningham was as energetic and ingenious a builder of backpacking gear as there was, and he frequently and generously shared his frontiering with readers of *Summit Magazine*. Gerry was, for a time, especially involved in the insides and outsides of the sleeping bag, and after a time a bemused group self-described as the Cougar Mountaineers (they lived on Cougar Mountain) undertook to bring technology to heel. In the pages of the magazine they put forth *their* miracle, a replacement for the sleeping bag— the *sleeping system*.

The "expedition" (four-season) bag has to be slept in to distinguish it from three-season look-alikes. A major difference, other than more filler, is the double-closure at the top—not only the around-the-head drawstring but another across the chest or neck.

The sleeper wore a war-surplus gas mask. Tubing carried his exhalations to a bag of anhydrous calcium chloride that absorbed the moisture from his breath and introduced the substantial heat resulting from rehydration. Tubing conducted the hot, dry air to what had been determined (by Cougar Mountaineers in their research laboratories) to be the body's temperature-control centers: the hands, the feet, and the small of the back.

Gerry found discrepancies in the scientific facts and brought them to the attention of *Summit* readers. The Cougar Mountaineers responded angrily and as fast as Gerry objected, they produced more facts, as fast as the typewriter could type. Support for the Cougar Mountaineers was expressed from California, Florida, New Jersey, and Chicago, from great universities in the East and little logging towns in the West.

The joke was at last exhausted, the Cougar Mountaineers never suspecting what they had wrought. Namely, two years later a major American chemical firm was granted a patent for the identical concept. Earlier, though, Gerry had published in *Summit* his own very sensible combination of a down half-bag, or "elephant trunk," reaching from foot to hips, and a down parka, covering torso and head. The system notion, a jest in the beginning, has proven pithy indeed.

Now and then, here and there, a supplier offers a complete system, composed, perhaps, of a Therm-a-Rest mattress, a summer sleeping bag that can be used along or inside a three-season bag that can also be used alone, and a Gore-Tex or heat-shield bag cover. Though the system is extremely versatile, in part or total serving every situation from balmy summer to polar winter, the cost appears so formidable that customer resistance is fierce. However, the concept remains valid, whether in Gerry's version (popular among climbers doing routes on the order of the Eigerwand) or in an individually tailored outfit, including some of the following components, liners and covers.

A *vapor barrier liner* for winter is said to enlarge the comfort zone of a bag downward 20°–30°F; 6 ounces, $25.

A *polypropylene liner*, a snuggly combed bunting, adds 10°F of warmth; 12 ounces, $50.

A *liner bag* is an extremely lightweight, skinny-mummy, simple bag meant to be inserted in a standard bag for extra warmth; in warm nights of high summer it can be used alone.

An *overbag* is an oversized bag meant to be slipped over a standard bag; it, too, can be used alone.

A *heat-shield cover* augments the bag's insulation by reflecting the body's radiated heat back to the source. One example is a Tex-O-Lite cover, the top and sides of ripstop nylon filled with PolarGuard, the bottom closing with Velcro tape to form a case for a sleeping pad (2¾ pounds, $95). In mild weather it is warm enough by itself; slipped over a basic bag on colder nights it adds 10°–15°F to the comfort zone.

A *Gore-Tex cover* repels rain and adds some 5°F of comfort. In one example the bottom and sides are coated nylon for waterproofness, the top breathable Gore-Tex; 1 pound, $70. When the cover grows more elaborate, it becomes a *bivy sack* (see Chapter 12).

A *combined Gore-Tex and Tex-O-Lite shell* repels rain, adds 15°–20°F of warmth, and in anything but extreme cold creates a swamp (1 pound, $120).

A *bivouac cover*, the pre-Gore-Tex ancestor of the bivy sack, has a low price that gives continuing appeal. A cover with a nylon-coated bottom and ripstop top adds 10°F of warmth (1 pound, $30). It was originally used by climbers planning to spend a night or two tied to a cliff sans the usual camp outfit. Where climate and terrain are kindly, a hiker employing one of these, and cutting a few other corners, and content to live on a pound or less of cold food a day, can ramble a week with a pack weighing no more than the usual rucksack load for a day hike. John Muir, given the chance, might have accepted this much luxury.

Sleeping Bags for Children

Saving the weight of an extra bag by letting a little kid snuggle in with Mommy—or with Mommy and Daddy in two bags zipped together (see "Zippers," above)—is often a disaster, what with the kicking and squirming, possibly the wetting, but not always.

Two adult-sized sleeping bags zipped together can make a very happy family burrow.

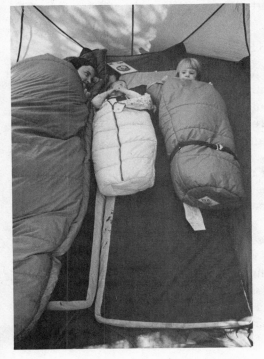

A family of bags big and little may better keep the peace, especially when there are two or more little people exercising territorial imperatives.

Longtime hikers with a basementful of old gear may take a worn-out bag, chop off the bottom, stitch up the gap and patch where needed, thus devising a child's bag with no cash outlay.

When a bag must be purchased, all the rules for adults apply to children. Polyester is recommended for two reasons: (1) accidents that with down are semitragic are mere incidents with the synthetic and (2) for a bag soon to be outgrown the investment in long-lived down is a waste.

Thanks to repeated baby booms, children's bags have become more available. An excellent example is a mummy filled with generic polyester. Weighing 2½ pounds and costing $50, it is good for bodies up to 4 feet 10 inches and comfortable to 35°F (actually lower than that since on cold nights Mommy and Daddy will be there for cuddling).

A bag "just like Dad's and Mom's," for bodies up to 5 feet, has PolarGuard fill, a comfort-rating to 25°F; weighs 2¾ pounds, $90.

CARING FOR THE SLEEPING BAG

There is no formula for predicting the life span of a sleeping bag. Every-night use for months on end, as during an expedition, may finish it off. If slept in only a few weekends a summer, it may last for years. However, more important than the amount of use is the manner. Proper care can greatly extend a bag's life, and carelessness can kill it while still new.

The nylon shell of the typical backpacker sleeping bag is strong but very thin and must be protected from wear and especially snagging. Therefore—and also to keep the bag dry—a layer should be placed between bag and earth, such as a tent floor, sleeping pad, or ground sheet, and the bag should be carried in a *stuff bag* (see Chapter 10). The hiker's repair kit should include a roll of ripstop tape for patching holes through which filler might escape.

Nylon shells must be scrupulously guarded against fire; even a tiny spark instantly melts a hole in the fabric—and could kindle a smolder in the filler. Using an unprotected bag as a seat cushion for campfire seminars usually leads in the course of an evening to several holes per cushion, despite constant cries of "Spark! Spark!"

Even more perilous is steaming out the residue of a rainstorm. All fillers require some time to dry, but down takes forever, and during the long process spark holes are inevitable. As patience becomes exhausted, one moves closer to the flames; the fabric is scorched and disintegrates. All the more reason not to let the bag get wet in the first place.

Fire aside, polyester is ruined by excessive heat. The bag should not be spread on a rock to dry in the hot desert sun (after a desert thundershower) or tossed in the car next to the heater.

The more a bag is allowed to loft, the longer it lives. Bags should not be stored in the stuff bag between trips. Tightly compressed weeks and months on end, the filler loses resiliency, thus loft, thus warmth. The bag should be loosely rolled and kept in a special large storage bag or, better, hung by the foot from a line in the basement or a hanger in the closet.

By the same token, a bag should be thoroughly fluffed before being slept in. The rule is, as soon as camp is reached and the tent or tarp rigged, the bag is unrolled, shaken vigorously, and placed under the shelter to finish attaining full loft.

Any bag, but down especially, should be air-dried after each trip to avoid mildew and rot and to prevent the filler from matting. Indeed, on multiday hikes the bag should be aired every day or two, weather permitting, to dry body moisture breathed into the filler at night.

How to Clean?

Ideally, a sleeping bag should be kept clean, not only for reasons of hygiene and social acceptability but to prevent the shell from rotting or being nibbled by small creatures (in the mountains or in the basement) lusting after salt and oil. Further, some people are allergic to the dust that collects on filler.

Polyester bags pose no problem; they must never be dry-cleaned (resins may be ruined; Hollofil and Quallofil may retain solvent) but can safely be washed in tepid water with a mild soap, Ivory or REI Loft or the like, but *never* a detergent. The only type of machine to use is the oversized, commercial, rotating-drum washer. Hand-washing is safer and not all that difficult. A drier, even at the lowest heat setting, may melt the polyester; the better method is to hang-dry on a line overnight, then 24 hours at room temperature.

Down is something else. Experts agree that more down bags are ruined by improper cleaning than by all other causes combined, including long hard use. Because of the perils, suspicious conservatives declare absolutely, "Never clean a down bag! If it gets too dirty for fastidious tastes, buy a new one."

However, sanitation is not the real issue. Body oils absorbed by down attract dirt, which mats the down and in time destroys its resiliency. Dirty down loses loft, and thus warmth, and if dirty long enough, it loses its power ever to be lofty again.

Nevertheless, there is merit in the argument of the conservatives. The hiker should not be a fanatic. With average use, one cleaning a year is sufficient to maintain loft and protect the down. The more the bag is cleaned, the greater the danger of quickly destroying it; still unsettled is the question how many cleanings, however careful, a bag can tolerate before the down turns to string.

Each of the two usual cleaning methods has advantages—and hazards.

Dry-Clean the Down—but Afterward Breathe With Care

Safest for the bag and simplest for the bag owner is dry cleaning, the method employed by manufacturers and retailers. However, these people know precisely what they're doing. Does the average hiker? Not often. Because cleaning solvents are toxic and have killed sleepers in the night, the U.S. Bureau of Standards warns against dry cleaning as altogether too risky. (Dry cleaning also kills Gore-Tex; bags including it *must* be washed following the manufacturer's instructions.)

Partisans say there is no danger if a mild petroleum-based com-

pound, such as Stoddard Solvent, is used and the bag completely air-dried afterward—for at least a week—until the solvent odor is gone. Though they admit the solvent lessens the water-repellency of the nylon shell and attacks the down's natural oils, already largely removed by processors, they think the harm done by one cleaning a year is acceptable.

But the chlorinated hydrocarbon (perchlorethylene) used by most dry cleaners turns down into string and remains lethal to living creatures even when the odor is barely noticeable.

Cautious hikers unwilling to trust their local dry cleaner say, "Better dirty than dead."

Wash the Down—but Gently, Sir!

Most experts recommend that the hiker clean his bag by hand washing, unquestionably safe for the hiker and safe for the bag *if done right*. At any of a number of points, though, one false step and the bag is wrecked. Following are precise instructions:

Use any of several brands of down soap (Fluffy, Loft). If such a product cannot be found, any *mild* soap (Ivory) may be substituted, but not detergent, which washes out the natural oils and destroys loft.

Dissolve the soap in 10–12 gallons of warm (never hot) water in a sink or bathtub or large top-loading washing machine (But *do not* use the wash cycle of the machine.)

Press the bag into the soapy water, starting at one end and keeping the other end dry (to allow air to escape more readily) until most of the bag is submerged. Gently squeeze out remaining air so the bag will stay submerged. Let the bag soak 1–2 hours (if longer, the fabric colors start to run), turning it *gently* a couple of times. (Once the bag is sopping wet it must *never* be roughly handled or abruptly lifted—the weight of the saturated down will instantly tear out the baffles and for all practical purposes the bag is a total loss.)

After the soaking period, scrub off the surface dirt with a sponge or soft brush. Drain the water from the tub or machine and press as much as possible from the bag by hand or, perhaps, foot. Refill the tub or machine with fresh warm water and gently knead the bag to work out the soap solution. Drain again, rinse again, and repeat for at least three water changes, until the water is clear and free of soap, residues of which will clump the down. Again remove all possible water by hand pressing. Lift out the bag—carefully, both hands underneath.

The safest and most economical method of drying, and one that gives excellent results, is air-drying. Gently *drape* the bag along a line (*don't hang it*) in a warm, dry place. After a day turn it inside out. As the down dries it begins to expand. Gently pat and shake the bag occasionally to aid the fluffing. Complete drying in the open air may take 3–5 days. If patience runs thin, after 2–4 days the job can be finished in a machine—*not* at home, *only* in a large commercial drier set on the lowest available setting ("Air"—meaning no heat). Toss in a pair of clean tennis shoes to break up clumps of matted down.

SLEEPING BETWEEN BAG AND GROUND: PAD, MATTRESS, GROUND SHEET

The bag is one of the three parts of every hiker's sleeping system. Another, the tent or tarp, is the subject of Chapter 12. The third is what goes between bag and ground.

The old-style backpacker sought to live off the land. In high meadows he luxuriated in one of the grandest of earth's mattresses, a clump of heather. In forests, when ground was wet or snowy, he cut branches from living coniferous trees to build a sumptuous bough bed.

Farewell, pioneer! There is not enough heather in the remaining wilderness of America, not enough greenery of trees, for these scarce resources to be utilized for *sleeping*. There is barely enough for *looking*. A friend of the earth must carry a complete sleeping system and not improvise a missing part by attacking the scenery with ax or knife or saw.

For Insulation Mainly—the Sleeping Pad

Recognizing the flaw of the sleeping bag—that bottom insulation flattens under body weight—manufacturers do not think of it as an article to be used alone on the trail. In assigning comfort ratings they assume a sleeping pad as not an optional accessory but an essential component of a complete system.

The most popular pads are *closed-cell foam*, in which neither air nor water moves through the individually sealed cells. The leader

THIS IS A "NO NO"

for years was Ensolite, a polyvinyl chloride (PVC) compounded with nitrile rubber. It's on the way out now, superseded by Blue-Lite, made of ethylene vinyl acetate (EVA), which is warmer and does not become brittle and crack when cold, as Ensolite does.

Pads come in various thicknesses: ⅜ inch is standard for three-season use. Winter campers lean toward ½ inch; hikers whose bags are polyester on the bottom may find ¼ inch enough. The pads are cut in many lengths, many widths. A ⅜-inch Blue-Lite pad 22 by 56 inches, adequate for the shoulder-to-hips area where most body weight rests, weighs 9 ounces, costs $6.

Some hikers prefer an *open-cell foam* (urethane or polyether) pad 1½ inches thick, which provides not only insulation but also cushioning. The objections are that open-cell foam is a sponge, sopping up water from every source and wicking it to the bag, and that a major effort is required to roll the pad to a diameter less than enormous.

For Cushioning Mainly—the Air Mattress

An air mattress gives more cushioning than a urethane pad and, being deflatable, makes less bulky baggage. However, despite also giving wetness protection, when used alone its insulation value is

Therm-a-rest mattress, inflated and ready for sleeping. Atop it, from left to right, a sleeping bag in stuff bag; a 1½-inch-thick sleeping pad of open-cell foam; and a ⅜-inch-thick pad of closed-cell foam.

minor; convection currents in the air cells efficiently carry heat from bag to ground.

Another disadvantage of some air mattresses is the evening and morning time needed to inflate and deflate. Another is the aggravating habit of letting the sleeper down in the night, either from a tiny puncture invisible to the naked eye, a valve failure, innate crankiness, or practical jokes by surly companions.

The Therm-a-Rest (see below) has driven old-style air mattresses out of trail country, though they continue to thrive at car campgrounds. Mattresses light enough and dependable enough for wildland use may exist; a survey for this edition found none. *Vinyl* mattresses occasionally manage to survive an entire night without puncturing; the repair kit of patches and cement may last two or three nights, providing hours of daytime entertainment. It is easily possible to manufacture a mattress of *coated nylon* that will last for years, and it used to be done, but not recently.

Beginning hikers often can't decide where to lay their heads at night. Polyester-filled pillows are a few ounces and dollars. On the principle that less is more, a better recourse is to fill the stuff bag with extra clothing. The Old Crock wraps a boot in a sweater.

For Both Insulation and Cushioning— Therm-a-Rest Mattress

No other invention of such elegant simplicity and logical inevitability has so completely captured so large a faithful following as the *Therm-a-Rest mattress*, a pad of open-cell foam contained within an airtight skin of waterproof nylon that is extremely durable and leak-resistant. Being patented, the device has no competition in America. (Abroad, the patent is flaunted by the pirates of a dozen nations.)

Upon arriving in camp, open the valve and the mattress self-inflates as the foam sucks up air and within a few minutes attains a thickness of 1½ inches. (More time is required in extreme cold; however, the moisture in human breath does no harm and a few quick puffs suffice to inflate.) Close the valve to trap air in the foam

and go to bed. The cushioning is superb, and since the interior air can't circulate well through the foam, so is the insulation.

In the morning, open the valve while getting final winks, and the body weight presses out much of the air. Finish the job by rolling up the mattress to a diameter of 4–6 inches, close the valve to prevent self-inflation on the trail, and away you go.

The standard-size mattress is 20 by 47 inches, weighs 1½ pounds, and costs about $35. The long-size model, which is better for camp use but preferred even on the trail by long people, is 20 by 72 inches, weighs 2¼ pounds, and costs $47.

A newer model, the Ultra-Lite, weighs just 1 ounce over 1 pound in the regular size, costs about $39 (in the long, 1¾ pounds, $50).

A 1-ounce "couple kit" joins two regular-length mattresses to form a double bed.

The mattress is extraordinarily dependable when given the most rudimentary care. Before spreading it out, inspect the ground to remove sharp rocks and twigs—weight pressing directly upon one of these can make a pinpoint hole that may deflate the mattress over a period of half a night. Keep the valve clean and remove any bits of sand or trash that creep in; most deflations result from a dirty valve that can't quite close. Even when a Therm-a-Rest fails, it usually does so considerately, allowing a person to wake up perhaps once or twice a night to give several quick puffs. The shop from which it was purchased can arrange quick repair, and the warranty is generous. Since any person may be careless enough to flop on a sharp rock, for lengthy trips the party may wish to carry the handy little repair kit, easy and quick to use.

For Moisture Protection—the Ground Sheet

For any sleeping bag—no matter what the filler—to get damp or soaked in the course of a trip is always a minor or major catastrophe, to be avoided by every available manner and means.

Neither pad nor mattress can be trusted to keep the bag absolutely separated from wet ground; during the night a shifty sleeper slops over the edges. The tarp camper therefore must carry a ground sheet. (The tent camper, with a floored tent, needs no sheet to keep his bag dry but usually wants one to prevent abrasion of the expensive floor.)

A 7- by 8-foot sheet of 3-mil polyethylene, large enough for two or three sleepers, weighs a pound or so, sells for so little as to be "disposable"—and that's the problem, the poly plague whitening the backcountry. Coated ripstop nylon is costlier but so durable as to be a better buy over several years than all those poly sheets that punctured or cracked, letting the bag get wet, and never quite burned up in the campfire, just melted on the rocks, nasty messes. (PACK IT OUT.)

12

Tents and Tarps

Look back several decades, deep in the memories of veterans still pounding trails despite trick knees and backs, arthritic hips, broken arches, inflamed tendons, sour stomachs, and other scars from the era of nailed boots, wooden packboards, wool sleeping bags, and half-stewed prunes and charcoal-crunchy oatmeal.

In the mind's eye, see a band of these pioneers sack out in a mountain meadow under a clear sky. What is between them and the stars? Nothing but the thin envelope of earth's atmosphere and millions of miles of space. See them fall asleep, and soon begin to shiver, and periodically, wakened by the cold, rolling over to find a closer approach to fetal warmth, glance up to make sure the stars remain bright. And when the stars turn watery, then vanish? Shivers lessen with the great tarp of clouds hung over the meadow, reducing heat loss by radiation. But sleep grows expectant, broken by frequent semiconscious glimpses upward, hoping for stars to sparkle through. Then, "pit!" Instantly alert, though still asleep, waiting for the "pat!" With "pit-a-pat, pit-a-pat" comes full consciousness. Then, "SPLAT!," and sadly they crawl from bags, gather gear in arms, stumble across the meadow to the forest edge, and snuggle up to trees, hoping it's not a three-day blow that will saturate the whole blessed world.

Why are these pioneers naked to the sky? Are they idiots?

In the mind's eye, see—on the same night in the same meadow— a second band of hikers smugly bedded down in tents. They sleep sounder than the others, partly because they are wealthy enough to own tents—and rich people always sleep better—and partly because they are much wearier from having hauled pounds of heavy fabric to the highlands. They are not wakened by the "pit," the "pat," or even the "pit-a-pat." But they stir with the "SPLAT" because the blob of rain is not stopped by the tent, only broken into a fine spray. After an hour of "SPLAT-SPLAT-SPLAT" they are awake and damp and miserably aware that if it's a genuine three-day blow, they will, despite their wealth, get as wet as the poor boys cuddling the trees.

The choice for backpackers then was between (1) carrying a heavy tent (assuming one could afford it) and thus reducing the miles-per-day traveled, punishing a back already suffering under the weight of other primitive gear, and gaining in exchange meager protection, and (2) carrying no tent or tarp at all, trusting to good weather, interwoven branches of trees, overhanging rocks, the trail cabins

and lean-tos then numerous and uncrowded, and accepting the inevitability of now and then being blasted right out of the wilderness in a retreat-from-Moscow stagger.

A few gimpy old troglodytes preserve the no-tent-or-tarp tradition, saying modern gear feeds the base lust to "conquer nature," that man is better for the humility of vulnerability.

In shelter as in so much else, World War II was the boundary between old and new. With V-J Day the backcountry of North America blossomed in a glory of orange and blue 7- by 11-foot liferaft sails of the miracle fabric, nylon, light and strong, coated to be waterproof, and given away by surplus stores for a dollar or two. Pioneers rigged them as tarps or converted them to tents, confessing their motive for trusting to luck in the past had been not asceticism so much as poverty.

Since then, in what some hail as the millennium and others as a warning of impending judgment, hikers of moderate means and load-carrying capacity have grown confident they can always build a snuggly wilderness home secure against any but the most fanatic attacks. The expectation is excessive in some climates, some elevations, some seasons. In general, though, it is true the backpacker of today can gain protection beyond the dreams of his grandparents.

Is this decadent, depraved, sinful? Perhaps. However, just as nobody really wants another Depression (also now said to have been ennobling), no hiker really wants to get soaked or frozen or bug-bitten to frothing hysterics.

Purism remains an option. The difference is, discomfort used to be compulsory. Now there's a choice.

CHOOSING A SHELTER

There still are hikers who cast off chains of comfort for the liberation of risk, and not all are doddering anachronisms; some are matured flower children who know they have not truly escaped the city as long as they haul with them its high-energy high-chemical high-price technology. The pendulum swings. The ball bounces. Bands of youths are even out in the wilds seeking totems, just as in the time of Hiawatha.

However, most beginners would as soon defer that initiation until they've learned to cope with blisters and black flies. They don't want to actually conquer nature but would like to avoid conquest of themselves and, to avoid being routed and put to the sword, are willing to tolerate bits of the city. Ordinarily, then, selection of shelter is one of the Big Four basic decisions. Two preliminary questions:

First, after battering by boots, pummeling by pack, stunning by sleeping bag, *how much money is left*? If next to none, a sheet of polyethylene costing several dollars thwarts enough of nature's nastiness to get through most nights. A 10- by 12-foot coated-nylon tarp, costing about $40, has been known to shelter an entire impoverished family of two adults and four little children and two impoverished dogs, providing, if not comfort, a semblance of survival. Tents? Well, except for the Asian alternative, the bargain basement is close to $100; the middle class $150–$200; and the baronial, out of sight.

Second, *what is the shelter for*?

Rain, of course, but how much, how often? A hiker who never will encounter more than summer drizzles (ocean beaches) and an occasional afternoon thundershower (High Sierra) is silly to spend the money and pack the weight to defend against ceaseless downpours (Cascades and Olympics).

Blizzards and monsoons? For those a person should look beyond the three-season tents emphasized in these pages to the "four-season" models.

Winds? Aside from Arctic gales, there are several species. Some drive rain and fog—or dust—through any manner of tarp rig, then shred the tarp and blow the bits to the next county. Even mild breezes are cooling; partly due to this, partly to the conservation of body heat, a tent interior is about 10°F warmer than the outside; in a strong wind, due to the wind-chill factor (Chapter 6), the differential is much more.

Sleeping under stars is one of the grandest experiences in backpacking. It may also be one of the coldest because the body-and-bag unit, together with all the rest of the world, radiates heat to the sky. On overcast nights the clouds usually reflect heat back to earth, but on clear nights it goes straight to outer space; especially in the thin air of high meadows the ground cools, and so do uncovered sleepers. The starry nights are chilly. They may also be wet when next-to-ground air is cooled below the dew point and beads of dew or crystals of frost form on the sleeping bag. A shelter, whether tent, tarp, or tree, greatly reduces radiation heat loss and gives a warmer (and drier) sleep.

In hot open country it is quite possible to get too much sun; a tent or tarp may well be wanted for a shady retreat.

In popular camps many hikers grow sensitive to being stared at by neighbors; a tarp offers a partial screen, but only a tent gives complete privacy, particularly appreciated by—for example—unliberated females and males who don't enjoy undressing in public. (However, beware of night activities in a candlelit tent that may draw crowds out of the bushes to watch what in the 1920s was called a "shadow show" and extensively legislated against; in some jurisdictions such performances are still felonies.)

Finally, in some places at some seasons the major menace is not moisture or cold or voyeurs but bugs, both those with wings and the creepy-crawlies. A tarp puts no obstruction in the paths of insects or small beasts; a floored tent with netting bars just about anything that lacks sharp teeth and claws.

Other questions arise:

How many people are there? A tarp of proper dimensions can cover any number, from a loner to a platoon. Most tents are designed for two adults, the most common combination on American trails, but readily accommodate a child or two. Big families have a problem. Another problem.

How much weight can the hiker carry, and how much does he want to? Shelter weights range from 0 pounds for the martyr-saint to the pound or so of a poly tarp to the 3½–6 pounds of two-person tents to the 10–12 pounds of circus tents. As a rule of thumb, *shelter weight should be no more than about 3 pounds per person*. Most backpacker tents are under the limit when occupied by the maximum potential population, too heavy if underoccupied. If the shelter is carried only short distances, a few extra pounds are a minor concern; on long jaunts every ounce matters and less protection may be accepted.

INTRODUCTION TO TENTS

To return briefly from technology to sociology, it is truly said that the past is a foreign country; backpackers of the 1980s resemble their ancestors of the 1940s about as much as scarlet tanagers do pterodactyls. Nowhere are the contrasts more evident than in camp. Those cold-blooded old reptiles felt feathers (tents) were for sissies; the gaudy-plumaged wildlander of today considers tarp-sleepers barely a figleaf from stark naked. Betraying saurian prejudices, the first edition of this manual discussed tents only after extravagantly praising tarps. However, public opinion has prevailed and here tarps have been shuffled off to chapter's end. Perhaps in another decade they'll have gone the way of the Trapper Nelson and tricouni and dehydrated spinach.

The typical beginner wants a tent, whether he needs it or not, and his decision is not necessarily an affront to reason and nature—or even the budget. Recent years have brought new designs and

sophistication that almost convert a reptile. Moreover, due to economies of production on a sizable scale, some of the prizewinners
cost less in constant dollars than hovels of the past.

In no part of the trail outfit has creativity so run amok—such tent
architects as Bill Moss are spoken of in the same breath as Buck-
minster Fuller. But the humble hiker innocent of esthetics needn't
be intimidated; with or without a refined eye, amid the wide variety
he'll find any number of very decent choices for his purposes.

Keeping personal purposes and goals clearly in mind is the key.
Meeting the customer halfway, outfitters have devised a categori-
zation that simplifies choice immensely. Before going into that,
though, some remarks are called for about matters common to tents
in general.

Materials: Skin and Bones

Cotton having been relegated to car camping, trail tents are nearly
all *nylon* of one sort or another. (For definitions of fabrics, see Chapter 9.) The floor typically is a tough taffeta, coated for water-repellency to the verge of waterproofness, usually with polyurethane.
The roof and walls are taffeta or ripstop or Nylsilk, uncoated, and
the rainfly, a coated ripstop or taffeta. *Dacron*, heavier and costlier
and with less stretch, is used in some large family-style tents. An
advantage is its superior resistance to ultraviolet radiation, which
in several years of frequent exposure can reduce nylon's strength
by half; a better recourse is to use the nylon rainfly even under the
driest skies and replace it when fatally sunstruck, a cheaper alternative than a whole new nylon tent.

Gore-Tex is employed in one category of tents. However, certain states have laws requiring tents to be flame-resistant, and because Gore-Tex (and polyethylene) cannot be so treated, some tents can't be sold in some states.

A tent lacking bug netting is a tarp. *Mosquito mesh* is inferior to *no-see-um mesh*, which repels everything larger than microbes and lacking sharp teeth.

The *frames* (*poles, wands*) are hollow, fiberglass or aluminum, the weights and strengths varying with the rigors of intended use and the price of the tent. They are held together by elastic shock cords (see below), which prevents the sections from straying apart and lets them be quickly snapped together. Some cheaper tents use solid fiberglass, no shock cord.

Details and Variations and Elaborations

A century of cerebration and experimentation (see "History," below) has developed niceties and frills from tent top to tent bottom and end to end. Lightweight, low-cost models embody the fewest; grimland, high-cost, the most. Only a few the average backpacker is likely to care about will be noted here.

In a tent with a *tub floor* the waterproof coating extends up the walls, and the floor has fewer seams, which are potential lines of leakage.

Some manufacturers seal all tent seams with heat and pressure in the factory for permanent waterproofing.

The rainfly may extend out from the door far enough to form a *vestibule*, for extra wind and rain protection, storing gear, and cooking; or the vestibule may be integral to the inner tent; or an add-on vestibule may be purchased separately. The result may be a "two-and-a-half-person tent."

Ultralight tents and a few others have an *integral fly*, permanently connected to the inner tent, with advantages of quick rigging.

Four-season tents often have a drawstring-closed *tunnel entrance* instead of a zippered doorway, providing a failsafe entry for high, cold mountaineering, merely adding weight and expense for summer use.

A *mesh roof vent* may be provided for better ventilation.

For guy lines, a *shock cord* of rubber stringers sheathed in nylon or cotton, stretches in wind gusts, then returns to its original length and tautness. Shock cords should *not* be used to guy an inner tent because they allow flapping, which strains the fabric; better in such cases to let the pole be bent. However, shock cord should always be used with a rainfly, which balloons in the wind and, being of a coated fabric, may rip unless the strain is transferred to the cord.

A *tent-cord tightener* is a device of nylon or aluminum that does the job of the traditional taut-line hitch, which probably only a handful of backpackers know how to tie or care to learn. With one of these gadgets on each tent (or tarp) line, ground pegs can be placed approximately and the proper tension in lines obtained by adjusting tighteners rather than repeatedly relocating pegs.

Color

When French *poilus* charged to the Battle of the Frontiers in 1914, full of *cran* and élan, they got their red pantaloons and blue jackets shot off and belatedly understood why the Germans wore uniforms of field gray, the British of khaki (the Hindu word for "dusty"), and Robin Hood of forest green.

During the 1960s, backpackers, formerly blending into the landscape like Leatherstocking, similarly began charging to wild frontiers in hues meant to catch the eyes of sharpshooters (with cameras). Disclaiming exhibitionism, though, they argued that vivid colors make a lost hiker easier to find, that in wet climates an orange or red tent gives a warm feeling, that in hot climates a blue seems to blunt the fury of the sun.

Maybe so. However, just as a city's honking horns rack nerves and murder sleep, so does *color pollution* disrupt wilderness. Grass is meant to be green, and snow, white, not orange and red and yellow polka dots. From miles away the paint-pot tent leaps out, grabbing the reluctant eye of a hiker who otherwise might enjoy

the illusion of owning the whole valley. To enlarge a shrinking world, we go slower. To enwilden a crowd-madding world, we hide.

By the 1980s, the pickup truck having yielded to the bicycle and the Eigerboot to the running shoe, manufacturers began to respond to the demand for *earth tones*. Gaudy tents are *out*. *In*, again, are forest green, khaki, field gray.

Care

Immediately upon buying a tent, the hiker should set it up at home. Several purposes are served. He learns *how* to set it up, better here than on a stormy night in the wilds. He confirms that the vendor has included all the promised parts. Finally, he takes the first and essential step in tent maintenance: using a compound sold by a backpacking shop, he paints and seals the seams, a process to be repeated annually.

Fire is the chief threat to tents (and tarps). If sparks from blazing logs are blowing toward the shelter, either the fire should be damped

or the shelter moved. To repair spark holes, rips, and punctures, part of the tent kit should be repair tape. Cloth tape 2 inches wide with adhesive backing is recommended for polyethylene, coated nylon, and other nonporous materials; 2-inch ripstop tape is standard for ripstop nylon.

Generally speaking, a tent is not meant to be cooked in. Moisture from steaming pots adds enormously to interior wetness, commonly to an extent that cannot be alleviated by cross-ventilation or breathing out through the fabric. More dangerous with many stoves is the chance of a flare-up that might instantly melt a huge hole in the roof. Cooking is best done outside the tent, or at least in the vestibule, if any. Expeditioners may have to take the risk frequently, but backpackers rarely. (Nevertheless, there are wildland veterans who always cook in tents when wind frustrates the stove or bugs devil the chef, not to mention when the weather is plain lousy miserable. But they do so *very carefully*.)

To protect the tent floor from gumming by pitch and abrasion by rocks, it is wise always to place a lightweight poly sheet underneath.

A tent should never be washed but may be sponged off with soapy water occasionally; better, really, to let it acquire a dignified grime and character.

However, gritty dirt tracked or blown inside should be scrupulously swept out to avoid sandpapering the fabric. Fastidious hikers carry a small whisk broom for the purpose—and a sponge to mop up puddles.

Grit can so damage the zipper as to prevent the slide from closing, requiring a trip to the shop for repairs; a zipper must never be trampled, especially with dirty boots.

The tent is better stuffed in the carrying bag without first being rolled up, the easier procedure anyhow and one that avoids the formation of creases that may develop into lines of weakness.

Moisture inevitably accumulates in a tent during a trip, if not from blown-in rain or tracked-in water then from exhalations of human bodies. Nylon and other tent fabrics will mildew if packed away wet. Therefore, before being folded (loosely) for extended storage a tent should be erected in the yard, in dry weather—otherwise, in the basement or spare bedroom—and thoroughly air-dried. (And swept clean.)

A QUICK HISTORY OF MODERN TENTING

Whatever else a tent does, most owners demand above all that it keep out rain. Not so difficult with modern chemistry's better things for better living. However, when tent pores are so tight the rain can't pound in, how does body moisture breathe out? Since a human exhales a pint of water a night, in a sealed tent the interior is damp by morning, a swamp by the end of a three-day blow.

This was the dilemma of the *single-wall tent* wrestled with by designers from the era of Whymper's scrambles in the Alps. Periodically a miracle fabric was invented, claimed to bar exterior moisture and release the inner, and mountaineers cried, "Hallelujah!" Then, in a year or so, rejoicing subsided to mumbling and soon no more was heard.

Later in this chapter the most recent single-wall miracle is given its due. However, currently accepted universally (almost) as the remedy for prolonged rain is the *double-wall tent*. The inner, or main, tent has walls of lightweight, breathable nylon that let body moisture exhale freely, and a floor—extending several inches up the wall—

of tough, waterproof nylon. The door is zippered (in economy models, perhaps merely tied) and backed with bug netting. To minimize the condensation that occurs in any tent (nothing's perfect), there are one or more ventilator windows with storm flaps and bug netting. The outer tent, or rainfly, is of a lightweight, strong, waterproof nylon. When the only protection desired is against fog, wind, radiation heat loss, voyeurs, flying bugs and creeping beasties, the rainfly needn't be rigged. For hard rain it is rigged, at some distance from the inner tent to allow airflow space: farther away in warm weather, when sun protection may also be wanted; closer in cold weather, when warmth too is thus provided. In balmy weather the fly alone may be rigged, as a tarp, to keep the moon from shining in the eyes, the morning sun from baking the bag.

So is defined the basic standard nonmiracle tent carried by nearly every backpacker. But so diverse are they in actuality that one is reminded of the zoologist who finished writing a definition of a dog, looked out the window, and saw the neighborhood pack romping— a St. Bernard, a Mexican hairless, a borzoi, a dachshund, a dingo. After reflecting on what an odd neighborhood he lived in, the zoologist wondered, "How do they all know they're the same thing?" Not by looking, that's clear.

The Way We Were: Rooted in Earth

From Whymper to the 1970s, when a hiker said "tent" he meant "A-frame," a structure of that geometry ("inverted V" would have been better) supported by poles and pegs solidly sunk in the planet. A century of experimentation confirmed the design; countless person-nights from summer forests of North America to icy ledges near the summit of Mount Everest provided a rigorous field test. Manufacturers pursued refinements—zealously, frantically, rather pitifully; there was a sense they'd gone about as far as they could go, were trembling on the verge of The Tent that would outlast the Pyramid of Gizeh, the shelter from within which good hikers would be summoned for their reward on the Last Day.

This was the way we were during the first edition. Short shrift

Example of the traditional A-frame tent, poled, pegged, and guyed. Inset: *With rainfly rigged.*

was given a competing design considered to evince aerospace on the brain.

To the consternation of historians who thought the pace was exceeding the healthy rate of mankind's pulse, the new designs—the Moon tents—proliferated so rabbit-fast that the third edition demoted the earth-steady A-frame to the back of the chapter, just ahead of tarps (which in *their* time opened rather than closed the chapter).

Several more years, a fourth edition, and the A is being measured for a niche in the museum.

It does survive on the trail (so many hundreds of thousands were sold, and they are so long-lived), and it is the choice of respectful novices who say, "That's how a tent is supposed to look." The 1984 catalog of official Boy Scout equipment has several models, in the two-Scout size as low as $114, weighing 5 pounds. Taiwan offers a $55 A.

State-of-the-art manufacturers have gone out of the A business.

Few shops have a single example in stock. The experts mourn the fact, saying "The A is still a terrific tent, if you can find one," but this is a manual of the state of the art and the popular, so with an obituary photograph the A is sent to join the Trapper Nelson.

Where We Are: In the Middle of the Air

When, in the 1970s, the free-standing tent, a canopy hung from a self-supporting frame of stressed poles, emerged from the workshops of furtive eccentrics, and the meadows came into geodesic bloom, scholars suggested the phenomenon as an addendum to Charles Mackay's classic of the nineteenth century, *Extraordinary Popular Delusions and the Madness of Crowds*.

Many outfitters resisted, bewailing the folly of blithely casting away a century of slow, steady advance toward (and very near) perfection to run after the new fad, addled as Toad when he saw his first motorcar.

Defenders of the old faith told with glee of domes tipped over by high winds and rolled like basketballs across the tundra, snatched in the sky and carried off to Oz. They warned that winds easily withstood by the semirigid poles of the A-frame would set flexible poles dancing, creating a scene of stark terror in the interior.

Prophets of the new confessed early faults but said they had been overcome, that advanced designs withstood side loads excellently,

and in case of doubt, the free-stander could be solidly guyed and pegged. Further, winds that smack and flap and crack the flat walls of an A flow quietly around curved walls.

Defenders of the old objected to the cost and weight of free-standers; disciples of the new told how the reduction in number of poles to two or three, and the economies of production scale, had brought the two species so close that the old one gave up the ghost.

The disciples concede that early poles were undependable, that a single snapping or bending made the tent defunct, then inform the customer that improved poles are quite trustworthy. Carrying an extra section still isn't a bad precaution. A pole-repair sleeve, 5 inches long, 1 ounce, can be slipped over a break in a pole to provide support to trip's end.

As free-standers were debugged, their virtues won the contest. They are faster to set up than the A and, in the newer designs, are becoming steadily simpler. Fit the pole sections together, slip them through sleeves or collars, clip rainfly to tent frame (no separate rigging lines necessary), move in the furniture, and go to bed. If the site proves too sunny or bumpy, no need to derig, simply pick up the erected tent and move it. When leaving, shake it clean. In calm weather, no guy lines to tighten, no pegs to trip over.

Finally, the A's straight lines and sharp angles permit far less roomier interiors than the new curvaceous geometry with half again more cubic inches for equal floor area. Lying down is not mandatory for most of the people most of the time; everyone can sit up to lace boots and drink soup and play hearts.

TAXONOMY OF FREE-STANDING TENTS

The banishing of the A-frame from the backpacking shop has by no means reduced congestion in the tent department. The array is as large as ever and even more diverse, and the bewildered eye of the novice can see no way to decide which is best for him. However, two questions will quickly winnow the choices to a few: What is the *season of intended use? How many intended users?*

Answer a third obvious question—*how much money can be spent?*—

and of the total five acres of tents only a half acre remains to be further examined, to decide on the *shape*, which is what sets the taxonomist to stroking his beard.

Seasons of Use

Tents sometimes are categorized as *entry*, for car camping and short introductory hikes; *backpacking*, what the average reader of this book has in mind; and *winter*, or *expedition*, which a few will move to later on.

The most generally used classification is by time of year. Since the thoughts of beginners normally turn to backpacking in late spring, the tent aimed at *one/two seasons*, meaning summer and perhaps bits of spring and fall, often is described as for *entry* (as may be any very low-priced tent).

A new star is the *two/three-season* tent, going by several names, including *ultralight*, an adjective earned by denying any ambitions to cope with early spring or late fall.

The *three-season* tent is dominant, serving from the end of the old year's snows to the beginning of the new.

The *four-season* models confront a renewal of the Ice Age complacently.

Size

About 95 percent of all tents sold are for two or three persons. If labeled as "two-person," space suffices for two adults, perhaps with some gear left outside in giant poly bags or under a poly tarp. If "two-three-person," the two adults have more sit-up space and can keep more gear inside. A third adult may be squeezed in provided some of the gear is stored outside under the tarp; a mother and father can fit in one or even two small children. If "three-person," the capacity is three adults and gear or two parents and two middling kids.

When capacity goes beyond three, the steam calliope strikes up and the elephants march and the circus tent comes on the scene.

Shape

First to capture the imagination of the crowds was the *dome*, in a smaller version called the *wedge*. (A subspecies, the *geodesic dome*, is constructed of a series of interlocking triangles.) This is the geometry with the *most volume* for the least surface—the most air space for the least weight. The frame flexes with the wind (giving rise to the description "part dome, part bird") but does not, as did the earlier models with the too-soft poles, tend to invert.

The *tunnel* is long, giving plenty of room for gear and legs, has much the head room of a dome and a lower profile, and is more resistant to high winds. Ventilation is better than in a dome. The hoop method of support employs fewer poles, saving weight. This is the geometric configuration with the *most floor space* for the least surface.

The *free-standing A-frame* is roomier than the old A, has no sharp angles and earthy tension, the shape smoothed to an aerodynamic

Example of a small dome, or wedge, shown here without the rainfly rigged.

Example of the most popular style of free-standing tent, the dome. Inset: *With rainfly rigged.*

Example of a variant on the dome, the geodesic dome or geo-dome, shown here without the rainfly rigged.

Example of a tunnel. Inset: *With rainfly rigged.*

Example of a free-standing A-frame design. As with many free-standers, some pegging is desirable if not essential. Inset: *With rainfly rigged.*

Example of one among many asymmetrical designs, this one somewhere between a dome and a tunnel. Inset: *With rainfly rigged.*

semitunnel. A model using a hoop pole in the middle is a crossbreed between an A and a pure tunnel.

Then, the *asymmetricals*. Some that are called "domes" have been stretched out to let people 6½ feet long unhitch their knees. Some are between dome and tunnel. Some are "modified" or "tapered" tunnels, high at the head end, low at the foot—weight-saving, space-efficient, storm-sturdy.

As a generalization, the more the headroom (dome), the pleasanter in good to moderate weather; the lower the profile (tunnel), the more secure when gales blow; the more difficulty a hiker has deciding, the more interesting the asymmetricals.

EXAMPLES OF FREE-STANDING TENTS

One/Two-Person; One/Two-Season

Korea, Taiwan, and other nations unencumbered by the minimum wage closely examine articles for which superconsumers pay $150 and manufacture copies that sell for $50. The hiker who expects to go tripping only in summer, with at most one companion, and perhaps isn't entirely convinced he'll wish to do it more than a few times, might reasonably investigate the advertised specials of Handy-Dandy Super-Drugs and Volume Discount stores, accepting the possibility the waterproofing won't keep the rain out and the stitching may separate in a wind. Aside from that, such a tent may be a true bargain as an entry to trail nights.

A few tents in this class are of a higher order. An example is the REI Hideaway 1, a modified half dome, rated two-season, one/two-person: weight, 6½ pounds, price, $80.

One/Two-Person; Two/Three-Season (Ultralight)

A new breed of the 1980s (actually not so new—there were ancestors) has so fired the imaginations of catalogers they've not agreed

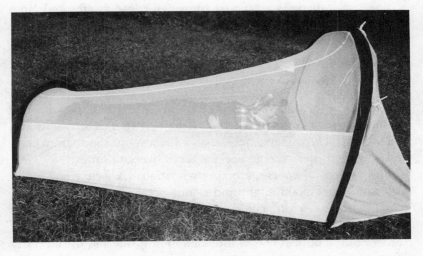

Example of a star-view tent (ultralight, tropical tent, bug tent). The person inside gazes out through a screen of no-see-um netting to swarms of mosquitoes and a heaven of stars. The integral rainfly, shown here rolled up and tied to the tent frame at the head end, can be spread out and pegged down in a matter of seconds.

on a single generic name. *Ultralight* applies because the features required by the times of snowing and blowing have been ruthlessly trimmed, giving not only low weight but quick rigging.

Tropical tent and *bug tent* are meaningful to those who have sought shelter from the sun on a baking plain and to those who have witnessed each column of heat rising from a steaming subalpine meadow carry with it millions of things with wings and stings. Finally, as tarp campers have ever reminded, the womb tent closes off the heavens; *star-view* is the description that is exciting the customers.

Though floor and lower walls are sturdy waterproof nylon fabric, the roof is netting, to keep bugs out and let the stars in. The rainfly, integral to the main tent and thus very quick to rig, is available to repel the rain or sun and to retain body-generated heat when the stars grow too cold. In regions where severe storms are unknown, rare, or of brief duration in the two/three seasons, warm nights are common, and bugs are on the move round the clock, this tent is a joy.

The usual shape is a tapered tunnel, for low weight and large skyview. A one/two-person model weighs 3¼–4¾ pounds, costs $130–$160. Two-person sizes run 4¼–5 pounds and $200–$225.

One/Three-Person; Three-Season

As for season of use, these tents can be trusted to cope with any conditions less extreme than the summit of Rainier or the South Col of Everest or a Tierra del Fuego williwaw—in short, anywhere, and anywhen, the average backpacker is likely to camp.

The sizings, of course, are approximations. A jockey and a ballerina on honeymoon might find a "one-person" tent commodious, while a "three-person" could cramp a solitary linebacker given to dreaming about quarterbacks. In choosing, the buyer must consider the size of the human bodies intended to fit inside and the intensity of their claustrophobia.

Most of the one-person models utilize Gore-Tex, since it is in this size the miracle functions best, and they will be treated in the miracle section below.

Example of a family circus tent, this one of dome design, spacious enough for perhaps four adults, or two adults and several small children and one dog. Inset: *With rainfly rigged.*

Tents classified as one/two-person are few, typically only one or two models being offered by a shop, if any. An example is the REI Half Dome, just over 5 pounds and $150.

Every manufacturer and shop puts the major emphasis in the area of greatest demand, the two-person tent. There are domes, tunnels, A-frames, and weirds, ranging from 3⅔ pounds (wow) to 7¾ pounds (whew) in weight and from $160 to $250 in price. The heavier the tent, perhaps the farther its capability reaches into the fourth season—or perhaps the more spacious it is—or perhaps the cheaper, exploiting less expensive and weightier materials.

In the three-person size the architects soar beyond constraints, and in the liberated upper atmosphere designs are more or less asymmetrical, giddy, thrilling. Weights and prices overlap the two-person class, but range higher, of course. Suggestive of the dispar-

ities that come from the competition between low weight and low price, the Sierra West asymmetrical dome is 6 pounds, $250, and the REI Hideaway II dome, 8 pounds and $100.

One/Three Person; Four-Season

Tents described as "moderate four-season" may weigh and cost no more than their three-season neighbors; terminology isn't that precise. The backpacker devoid of winter ambitions may benefit from studying these, for comparison with what he's buying, and even the "extreme four-season" for the esthetics, and perchance a bit of dreaming, as when, say, gazing upon the JanSport China Everest, for two/three person (15½ pounds, $500).

Circus Tent; Three-Season

Parents with more than the permissible 2.1 children may find that at a certain age and size they won't lie inert all night the way sardines are supposed to, yet aren't quite ready to go off to a separate tent to face the lions and tigers and bears. The "family" tent with plenty of wiggling room is particularly appreciated then, as well as during days of rain, when each squirming kid must be kept from bloody

war by being assigned an inviolable territory. In another sort of ménage, companionable adults may not wish to pair off but stay in a group—for bridge tournaments, recorder quartets. In either case, though the weight (and price) of a circus tent may seem formidable, the individual share is often less than with a multiplicity of two-person tents.

The succession of American baby booms has enormously enlarged the circus offerings, with models ranging in size from four-person to six-person. The array includes domes, hexagons, free-standing A's, and Taj Mahals—only yurts and teepees are lacking. They weigh as much as 15 pounds, or as low as 11, and the cost ranges from $175 for a four-person tent to $350 for a five-person to $450 for a six-person. The prospective purchaser needs to get inside the tent, lie down, sit up, squirm around, deal a hand of hearts; visualize living there on a windy night or a rainy day with a band of children or friends; study the weight per person; check the price tag.

A person may wish someday simply to see, if never own, the Bill Moss Trillium, centered on a sociability area from which radiate three carrels, each a two-person compartment with separate entrance, a six-person pleasure dome that would grace the skyline of Xanadu. Weight—a mere 14 pounds. Cost—if you have to ask, you can't afford it.

Something Completely Different: Gore-Tex

The Gore-Tex principle is that body heat pushes water vapor out through the fabric—of the clothing (Chapter 9) or sleeping-bag cover (Chapter 11). The problem in using it for tents is that much of the time the bodies are inside sleeping bags, keeping their heat to themselves. Moreover, in warm weather and high humidity (as, say, summer in the Appalachians or on an ocean beach), there is no "push" because wet air inside can't be forced into wet air outside. Further, in freezing weather the pores clog with frost, breathing ceases, and the pint of water perspired per person per night swamps the tent floor.

Nevertheless, designers have persevered. The simple solution is to keep the tent very small to help the "push." No nonsense, here, about sitting-up space and elbow room. The shapes are few, mostly tapered tunnels. Capacity is limited to two persons—and they must be two persons exceedingly considerate and tolerant or who like each other a lot.

Example of a Gore-Tex single-wall tent, kept chummily small, almost of bivy-sack size, in order for the "heat pump" to work.

The compensations are several. Being single-wall tents and kept small, they are light on the back and very easy to rig. Thanks to the aerodynamic shape—and the single wall—they spill fierce winds and shed heavy snowfalls, and are applauded for Arctic winters. The absence of a rainfly means one less thing to worry about in a hard blow. Though usually designated four-season, Gore-Tex tents might better be called two-season—winter plus bits of late fall and early spring.

Not every innovator has given up on Gore-Tex for large tents; a few spacious domes and the like are on the market. The jury is still out, though most members have decided how they'll probably vote.

Not every innovator thinks Gore-Tex is anything but a tribute to the maxim of J. P. Barnum ("one born every minute"). The leading skeptic has long been Jack Stephenson, whose Warmlite tents are single-wall. A rear vent close to the floor lets in cold dry (winter) air; a front vent by the roof lets out warm wet (from the bodies) air. The "push" of human heat provides flow-through ventilation. Interestingly, Marmot Mountain Works hedges its bet, using Gore-Tex but also low-high vents—and saying the flow-through is more important than the miracle!

Wherever it is used, Gore-Tex skyrockets the cost—in tents, perhaps $100 or more over a comparable product without it. However, the prices of some are within reach of the common man, and at attractive weights. Several examples are the Early Winters Light Dimension, 3¾ pounds, $300; Marmot Twilight (described as a bivy sack for two, meaning a very small tent), 3¾ pounds, $270. These are not intended for the depths of winter.

In the mid-range of weight and price are the Early Winters Winterlight 4¾ pounds, $350; and the REI LR2-GT, which with the optional vestibule recommended for winter is 5 pounds, $370.

The Marmot Taku weighs under 5 pounds, very little for a structure built to withstand the worst Aleutian howlers can throw at it, and costs $450.

Bivy Sack

Sleeping-bag covers (Chapters 11) have been around as long as sleeping bags, simple add-ons for extra warmth. Bivouac bags or covers are equally venerable, carried by climbers for nights on the Great North Walls. With the arrival of Gore-Tex, the covers/bags became able not only to reduce heat loss but to repel mists and rains—a new species of shelter, almost (but not quite) a tent, the Gore-Tex bivy sack.

The beginnings were simple envelopes weighing about 1 pound—the old bag covers plus the Gore-Tex. Subsequent models grew more commodious, a very few expanding to a two-person size, properly considered a tent. In some the floor is of coated nylon for durability, perhaps at the expense of inner wetness from body moisture, and only the roof is Gore-Tex laminate; in others the laminate is all around, perhaps at the expense of floor durability. On a night merely dewy the sack can be crawled into as a bag cover, keeping

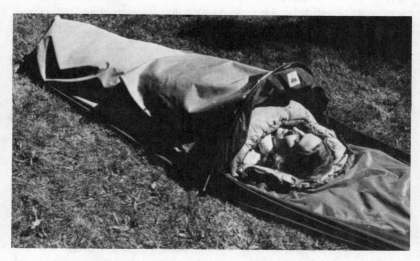

Example of a Gore-Tex bivy sack, here used only for warmth and to keep the dew off the sleeping bag. When needed, the bug netting can be zipped in place over the sleeper's head, and also the head of the "roof."

out the wet and adding some 10°F of warmth. In wind and rain the fiberglass wands and the guy lines support a hood for headroom, for eating breakfast or gazing smugly out into gray dripping heather. Bug netting is standard, and there's a mercy. Most models cost around $150, weigh a bit below or above 2 pounds.

Make no mistake—the sack is not a tent. One could save a person's life in a cold storm, but after a couple of days inside he might not care. However, a lone hiker can dispense with tent or tarp; when morning comes he can crawl out in the storm and run for it.

TARPS

Three species of hikers habitually sleep under tarps. One is the creaky Old Crock whose 7- by 11-foot war-surplus life-raft sail is enshrined in memory with his Model A and who always has felt tents are for (1) winter, (2) nights in the summit crater of Mount Rainier, and (3) girls. The second is neither creaky nor old but has been on the trails long enough to comprehend that tent-campers are retreaters-to-the-womb, that tarp-campers, livers-with-nature, intimately know not only wind and bugs but also sights of moonlit clouds and shooting stars and dawn, scents of pine needles and flowers and grasses and prowling skunks, sounds of little feet scurrying in the darkness over sleeping bags and faces. They experience more of everything except claustrophobia, and in retrospect their wilderness nights are as memorable as their days. The third tarper is the beginning backpacker who compares weights and prices and decides (shrewd chap) that tents are for rich donkeys.

These are the free spirits, a select band, smaller and more select by the year, who ask protection only against downward rain, heat loss and dew accumulation through radiation, and the hot sun. The creepy-crawlies they accept, perhaps becoming inordinately fond of beetles, and the buzzing wings they foil with a "habitat" of no-see-um netting (Chapter 15). Mild breezes they welcome, and the gentle mists they may carry, bathing the brow. And as part of the bargain they accept the occasional Armageddon when forces of evil

rage in the night, chewing up tarps and spitting them out, sending naked-to-the-sky refugees fleeing through the tempest, whimpering.

Tarps are inconspicuous in today's backpacking shop or absent and, even if in the shop, are often omitted from the catalog. Merchandising space costs money; low-price, low-sales products don't pay their share of the rent. Equally prejudicial is that by 1980s standards the tarp is ignominiously low-tech. (*Sic transit gloryosky* for the sheets of war-surplus nylon that in the late 1940s were the highest of tech.)

As a consequence, novices are repeatedly reminded that tarps are cheap; tarps are good enough shelter for a large proportion of the world's wildland camps; tarps are funky. But nobody tells them how to get into tarpery, and after a catastrophe or two they buy a tent that costs and weighs five times more but comes with a set of instructions. Herein, then, is a treatise on tarps—to preserve, for the discriminating few, the alternative.

The Tarp Kit

A canny old tarper can find any number of waterproof plastic sheets sufficient for the purpose. The beginner, however, is liable to be led astray in a hardware store by lightweight films that cost very little and aren't worth it, coming apart at the touch of a twig or a breeze. The backcountry is littered with shredded plastic abandoned during flight in a wild night, subsequently chewed on by small animals, some of whom die, poisoned.

Backpacking shops, if they stock tarps at all, do a proper job of it. At the low end of the price range they have polyethylene sheets 0.004 inch (4 mils) thick, a translucent white to reflect sunlight; Visqueen is a common trade name. A 9- by 12-foot size weighs 2 pounds, costs about $8, handsomely shelters two adults, a child, a dog, and packs. The 12- by 12-foot size, for two adults, four kids, and two dogs, weighs 3 pounds, costs about $10.

These tarps lack grommets, and a means must therefore be devised of attaching guy lines to the fabric. Bunching up the corners and wrapping lines around is simple, but a four-corner support, though adequate in mists and breezes, cannot hold the tarp close to the ground in a wind or prevent it from sagging under a heavy rain. A better improvisation, one that permits attachment of lines anywhere along the tarp edge, is to push a pine cone, rock, or wad of paper against one side of the fabric to produce a bulge on the opposite side, then wrap a rigging line tightly around the bulge. By far the best method is the Visklamp, sold by any shop that sells tarps, though it may be kept under the counter with the Stephenson catalogs. The device consists of a small rubber ball and a metal circle

the diameter of the ball, one side of the circle extending out in a narrower extension. The rubber ball is pushed against the fabric, carrying it through the circle; ball and fabric are then slid out of the circle into the narrower extension, where they wedge in securely, firmly connecting Visklamp to tarp and providing a "grommet." The Visklamp costs $1.50. For windproof rigging of a large tarp, eight are required, as discussed in the following section.

A step up in weight and price, and strength and convenience, is a poly tarp that has nylon-thread reinforcements imbedded in the plastic and grommets at corners and along sides. The 10- by 12-foot size is $14 and 4 pounds; the 12- by 14-foot, $20 and 5¾ pounds.

Poly decays in sunlight faster than nylon; a tarp of coated nylon is initially costlier but in the long run more economical than a succession of plastics. Equipped with eight grommets, the 8- by 10-foot size, (two persons and gear) is 2 pounds, $26; the 10- by 12-foot, 4 pounds, $36.

Ripstop nylon can be lighter for equal strength, so that a 9- by 12-foot tarp weighs only 1¼ pounds (but costs $48); at 10 feet by 12, 2¾ pounds, $56.

High-tech has not utterly shunned the tarp; the wonder of the age, fit company for his Trillium, is the Bill Moss Parawing, a hyperbolic paraboloid cut on the bias. The 19- by 19-foot on the diagonal size, spacious enough for a wine-tasting party, weighs 5 pounds, costs $162, dirt-cheap as hyperbolic paraboloids cut on the bias go.

To tarp and grommets (built-in or Visklamp), the tarper adds:

- A 50-foot length of strong, not-too-stretchy rope to serve as the *ridge line*. Ample for the purpose is ¼-inch braided nylon, breaking strength 1,200 pounds; under ½ pound, $5.
- A 100-foot hank of ⅛-inch braided nylon, 260-pound test, to be cut into *guy lines*—(and bootlaces, lashings for broken packs, and dog leashes); a bit more than ¼ pound, $5.
- A roll of 2-inch *cloth tape* with adhesive backing to repair rips and holes, notably those caused by flying campfire embers (tarpers have a proclivity for wood fires), and to reinforce lines of developing weakness.
- Six or eight *pegs*, weighing and costing little. The least expensive are skewer stakes, the most versatile are high-impact plastic, 9 inches long. Though stakes can be improvised by whittling sticks, rarely is this possible in the middle of the night when lightning flashes and hail pounds. Frequently some of the guy points can be bushes, rocks, or roots but a half-dozen pegs make the tarper independent of luck.

Rigging the Tarp

As the trail day is ending and camping time is nigh, the tarper—unlike the tenter, who is self-sufficient—keeps an eye out for help from the terrain.

The simplest-quickest design is the *shed roof*, requiring only two trees reasonably close together to support the high side; pegs anchor the low side at two to four points. The shed fends off misty rains and, with the low side pegged flush to the ground and the high side faced leeward, even downpours if the wind blows consistently; gusting and eddying and swirling make the shed a sail.

Polyethylene tarp rigged as shed roof, adequate protection against gentle rains, radiation heat loss, and glaring sun.

The experienced tarper, if he feels the need for any shelter at all (experienced tarpers lie out under the stars as often as possible, which means they often do their rigging when the stars dissolve), erects the *A-tent*, as follows:

Step one: Locate two trees, or a tree and a tall boulder, or two boulders, some 10 to 20 feet apart, suitable at a height of 6 or 8 feet from the ground for attaching ends of the ridge line. There must, of course, be sleepable terrain between—not too sloping or rocky or bushy.

Step two: Tie the ridge line at the two ends and draw it taut. (As time passes and a load is placed on it, some stretching will occur.)

Step three: Drape the tarp over the ridge line, the longer dimension parallel to the line.

Step four: From the two grommets (or the two Visklamps you have affixed) that now lie on the ridge line, run guy lines to the end supports and tighten them to draw the tarp to its full length along the ridge. (Failing this, the tarp will sag along the ridge line, reducing the protected ground by several feet at each end.)

Step five: Tie guy lines to grommets (or Visklamps), then to pegs, and step or pound these into the ground. In windy weather the lines should be short to keep pegs close to the tarp edge to hold it down; in calm weather they can be longer for a more spacious interior. For still more space, when weather permits, bushes or trees or other anchor points high off the ground may be substituted for ground pegs.

The despair of the novice is terrain that volunteers no help, no natural feature taller than driftwood or a tuft of grass. Here the canny old tarper reaches in his bag of tricks and pulls out the *bipod*.

Step one: Scout around for four poles, 5–7 feet long, swept down to the cirque floor by avalanche, washed up on the creek bank by

Polyethylene tarp rigged as A-tent, using Visklamps at the corners to attach guy lines and also at both ends of the ridgeline to keep the tarp from sagging inward. In windy weather the tarp edges should be flush with the ground and held by three or more guy lines per edge.

flood, thrown onto the beach by waves. The poles need not be particularly sturdy; they can be crooked and limby and limber— almost anything long enough and not thoroughly rotten will work.

Step two: Tie one end of the ridge line to a peg and stamp it in the ground.

Step three: Stand a pair of poles upright in the A (inverted V) mode and wrap the ridge line around the junction, two turns horizontally and two vertically, lashing together a bipod.

Step four: From this bipod stretch the ridge line far enough to accommodate the tarp's longest dimension plus a foot or so extra on either end.

Step five: Lash the ridge line to the second pair of poles—the second bipod.

Step six: Draw the ridge line taut, tie the end to a second peg, and pound it into the ground.

Step seven: Rig the tarp over the ridge line as described before.

With this treatise in hand, nobody has any excuse for buying tents simply because they are there. Let tarps now be fruitful, and go forth and multiply.

13

Kitchen Gear

Time was when hikers planning wildland kitchens were inspired by a popular genre of American art, the calendar painting. There, all in florid color, they saw a band of hardy woodsmen gathered around a wall tent and massive stone fireplace, wearing pistols and Bowie knives, surrounded by double-bitted ax, chopping block, crosscut saw, rifles, fishing poles, cast-iron frying pans, iron kettle, two-gallon coffeepot, sides of bacon and sacks of flour and salt and beans, table and chairs hewn from logs, laundry lines strung between trees, antelope suspended from a pole tripod, smokehouse full of trout, faithful Indian guide skinning out a bear—and the herd of horses or fleet of canoes that carried the ton of gear and supplies.

Led astray by such portraits of a largely imaginary past, many a person once sought to duplicate, to the limit of his carrying capacity, the ideal frontier kitchen. However, that old ideal is as long extinct as passenger pigeons darkening the sky and bison blanketing the prairies. The new ideal, that of the modern ethical hiker, is a kitchen kept as simple as possible to avoid damage to fragile ecosystems. And his back as well.

After the anguish of selecting boots, pack, sleeping bag, and tent, the beginner can relax when assembling his kitchen. The few, light, inexpensive elements are (1) a fire, (2) cooking pots, (3) eating tools, and (4) miscellaneous accessories. A number of handy gadgets are available for gracious living, but the novice does well to start with nothing but the basics and add frills very gradually, if at all.

FIRE—WITHOUT STOVE

Wood Fire

As explained in Chapter 4, the backpacker is by necessity growing accustomed to camps and kitchens lacking that old symbol of the wilderness home, the wood fire. It's sad to see grand traditions recede into ancient history, but the world changes and only sometimes for the better. Still, a wood fire is not yet everywhere morally a sin or legally a crime. To cook with wood several bits of equipment should be carried.

Cooking with a wood fire, using a lightweight metal grate. On driftwood-littered beaches, wood fires will long be possible in good conscience, unlike many other provinces of American trail country.

Matches, of course, a main supply in a poly bag, an emergency reserve in a waterproof box of foil, plastic, or metal. Regular kitchen matches, if kept dry, strike easily on a dry rock. Waterproof matches won't ignite if the striker on the box is damp. Over long stretches of wet weather all matches get soggy and useless; a *butane lighter*, ever faithful, may be no frill but essential.

Gadgeteers may be intrigued by a "metal match" or "flint stick" that, when struck or scraped, emits a shower of high-temperature sparks. For sport on a layover day, a few hours with an official Boy Scout kit for making fire by friction ($6) or with flint and steel ($4) will instill respect for ancestors, even awe.

Hikers depending on a wood fire in wet country should carry one or another sort of *fire starter*. Nothing beats a splash of kerosene or white gas, should these be in supply for stove use; the splash must be small, *must* be made before the first match is struck, and *never* over so much as a single glowing ember lest flames race to the fuel container and blow up the camp. Stove fuel lacking, there are solid hydrocarbon "fuel tablets," jellies that squeeze from tubes, wax-impregnated fiber squares, and so on. Among the most efficient are Esbit Heat Tabs, Fiber Squares, Fire Ribbon, Fire Up, Zip Fire, Firelite, Flame-O-Magic, and Sterno.

The easiest way to cook on a wood fire is with a metal *grate* or grill. Weight should be less than ½ pound, the width narrow enough to slip easily into a pack (carried in a nylon or poly bag to avoid sooting the interior), and legs omitted as worthless. Few, if any, outdoor shops stock usable products. The best—a rectangle of three stainless-steel tubes 15 inches long and 5 inches wide, weighing 3½ ounces and costing $7—seems recently to have vanished from the mercantile face of the earth. However, in the kitchenware section of a variety store excellent grates can be found, weighing and costing next to nothing, though when the plating burns off they rust and must be replaced. They are called *cake racks*.

Recommended in some jurisdictions is a *fire pan*; one example is a cake pan 8½ by 12½ inches at the bottom, with sides 2½ inches high, flaring to 10 by 14 inches at the top. Though the pan does not eliminate soil sterilization and charcoaling, it confines the fire to a modest size and simplifies the subsequent scattering of ashes. Where established fire rings are officially condoned, a pan serves no purpose, but in virgin-seeming sites it helps achieve "no-trace camping. One has to wonder, though, whether so dinky a fire is better than none at all.

Solid Chemical Fuels

The fuels mentioned above as fire starters can be used for rudimentary cooking by igniting them between two rocks arranged to support a pot or cup. A person intending to use the fuels regularly will enjoy an *Esbit pocket stove*, weighing next to nothing and giving wind easy pot support.

Though these fuels generate relatively little heat, they can serve well enough for a hiker dining alone, wishing only to warm a can of Vienna sausage or coddle an egg. In wind-free conditions some boil a cup of water in 5 or 6 minutes or less; the winner in tests by the REI Quality Control Department was Fire Ribbon, in 3½ minutes. In other tests the Esbit stove and heat tabs boiled a quart of water in 8 minutes.

STOVES

Backcountry cookery used to be on a wood fire or a Primus, the name of that company being a synonym for stove, no other caring to bother with so minute a market. A few Primus stoves survive, though thanks to corporate rearrangements now mainly under the name of Optimus. However, a market no longer tiny has drawn the interest of competitors and for every Primus-Optimus relegated to the museum for lack of demand, several new models reach shop shelves.

In choosing from among the dozens, the backpacker must ignore the heavy ones, intended for car camping, canoe camping, and other trips where weight doesn't matter, and focus on those of 2 pounds and under. He must then decide which fuel he prefers: white gas, kerosene, butane, or several fuels in a single versatile stove.

Cooking on a stove, no fuss, no muss. When the party leaves, no sign of its stay will remain except temporarily flattened grass

The accompanying table compares the weight, cost, and efficiency of the currently most popular stoves, and the following pages discuss the characteristics of the individual fuels and the virtues of the different models. First, however, some general observations.

Cooking With Liquid Hydrocarbons

Through all the generations of Primus dominance the choice in fuels was between white gas and kerosene. In the early 1960s butane stoves appeared in America and for a time outsold all others. Subsequently, however, new gas stoves regained popularity for that fuel. Kerosene continued to have devoted adherents. Then arrived the multifuel stoves, some of which can use white gas, automotive gas, kerosene, stove oil, or anything else that originates in an oil well.

At present, a representative large backpacking shop finds that of its five best sellers, three, including the top two, use white gas, the third spot is shared by a multifuel and a butane, but that the second rank of stoves is well entrenched, new inventions are arriving hourly, and the situation continues in flux.

BACKPACKING STOVES

Stove Model	Approximate Price, without fuel or fuel carrier	Pot Stability	Stove Stability	Compactness	Cold-weather Use	Ease of Operation	Water Boiled per Pint of Fuel (quarts)	Average Boiling Time* (minutes)	Burning Time at Maximum Flame (minutes)	Fuel Capacity (pints)	Stove Weight Without Fuel (ounces)
White gas											
Coleman Peak 1	$37	G	E	G	G	G	29.8	3.4	70	0.69	29.2
MSR Firefly	$60	E	E	G	G	G	28.3	2.9	106‡	†	18.2†
MSR WhisperLite	$40	E	E	E	E	G	28.7	3.8		†	12
Svea 123R	$40	E	P	E	E	G	23.6	4.1	29	0.30	18.2
Optimus 8R	$44	F	G	G	F§	G	22.4	4.1	23	0.25	22.4
Optimus 324 Rider	$40	P	F	G	F§	G	24.2	3.9	33	0.35	24.4
Kerosene											
Optimus Camper 00	$50	E	E	E	E	F	27.8	3.7	107	1.04	27.6
Butane											
Gaz C-206	$21 / $80	G	F	F	F#	E	21.5‖	8.5	183	‖	11.6

Stove Model	Stove Weight Without Fuel (ounces)	Fuel Capacity (pints)	Burning Time at Maximum Flame (minutes)	Average Boiling Time* (minutes)	Water Boiled per Pint of Fuel (quarts)	Ease of Operation	Cold-weather Use	Compactness	Stove Stability	Pot Stability	Approximate Price, without fuel or fuel carrier
Multifuel											
MSR X-GK											
Kerosene	18.8†	†	116‡	3.0	30.0	F	E	G	E	F	
White Gas	18.4		128‡	3.4	29.2	G	E	G	E	F	
Optimus 199											$60
Kerosene	31.4	0.25	27	4.4	24.5	F	G	G	G	G	
White Gas	31.4	0.25	32	6.0	21.3	G	F	G	G	G	
Alcohol	31.6	0.25	37	13.2	11.2	G	P	G	G	G	

NOTE: The stoves in the table are currently the most popular among the models available. The tests were conducted by REI Quality Control Department.

E = Excellent; G = Good; F = Fair; P = Poor.

* Water at 70°F in covered pot, in still air at sea level.

† MSR fuel bottle: weight 4 ounces, capacity 1.29 pints; 0.6-liter Sigg Bottle: weight 2.6 ounces, capacity 1 pint; 1-liter Sigg Bottle: weight 3.9 ounces, capacity 1.97 pints.

‡ With MSR fuel bottle.

§ Stove must be insulated from snow or cold ground unless Optimus Mini-Pump is used.

|| 6.7-fluid ounce cartridge (empty weight, 3.3 ounces).

Fuel cartridge must be kept above 30°F.

Fuel cost is not the factor it once was because none is any longer really cheap; in any event, the amounts used are so small that even with the costliest fuel the average hiker's outlay for cooking during an entire summer would run about the same as for a package of freeze-dried porkchops.

Fuel availability must be considered. Under such brand names as Coleman Fuel, white gas is sold in sporting-goods stores and department stores across America; outside the United States, though, it scarcely exists. Kerosene, sold everywhere in America, is also the universal fuel of the Third World and thus an excellent choice in Mexico, South America, and Nepal. Butane cartridges are sold in Europe at every grocery store, hostel, and campground and are ever more available in underdeveloped nations, competing with kerosene.

Of minor consequence on short hikes but very important on the long ones are *fuel consumption* and *heat output*, as shown in the table. These statistics are basic to the determination of *fuel needs*. In theory a supper for three persons, at low to medium elevations, in reasonably calm weather, can be cooked—if quite simple and carefully scheduled—in about the time required to bring 3 quarts of water to a boil, each quart separately. That is, first a pot of soup, then a main course, then the water for coffee, cocoa, or tea. Thus, to use the Coleman Peak 1 as example, burning time for supper might be as little as 12 minutes, perhaps half that for breakfast. One 0.69-pint filling of a Coleman, with a burning time of 70 minutes, therefore might cook (on the average) four suppers and four breakfasts, and a full tank plus a full pint fuel carrier would suffice for a three-person 9- or 10-day trip.

That's the theory; the practice is conducted where foods perhaps have to be boiled a while, especially at higher elevations, where some gas is spilled, some burning time wasted, and the wind is blowing. The theoretical figure might best be doubled—*two* pints of extra gas allowed.

Beginners on short trips should carry plenty of fuel, far more than required, and learn how much they need for the long trips. Studying the table is also helpful.

Gas Stoves

With the exception of the multifuel model discussed below, gas stoves don't burn automobile fuels, which contain lead—or, if unleaded, other additives—that clog the mechanisms. The proper fuel is pure naphtha, better known as "white gas," sold under such names as Coleman Fuel, Blazo, and Pressure Appliance Fuel. Unlike the white gas that used to be sold by gas stations, these products are

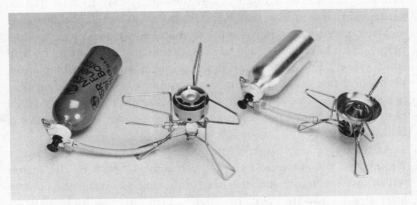

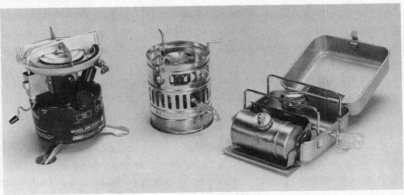

Popular gas stoves. Top, left to right: *MSR Firefly, MSR Whisperlite.* Bottom, left to right: *Coleman Peak 1, Svea 123R, Optimus 8R.*

filtered clean and stabilized with additives to stay good for three years in a sealed can or six months after being opened.

The flash point—ignition temperature—is − 40°F, making it the easiest of backpacker fuels to light and the most dangerous. Molotov cocktails used to disable Tiger tanks; a mishandled gas stove can wipe out a tent.

Advantages are that spilled fuel evaporates readily, not soaking into clothes and gear; the same fuel used in operation is used for priming; and in the United States the fuel is easy to buy. Disadvantages are that spillage can be catastrophic, as can sloppy priming.

The current best seller is the Coleman Peak 1, weight 2 pounds, price $37. The stove is easy to start thanks to a built-in pump and quicklighter. The flame ring is large and the burner control sensitive, permitting fast boiling or slow simmering as wanted. Pot support is stable, noise level, low. Boiling speed is faster than average (even better with a Sigg Cooker, discussed later.) However, the stove is bulky and heavy.

As for operating characteristics, when starting it in even a slight wind, turn the stove on before the match is struck or the match will blow out before fuel reaches the burner. Turning the control lever slightly toward "run" or "high" during preheating helps keep the flame alive, but turning to "run" position too soon may cause flooding and a scary flare-up. Though priming is not required, in a wind a small amount of fuel ignited on top of the burner helps get things going.

Second in recent sales has been the MSR Firefly, 15 ounces, $60. Add 4.5 ounces and $5 for the 22-ounce-capacity aluminum fuel bottle essential for operation. (A fuel bottle is, of course, also essential to any other stove on any trip longer than a weekend.) Despite the Rube Goldberg appearance, the stove is quick-starting (a pump is in the fuel bottle), fully adjustable from simmer to roar, and boils 1 quart of water in under 3 minutes. The tripod base and pot support is stable. The main objections are that the operation is very noisy and the wind screen flimsy, perhaps minor quibbles in view of the fact it's one of the few stoves that function at all in a high wind.

A maintenance kit, $6, permits repairs in the field. A suspension kit, $12, lets the stove be suspended from a tree branch or piton.

New on the market and predicted to replace the Firefly is the MSR WhisperLite, 12 ounces (including pump), $40. The stove is cheaper and lighter than the Firefly, boils water nearly as fast, is so compact it can fold up and fit in a cooking pot, and is *quiet*.

Still selling well to sentimentalists is the old favorite, Svea 123R, 15 ounces, $40, the package including a wind screen and a small pot that forms a cover and a pot lifter. Priming is necessary, though not pumping; however, the Optimus Mini-Pump, $9, helps start the stove in cold weather. The boiling speed is slower than average, tank capacity is small, which means frequent halts to refill.

Another ancient favorite somehow managing to hang on is the Optimus 8R, 1½ pounds, $44, which packs in a convenient metal box, the lid forming a windscreen. The stove starts easily in wind by use of the screen, requires no pumping (though the Optimus Mini-Pump is a help), has a boiling speed slower than average, and a small fuel capacity. Stove stability is good, but the pot support is so narrow the soup pot can easily topple.

A new entry from the old firm is the Optimus 324 Rider, 1½ pounds, $40. Intended as the answer to the Coleman Peak 1, it has half the fuel capacity, lower efficiency, less stability, and in the field has been found to be not as reliable as the Optimus-Primus stoves of former years.

Using a White Gas Stove (Some Remarks Applicable to Other Stoves)

The fuel for gas stoves (and kerosene as well) must be transported in a leakproof metal container—not glass, which breaks, and not poly bottle, leakproof for many other liquids but not fuel. With MSR stoves the fuel carrier is also the stove's fuel chamber.

The favorite is an *aluminum fuel bottle* with the standard screw plug replaced by a *Super Pour Spout* ($4) that is plug and pouring spout all in one, eliminating the need for a funnel to avoid spillage. The bottle is very sturdy and fits neatly in an outer pack pocket—the best place to carry fuel, since some fumes inevitably escape, and if within the

Aluminum fuel bottle, the standard screw plug replaced by a Super Pour Spout for non-spill pouring.

pack, permeate food and clothing. The bottle should never be filled to the brim. Leave an air space of at least 1½ inches to allow for the expansion of fuel if warmed in the sun; otherwise, the bottle neck could rupture. The plain-finish 0.6-liter bottle weighs 4 ounces and sells for about $4.50; the liter size weighs 5 ounces and costs a bit more. Lacquered bottles are corrosion-resistant.

Before firing up any stove the camper must read the instructions, follow them. None is proof against a resolute fool.

The first step with a gas or kerosene stove is to fill the tank—but to no more than 75 percent of capacity; with a too-full tank the fuel lacks proper room to build vapor pressure for optimum operation. Also, when a gas stove gets hot, the expanding fuel shoots from the burner in a frightening flame, leaks from the cap, and ignites, making a generally hectic kitchen. In the case of kerosene, a too-full tank prevents bleeding air to the outside to lower the flame.

The next step is to clean the fire hole. Many gas stoves have a *built-in self-cleaner*, a rack and pinion device; turn the knob and tiny bits of soot or whatever are pushed out through the nipple. When a stove malfunctions, the hiker's typical reaction is to disassemble the self-cleaner, usually a mistake because a failure to reassemble it correctly results in fuel leaking out around the burner rim. Any shop that sells stoves can give simple over-the-telephone instructions for getting the teeth in the proper grooves.

Some models (the MSR Firefly and XGK) are equipped instead with a *separate cleaning wire*. This should be plunged two or three times into the gas vent in the burner head to ensure free passage for the vaporized fuel. The wire pushes tiny trash out of the way; however, interior pressure may push large trash back to the vent once operation commences. When a stove grows impossibly cranky it is usually because of such chunks; the cleaning wire avails naught and the only recourse is to remove the nipple and clean out the cavity below, as well as the orifice in the nipple.

A gas stove with a *built-in pump and quicklighter* (Coleman Peak 1, Optimus 324) is safe when used correctly but unforgiving to the careless. The instructions must be followed precisely; failure to do so can lead to all sorts of troubles, including a terrifying fireball.

A stove with a *built-in pump but no quicklighter* (MSR Firefly and X-GK) is started by opening the valve a few seconds to run a small amount of fuel into the priming cup, then closing the valve and lighting the priming fuel. As it burns low, open the valve slightly until the stove burns with a blue flame. The valve may then be fully opened.

A *no-pump stove* (Svea 123R, Optimus 8R) operates on self-pressurization from heat. The first step in start-up is to preheat the vaporizing tube located between the tank and the burner head. One method is to extract gas from the tank or fuel bottle with an eye-dropper, fill the small depression at the base of the vaporizing tube, and (with the control valve in closed position for safety) ignite. (Alcohol is much cleaner, since it leaves no soot.) When the outside gas (or alcohol) has nearly burned off, open the control valve; with the gas in the vaporizing tube now heated to the vaporization point, the stove—maybe—roars into life. If not (as perhaps in cold wind), try again. If the priming flame goes out before the burner lights,

strike another match (or flick the butane lighter). The goal is to get
the stove hot enough to vaporize the fuel before it comes out of the
nipple.

Useful as the Optimus Mini-Pump often is, in the hands of a
sloppy operator it can turn a Jekyll of a stove into a Hyde of a
bomb. Hikers in ordinary spring-summer-fall conditions never need
it and shouldn't bother. Climbers and cross-country skiers and others who travel much at high altitudes or in the cold (25°F and below)
may well find it indispensable—but must take pains to learn safe
usage. The proper procedure is as follows: Attach the Mini-Pump
to the stove; pump no more than two or three strokes (at 0°F and
below, several more may be needed); let enough gas drip down to
fill the priming cup; close the control valve to halt fuel flow; continue
with the normal start-up as described above. If during cooking the
stove starts to sputter, and the tank is not nearing empty, give the
pump two or three strokes. *Do not overpump*—better a late supper
than an explosion.

In windy weather the cooling may make pressure generation difficult and gusts may repeatedly blow out the flame, requiring the
stove to be shielded by rocks, logs, or aluminum foil. However, the
shield must not be so effective as to risk the stove overheating and
blowing the safety valve. A stove must never be buried in dirt or

tightly walled by rocks and logs. A Svea must never be used with its own windscreen inside a Sigg Cooker—or a meltdown will result.

On wet ground or snow the tank of any stove may need bottom insulation to maintain pressure; a small square of closed-cell foam of the sort used for sleeping pads may be carried for this purpose.

For several reasons the flame of any stove—but especially one burning gas—should be regulated by the control valve to somewhat less than maximum output:

First, flame pouring out around the sides of the cooking pot wastes heat and fuel.

Second, overheating of a gas stove can blow the safety valve. Usually the valve prevents the tank from exploding like a bomb, but the scene is only a little less dramatic when a valve lets go, releasing vapor which instantly ignites in a 3-foot stream of fire. When this happens, the proper action is to kick the stove off into the weeds or run like hell.

Third, the major cause of stove malfunction in the Svea 123 and Optimus 8R is a scorched wick. The cotton wick draws up fuel from the tank into the vaporizing tube, where, on contact with hot metal, vaporization occurs. If a stove operating wide open and very hot abruptly runs out of fuel, the now-dry wick is scorched and loses wicking capacity. The relit stove sputters and stutters.

Gas stoves—and stoves in general—are simple contrivances but tricky, and only practice makes perfect. The beginner should try his under ideal conditions, such as in the yard at home, before depending on it in a dark and stormy wilderness night.

Any stove should be kept clean, and the fuel, free of impurities. When the stove is left unused for extended periods, the fuel should be drained from the tank to prevent accumulation of clogging lacquers.

In case of malfunction and attempted field repairs, never fiddle with the pressure-release cap on any stove. This safety device is precisely set at the factory to ensure that above a certain pressure the cap will vent the excess. A cap with problems must be replaced.

A gas stove—and the gas—must at all times be treated with caution. Never fill the tank near an open flame. Never refill a hot stove—

let it cool first. (That's why the tank should be filled before starting a meal, to avoid having to stop in the middle, letting half-cooked food cool. Never operate any stove in a tightly sealed area, whether tent or snow cave. Fumes may cause sickness; oxygen starvation and carbon-monoxide poisoning can be fatal. When a stove is used in a tent, be supercareful, keeping in mind that house and home and all worldly goods might vanish in a flash; since the start-up holds the most potential for drama, conduct the operation outside the tent—if the wind allows.

It has been observed that backpackers who for one reason or another insist on doing a lot of cooking inside tents tend to prefer kerosene or butane, fuels that are much less dramatic than gas.

Kerosene Stoves

Kerosene has approximately the same BTU rating as white gas. With a flash point of 110°F, compared to −40°F for white gas, it's

Left: *The Optimus 00, the last kerosene stove still much seen in the backcountry, shown with a bottle of priming alcohol.* Right: *The overwhelmingly dominant model of butane stoves, the Gaz C-206 Bleuet, shown with cartridge in place.*

a bit harder to nourish to healthy flame, but by the same token, is far less likely to explode, making for greater peace of mind inside a tent—though care must still be taken in starting and using, since if not sufficiently preheated a stove can flare up. An objection to kerosene is that when spilled it doesn't evaporate readily but soaks into gear and stinks. On the other hand, spilled fuel doesn't readily ignite. The fuel is on sale everywhere, yet is often difficult to obtain in small quantity; kerosene stoves will operate on stove or diesel oil should kerosene be unavailable.

The only model practical for backpacking and widely sold is the Optimus 00 Camper, with roarer burner, weighing 1¾ pounds and costing about $50. It lights easily in wind if the windscreen opening is faced into the wind. Fuel capacity is large, boiling speed faster than average.

The stove requires priming; Optimus makes a Priming Paste, but alcohol, carried in a metal can, is better. A small amount is poured in the cup at the base of the vaporizer and ignited. Once the vaporizer is hot, the air valve is closed and pressure is hand-pumped in the tank, the kerosene begins to burn. If necessary, use a match to light the burner.

The stove doesn't have a control valve. More flame is obtained by using the built-in pump; less, by opening the air screw on the tank. A safety valve is unnecessary, since kerosene doesn't build up dangerous pressure.

Butane Stoves

Butane stoves outsell all others in Europe and were for a time the best-selling stoves in America before a new generation of gas stoves arrived. Now they are perhaps third or fourth in the United States, topped by one or two gas models and a multifuel.

The fuel is a liquified petroleum gas contained under pressure in a thin metal cartridge; fuel vaporizes inside the cartridge and flows out as a gas; apply a lighted match and the stove is going. Butane stoves are quick and easy to start, dependable, virtually free of tricks, "tent safe," and the fuel is conveniently carried with no fuss, no mess. The stove can be readily adjusted to simmer or sauté or to fry a decent egg or pancake. There is no noisy roar—the silent butane flame lets one hear the birds.

Backpackers appreciative of the virtues have learned to eliminate the vices. Problems and solutions:

1. Butane has no vapor pressure at 15°F, and *at sea level* doesn't freely vaporize below 32°F, and thus the stove operates poorly in the cold of winter and strong winds. (Insulate the tank bottom from snow or cold ground by setting it on a sleeping pad or the like. In freezing conditions—*but not on warm days*—shield the tank with aluminum foil to reflect back heat. By such means the stove can be run beautifully to 20°F or less at sea level. Before mealtime, though, it may be well to warm the cartridge inside a jacket, next to the body. Or sleep with it for the sake of a fast breakfast. Now—attention, mountaineers: Because the butane is pressurized at sea level, the higher the elevation the greater the pressure differential between cartridge interior and exterior, the hotter the flame, the lower the vaporization temperature—at 10,000 feet, as low as 12°F.)

2. There are those dang cartridges to carry. (For a gas or kerosene stove there is the dang fuel bottle to carry around.)

3. Fumes leak from an opened cartridge and have a retchy perfume smell. (Tape the orifice. Carry opened cartridges in poly bags, in outside-pack pockets. Fuel bottles also leak. Gas and kerosene stink too.)

4. "Disposable" cartridges garbage up the backcountry. (PACK IT OUT.)

5. Even an "empty" cartridge, not to mention a full one, contains enough energy to wipe out a machine-gun nest. (Do not be stupid—do not change cartridges by a campfire or another stove in operation or any other open flame.)

6. Since butane emits less heat than gas or kerosene, boiling speed is slower than average (may never happen at all in a wind), cooking time is substantially longer; also, as pressure

drops in the cartridge, the heat output drops—the last supper may be lukewarm. (This is true at and near sea level, but the higher butane cartridges climb, the hotter they burn, as hot as any other fuel, and that's why the stoves are used on Himalayan expeditions.)

7. Though the stove lights easily in wind, if the burner is turned on before the match is struck, the longer the stove runs, the worse it runs because the fuel vaporizes inside the cartridge, the evaporation steadily cools the cartridge, and the flame gets steadily weaker. (Cartridge temperature can be maintained by setting the stove in a pan of lukewarm water.)

8. In the absence of a scale one never knows how much fuel remains in a cartridge. (Some things you just have to learn to live with.)

Shops that service stoves say butane models are rarely brought in for repairs. Virtually the only problem is cartridges that leak because the top recess has been dented by rough handling (don't buy or use a cartridge so dented).

The pioneer model on the American market and still the overwhelming favorite is the French-made Gaz C-206 Bleuet, bulky and tall, requiring care to position it on an absolutely flat surface. Without cartridge the stove weighs 12 ounces, costs about $21, the optional windscreen is ¼ pound and $4. Gaz C-206 cartridges, good for 3 hours, weigh 10 ounces full (5 ounces empty) and cost about $2.

The Gaz is a *vapor-feed* stove; the butane goes directly from cartridge to burner, meaning that for efficient performance the entire cartridge must be kept warm. Other vapor-feed models are available here and there, using either a Gaz cartridge or a Ranger, Optimus, or other. Many of the stoves are cherished by owners, but distribution is sparse and models come and go on the market with few to notice.

In a *liquid-feed* stove the butane flows from cartridge to a vaporizing chamber. Since the chamber is the only part that must be kept warm for steady operation, there is little loss of efficiency in windy or cold weather. However, during start-up these stoves have a disconcerting tendency to flare. They've never caught on and continue to be sold here and there, but not in any quantity.

Multifuel Stoves

When the first MSR stove emerged from a home workshop, the backpacking world burst out giggling, "That's not a stove, that's a contraption." However, those who came to chortle stayed to gape as the contraption boiled water faster than an erupting volcano. Even when competing stoves improved their performance, one model, the MSR X-GK, continued in favor because of its ability to burn white gas, leaded or unleaded automotive gas, aviation gas, kerosene, No. 1 or No. 2 diesel oil, No. 1 stove oil, Stoddard Solvent, and what-have-you.

The contraption consists of a fuel-carrying bottle that doubles as a stove tank; a pump that screws into the bottle and connects to the burner by a "pipeline"; collapsible wind and heat-reflector; a burner

Multifuel stoves. Left: *MSR X-GK, burning any sort of gas, kerosene, stove oil, or other petroleum product.* Right: *Optimus 199, burning white gas, kerosene, or alcohol.*

assembly; a built-in sparker for gas fuels; and an aluminum cup-cover. For use with kerosene a priming-fuel bottle is included as the alcohol carrier. Also in the package is a cleaning pin. Weight, 1 pound; price $80. Add 4 ounces and $5 for the aluminum fuel bottle.

Boiling time is so fast in every clime, from deep winter close to home to high elevations far away, the fuel versatility is so amazing, and the field maintenance kit ($6) renders it so independent of repair shops that the X-GK is especially liked by people who go in for winter mountaineering and foreign journeys to big mountains.

More conventional is the Optimus 199, 2 pounds, $60. The aluminum carrying case (the top serving as saucepan) compactly holds stove, mini-pump, and windshield. Unlike the omnivorous X-GK, it accepts only three fuels, but one of these is alcohol (the others being white gas and kerosene). Boiling speed with white gas and kerosene is average, respectable with alcohol when a large orifice is used and the air restrictor (supplied) inserted in the burner. It's a silent stove, and that's a blessing.

POTS AND PANS AND ALL

A cooking kit can be improvised from kitchenware dug out of the basement or picked up at thrift shops and garage sales for nickels and dimes. The pots stocked by backpacking shops have many advantages, such as bails or handles, tight-fitting lids, ease of cleaning, and the compactness of nesting sets. They are also very light. (Be sure to avoid the heavier sets intended for car camping, canoeing, or horse packing.)

A loner needs nothing more than a small kettle and a cup. Two or three people usually want several pots in various sizes, and four or five people, a couple more. Outdoor shops offer a number of sets of different materials and prices; a few may be cited to suggest the alternatives.

The classic favorite is a set of *nesting billies*, three aluminum pots with capacities of 1, 2, and 3 quarts, individual lids that double as plates, fry pans, or saucepans. The lightest and least expensive of the common sets weigh 1¾ pounds, cost about $18 and have a life span measured in decades. Three to four people can be served quite decently. The large pot can be left home by two-person groups. A lone hiker may want only the small pot.

If stainless steel is preferred, the *Sierra Cook Set* has a 1.4-quart teapot, pots (with lids) of 1.4, 1.7, and 2.1 quarts, fitting into a nylon carrying sack and weighing just over 2 pounds, costing about $30.

Another classic and favorite is the *Sigg Tourist Cooker* (or *Cook*

Top: *Sigg Tourist Cooker (the Svea version), on left disassembled; on right assembled for carrying, stove and all.* Bottom: *Nesting billies, disassembled on left, assembled for carrying on right.*

Kit), aluminum pots of 2½- and 3½-pint capacity, a lid which can serve as a fry pan (and makes a good double boiler, with any pot beneath, for fondues), a stove base (for reasons to be explained) and windscreen, and a pot lifter. By itself the set suffices for two or three people—more by adding a pot or two. Total weight is 1½ pounds; cost, $30 in one version, about $35 in another. The distinctive feature of the Sigg is a symbiosis with a stove, the pots being designed for the stove to nest inside, the pot support and windscreen to marry the stove to the pots in use. Three versions are presently sold; one to combine with the Svea 123R; a second with the Coleman Peak 1; and a third with the MSR Firefly, MSR WhisperLite, and Gaz C-206 Bleuet.

A different species of cook kit may include plates and cups in combinations to serve a solitary Scout, a family, or a whole Scout troop.

A desirable accessory to avoid burned fingers and dinner spilled on the ground is a *pot lifter*. The best is a spring-loaded steel model that gives a strong grip on loaded pots. Some hikers prefer a pair of *pliers*, which can also be used to work on the stove, open jammed fuel bottles, repair packs, and extract teeth.

A *stirring spoon* with a long handle keeps the hand comfortably distant from flames; wooden ones don't melt or get so hot they burn the hand if left in the soup.

Hikers who do a lot of frying, as of fish, hotcakes, and omelettes, become disenchanted with lids of nesting pots and carry an honest-

Top: *Typical four-man cook set. Everything nests into the large kettle for carrying.*
Bottom: *Typical two-man cook kit, disassembled.*

to-gosh *fry pan.* Some declare it's impossible to fry properly except
with steel; a pan 8¾ inches in diameter, weighing 12 ounces, costs
$10; a light steel spatula completes the unit. Others like an easy-to-
clean Teflon-coated aluminum pan, 9½ inches in diameter, weighing
14 ounces complete with the nylon spatula that must be used with

Teflon (wood is also suitable); cost, $10. Fanatic fry cooks, including parents and Scoutmasters who love to show off by making hotcakes for the whole crowd, favor a *griddle* of thick aluminum, 10 by 16½ inches, 1¼ pounds, $20.

Heavy-duty aluminum foil, a square yard or so, can be crimped into an oven, usable with wood fire or stove. Carry a little sack of Bisquick and there can be biscuits for breakfast. Pick fresh huckleberries and have coffee cake for the night's dessert.

High-altitude hikers may consider a *pressure cooker*. At sea level, water boils at 212°F; at 5,000 feet the boiling point is 203°F and cooking time is increased by half or more; at 10,000 the boiling point is 193°F and cooking time is nearly quadrupled. Those who frequently camp at 10,000 feet, as in the Wind River Range, High Sierra, Colorado Rockies, Peru, and Nepal, may appreciate the pressure cooker's ability to cut cooking time approximately in half. A 4-quart cooker suitable for four people, of heavy-duty aluminum,

Kitchen accessories. Clockwise from left: *Optimus Mini-Oven (three pieces), a good idea but hard to find on the market, requiring camp bakers to improvise with aluminum foil; pressure cooker, of interest only at very high altitudes; an excellent grate, also scarce in the shops, replaced on the trail by the dime-store cake rack; and pot gripper, pliers, stirring spoon, and Teflon-coated aluminum fry pan with nylon spatula.*

with two perforated separators and a solid one for segregating foods, 6½ inches high, 7½ inches in diameter, weighs 2¾ pounds and costs about $55.

EATING TOOLS

Any number of methods convey food from pot to mouth. There are hikers who cannot eat happy unless all solid elements of the entire meal are spread before them at the same time on a *plate*. The lids of billies and other kettles can be employed, or the plates included in cooking sets and kits, or pieces of aluminum foil, or plates of plastic or aluminum. Other hikers cannot abide cereal except in a *bowl*—the shops have them, mainly plastic.

Many experienced hikers do all their eating from a *cup*—whether the food is soup, coffee, steak, pancake, or salad. While plate-eaters move now to this item, now to that, back and forth, everything getting cold, cup-eaters go one course at a time, finishing this before starting that. Plastic cups, light and cheap, are most popular; stacking (nesting) mugs of large capacity weigh ¾ ounce, cost a dollar or so. A measuring cup with quarter-cup graduations doubles as a

Eating tools. Top row: *Plastic plate, bowl, and cup.* Bottom row: *Cutlery, pocket knife, and stainless-steel cup.*

chef's tool, saving guesswork about quantities of ingredients and avoiding watery puddings.

A traditional favorite is a stainless-steel cup with wire handle (called "Sierra Club cup" in California, and among Northwesterners of long memory the "Ome Daiber cup"). It can serve as a small pot, to heat water for a spot of tea. Weight is 3 ounces; cost, about $3. The capacity is 9 ounces—a good thing for the cook to remember (1 cup equals 8 ounces).

Plastic cups have the enormous virtue of the "cool lip" but cheap ones (hot polycarbonate) may absorb and retain tastes of certain foods. Steel cups, cool at the rim but not elsewhere, are easy to keep clean and pure. Aluminum cups are a disaster—when the soup is hot the edge burns the lip, and when the edge is cool enough for the lip, the soup is cold.

The *pocket knife* every hiker must carry (see Chapter 15) serves ordinary cooking and eating needs. If it lacks an effective *can opener* and the menu contemplates the contents of a can, a separate one must be included in party gear. On a day when business was slow the REI Quality Control Department looked into the matter. In a test, opening 6½-ounce cans of tuna fish, the fastest model (20 seconds) and all-over best, leaving no ragged edges, was the Swing-A-Way. The opener on the Victorinox Swiss Army knife did well, 31 to 34 seconds. The "Boy Scout knives" ranged from 38 to 73 seconds.

A *spoon*, stainless steel or plastic, transports food to the mouth.

The best is a lightweight yet rigid and sturdy, not plastic-limp, polycarbonate spoon that won't crack, won't chip, won't stain, won't sag under a load of oatmeal. Some hikers carry a *fork* as well, to spear meatballs. *Chopsticks* are superb for noodles once you get the hang of them, but tricky with peas.

FOOD CONTAINERS

Backpacking shops stock many kinds of plastic bags, bottles, and jars for hauling foods, including water.

Strong, light, transparent *poly bags*, in sizes from 5 by 8 to 15 by 18 inches, costing pennies, have many uses noted in Chapter 4 and elsewhere in this book. Cheaper and lighter sandwich bags and those in which bread and produce are sold can be doubled for fairly decent durability. Bags may be closed by rubber bands, or, better, paper-wrapped wires—several of which should always be in every hiker's pocket to replace the ones that disappear in thin air.

Polyethylene bottles in shapes from oval to round, with capacities of 2 to 32 ounces (1 quart) to 2 quarts, the prices from under $1 to $3, serve as containers for liquid detergent, cooking oils, or the ingredients of an aperitif, as shakers for mixing the morning-after orange juice, and so on. The larger sizes are the standard canteens nowadays; only a few traditionalists carry the old "canteen-shaped" canteens of aluminum or rigid plastic. *Nalgene* bottles, of high-strength polyethylene, don't absorb contents as the lighter-weight poly does, but become brittle at 0°F, compared to −100°F for the other, and must be handled gently in bitter cold. For most purposes *wide-mouth* bottles are preferred to the narrow, to dump juice powder and cram snow in. *Loop tops* cannot be misplaced or lost; a flexible plastic ring keeps bottle and top together. *Rectangular* bottles fit snugger in packs.

Poly boxes or *jars*, square or round, Nalgene or plain poly, with snap-on or screw-on lids, are good for lettuce, grapes, tomatoes, peanut butter, and other crushable or sloppy foods. *Poly vials* handle pills and spices and secret ingredients. *Poly squeeze tubes* are excellent for jam, honey, peanut butter, margarine, and other oozy foods—

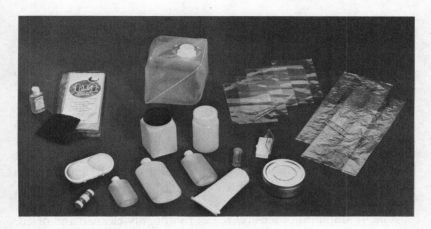

Dishwashing gear and food carriers.

except in cold weather, when contents refuse to squeeze. The tube has a bottom clip to permit refilling and washing.

A plastic two-compartment *salt and pepper shaker* is convenient. If a larger supply of salt is carried separately, as customary on long hikes, the other half of the shaker can be filled with garlic salt, lemon pepper, cinnamon, or some other favorite spice. Film cans are excellent carriers.

Desert or hot-mountainside camps may be bone-dry, requiring water to be brought from far away and in large quantities. In fragile ecosystems a major source of damage to vegetation and soils is the back and forth trampling from camp to creek. Increasingly, therefore, hikers include a *water carrier* in the party gear so that not twenty or thirty but one or two trips must be taken to the soft-soiled creek bank. As a serendipity, camp can be made high on a dry, sublimely scenic ridge, superbly lonesome, rather than down in a dark, dank hole with the madding crowd. Collapsible plastic "tanks" holding 1½, 2½, and 5 gallons weigh about ½ pound and cost $4–$5. A flexible water sack that folds flat in the pack has a nylon taffeta skin to protect a replaceable poly bladder; capacity is 3 gallons, weight ¼ pound, cost $5.

DISHWASHING

The tools of dishwashing are simple enough.

First is some device to loosen food particles (and charcoal) from utensils, particularly cooking pots. Oldtimers did the job with sand and gravel; much neater is a plastic or metal scouring pad.

Second is some means of cutting grease. Hot water alone serves very well, but a small amount of soap or biodegradable detergent, liquid or solid, speeds the process, and minimizes consumption of hot water, which may be in short supply when the cooking has been done on a stove for which the fuel has been carried a long, long way.

Note: If aluminum utensils are not thoroughly cleaned and dried, acids will form that dissolve the metal with startling speed. Foods containing salt are highly corrosive, as is chlorinated water; pots must be washed thoroughly after cooking and completely dried.

A tip: Tests by the REI Quality Control Department show blackened pots heat faster than shiny ones. Wash away the soot on the exterior but do not polish.

Final note: None of the above is to be done beside the lake or creek. Carry water up in the woods or out on the moraine and wash dishes there.

14
Food

Once upon a time in the Great Depression a CCC crew was building a road near Hood Canal. Several of the guys, all from Eastern cities, began wondering about the interior of the Olympic Mountains and decided to spend a holiday exploring. None had ever seen a mountain or trail before, so they asked an experienced hiker how such a trip should be done. After hearing the complexities of packboards and food lists and boiling oatmeal and rice on campfires a mile above sea level, they said, "The hell with it, we won't take any food. We're only going to be gone three days."

Off they went in Olympic wilderness, fifty miles up and down valleys and over passes and along ridges, and nothing to eat. In the Depression, many Americans learned that a mere three days of fasting wouldn't hurt. In fact, a person in average health can miss a lot more meals than that without harm; from a perspective of history and a glance around the world one might say that on the ordinary hike of up to a week or so, food is a frill.

To make a fast retreat before the gathering wrath of mountain rescuers: Lacking a fairly constant supply of calories, the body slows down and weakens and becomes prone to stumble, the mind tends

to make errors in judgment, and the system loses resistance to cold. Hikers should keep stoking for reasons of safety if not pleasure.

Still, it is true that most backpackers worry excessively about food. The first common mistake of novices is to haul too much of it—twice as much as they can eat and four times more than they need. The second mistake is to fret about the proper mix of protein. vitamins, and minerals—not realizing that on any hike up to a week or two in length, the only important physiological need is calories (unless one tends to suffer from constipation and requires a certain amount of roughage, in which case a cup of prunes a day keeps the suppositories away). To be sure, with an exceptionally bizarre diet, minor vitamin deficiencies could occur, perhaps causing night blindness, but in so short a time there is absolutely no risk of scurvy, beriberi, or rickets. And anyway, whatever foods are carried (unless one tries to subsist solely on sugar cubes) will have enough of the essential elements to prevent significant imbalance. As for fears of a deficiency in protein, even during strenuous exercise the body uses relatively little for muscle replacement; Americans happen to like and be able to afford protein and consume vastly more than the world average, but most of it is converted to energy (and fat), not muscles.

Before leaving the point, let it be noted that Americans of the affluent class that does the bulk of the backpacking generally can well afford to drop surplus pounds in the wildlands by deliberate undereating—which reduces not only body but pack weight.

The above discussion omits something: it's a pleasure to eat. And never more so than on the trail. Indeed, some longtime backpackers confess they are not sure whether they eat to hike or hike to eat. Though perhaps never in their city lives having visited a gourmet restaurant, and at home hardly able to recall at breakfast what they had for supper, they will rapturously describe the famous hoosh they created at Pretty Meadows on a magic evening twenty-five years ago.

Whether necessary or not, then, eating is a diversion only the most ascetic totem-seeking hikers forgo. But what to eat? There is the question with a thousand answers, all correct. The choice is almost entirely determined by personal tastes, including passionate likes and dislikes that develop with age and experience. Assemble a seminar of Old Crocks and ask them to reveal the secrets of their trail success, and they'll talk boots and pants and packs—but eventually will end up in loud debate about the virtues of Logan bread versus pilot bread versus pumpernickel and how many smoked oysters per person are essential for a nine-day trip. Then they'll settle down to swapping recipes, which leads to arguments about brown versus white sugar, the ideal way to rehydrate a meatball, and whether the one-pot supper is the greatest invention of mankind or a sign that civilization is rushing toward total and richly deserved collapse.

Indeed, try to plan a week's menu that will perfectly satisfy each of four trail veterans, and chances are the party never will leave town. Two may insist on Thuringer sausage, one can't abide anything but salami, and the other vows to boycott all lunches lacking Goteborg. More has been written about food than all other aspects of wilderness travel combined. Most manuals have an enormous lot to say, and myriads of books and booklets and pamphlets are devoted exclusively to trail cookery, offering googols of recipes for kabob, gorp, charcoal bread, fried grass, boiled owl. The number of cookbooks written is roughly equal to the number of camp cooks; the number published is only slightly less; the number stocked by backpacker shops is limited solely by the need to allow a bit of space for boots, packs, and all that. The plethora is a delight to novices flitting from dish to dish, restlessly questing for ambrosia. However, as they mature, they typically decide that the spice of variety is overpraised and settle into a single menu of a few dishes, repeated over and over, liked better every passing year. (Arctic explorers used to eat pemmican and pemmican alone for months at a time; upon returning to headquarters and sitting down to meals of moose steak and peas and potatoes and biscuits, they sighed for—pemmican.)

The following exposition does not probe deeply into trail cuisine and is not intended for the experienced backpacker, who already knows what he likes and is certain to object more or less violently to whatever is said on the subject. Rather, the treatment is aimed at the absolute novice and is designed solely to assist in selecting the first trail meals. Having fed himself a few times in surroundings beyond electric stove and refrigerator, he will soon make stupendous discoveries, become as opinionated as the veterans, start pressing recipes on strangers encountered in wilderness camps, and submitting cookbook manuscripts to publishers.

THE SHORT AND THE LONG OF IT

Opening a can is within the capacity of the majority of beginning hikers, given a can opener. Nearly all are able to strip a banana and assemble a jelly sandwich. No higher skills are required to make out well enough on short trips. As miles and days mount, though, cookery becomes slightly less simple—but nowadays never really complicated.

Day Hike

For an afternoon stroll a chunk of chocolate or an apple or packet of nuts may add to the pleasure of a rest stop; food, however, is purely optional.

On a full-day hike the only meal is lunch, usually consumed in several installments from second breakfast through high tea—and supper and breakfast, too, if an accident or loss of route forces an unplanned night out. Any menu will do—sandwiches, crackers and cheese, smoked salmon, grapes, cookies, carrot sticks, cherry pie— whatever the people enjoy. Any amount will do as long as there is enough for a possible emergency—too much is unlikely to damage the back. (Unless the example is followed of a group of climbers who once hoaxed an Eastern photographer at a lunch stop high on the Nisqually Glacier of Mount Rainier, and through him the readers of *Life* magazine, by casually pulling watermelons from rucksacks and slicing them up as if this were standard alpine fare.)

Even in well-watered (and pure-watered) country the party should have a canteen supply, if not to drink (perhaps mixed in the cup with lemonade powder) then for first-aid purposes. For thirst alone, canned fruit juices or carbonated beverages are delightful; they also give a quick shot of sugar to cure an acute case of that pooped feeling. Gatorade and the like (Gookinaid ERG, for "electrolyte replacement with glucose") claim to replenish the sodium, calcium, and magnesium salts sweated out in heavy exercise, attacking other basic causes of the poops, as well as curing leg cramps better than salt tablets. However, some research suggests these aids don't work— nothing beats plain water and a candy bar.

Do not drop along the trail or toss in the brush candy wrappers, orange peels, or cans. And don't bury them. PACK IT OUT! PACK IT *ALL* OUT!

Overnight

The same rule that applies to day-hike lunches extends to weekend lunches—and breakfasts and suppers. The rule is, there is no rule. Too little food doesn't cause intolerable misery and indeed adds zest to hamburgers and milk shakes at the drive-in Sunday night. Too much rarely leads to a permanent stoop.

However, a basic choice must be made prior to the trip: between walking far and fast or eating in the mode of the last days of Pompeii.

At one extreme are meals that are essentially a succession of quick lunches. Ham sandwiches make a satisfying supper, and unheated hash fresh from the can resembles dog food but is amazingly tasty, especially with a splash of ketchup. To quote a maxim of climbers: "Though the food is cold, the inner man is hot." Civilized stomachs are conditioned to feel vaguely incomplete lacking at least one hot meal a day; amid grand scenery the sensation passes.

At the other extreme is wilderness feasting, where backpacking miles have as their goal the sharpening of the appetite. Sybarites may devote the afternoon and evening to a supper of aperitif of choice and hors d'oeuvres of sesame crackers spread with truffled pâté; tossed salad or slices of lemon-washed avocado; Cornish game hen foil-roasted in coals and served with corn on the cob; biscuits baked in a mini-oven and topped with frozen strawberries and whipped cream; wines and brandies and cheeses at the discretion of the maître d'.

The average weekender meals fall someplace in the middle. For example, supper may be cherry tomatoes, soup, canned beef stew, bread and butter, stir-and-serve pudding, and instant coffee, tea, or milk. Breakfast may be orange juice, oatmeal "cooked" in the cup by the addition of hot water, and instant coffee or cocoa. Thousands of other menus have been published. Ad infinitum, ad nauseam.

High-Tech Packaging

The problem in having engineers on the company payroll is the impossibility of turning off their ingenuity. One might have thought they'd have called it a good job and quit after inventing the tin can, or surely after freeze-drying, but the advertising agencies kept crying for more. Two innovations of the 1980s do not save weight, as do dried foods, and therefore are better suited to short trips—day or weekend or perhaps 4–5 days. Their appeal is bringing "like fresh" taste to the backcountry.

In *retort packaging* the food is placed in a three-layer retort pouch, polyester on the outside, foil in the middle, polypropylene on the inside—a "flexible tin can." The air is pumped out, the pouch sealed, the food cooked. All the natural moisture is retained so the food is heavier than dried food, though the overall package is lighter per unit of food than with a metal can.

The food is as easy to prepare in camp as freeze-dried, but (the bad news) costs more. Shelf life is 1–2 years. Meats and such taste better than canned (which are cheaper).

Sterile boxes contain fruit juices that taste fresher than those in cans or reconstituted from powder—because they are fresh. Shelf life is 1½ years. The boxes (fragile—easily damaged in the pack) can be dropped in a creek for cooling. Looming on the technological horizon is fresh milk that will keep an entire summer and perhaps the next, too.

Long Backpack

Beyond a 3-day weekend, eating demands thought. Depending on the backs and appetites involved, somewhere around 4 or 5 days and certainly by 6 or 7 days, the distance from the road forces a qualitative change in cuisine.

Above all, it becomes essential to *go light*. An extra half pound per person per meal matters little on a weekend with a maximum of 4 meals, but matters much when the meals number 12 or 27—

6 or 13 extra pounds on each suffering back makes for a slow and painful pace.

Through use of dried foods and those naturally low in water content, shucking cardboard packaging, and moderately careful menu planning, it is possible to feed the average hiker to repletion on 2 pounds of food per day. By more precise planning, the job can be done with 1½ pounds. And if party members are willing to leave a bit of lard along the way and endure pangs while stomachs shrink, with 1 pound. At this point, though, about the fifth evening the hiker will look into the setting sun and see not the drama of day's end but only a great fried egg dripping hot butter.

This general rule concerning pounds of food per person has so many exceptions that it is hardly a rule at all. Exercise stimulates the appetites of some, who grow ravenous several days out and go mad at the aroma of peanut butter and begin to lust after chipmunks and prowl tidal pools for edible seaweed. Others eat less the harder they work—perhaps because their systems, freed from neurotic overstuffing, are slimming down for the sane life of the wilderness.

And, of course, an 80-pound human requires less fuel than a 250-pounder. Although, contrarily, a person with hyperactive metabolism, the sort who eats and eats and is always skinny, needs more food than the person whose inner plant is so efficient that a single kipper adds an inch to his girth.

And again, on extended backpacks as on day walks, the choice must be made between lightness and luxury. On long trips, lightness dictates most decisions, but there are no words to praise salted cucumber slices six days from the road; the extra ounces of such an occasional special treat may be worth the strain.

Cooking time is another consideration. When the intent is to cover a lot of ground, walking every day from early morning to late afternoon, and/or when all cooking is to be done on a stove, most meals should be medium-fast and some instant-quickies, requiring only hot water for supper and cold water for breakfast. On less frantic trips, though, a few meals should be fancy—for rest days or days of rain at camps where wood fires can be built. For example, the ingredients of a pancake-bacon-eggs breakfast contain no surplus water and are very efficient in the ratio of weight to calories. A pancake breakfast ordinarily lasts to lunchtime, but when mists are driving through the flowers, or rain drizzling among the trees, or the camp is paradise, and there is no need to march on, who cares?

For obvious reasons the subject of foods for long backpacks is the most controversial among veterans—and the most baffling to novices. Thus, to guide through the confusion, a new section must begin. In fact, four sections, one after the other.

LONG-HAUL FOODS: SUPERMARKET

Forty-odd years ago, before food processors ran amok, the diet of the long-distance backpacker was restricted and his cookery a formidable art. Few dried foods were available (it was possible to get quite sick of prunes and chipped beef) and those naturally dry were not treated for quick cooking. Pasta (noodles, macaroni) was relatively easy to make digestible, but rice took an hour or more at high altitude and usually ended as a gruel punctuated by tiny pebbles; beans were an overnight project. Even oatmeal and farina required an eternity of smoke swallowing and stirring and generally burned on the bottom.

A sampling of long-haul foods available in supermarkets. Top: *Breakfast ingredients.* Center: *Lunch things.* Bottom: *Supper stuff.*

Nowadays, however, supermarkets are cornucopias of low-in-water, fast-cooking products. By prowling the aisles and checking cooking times carefully, avoiding tempting packages that call for a 400°F oven, the backpacker can assemble any number of light-weight, nutritious, delicious, alacazam meals. To stimulate the imagination, following are some of the innumerable supermarket foods suitable for long-haul backpacking:

For breakfast: quick-cooking and instant-in-the-cup oatmeal and farina; compact no-cook cereals such as Grape-Nuts; pancake flour; bacon; dried fruits; powdered juice mixes; "instant breakfast"; sugar; dried milk; instant cocoa and coffee.

For lunch: dense and durable breads and crackers; margarine; cheese; peanut butter; jam and honey; candy; nuts; dried fruits; sausage; powdered juice mixes.

For supper; dried soups; instant potatoes and dry gravy mixes; quick-cooking noodles with cheese (Kraft Dinner); super-fast-cooking Oriental noodles (Top Ramen); Minute Rice, which requires no boiling, only steaming; canned meats and fishes; hard sausage; chipped beef; cheese; instant puddings; cookies; instant coffee; tea bags.

The big problem is deciding how much of any particular food is enough for a certain number of people; the "serves four" on a package may mean four finicky mice. Trial-and-error experience gained on short hikes, where mistakes in calculation are not serious, is the best way to learn how to buy. If a shortcut is wanted, exact amounts of ingredients required for myriad menus are given by backpacker cookbooks.

Before we leave the supermarket, a word needs to be said in defense of canned meats. First, they cost enormously less than the freeze-drieds lauded below. Second, because the freeze-drieds contain little or no fat (4,000 calories per pound, compared to merely 1,600 for protein), they may offer less nutrition per ounce on the backpacker's back, even taking into account the weight of canned meat's water and metal. The advantage is greatest, of course, with fatty Spam-like meats and oil-packed fish.

DRIED FOODS

Time out now, before proceeding from supermarket to backpacking shop, for a bit about the background of dried foods, which generally weigh merely a third or a quarter or less of what they did before processing.

Man's earliest means of preserving food was sun drying, dating to prehistoric times and the original method of making raisins, prunes, dried peas and beans, beef jerky, and the like. Freezing came perhaps not much later, as man moved into lands of cold winters. Probably the first use of artificial heat was in smoking meat and fish. The technology of preserving without tinning advanced little beyond this level until the twentieth century, when experiments with other techniques, stimulated by military requirements during and after World War II and the police action in Korea, led to the current state of the art.

Hot-Air Drying ("Dehydrated" Foods)

Hot-air drying was once done in ovenlike chambers by the batch, requiring much handling and consequent expense. An improvement was *tunnel-drying*, where foods are placed on trays and passed slowly

THIS WILL FEED BOTH OF YOU FOR FIVE DAYS

through a long tunnel in which hot air blows end to end; emerging after 6 hours or less with a moisture content below 10–12 percent, the food is transferred to finish-drying bins, where moisture is reduced to less than 5 percent, the point necessary for storage stability. Demanding more complicated equipment but offering greater efficiency and economy and providing better quality control and thus gradually replacing tunnel-drying are various *continuous processes*. An example is spreading the food on a wire-mesh belt that moves through a chamber perhaps 120 feet long; the air blowing through the food from various inlets may be very hot early on, then cooler. In 3–4 hours for large vegetable dices and 30–45 minutes for leafy vegetables, moisture is usually less than 5 percent, often eliminating the need for finish-drying in a bin.

Dehydration of highly concentrated fruit or vegetable purees, such as mashed potatoes, yams, applesauce, tomatoes, and so on, is by *drum-drying*, the "mash" spread on the stainless-steel outer surface of a large, internally heated, rotating drum, automatically scraped off into a hopper, and spread on another drum, and so on, until done.

Some fruits (apples, apricots, peaches, prunes) may be processed by *vacuum-drying*, basically with hot-air methods but in a partial vacuum to avoid excessive oxidation and resulting discoloration. The older and still-common and less-expensive alternative is to replace the air in the chamber with sulfur dioxide gas; the taste and odor inevitably linger.

Spray-drying, conducted in a tall tower into the top of which tiny droplets are sprayed, dehydrating as they fall through heated air, is customary for powdered milk, coffee, and vegetable and fruit juices.

Upon rehydration, foods treated by hot-air methods generally do not closely resemble the original in appearance or flavor, largely because when a plant or animal is air-dried to less than 10–15 percent of its natural moisture, the cell structure tightens up irreversibly. A stewed raisin is nothing like a grape, and rehydrated spinach flakes are only distant cousins to leaves fresh from the field. But then, a raisin is excellent eating in its own right, and some hikers prefer trail spinach to garden spinach. Air-dried foods can be delicious and have the advantage of much lower cost than the freeze-dried.

Intermediate-Moisture Food

On the horizon for the backpacker, though already on the floor for consumers of "moist and meaty" dog food, is "intermediate-moisture food," prepared by removing enough water to prevent growth of mold and fungus, while leaving in enough water to preserve the texture. This residue must be physically combined with a "humectant" to prevent growth of bacteria; sugar is the one used in dog food, which thus is very sweet for human tastes. If research finds better alternatives, the trail kitchen may be enriched. Meanwhile, there's "moist and meaty"—and to stop smiling for a moment, social workers testify it's already a regular item in the diet of elderly Americans on miserly pensions.

Also still on the horizon—and firmly held there by government regulations—is the fulfillment of a hiker's fantasy—Beer Kool-Aid. The Japanese have perfected a method of encapsulating alcohol in powder form. Resulting products, available now outside the United States, can be reconstituted on the trail to make beer (using solidified carbon dioxide for the bubbles, as in Pop Rocks), hot spiced wine, martinis, or, for the morning after too many of these, Bloody Marys. But until a host of bureaus and boards have pondered and approved, American hikers must keep a stiff upper lip. (However, as the Noble Experiment proved, old Adam will not be forever denied—should the feds delay too long, there may again be fleets of swift black boats arriving by night on secluded American beaches.)

Vacuum Sublimation (Freeze-Dried Foods)

Vacuum sublimation, called the greatest breakthrough in food preservation since the tin can, combines the flavor-retention of freezing with the lightness of dehydration.

The food, cooked or raw depending on the product, is flash-frozen so that ice crystals cannot grow large enough to distort the cell structure, then placed in a high-vacuum chamber at very low temperature, perhaps down to − 50°F, and exposed to radiant heat. The combination of heat and low pressure forces some 97 percent or more of the moisture to sublime—that is, pass directly from solid to vapor without ever becoming liquid, again preventing damage to the cells.

For millennia the Incas of the high, cold, sunny Andes successfully freeze-dried potatoes, and the Indians of Alaska in winter did the same with salmon. Not until recent years, however, mainly as a result of military needs, has a modern refinement of the technique become economically practical.

Partly due to the inefficiency of batch-handling, freeze-drying is the most expensive method of food preservation; if engineers would quit fooling around and perfect an assembly line, the cost would drop considerably.

Not even high prices discourage affluent backpackers, who like freeze-drieds because they rehydrate quickly to virtually pristine shape and flavor, retain more nutritive value than air-drieds, and if correctly packaged and stored in cool, dark places, keep indefinitely. The technique works beautifully on meat and fish, most fruits and vegetables, coffee, and a great many other foods—though not all; cheese, for example, crumbles to dust.

Packaging

Many dried foods are shipped from manufacturer to retailer in large tight-closed tins and packaged in poly bags shortly before sale. (Some shops sell full tins of vegetables and fruits for big-time eaters.) A few dried products last for months in the poly, but because the plastic is not absolutely impervious to passage of air, many start to deteriorate in a matter of weeks. Dry fruits and vegetables stored in a cool, dry spot—ideally a refrigerator, otherwise a corner of the basement—may last a year or more before providing odd new taste sensations.

Eggs packaged in poly definitely must be used the same season purchased. So should such foods as flour and beans; they will not spoil but over a long period may develop weevils, which do not lessen food value, and indeed increase the protein content, but are widely considered unesthetic.

Though aluminum cans are occasionally used, the most common container for freeze-dried meats and meat products and some vegetables is the *shrink pack*, where the food is placed in laminated aluminum foil, the air drawn out by vacuum, nitrogen gas pumped into the food to replace oxygen-containing air and thus increase shelf life, and the sealed foil covered by an outer layer of tough plastic. The package is very durable if protected from puncturing and preserves contents indefinitely. Even a tiny, perhaps invisible, hole, however, permits freeze-dried meats to rehydrate, in which event they quickly spoil; if the food stinks or looks strange, it must *not* be eaten.

LONG-HAUL FOODS: BACKPACKING SHOP

Where the supermarket leaves off, the backpacking shop begins, offering dried foods and specialties with limited appeal, if any, for city use but enabling a variety, convenience, and quality of wilderness eatery inconceivable to oldtimers.

Generally, because of special processing (particularly freeze-drying) and packaging, a menu entirely drawn from backpacking shop supplies is considerably more expensive than one depending partly on the supermarket. The hiker must let his pocketbook be his guide.

Separate Ingredients

A wide range of fruits, vegetables, meats, and miscellaneous foods are packaged separately, to be eaten alone or in combination with others, such as:

Air-dried and freeze-dried fruits and vegetables, from apples to peaches, from beets to peas and carrots (but rarely, nowadays, yams or spinach).

A sampling of long-haul foods sold by backpacking stores. Top: Separate ingredients, some normally eaten alone, others commonly mixed in hooshes. Center: Complete dishes, all required components in the package. Bottom: Complete meals, the easy way out for confused and wealthy novices.

Freeze-dried meats, from meatballs and hamburgers and diced beef and ham and chicken to beefsteaks and porkchops and tuna salad.

Beef jerky, dehydrated bacon bar and meat bar, powdered eggs, freeze-dried cottage cheese, meat-flavored vegetable-protein (soya) chunks.

Fruit pemmican, English mint cake, maple-sugar candy, fruit-nut bar, powdered beverages, pilot bread, yogurt.

And more.

Complete Dishes

A number of firms (Dri-Lite, Alpine Aire, Rich-Moor, and Oregon Freeze-Dried Foods, with the Mountain House label) package complete main courses and side dishes that are delicious and nutritious or at least edible and so simple to prepare as to be virtually foolproof; some require only the addition of hot or cold water to be ready to eat. To cite a very few from a great many:

For breakfast there are omelettes, pancakes, cereals, sausage patties, hashbrowns.

For supper there are rice-beef-vegetable mulligan, beef stew, chili, lasagna, beef Stroganoff, beef Stromboli, beans and franks, chop suey, shrimp creole, creamed chicken, Boston-style beans, ham and potatoes, noodles and beef, cheese Romanoff, turkey Tetrazzini, beef almondine, tuna à la Neptune. And for dessert, puddings and gelatins, apple compote and raspberry cobbler—and no-bake pineapple cheesecake with graham-cracker crust!

And drinks, snacks, and goodies galore.

Many of these dishes cost two or three or five times more than the hooshes (nowadays vulgarly called "glops") a hiker concocts from supermarket foods—which doesn't matter to the wealthy or occasional camper but certainly does to the impoverished, inveterate long-distance walker, who mostly eats at the Kraft Dinner level and considers freeze-dried hash a holiday treat.

It must be noted that most of these foods are unappealing in the city, barely tolerable on weekends, and don't become genuinely appetizing until about the fourth day on the trail. Moreover, an increasing number of disenchanted hikers report that despite the ravishing names, after a while they all taste the same.

Complete Meals

Several of the firms mentioned above provide the ultimate in convenience by packaging complete meals carefully tailored to the high-calorie, low-weight, easy-cooking requirements of the hiker and accompanied by exact directions, which can be followed by anyone able to boil water and scramble an egg.

Among the fans of complete meals are Scoutmasters and other trail bosses who have neither the energy (or perhaps experience) to puzzle out a menu and shopping list for a dozen or a score of gaping young mouths; using the shortcut, they can buy food for a week in minutes and feed the troops very well.

This convenience, of course, has a price, and after the beginner has developed personal eccentricities he doubtless will prefer to structure his own menus. However, through packaged meals he receives on-the-job training in backpack cookery taught by experts.

THE CUISINE OF AN OLD CROCK

The eating habits of ancient mountaineers really are better left to silence. For example, the man who led REI through its early decades was noted for climbing a boggling number of tough peaks in typhoons and blizzards—and notorious for feeding himself three meals a day by reaching into a huge and greasy sack of sandwiches from home; by the fourth or fifth day of a peak-bagging expedition, companions insisted he go off to a separate glacier to eat.

Nevertheless, readers have complained that previous editions of this book failed to satisfy their prurient curiosity about the private habits of Old Crocks. Following, therefore, is the typical menu of one such in his forty-sixth summer since days as a Tenderfoot cooking kabob on a stick and hunter's stew in a coffee can.

Breakfast

When alone or wishing to get out of camp and on the peaks at the crack of nine o'clock, Old Crock eats the identical breakfast every morning: a packet (two if ravenous) of instant oatmeal stirred in the cup with hot water, Milkman, and brown sugar. Two cups instant coffee with white sugar and nondairy creamer. Companions have black coffee, coffee-cocoa, or plain cocoa.

When the party includes Mrs. Old Crock, who invariably arises mad to cook, breakfast starts with coffee, moves to bacon, progresses to a primitive (but good, but good) omelette of powdered eggs, cheese, bacon-flavored soya, and mushrooms (gathered fresh or re-constituted from an earlier harvest dried at home—Mrs. O.C. spends all winter fiddling with her food drier). Finally, the box of Bisquick comes out and hotcakes begin, topped with margarine and straw-berry jam, brown-sugar syrup, or (in season) huckleberry syrup. It's then time for lunch.

Lunch

The everyday staple is Royal Kreem, preferred for tastiness over Sailor Boy pilot bread, which is, however, more durable. Spread with margarine, peanut butter, cashew butter, strawberry jam, yel-low or white or blue or cream or stinky cheese, hard salami, smoked oysters, spiced herring—not all at once.

For sweets (again, not all at any one meal), Callard and Bowser licorice and toffee, Cadbury chocolate, home-dried fruits, candied papaya and pineapple slices, and a sack of "squirrel food" (the orig-inal and legitimate name, though now incorrectly called "gorp," a wretched neologism) of M&Ms, candy corn (which Mrs. O.C. can't abide), and cashews (which Young Crock abhors), and absolutely no raisins (which Mrs. loves but Mr. calls "dried flies").

A jug of punch from a packet of Wyler's—the favorite flavors used to be cola and root beer, and will be again when Wyler comes to its senses and resumes making them.

Though the supermarket is the main source, and the backpacking

shop supplies several key items, any long trip requires crucial items only available at Puget Sound Consumers Co-op and an array of delicatessens, including Brenner Bros. for Jewish foods, Uwaija-maya for Asian, and Liebchen for German and other European. Of course, in other areas the names are different.

Supper

The first course is soup from a country that knows how to make it right—Germany, Switzerland, France, Norway, Japan, or Israel, among others, not including the United States.

Because when denied greens Mrs. O.C. gets down on all fours and attacks the flowers, the next course flatly renounces the Law of Dry and Light. Early in the trip there is a nightly salad of lettuce, tomato, avocado, marinated artichoke, and oil-vinegar-spices mixed at home. When these are gone there are cucumber slices in vinegar.

The main course is a hoosh. The current favorites:

- Top Ramen noodles: beef-flavor with a can of corned beef, or Oriental-flavor, with cans of shrimp; plus a dollop of soy sauce and a bit of sesame oil.
- Kraft Dinner with extra cheddar cheese sliced in and a fresh green pepper, diced. Season in the cup with lemon pepper.

- Minute Rice with cans of tomato paste and tuna fish; Minute Rice and tuna fish and packets of dried crab soup and lobster sauce.
- Span-Yam-Bam nonhoosh dinner, the Spam fried separately, the yams reconstituted from canned yams dried at home, boiled with brown sugar to taste.
- Hungarian goulash soup, beef soya bits, that box of Bisquick brought out to make dumplings—and loud yowls of ecstasy echoing from the cliffs.

Now that dried spinach, the traditional staple, has been ruthlessly removed from the market, side dishes (not every meal) may be dried carrots; peas topped with hollandaise sauce made from a packet; or—hang the expense—freeze-dried cottage cheese.

Dessert is usually instant pudding (pistachio the favorite) with Dream Whip topping from a packet. One or two nights, store cookies instead. At least once during a week, out comes the Bisquick and a roll of aluminum foil and Mrs. O.C. bakes cookies over the coals of the campfire: a packet of spiced instant oatmeal with home-dried apricots, Milkman, margarine, and cinnamon.

For hot drinks in the evening cool: coffee, real or caffeine-free, Postum, instant cocoa, tea, fruit soup, peppermint tea. Cinnamon sprinkled where appropriate.

And so to bed.

Old Crock Alone

With the passage of time and the fossilizing of eccentricities, Old Crock has increasing difficulty recruiting companions for the trail and frequently goes off to wildlands alone except for three or more dogs, some of them getting old and all quite eccentric. Meals, he finds, are no longer social occasions (discounting the six or more canine eyes riveted on every bite that enters his mouth); there's no fun in tossing a spectacular salad, chefing a stupendous glop. His meals are fading away as inexorably as the state in an anarchist's dreams.

In an entire week he may have hot food only four or five times. This or that morning he may hanker for a cup of coffee and heat water on a fire of Esbit Heat Tabs or a handful of twigs. That or this evening he may have picked up some puffballs or coral mushrooms along the trail and decide to boil them in a pot of instant (hot-water-only) soup, adding a can of Vienna sausages.

For the rest, he has learned that instant oatmeal is nearly as good cold as hot, and instant breakfast shaken in a poly bottle with Milkman is delicious. Who needs more breakfast?

As for supper, most nights it's simply another installment of lunch—which he probably forgot to eat anyway, full as he is of oatmeal and chocolate milk.

Thanks to the meals being minimally delicious, he saves much weight, eating on an average substantially less than 1 pound of food a day—lucky, because the dog food is heavy.

NATURAL FOODS

Many a hiker who flees the chemical-filled air and water of the city is chagrined to find, upon reading ingredients on a food package, that he is consuming the equivalent of the Houston Ship Canal. A search for the pure and "natural"—low-sugar, low-sodium, non-chemicalized, or whatever—can be arduous. Large supermarkets typically have small sections catering to special dietary needs and desires. A few communities have consumers' co-ops whose members pool buying power to obtain natural foods at low cost; they may have connections with farmers (retired hippies or other counter-culturists) who grow fruits and vegetables by "organic" means. Backpacking shops increasingly are featuring such natural foods as wild rice and raw nuts. They also have a large selection of vegetarian meals, such as whole-wheat pasta stew, mushroom pilaf with almonds, spinach noodle Stroganoff, curried bean pilaf, Loch Ness stew—good to eat and presumably good for you.

WILD FOODS

Living off the country cannot be condoned or encouraged now that people pressure is crushing the small scraps of wilderness remaining in North America. Still, in proper places at proper times hikers may gently crop the wildland without harm.

Fishing in lakes and streams is an obvious example, and gathering clams and other shellfish from ocean beaches. A person may harvest all the edible berries he can find without upsetting the natural order (though perhaps a bear) and thus explode a tart moisture in a dry mouth or, by saving a cupful for camp, boil up a topping for pancakes.

Mushrooms sautéed in margarine add a gourmet touch to any outdoor supper. With a little study a half-dozen supersafe varieties can be learned.

Similarly, a number of greens may be harvested for a wildland salad—miners' lettuce and sorrel are famous. The tips of the year's new growth of salmonberry canes, easily peeled of thorns and skin, yield "Indian celery." For fresh vegetables there are such delicacies

as boiled nettles and skunk-cabbage leaves and sour dock—picked at the proper stage. *Stalking the Wild Asparagus* and sequels by Euell Gibbons are story-style introductions to enlivening the diet. The edible plants native to various parts of America are described in a number of regional booklets sold in bookstores and backpacking shops. The backpacker does well to know some of the common edible plants in the area of his customary travels, not only to vary menus on long trips but to gain the increasingly rare experience of eating absolutely natural, completely unchemicalized, perfectly organic foods.

15
Essentials

Mercy!" pleads the newcomer. "Chapter 8 emptied my wallet and Chapter 9 my left shoe, the good old getaway money. My savings account was closed out by 10, 11 took the silver ingots I had buried under the old oak tree, the second mortgage barely covered 12 and 13, and 14 broke the piggy bank. Enough!"

Not quite. A final few items remain, costing and weighing little compared to what has been suffered earlier. However, they must not be omitted. They are called "essentials" because they are—for safety, for comfort, or in a few cases, for the fun of it.

THE TEN ESSENTIALS

Back in the 1930s, when the Mountaineers began presenting an annual climbing course, the faculty soon discovered that while students were eager to haul axes and ropes and pitons, they saved weight by eliminating less glamorous stuff. Novice Homer and Novice Chuck, inseparable companions, would arrange for one to carry a flashlight, the other a map and compass. Then the party scattered on the descent from a peak, and the buddies were separated from each other and everyone else. Darkness came and Homer could see to walk but didn't know which way to go; Chuck knew which way to go but couldn't see to walk.

From innumerable such incidents, many miserable and not a few tragic, the Mountaineers drew up a list of Ten Essentials to be carried by every climber on his person or in his pack at all times. The list was really just a teaching device, since no experienced wilderness climber then or now would ever be caught without the Ten.

The rule is absolute for climbers; for hikers there is a sliding scale of necessity. The afternoon walker on a broad, well-marked, heavily populated trail often can do without a single Essential. The overnight backpacker who sticks to turnpikes may need only several. Those who probe deep into wilderness, away from the quick support of rangers or other hikers, and especially those who strike off cross-country, must have the full Ten.

A further qualification. A family that invariably stays together in a tight bunch may need some of the Ten only *as a group*. The

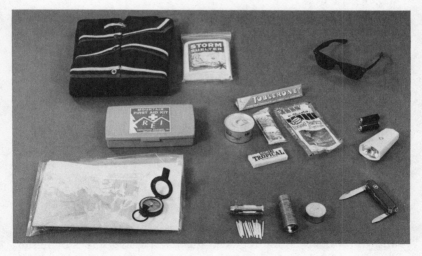

The ten Essentials. Top row: *Extra clothing (here, a sweater and a storm shelter), sunglasses.* Middle row: *First-aid kit, extra food, flashlight (and extra cells).* Bottom row: *Map, compass, matches, fire starters, knife.*

more independent the party members, the more important that *each person* carry all Ten.

One: Extra Clothing

Chapter 9 sufficiently makes the point, which is to have in the pack more clothing than seems necessary when setting out on a sunny morning; the afternoon may be windy and rainy, the night stormy and freezing, and though the hiker doesn't intend to be on the trail then, a sprained ankle may leave no choice.

In wet, cold country each person must have *wool* or other *warm-when-wet* clothing and some sort of protection from moisture of sky and ground in case circumstances force a bivouac without camping gear. A sheet of polyethylene serves as a storm shelter; a "space blanket" or "emergency blanket" of aluminized mylar additionally reduces heat loss by radiation, weighs 2 ounces, costs $4.

Two: Extra Food

The day hiker's lunch may have to be stretched to a supper, a breakfast, another lunch—while the lost route is being found or the rescue party summoned. Thus the lunch must be substantial; the test is that on any trip *without* misfortune there should be food left over.

A can of fruit-nut pemmican stowed permanently in the pack serves the purpose; few people will eat it in anything but an honest-to-gosh emergency. One Northwest climber carries a packet of dry dog food.

Three: Sunglasses

In forest travel, sunglasses are not essential; they surely are in desert country and open alpine regions, such as massive screes or felsenmeers (boulder fields) of light-colored rock. The extreme case is snow, where sunglasses are mandatory on bright days to prevent discomfort, pain, and even *temporary blindness and permanent damage*.

For ordinary hiking, any model that filters out about 65 percent of available light will do. For extended snow travel, more care must be taken in selection. First, side shields are important. Second, glass lenses are recommended because they filter out both ultraviolet and infrared rays; some cheap plastic lenses are virtually useless and even the best, made of CR-39, don't stop infrared. Except in fog, where yellow lenses improve contrast, helping distinguish holes from bumps, green or gray-green are best because they don't alter the color balance of visible light. Persons who wear prescription glasses should be careful to buy sunglasses that fit comfortably over regular lenses; few do, and none of the clip-ons are dark enough or have side shields, and that's why myopic snow trompers usually end up having an optician make them a pair of prescription sunglasses.

Four: Knife

Except for small children, each hiker should carry a knife. Uses include eating (opening that can of pemmican), first aid, whittling kindling to start a wood fire (for cooking or for emergency warmth when trapped in a storm or at night by accident or loss of route).

No backpacker needs a "hunting knife" or cutlass or scimitar. Big blades are for hunters, fishermen, and guerrillas.

While on the subject of weaponry—the backpacker has no business hauling an ax or hatchet; they are heavy, unnecessary, and inevitably lead to clear-cut logging of campsites. And just as an ax triggers a compulsion to chop-chop-chop, a lightweight folding saw may cause even the sensitive hiker to engage in an orgy. It was a sign that a frontier town was coming of age when the sheriff required transients to check their guns at his office, and it is high time now for wildland walkers to check their steel at the trailhead. If Sonnyboy is going out of his mind for a chance to try his new hatchet, keep him away from the trees, send him off to whack at subdividers' survey stakes.

Returning to knives, for decades the trail standard was the "Boy Scout" type, officially designed for the organization and subsequently imitated. Many models are on the market, with single blade,

can opener, cap opener–screwdriver, and awl, or other assortment of tools, costing very little or quite a bit depending on quality. The cheapest is best for children, who lose knives instantly.

Nowadays, though, what the pin is for the Greek and the tooth is for a Moose the Swiss army knife is for the backpacker. It's a very good knife, sturdily constructed of stainless steel and featuring a spring system that revolutionized knivery in the late nineteenth century, displayed by the Museum of Modern Art as an outstandingly well-designed functional object. Models more or less elaborate range from $10 to $40, the latter an excellent conversation piece. A thread of controversy has woven into the history. The Swiss Army buys from two firms; Victorinox makes "the original," and Wenger, "the genuine." Innumerable other manufacturers produce lookalikes, which are not purchased by the Swiss Army. Less fastidious is the "Taiwan Army knife," with fork, spoon, eyebrow tweezers, and fishing pole, unsurpassed for keeping a little kid amused.

The hiker should own but not necessarily carry a whetstone for occasionally sharpening the blade.

Five: Fire Starter

Even where the wood fire is obsolescent or prohibited, it continues to have a role in emergencies. To be able to start a fire when one is urgently needed, as in a rainstorm when the hiker is lost and the wood wet, each person should carry one of the fuels noted in Chapter 13.

Six: Matches

To start the fire starter, matches are required. In addition to those carried for routine purposes, each person should have an emergency supply, either waterproof or in a waterproof container; windproof matches can be lifesavers in foul weather. So can a butane lighter.

Seven: First-Aid Kit

Ideally, every hiker venturing more than a few miles and hours from civilization should have first-aid training and a complete kit; certainly anyone who spends much time in the backcountry should avail himself of instruction offered by the American Red Cross or mountaineering clubs, and assemble a kit with sufficient materials to cover a wide range of eventualities. If unable to take formal instruction, he should study such books as *Mountaineering First Aid* by Dick Mitchell, describing contents and use of the first-aid kit, and *Medicine for Mountaineering* by James A. Wilkerson, a detailed "doctor book."

At the very least, the novice must be equipped to handle common ailments of the trail, some of which can be disabling even though not "serious" in a medical sense. If each hiker carries a small kit, supplies can be pooled for crises; if the group (say, a family) carries only a single kit, it should be correspondingly more elaborate.

The following items constitute a *very minimum, one-man* first-aid kit:

- Band-Aids—several, for minor cuts
- Gauze pads—several, 3 inches and 4 inches square, for deep wounds with much bleeding
- Adhesive tape—a 1- or 2-inch roll for holding bandages in place, covering blisters, taping sprained ankles, etc.
- Salt tablets—to prevent or treat symptoms of heat exhaustion (including cramps) when sweating heavily
- Aspirin—for relieving pain and reducing fever
- Needle—for opening blisters, removing splinters
- First-aid manual—a booklet discussing diagnosis and treatment (supplied with kits at backpacking shops)

Such a kit can cope with only the simplest problems; after a hiker has gained a bit of sad experience, he will want to add many of the following:

- Moleskin and Molefoam or Second Skin—for covering blisters
- Razor blade, single-edge—for minor surgery, cutting tape and Moleskin to size, shaving hairy spots before taping
- Gauze bandage—a 2-inch roll for large cuts
- Butterfly Band-Aids—for closing cuts
- Triangular bandage—for large wounds
- Large compress bandage—to hold dressings in place
- Water purifier (Chapter 4)—for treating drinking water of doubtful purity
- Antacid—for settling stomachs upset by overexertion, unaccustomed altitude, and the cook's mistakes
- Wire splint—for sprains and minor fractures
- Elastic bandage—3 inches wide, for sprains, applying pressure to bleeding wounds, etc.
- First-aid cream—for sunburn, itches, scrapes, and diaper rash
- Antiseptic—Bactine, Zephiran Chloride, or other, for cleaning minor wounds
- Antihistamine—for allergic reactions to bee stings
- Oil of cloves—for toothache
- Darvon—for severe pain (prescription required)
- Antidiarrhetic pills—for terrible cases of the trots (prescription required)
- Laxatives and/or glycerine suppositories—for prune-resistant constipation in persons congenitally suffering from this affliction
- Snakebite kit—see Chapter 5
- Tooth-repair kit—for extended trips

Backpacking shops stock small kits containing some of the above items, weighing under 1 pound, costing from $9 to $25. The beginner should purchase one of these for a start and build from there.

Eight: Flashlight

As an Essential the flashlight is primarily to permit continued travel when caught by darkness. With the exception of small children, who will never be far from parents, each person must carry his own light. (One in the party is not enough even if the group stays scrupulously together; many modern flashlights are notoriously undependable.) the obscurity of a forest night is total, and the only safe way to navigate an unlit trail is on hands and knees, which makes for a very slow pace.

Almost every year, somewhere in America, a benighted lightless hiker keeps walking in an attempt to reach his destination, perhaps minutes away, and steps off the path, over a cliff, into eternity. And every year other hikers wisely give up the attempt and sit out long shivering hours while relatives worry and rescue parties mobilize; these hikers nevermore leave the flashlight home to save weight.

There must be light to walk by night. There also must be light for orderly habitation of camp—cooking late suppers or early breakfasts, taking short trips into the bushes, and keeping a happy tent. The demands of camp light and trail light are quite different, as may be those of outside camp light and inside tent light, and trail

Left to right: *Candle lantern for camp use; four high-tech handlamps representative of the dozens trying to convince hikers they are dependable.*

light and icefall- and cliff-climbing light. Selecting the right light requires the backpacker to think about several matters. He wants enough *useful light* for his varied purposes, whether walking trails or reading in the sleeping bag, and for the number of nights he is out. He seeks the *least weight and cost*, yet will pay a premium in both for *dependability*. No one product is all things to all hiking situations. A person has to study and ponder a number of things.

Camp Light

As discussed in the next section, a battery yield of 1.8 volts has been found to be about the lowest level providing enough light to follow a trail, while 1 volt gives sufficient light around a campground or inside a tent. Even when batteries have faded far below pristine strength they do well enough for stirring pots and finding the tent door.

Any of the trail lights serves in camp, of course. One of the midgets, marginal for traveling, may be carried as a camp extra, weighing little and fitting handily in a pocket.

In addition there are midgets that verge on gadgets: the teensy Pinchlight, 1 ounce, 2.50; the Cyalume Light Stick, which gives instant light without batteries (fireflies?), 1 ounce, $2; the Lightning Bug (not a real one), ½ ounce, $3; a fluorescent cylinder for diffusely illuminating a tent, 4 ounces, $15, not counting batteries.

Finally, nothing is so wild-woodsy as candlelight. If lit in a cup or on a rock unprotected, a candle tends to burn too fast in breezes, dripping and wasting wax, or to get blown out in the wind. A craftsman with a Swiss Army knife and an old tin can will enjoy fashioning a wind-guarded candlestick or even (see below) a genuine Boy Scout "lightning bug." Much more elegant is a pretty little candle lantern, 6 ounces, $14, that keeps wind out and drippings and flame in. It can be hung from a tent ceiling to illuminate the interior, from a branch to shed light around the kitchen, or placed close to a book for reading. A package of three candles, each lasting up to 8 hours, weighs 5 ounces, costs $2.

Batteries and Bulbs

The first consideration in batteries is the *electrochemical constitution*. The accompanying charts clearly show the inferiority, for back-packing, of *carbon-zinc* cells, whether standard or heavy-duty. Though the least expensive, the short life means relatively little useful light for the weight. At 70°F the standard permits trail walking (that is, it yields 1.8 volts) for barely 3 hours; the heavy-duty for 11; the *alkaline* is good for 25. At 0°F the standard carbon-zinc drops dead almost immediately, the heavy-duty holds out for 2 hours, the alkaline continues for about 6 hours.

It should be noted that the tests were for continuous use; the switch was never off. During intermittent use the batteries have time to percolate chemicals and recover some strength, thus giving more hours of light than the test charts show. Further, batteries run down all the way to dark death can be revived by warming, in the hot sun or near (not *too* near lest there be an explosion) a campfire. In a test where alkaline batteries were run down to a yield of 1 volt at 0°F, then rewarmed, D cells gave 8 more hours of 1.8-volt life with a PR2 bulb, 16 hours with a PR4.

Lithium cells are hailed by catalogs as "satellite tech . . . pacemaker-tech, where reliability is life or death . . . state of the art . . ." A

BURNING TIMES OF BATTERIES

Tests by REI Quality Control Department, using PR6 bulb, comparing D-size cells: a single Eternacell lithium and pairs of Mallory alkaline, Eveready heavy-duty carbon-zinc, and Mallory standard carbon-zinc.

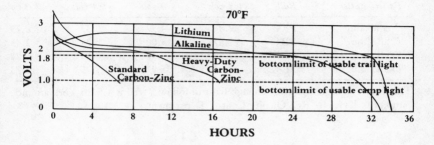

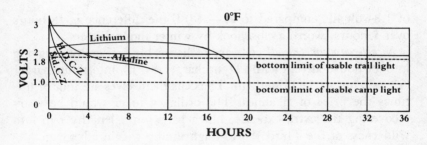

chemist can demonstrate mathematically a five to one advantage in longevity over alkalines, which would make the cells a bargain for backpackers, even though the cost is also five to one. (A standard flashlight that uses a pair of alkalines costing about $2.50 takes a single lithium cell plus a dummy, for about $13.) Unfortunately, whatever the results in satellites and pacemakers, tests in backpacking situations don't confirm the mathematics. A percentage of the cells are very erratic. Some don't work at all. Nobody knows why—if they did, they'd fix it. Until they do, lithium cells must be considered experimental. Nevertheless, though their performance at 70°F is not notably superior to that of alkaline—33 hours

BURNING TIMES OF THE MOST COMMON
ALKALINE BATTERIES

		Continuous Burning Time (hours)			
		70°F		0°F	
Pair of Batteries	Bulb	1.8 volt	1.0 volt	1.8 volt	1.0 volt
AA alkaline	PR4	2.88	4.37	0.33	0.73
C alkaline	PR4	9.67	15.00	0.25	2.43
D alkaline	PR2	11.80	19.47	0.75	4.77
D alkaline	PR4	30.33	35.92	3.75	11.23

The lowest voltage that gives enough light to follow a trail is 1.8; to work around camp, 1.0. Tests by REI Quality Control Department.

of 1.8-volt life compared to 25—at 0°F the difference is 18 hours over 5 hours, worth a close look by winter mountaineers.

Nickel-cadmium (nicad) cells are rechargeable, either by plugging into the house current with a Dynacharger ($15) or into a Suncharger ($25) set out in the bright sun. The cells themselves are four or five times the price of alkalines. The ordinary hiker would be years recovering the extra expense, but a party on a lengthy trip into wilderness or the Third World might find a weight advantage.

The alternative to batteries is a *hand-powered generator*. The Dynolight, (8½ ounces, $15) continues putting out light as long as the hand keeps squeezing.

The second consideration in batteries is *size*. The little AA cells cost minimally less than the larger C and still larger D; for packages of two, about $2, $2.50, and $2.50, respectively. They weigh much less, of course, and thus are used in midget lights, and some others too. As the table shows, the size (and weight) reflect how much "juice" the alkaline contains. At 70°F, with a PR4 bulb, a pair of AA yields 2.88 hours of 1.8 volts, while the C yields 9.67 hours, and the D, 30.33 hours. The D, though a bit heavier than the C, plainly offers the most hours per ounce.

In choosing size a person must decide how many hours will be spent walking by night, which requires 1.8 volts, and how many hours fiddling around in camp or tent, where 1 volt suffices. Whichever cell is used, the self-reliant, prudent hiker carries a spare pair—or, a standard flashlight plus a midget. As the chart shows, when alkalines (and lithiums too) sicken, they die almost immediately, and exterior examination tells nothing about inner health.

The *bulb* affects battery life. The smaller the bulb number the more current it draws, the brighter light it gives, the quicker it exhausts the cells. As the table shows, a PR2 gives 11.8 hours of 1.8-volt life with the D alkaline; the PR4, 30.33. Other bulbs, in order of declining luminosity and increasing thrift, are PR6, PR222, and PR311. Anything much dimmer than a PR6 may be marginal for trails, though abundant for locating the toilet. A climber standing in inky night on the brink of a crevasse a rope-length wide, wondering if the snow bridge goes clear across, is not going to be satisfied with a PR4, or really happy with anything less than searchlights and Roman candles.

Headlamps

Setting off across that snowbridge to see where it goes, the climber wants both hands free for handling rope and ax, especially when the bridge groans underfoot as if about to collapse, and therefore he is likely to be wearing a headlamp. Hikers have avoided climbers' headlamps because to cast a long, bright beam they must be heavy and cumbersome—lamp on forehead, batteries in a pocket, the connecting cord forever tangling in brush and whiskers.

However, on long night hikes or lengthy camp evenings the headlamp has distinct convenience, and new models have reduced the weight and eliminated the cord. One example is a mini-headlamp that weighs less than 5 ounces, including two AA alkaline cells, and costs $10. Thanks to the use of AA cells, the whole package rests comparatively lightly on the head, though in time it grows irksome. Thanks to the use of a PR14 bulb, some 4 hours of light are provided—some of it useful for trails, the rest for camp.

Another cordless headlamp weighs more, gives more light longer, operating on four AA alkalines with a PR14 bulb. Weight, complete

A cordless and fairly light-weight headlamp using AA alkaline batteries, worth considering for ordinary backpacking.

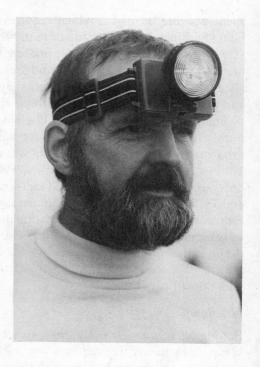

with cells, is 8 ounces; cost, batteries excluded, $12. Light useful for trail or camp lasts about 8 hours.

Handlamps

The customary hiker's choice is a hand-held two-cell flashlight. In olden days, when so much American life was out of doors at night, walking home from school on a country road, bringing in an armload of wood for the stove, getting out of bed to see why the chickens were making a fuss, running to the privy in emergencies, a flashlight was expected to be as solid as the Rock of Gibraltar, and was, and if it should fail, was readily fixable by anyone possessed of a Boy Scout knife. Latterly the product has so deteriorated that a hiker who depends on supermarket and drugstore models does well to carry two and insist on his companions doing the same, so that, say, in a party of five there may be, at the time of crisis, one of the ten still functioning.

A lone hiker who doesn't wish to carry several flashlights may take a few candles as backup. On any much-used trail a Ten Can often can be found around long-established camps. A nail (from the emergency kit) is used to punch a hole in one side of the can, halfway between bottom (back) and top (front), and the candle is wedged tightly in the hole. Smaller holes are punched at back and front to insert a wire or cord (from the emergency kit) for a carrying handle. This genuine old-style official Boy Scout "lightning bug" casts a wide, diffuse glow ideal for trails and is almost windproof.

A major problem is that as wildland trails grow cleaner, Ten Cans and other useful garbage grow rarer, so that lightning bugs may be available only to ancients who carry their own Ten Cans because to them food doesn't taste right cooked in a billy. The average hiker will thus forget it and select his lighting system from among three categories of handlamps.

The *old ordinaries* sold in supermarkets, drugstores, and gas stations are good enough if a party has enough of them. In remarkable instances they last for years, though usually only hours or minutes—and there's no way to fix the circuitry or switchery. They are light (with batteries, under ½ pound) and cheap (without batteries, under $7 or so).

The *indestructibles* (well, almost) often come with guarantees, for whatever satisfaction *that* is when on a dark and stormy wildland night they do, indeed, fail. Weight is usually the same or less, but sometimes more, than that of the ordinaries. Cost is higher. Backpacker shops mostly prefer not to recommend one or two models but to present the vital statistics and manufacturers' claims and let the hiker study such information as is presented by the charts and table in this chapter, become somewhat knowledgeable about electrochemistry, ponder personal needs and desires, and sally forth to learn from experience, some of it doubtless bitter. What the shops *will* do is discontinue any flashlight that turns out to be a perennial troublemaker.

The third category, the *midgets*, is not readily separable, since some are also indestructible, and the same firm may offer a range of models, from very lightweight to very long-life.

Tekna, for example, has these: Micro-Lite, 1.76 ounces, $5.50 (no batteries), "lots of light" from a pair of N (that's very small) alkaline batteries; Tekna II, 1.5 ounces, $9 (no batteries), using a PR222 bulb and two AA alkalines, giving "four hours of light"; Tekna IV (5 ounces, $20, no batteries), using a PR13 bulb and four AA alkalines, the beam "intense—for 1½ hours"; and Tekna II Micro-Lith, 1.4 ounces, $16 (including a lithium cell), operating "3–4 hours."

Durabeam "never will let you down" with: the Compact, 3 ounces and $4 (including two AA alkaline batteries and a PR6 bulb) and the Regular, 15 ounces, $8 (two D alkalines not included), using a PR2 bulb, the "switch guaranteed for a lifetime" and the "ABS plastic construction unbreakable."

The PeliLite, 7 ounces, $20 (including two C alkalines), is "guaranteed to last a lifetime," can be submerged in water to a depth of 2,000 feet, runs 2 hours on a set of batteries, and the high-intensity Krypton bulb lasts 30 hours (15 sets of cells).

Mag-Lite offers "the toughest flashlights made," waterproof and shockproof, unbreakable lens, and the beam "can be focused from full flood to narrow spotlight in a split second." The two-cell (C) model weighs over ½ pound, costs $23 (no batteries).

The Starwood is "trusty as it is handsome," suitable for trail or den. It uses alkaline, lithium, or nicad C cells, has a "night-slicing Krypton beam," weighs 6 ounces, costs $50 (no batteries). A monogram is $4 more.

The Super QXL-Lite uses three C cells, alkaline or rechargeable nicads, with "a quartz-halogen bulb whose beam pierces smoke and fog." Weight 10 ounces, cost $22 (no batteries).

There are others, too.

Nine: Map

The kinds of maps and their use and where to obtain them are discussed in Chapter 16. Here, suffice it to say that a party, and preferably each individual, must have a map of the area being traveled—and know how to read it!

Ten: Compass

The natural companion to the map is the compass, use of which is also treated in Chapter 16. The hiker should avoid the expensive precision instruments intended for complex navigation; he can do very well with a simple compass costing around $7 to $13 as long as it has a clear base with grid lines that can be aligned with a map reference line for orientation.

The *altimeter*, to climbers and cross-country roamers a route-finding aid often more valuable than a compass, is hardly necessary for ordinary trail hiking but does serve as a barometer. Instruments calibrated to 16,000 feet or higher in 100-foot graduations are available for $25 to $150.

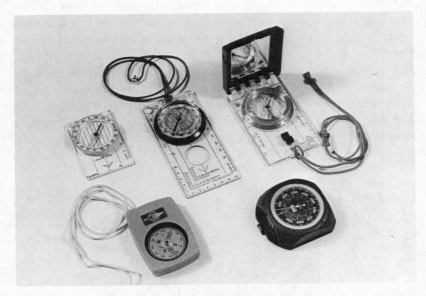

Representative compasses popular with hikers. Top row: *Silva Polaris, Suunto Boy Scout, Silva Ranger.* Bottom row: *KB-20, Thommen altimeter.*

OTHER (FREQUENTLY) ESSENTIALS

There is another category of items whose lack rarely imperils life or limb but can lead to major discomfort or inconvenience.

Whistle

Rescue authorities wish every lost hiker had a whistle, since the shrill blast carries farther than a yell and takes less effort. Parents often issue whistles to offspring—after sternly emphasizing they are *not* for scaring birds and aggravating neighbors but solely for emergencies.

Sunburn Preventive

See nature boy strip to shorts and T-shirt in morning and walk meadows or desert or beach, joyously soaking up rays from the life-creating sun. By afternoon he notes that his skin feels warm even when a cool wind blows, but is unaware of catastrophe until, in camp that evening, companions cry out aghast at the sight of him. Through the night he lies sleepless on his bed of pain. In morning he cannot move legs or head without wincing, and to hoist pack on back is to scream and whimper. He will not again seek oneness with the solar furnace, this miserable nature boy. Next time he wants a tan, he'll buy it at the drugstore.

In woodlands and poor weather a hiker is unlikely to receive more radiation than his skin can readily tolerate. But in all-day brightness, especially at high elevations and/or in snow, a burn can become a true medical emergency, requiring first aid with soothing creams and painkillers and sedatives plus aspirin to reduce fever, possibly an unplanned layover, or in the extremity, evacuation to a hospital. Persons with dark complexions or deep tans slowly acquired can stand more sun than those with fair skins freshly exposed after months of encasement in city clothing, but not as much as they think; even people with multimillennia of genetic adaptation to tropical sunlight can become gravely burned.

During the first bright trips of summer a hiker should cover up with shirt and trousers after no more than 2 hours or so; gradually the time of exposure can be lengthened, perhaps to a full day. The uncertain beginner should apply sunburn preventive to exposed areas at the very start of an extended walk in the sun and every hour or so during the day and definitely *not wait* for "hot skin" or "red skin"; by then, it's already 2 hours too late to avoid agony.

Unless a hiker spends a lot of time in snow or is supersensitive to sunlight (a condition likely discovered early in life), he doesn't need the clown-white or glacier cream favored by climbers and skiers. The standard screen, the active ingredient in most current preparations, is para-aminobenzoic acid, PABA for short. At a concentration of 5 percent, the ultraviolet is totally blocked and the skin neither burns nor tans. Lower concentrations for "tanning without burning" (an impossibility) suffice for most hikers most of the time. The main thing is to have *some* burn preventive—and to *use* it. Experience (a certain amount painful) tells how much protection is required. Preparations are usually labeled with their SPF (sun protection factor), ranging from 2 to 15; individuals with sensitive skin ordinarily prefer a rating of 8 or higher. Some people learn to their chagrin that they have an allergic reaction to this ingredient or that; perhaps worse, they may have a phototoxic reaction, the cream itself giving them a bad burn with any sun exposure whatsoever.

A person whose lips are prone to burn and chap should carry a lip salve or Chapstick. (Lipstick works fine for women, but men risk misunderstandings.) Similarly, people with flaring nostrils may appreciate one of the preparations available to prevent interior burns that cause runny noses.

Insect Repellent

It is possible for hikers to be totally incurious about the water ouzel, golden eagle, varied thrush, and hummingbird. However, none is so stolid of soul and tough of skin as to lack a lively interest in mosquitoes, flies, gnats, no-see-ums, ticks, chiggers, and others of the afflictions visited upon man as a consequence of his fall from grace. These instruments of the Lord's anger, which drove Adam and Eve from the Garden of Eden, are considered at gruesome length in Chapter 5.

Though no repellent answers the hiker's prayer for a zone of quiet, application can reduce the incidence of bites; the attendant cloud of wings just has to be lived with.

Still on the market and still with faithful adherents are liquid and rub-on stick repellents, dating from World War II, whose principal active ingredient is ethyl hexanediol; there are also arcane potions concocted by North Woods medicine men and transcending science. Vitamin B-1 taken orally has long been thought by some hikers to drive bugs away, and has long been known certainly by all hikers to give a sweating body a distinctive aroma that drives people away. Marketed as an "oral repellent," the tablets are priced many times higher than those sold in drugstores as just plain vitamins. The nicotine reek of tobacco addicts is also reputed to offend bugs and other nonsmokers.

For all that, in the late 1950s the bug experts of the U.S. government concluded after extended research that N,N-diethyl-meta-toluamide (DEET) is the most effective known chemical (safe for application to the human body) for discouraging insects. Because no successor is in sight, and because once a candidate is identified the federal safety tests take years, the status is likely to stay quo for decades. (However, the U.S. Army is working to develop a time-release packaging to release small amounts of repellent over 12 hours.) DEET is not without flaws—it attacks the plastics in watch crystals, glass frames, and handles of Swiss army knives, and is a suspect in mysterious allergic reactions.

The most potent form and least expensive is Jungle Juice in a 100-percent alcohol solution. The alcohol quickly evaporates, but the odorless, invisible chemical remains and works for hours unless washed off by sweat or rain. The compound is so strong in this concentration that care must be used around the eyes, where it may be carried by sweat and sting like fury. It may also irritate the tender skin of infants.

Other brands have lower concentrations, at prices that by comparison seem exorbitant. Nevertheless, the oil base of Off and the cream of Cutter are preferred by many hikers, some because they like the feel, some because they fail to understand it's not the palpable oil and cream that fend off the bugs but the invisible DEET. Aerosols and foams have more gas and package than repellent, and weigh and cost too much for backpacking.

Tundra in mosquito time, forests in fly time, may drive a hiker to cower in a tent barred at every opening or cover up completely with clothing supplemented by a *head net*. More commodious for sitting around camp or trail, and highly recommended for tentless sleeping, is the *"habitat,"* a piece of no-see-um netting wide and long enough to drape over head and torso; from within, dreaming peacefully or nibbling pilot bread and peanut butter, one looks smugly out to the wing-crowded world. Praised by walkers and canoeists in the Far North, where mosquitoes work around the clock in numbers endangering sanity and life, is the *"shoo-bug jacket,"* a light fishnet garment with elastic at wrists and waist and a drawstring hood. To prepare for use, place the jacket in a ziplock plastic bag, pour in a bottle of Jungle Juice, and zip the bag tight for 6 hours, during which period cotton fibers interwoven in the nylon fishnet soak up the juice. The treated jacket frees the wearer from bites for up to 2 weeks without a recharge.

Repair Kit

A hiker awakes to find that during the night a goose apparently died a violent death inside the tent; then he notes the rip in his sleeping bag, exactly where he dried it by the campfire. On the trail he carelessly dumps pack from weary back, the frame hits just right (wrong) on a rock, a joint separates, and there seems no solution but to send out for a wheelbarrow. Nearing the road, he lengthens stride and overstrained pants rip, and modesty forbids him to enter mixed company.

These are only a few of the ills the best of gear is heir to, reasons experienced backpackers carry some sort of repair kit. Following are typical components and examples of uses:

- Cloth tape—for repairing tarps
- Ripstop tape—for mending ripstop nylon parkas, sleeping bags, and tents
- Thread—a spool of heavy cotton-covered polyester for mending clothing and sewing on buttons
- Needles—several in various sizes
- Awl and very coarse thread—for sewing packbags, tent floors, and other tough fabrics

- Safety pins—several large ones and lots of little ones for such emergencies as a zipper that goes off the trolley
- Clevis pins and wires—for pack-frame problems (see Chapter 10)
- Nylon cord—⅛-inch or so, for lashing together broken packs and sick boots
- Light steel wire—for field reconstruction of gravely wounded pack frames
- Nails and screws—a small assortment for heavy engineering
- Pliers—for manipulating recalcitrant materials, in addition to kitchen use and expedition dentistry

Toilet Kit

A folk hero brags in an old ballad:

> I clean my teeth with river sand,
>   Comb my hair with a tree,
> Wash my face whenever it rains,
>   And let my wind blow free.

His gamy descendants know neither soap nor comb nor toothbrush nor handkerchief from start of trail to end, when they again submit to cleanliness and godliness.

Years of wildland wandering are necessary to live unsoaped and uncombed, and TV training is so ingrained that most people can never bring themselves to blow their nose in the old way, finger against nostril. And in an age when sweating in public is a penitentiary offense, who dares spit anymore? Women especially, because of the sugar and spice sexism too many of them share, adjust very slowly to an environment of natural, healthy dirt.

Eventually the steamroller of the Neatness Industry must be halted and a compromise found that allows people to pass downwind of each other without being stunned, yet permits rivers to flow suds-free to unpoisoned oceans.

Granted, a clean body, even if it does not lead to a clean mind, has certain health values; the following simple toilet kit is environmentally tolerable if used in moderation:

- Toothbrush and paste in carrying case
- Soap or biodegradable detergent—a plain old bar or a tiny bottle of concentrated liquid solution—either of which doubles for dishwashing
- Small cloth towel, reusable paper towel, or a packet of Handiwipes
- Polished-steel mirror
- Comb
- Handkerchief—if not for nose blowing, for cleaning glasses, wiping sweat, binding wounds

Finally, a word about what formerly was called the Eleventh Essential. Toilet paper, which started to be widely used only in the past century, can be dispensed with by employment of available greenery—avoiding, of course, the likes of poison ivy. Whereas human wastes are biodegraded in weeks, the paper may last for years in a dry climate—and not out of sight, because critters dig it up and winds blow it here, there, everywhere. A caring hiker does well to substitute natural greenery for paper whenever feasible, and when not, to hold a small paper fire on the spot. (Beware of Smokey the Bear!) In densely inhabited camps lacking toilet pits, the deeply caring hikers are beginning to employ, on the pattern of garbage bags, "sewage bags." (PACK IT OUT. PACK IT *ALL* OUT.)

NOT ESSENTIAL BUT SOMETIMES NICE

The reader who entered this chapter impoverished and distraught is surely about to emit a primal scream and run off naked as an ape to look for a cave and some bananas, and a plague on the rest of it. Wait a bit. The *fun* is about to start.

Camera.

Fishing tackle.

To expand horizons, ice ax, rope, snowshoes, and skis (Chapters 17 and 19).

Binoculars aid in puzzling out cross-country routes, identifying distant peaks, and studying birds and animals. A good choice for a backpacker is a set with a magnification of 6 or 8, weighing about ½ pound, costing around $75–$100. A monocular can be had for ¼ pound and $35, a telescope, for ½ pound and $20. At the other extreme of the dimensional universe are an 8-power hand lens for 3 ounces and $5, a 100-power pocket microscope for 3 ounces and $15.

The weather—past, present, and future—has unfailing interest. For ounces you can have a pocket thermometer that tells how hot/cold it is now, a maximum/minimum thermometer that in the morning explains why you shivered all night, a wind gauge that will teach you to distinguish a brisk breeze from a whole gale, a rain gauge that will support your story that you really *did* see Noah's ark float by in the night, a hygrometer to confirm that the summer humidity from the Rockies east to the Atlantic is always 100 percent. A "mini-weather station" monitors wind speed and direction, temperature, and rainfall, all for ½ pound.

Leaving the watch in the car is a stimulus to learning to mark the passage of time by the motion of heavenly bodies. However, approximations can be grossly awry in climates that conceal heavenly bodies days and nights in a row. If boats or buses are to be met, a watch should be carried. Two watches.

There is nature study, to enlarge knowledge of wildlands and deepen appreciation, using guides to birds, animals, animal tracks, flowers, trees, mosses, mushrooms, liverworts, rocks and minerals. A planisphere locates planets and stars. An Audubon bird call lets a birder talk back, as does a beautifully crafted Brazilian bird whistle.

Nobody should ever grow too old for toys. The Frisbee and other kinetic fripperies absolutely must be banned from meadowlands and quiet lands, as must touch football and soccer. However, flying a kite from a tall peak gives a feel for winds and sky and, except for interesting the eagles, scarcely disrupts the natural order—though on the beach a Chinese dragon has been known to cause gulls and crows to riot.

Fulfill a childhood ambition—learn to juggle, using instruction booklet and practice kit. Off in a rough moraine, where the boulders can withstand your boots, master the boomerang.

Therapy toys? Take along Body Bliss Beads, a Massage Tractor, or a Backstroke and while away the storms exchanging back massages to relax those tense muscles.

A few days from the city, compulsively literate folk become inordinately fascinated by lists of ingredients on food packages, a symptom of printed-word hunger. The syndrome can be controlled by carrying a paperback book, preferably with maximum words for minimum paper and slow enough going not to be run through hastily. An Ian Fleming or Stanislaw Lem fills a mere afternoon; for little more weight a single volume of Gibbon's *Decline and Fall* occupies the entirety of a three-day blow and then some; a Bible is unsurpassed in weight-to-content ratio; what with memorizing soliloquies and reciting them to tent-bound companions, a collection of Shakespeare's tragedies can last a whole expedition, or even end it.

Confined to tent or tarp by days of miasma, hikers will, of course, sleep, until that's worn out. They next will talk, until hostilities tend toward confrontations. Best, then, to bring out a backgammon board, pocket Scrabble, or dice. Or a deck of cards for a game of hearts ("Smoke it out! Smoke it out!") that harmlessly releases tensions. Or a pocket chess set to do the same at a lower noise level, though risking years of smoldering animosity.

The scene may bring out latent artistry: Carry a watercolor pad and paints, crayons disguised as children's playthings.

Make music with a harmonica (instruction book included); a "magic" flute (also with teaching guide); an African kalimba (thumb piano); an Andean reed pipe, excellent for soothing your restless llamas.

Include in party gear a catalog of Early Winters, Ltd., to see how much fun you could have had with the right games and musical instruments. And a Jack Stephenson catalog for close study of the vapor barrier.

Finally, a notebook and pencil stub. For leaving notes when the party is traveling in two or more sections. For keeping a trip log or diary. For capturing those lines of verse, those philosophic insights, you think you'll remember but won't. For composing letters to the custodians of this book, telling the Old Crock where to get off.

Part III

Elaborating
the Art

16
Routefinding

Many hikers, even some with years of trail experience, stay on course entirely by watching the heels of the companion immediately ahead and never need any routefinding skill except that of boot identification, to avoid switching to the wrong boots at a crowded junction and following a stranger up the wrong valley.

However, the method has serious faults. The heels may disappear around a bend and be seen no more. They may themselves be lost. Finally, even should the heel watcher always get where he wants to go, he never feels independent and self-reliant, is always somebody's caboose.

Mastery of wilderness navigation requires considerable time and study and is too complex for extensive treatment in these pages. A text recommended for anyone who expects to leave turnpike trails for byways is *Be Expert With Map and Compass* by Bjorn Kjellstrom. But even the raw novice should learn the fundamentals discussed here in order to have a fighting chance to reach his objectives—and return without the assistance of a search party.

TOOLS OF THE TRADE

The basic equipment of routefinding is built into the human body; the skilled navigator, by use of eyes and ears and other senses, and through habits of always watching where he's going and where he's been, constantly filing mental notes about landmarks, maintains a sort of internal gyroscope.

However, the instrument occasionally gets out of whack, particularly in fog or darkness and unfamiliar terrain, and other tools must be brought into play.

Compass

The compass needle always points north—right? Wrong. The needle has two ends and one points south; to avoid very gross errors, the distinction between the ends must be kept in mind.

The north end of the needle always points north—right? Wrong. It does not point to *true* north—that is, the North Pole—but to *magnetic* north—that is, the North Magnetic Pole, located about a thousand miles to the south in the Canadian Arctic. The difference between true north and magnetic north is the *declination*, and unless this is known for the area being traveled, the compass merely confuses the situation.

For example, the current declination in the state of Washington is approximately 22° east (that is, the needle points 22° east of true north) and in the state of Maine approximately 20° west. Some maps give the local declination, but some don't, in which case the information must be obtained elsewhere before the trip. Trail navigation is not so precise that the hiker must fret about declination down to the last several degrees. However, failing to distinguish between east and west, and thus adjusting for declination in the wrong direction, is a good way to see a lot of unexpected country.

Before it is used, the compass must be oriented. Set it on a flat surface or hold it carefully in the hand, making sure no metallic

WASHINGTON   MINNESOTA   MAINE
22-23°E.   7-8°E.   20-22°W.

SOUTHERN   COLORADO   EASTERN
CALIFORNIA   14-15°E.   TENNESSEE
15-16°E.   0°

Compasses oriented for various parts of America, showing declination.

objects are close, since their slight magnetism may distort the reading. When the needle stabilizes, rotate the compass to the proper declination—that is, for Washington, until the north-pointing end of the needle points 22° east (right) of the north symbol on the dial, and for Maine, 20° west (left) of the symbol. The compass is now oriented and the north symbol on the dial indicates true north.

True north can also be found by spotting the North Star on a clear night. True south can be found with a watch: point the hour hand (standard time—not daylight saving) at the sun; true south lies halfway between the hour hand and 12.

Through experience a hiker learns to identify certain characteristics of his home hills with certain directions—a greater frequency of cirques, avalanche paths, and snowfields on north and east slopes, or dry-habitat trees and shrubs on south and west slopes. But the lore is much less dependable than always carrying a compass and always knowing the local declination.

Altimeter

In areas accurately contour-mapped, knowing the elevation often permits climbers and off-trail ramblers to puzzle out their position even in thick fog. The altimeter has less utility for the average hiker but may serve such purposes as gauging progress when he ascends a trail in dense forest.

An altimeter does not directly indicate distance above sea level but rather, being in fact a barometer, measures atmospheric pressure, which varies not only with altitude but with weather changes. Readings are therefore approximate; while sitting in camp, a party may be informed by the altimeter it is gaining elevation at a mad rate—unsettling news, meaning air pressure is falling rapidly and a storm is roaring in.

Binoculars

In cross-country travel a close-up look at distant terrain is extremely valuable in choosing a route or campsite, identifying landmarks needed for orientation, finding a skimpy trail invisible to the naked eye. Trail hikers use binoculars more often for nature study.

Maps

Anyone who paid moderate attention to geography lessons has at least a rudimentary ability to interpret maps, sufficient for the elementary demands of trail travel; though only field practice makes perfect, mainly a novice needs to know which maps to use and where to get them.

A *planimetric* map shows lines (roads, trails, rivers, and perhaps ridge crests) and points (camps and peaks) in their horizontal relationship but without "depth." A familiar example is the highway map normally required to escape civilization.

A number of federal and state land-managing agencies and some private firms publish planimetrics. Most widely used are those from the U.S. Forest Service, sold at ranger stations and (by mail) head-

quarters of National Forests, normally obtained by a hiker along with a wilderness permit. Government planimetrics are revised fairly frequently and provide the most up-to-date information about roads and trails and other works of man.

A *topographic (contour)* map contains all the data of a planimetric, and in addition portrays the vertical shape of the terrain with *contour lines*—lines upon which every point is the same elevation above sea level. With experience a hiker develops stereoscopic vision that allows him to look at a topographic map and clearly distinguish ridges from valleys; however, even a novice can readily learn from the contours such crucial matters as whether a planned camp is at 6,000 feet rather than 2,000, or whether the trail ahead gains a lot of altitude or very little.

Topographic maps of the United States are produced and sold by the U.S. Geological Survey. For areas west of the Mississippi River, order from U.S. Geological Survey, Federal Center, Denver, Colorado 80225; for areas east of the Mississippi, from U.S. Geological Survey, Washington, D.C. 20242. Index maps of the sheets available for individual states are free on request. The newer Forest Service maps of dedicated wildernesses are also topographic.

Topographic maps of Canada may be purchased from the Map Distribution Office, Department of Mines and Technical Surveys, Ottawa, Ontario.

Backpacking shops stock selections of topographic and other maps in their areas.

Pictorial relief maps, giving a bird's-eye view of the land, and sketch maps published in guidebooks and alpine journals often offer supplementary data not found on the basic maps.

Rare is the map that merits absolute, unquestioning trust. Several factors determine the reliability. First is the reputation of the producer, the U.S. Geological Survey standing at the summit and other agencies at varying positions downward. Second is the date of the survey on which the map is based, usually noted on the sheet. Particularly in areas being heavily logged, such as multiple-use zones of U.S. National Forests and most of Canada, roads are constantly being built and trails obliterated, and maps more than several years old may be ancient history. Third is the scale, since the larger the area represented by a map, the smaller the amount of the fine detail and the less painstaking the preparation.

Though maps are inexpensive and can easily be replaced in the city, not so during a wildland storm, precisely when hikers may be wondering where in tarnation they are and how to get out; maps should thus be protected by being carried in a polyethylene bag—in windy, rainy weather the map can be folded for reading without removal from the bag.

Verbal Information

Maps condense an enormous amount of data in a small space but cannot tell all a hiker may wish to know about a trail—the attractions that make it worth walking, where the bears hang out, the elevation of the timberline, the season when the snow melts off, the season when bugs are least vicious, the season when the flowers are brightest, the legal and the preferred campsites, the rules and regulations, the confusing junctions, and so on. For this there are hiking guides, more every year; few portions of the continent now lack "cookbooks."

Climbing guides should not be overlooked from a sense of humility; in describing approaches to basecamps for summit ascents,

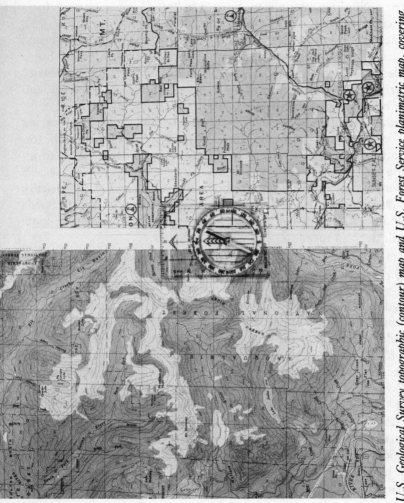

U.S. Geological Survey topographic (contour) map and U.S. Forest Service planimetric map, covering approximately the same area. Both are properly oriented by the compass.

they often provide excellent recipes for trail trips and off-trail roamings. However, the hiker must not be tempted beyond his abilities; when a climbing guide says a route is "easy" it means easy for a trained climber, not every casual pedestrian.

Each guidebook must be checked for publication date, field-tested for accuracy, and accorded only the degree of trust it earns. Some guides are sloppy ripoffs, and even those of the highest integrity invariably include mistakes in observation, typographical errors, and data rendered obsolete by time and bulldozers.

Other valuable sources of verbal information are mountaineering and conservation journals, annuals, and magazines, which frequently print narratives of tempting hikes, and descriptions of inviting country.

But only by talking (in person or by letter) to local folk—usually the rangers—can late news be learned—such as that spring floods took out a key bridge or that due to an exceptional winter the snow is still deep in meadows ordinarily in flower.

ORIENTATION

Rescue-wearied, sleepless rangers, besieged by worried relatives calling about overdue parties, sometimes suspect that a majority of travelers abroad on the trails know their location only to within several miles and that if a dense mist were to settle on the land, the backcountry mortality rate would approach that of the Black Death.

Even the hiker who intends never to stray—on purpose—from well-beaten paths must learn the basics of orientation (determining present position in relation to surroundings) and navigation (getting from one known point to another). Getting from one unknown point to another is called being lost and requires no elaboration beyond that in Chapter 6.

Any honest veteran will admit that more than once he has been, if not lost, badly confused and has felt the unreasoning panic of brain-spinning disorientation. Once or twice is enough; the mark of the veteran is that whenever he walks a few minutes without knowing exactly where he is, legs automatically halt, suspicious

eyes rove. And if a sure sense of direction does not come quickly, he pauses for orientation. The following brief outline is the merest introduction to the most elementary techniques of a complex science-art.

The first step is to *orient the map*, most easily done by lining up known landmarks with their symbols on the sheet. This failing, as in unfamiliar country, the compass is brought out. Spread the map flat and lay the compass on the sheet, dial north with the true north arrow of the map (almost invariably true north is the top of the map). Rotate map and compass as a unit until the needle points the correct number of degrees east or west of dial north, in accordance with local declination. Compass and map are now oriented.

The next step is to *orient the hiker*. If he *knows the precise point* of his present location (river crossing, trail junction, mountain summit), any visible feature (peak, pass, valley) can be identified by placing a pencil (or other straightedge) on the map touching the known point, aiming the pencil at the visible feature, and examining the map to see what features are intersected by the pencil. Similarly, if the hiker wants to find the position of an invisible feature (hidden by trees or fog), he places the pencil on the map to intersect his known point and the invisible feature, which then lies in the direction indicated by the pencil.

Orientation is more complicated when the hiker *knows only he is somewhere on a certain line* (trail, river, ridge). He must be able to identify at least one distant feature—say, Bald Mountain. A simple procedure, not as craftsmanlike as the methods of Kjellstrom and other masters, is to place the compass on the map with the compass center exactly atop the symbol for Bald Mountain, orient map and compass as a unit, place the pencil on the compass center, and point it at the actual Bald Mountain. The intersection of the pencil with the known line (trail, river, ridge) is the present location—*approximately*. A second distant feature is desirable for verification. Comparison of the surroundings with the map determines if the results are reasonable.

When a hiker *knows only that he is in a certain area* (perhaps on one of several possible trails, rivers, or ridges), at least two distant features must be identified, and the technique is beyond the elementary; see Kjellstrom.

And if no distant features are visible, as in fog or deep forest? Or none can be positively identified? Time then for advanced navigation methods. Either that or sit down and wait for the search party, as discussed in Chapter 6.

STAYING ON COURSE

The beginner may say, "I don't need to bother about all this route-finding stuff because I'm always going to stick to trails." Well and good—if he can. But sticking to the trail, and finding it in the first place, isn't invariably a cinch.

For openers, in multiple-use public lands of the United States, and in the entirety of Canada outside National Parks, the trailheads often lie amid a maze of logging roads, either completely unsigned or, in some National Forests, marked only by cryptic numbers meaningless unless one has obtained the secret-decoder Forest Service map. Stops may be necessary at junctions to consult map and guidebook, which perhaps are obsolete because of new roads built and old ones abandoned. At length finding the presumed start of the wanted trail, a party may see naught but a chaos of logging slash, or perhaps several paths heading in different directions, and

no signs. Again map and compass may be required even before leaving the road, and possibly short scouting trips.

Once his boots are pounding a broad, well-maintained, heavily used trail, usually the hiker must only avoid walking with eyes steadily on the path underfoot and failing to see a junction and hours later having to ask a stranger, "Pardon me, but do you know where I am?" Similarly, ground-watchers have been known to walk blindly off the end of a switchback and plunge stupidly forward into brush.

Many otherwise distinct trails require frequent reference to the map because they lack signs at junctions, or have signs so mauled by bears, chewed by porcupines, or shot up and chopped by idiots to be past deciphering. At any dubious junction the party should assemble, particularly if the rearguard members are inexperienced or notorious, given two choices, for instinctively taking the wrong one.

Traveling old, little-used trails is more akin to cross-country roaming than trail-following. On some the tread periodically vanishes in blowdowns, meadows, marshes, and rocks; on others frequently divides and redivides, myriad tracks beaten by deer, elk, goats, sheep, or cattle. There may be blazes on trees—but also "lost-man blazes" made by falling trees and rocks (and lost hikers). There may be cairns or ribbons—helpful if placed by people who knew where they were going, and if where they were going chances to be where

you want to go. Often a hiker can steer through the maze by figuring where he would have built the trail if it had been his job. The second and third in line should pay as much attention to routefinding as the leader, who in forest may not see a blaze or sawn log off to one side and on a fogswept ridge fail to note diverging spurs.

When a path disappears and does not immediately resume, the party should *stop*. The temptation is to forge straight ahead, hoping to pick up the way, but if the trail takes a sharp turn somewhere in the missing section, every forward step leads farther into nowhere. With the party halted and assembled, two or three members (more just muddle matters) should fan out and scout for tread, blazes, sawn logs, and the like, staying in communication so that any of them can sound the recall; the scout who goes beyond intelligible voice range may return to fuming companions who found the trail a half hour ago and have been yelling their heads off.

Several rules are important when traveling sketchy trails and wandering away from trails, particularly in poor weather. *Keep the party together*, every member in sight or sound of others at all times.

Maintain constant orientation, at every step observing close and distant landmarks, periodically relating them to the map.

Though getting there may be half the fun, the other half is getting home, so prepare for the return by noting prominent boulders and trees, cliffs and creeks. *Look over the shoulder* frequently to see landmarks as they will appear on the return. If terrain is complicated or visibility limited, mark the route at critical points with toilet paper draped on trees or shrubs. *Plastic ribbons* are more durable but *should not be used unless faithfully removed later on*; paper markers should also be picked up on the return, but if circumstances forbid, remember that toilet paper disintegrates in the first rain while "surveyor's tape" lasts for years. Wilderness managers hate "tapers" because their pioneering encourages boot-built trails, often on fragile lands where there should be no trails.

A final rule: a good leader should take it upon himself to train less-experienced party members in routefinding—especially children who otherwise may never progress past heel-watching.

Everybody is a beginner sometime and the only way to master wilderness navigation is doing it. By maintaining constant orientation, probing cautiously, invariably keeping open the line of safe retreat, inexperienced hikers can venture some distance into uncertainty without unreasonable risk. Yet it should always be remembered how unpleasant it is to be lost.

17
When the Way Grows Rough

The elements of walking and camping are best learned on well-marked, well-manicured trails. Indeed, most hikers, immune to the charms of nastiness and danger, never stray from friendly turnpike terrain. They feel no need to prove their bravery and fortitude, which they do every workday driving freeways and breathing city air, and gladly renounce adventure for peace.

Others, though, having put a few hundred miles on their boots, hear the call of the wild so loud and clear, are so driven by a force stronger than good sense, that they climb above trails through brush, up rocks and snows, to tall summits. Such berserkers must look elsewhere than here for instruction; one place is *Mountaineering: The Freedom of the Hills*, the standard American text since the publication of the first edition in 1960.

Between the modes of easy-trail hiker and wilderness mountaineer is the subject of this chapter—a middle way that leaves the beaten track but stops well short of "technical climbing."

Actually, no hiker is so timid that he will not occasionally abandon tread to wander a meadow valley, a tundra ridge, an open desert, a wave-washed beach. But the more ambitious, studying maps, see how little wildland is traversed by trails—they wonder about all those other valleys and ridges, peaks and basins, streams and lakes. Thus they graduate from trail pounder to cross-country rambler.

Without ever leaving trails, a hiker may be challenged to something more than hands-in-pockets walking. In maritime mountain ranges of the Northwest even turnpikes are completely snowfree only a few weeks of summer; ability to cross a lingering snow patch safely can make the difference between continuing to the planned destination or turning back disappointed. Similarly, trails frequently come to riverbanks and quit; the hiker must either ford or go home. And a good many paths, including some very popular ones, have been built solely by boots and hooves and nary a stick of dynamite, and are interrupted by short stretches of rock that require hands as well as feet.

Let it be stressed that rough country is not for everybody and surely not for the beginner. When the next step can be taken only at the risk of becoming a statistic in the annual report of the local mountain rescue organization, the mandatory decision is: *Don't take it; turn back*.

Further, reading this chapter does not give certification as an expert wildland rover; for that, one should seek personal tutoring from veterans, best done by joining an outdoor club.

However, by adding a few items to his outfit and learning a few simple techniques, a hiker who has served his trail apprenticeship can greatly increase his safe hiking range. These tools and techniques will not be described here in detail, but rather introduced, their potential suggested, and the reader referred elsewhere for more information.

ICE AX AND ROPE

A hiker may feel presumptuous even to think about carrying ice ax and rope, symbols of the climber, yet through their use he frequently can pass otherwise dangerous obstacles with no more risk than walking a broad trail. So what if somebody does accuse him of dressing up for a masquerade? It's his neck.

Ice Ax

The ax at work is discussed in following sections; here, several remarks about the instrument itself.

The ice ax is a dangerous weapon; one was used to assassinate Leon Trotsky in his Mexico City hideout, and others have accidentally wounded and killed climbers on many a mountain. It must always be handled with care so as not to inflict injury on companions or self.

The refinements of models designed for icicle climbers and Karakoram craggers have no utility for the hiker, who should buy the simplest and cheapest he can find. The shaft should be just long enough so that with carrying arm hanging loose, hand gripping axhead, the spike firmly contacts the ground; however, several inches this way or that make no appreciable difference.

If a hiker is sensitive to the sneering and gawking occasioned by an ice ax miles from the nearest snow—even though, as noted below, the value is not limited to snow and indeed is very great on slippery driftwood of an ocean beach—he may prefer a steel-tipped cane that does much (but not all) the work of an ax and with less threat from errant metal.

The alpenstock cherished by oldtimers serves some of the same purposes, as does a bamboo staff or a sturdy stick picked up in the forest and discarded when no longer wanted.

Rope

A snow patch, a steep bit of rock, a footlog, a cliff of slick grass may bother some members of the party not at all but force others near or over the line of mortal peril. The weeping and the whining, the silent fear frozen in a face, must never be ignored by the strong, the brave, the sure-footed. By tying a rope to the frightened and thus endangered child, wife, husband, or weary friend, they can often remove the risk of tragedy from what is, after all, a pleasure trip. The cost? A few extra minutes—nothing compared to the time spent on a rescue.

Even if the risk is merely imagined, the terror is real, and except in small, infrequent, controlled doses the average hiker gets no fun from terror.

Unlike the climbing rope, the "hiking rope" is intended strictly for short pitches, where the only falls possible would develop relatively minor forces. A good choice is 50 feet of ⅜-inch nylon weighing about 2 pounds. The breaking strength is around 4,500 pounds, which may sound like overkill, but, keeping in mind that a knot reduces the effective strength by as much as half and that a 150-pound person in a free fall of 10 feet gains a kinetic energy of 1,500 foot-pounds, really is about the safe minimum.

Totally lacking any notion of how climbers tie into a rope and establish belays, a hiker can fumble up some way to attach the rope securely to the waist of a companion and find a solid stance for safeguarding his passage. Obviously the job can be done better with knowledge of knot tying and rope handling; for hiking (but not climbing) purposes, enough can be learned from books—see *Mountaineering: The Freedom of the Hills*.

WALKING ROUGH GROUND

When the route leaves trail for untracked forest, steep meadow, talus or scree or moraine, rock slabs, brush, marsh, or snow, the hiker accustomed to having decisions made for him by established tread tends to stop after each step to plan the next; the pace slows to a creep and the sun goes down with camp still hours away.

What centrally distinguishes cross-country rambling from trail tramping is that the hiker must constantly look and think ahead, or *hike with the eyes*, a three-part process: Periodically he halts momentarily to survey the area and choose the broad line of approach; while moving, he scans the terrain a dozen yards in front to pick the easiest going; simultaneously he examines the ground of his next several steps. With practice the long-, medium-, and close-range studies fall into an automatic routine and the pace is almost as fast and rhythmic as on a trail.

To reveal a secret about the ice ax: Even a climber uses it maybe

1 percent of the time for chopping steps in ice, perhaps 9 percent for security on snow, and 90 percent purely as a walking stick. Old climbers are accused of carrying axes on trails and beaches out of snobbery so they will not be mistaken for mere hikers, but in truth, take away the old climber's ax and he walks off balance, pawing the air with his empty ax hand, falling down a lot.

On any steep and/or slippery terrain, not just snow but also wet heather, mud, moraines and talus, streambeds, footlogs, brush, and driftwood, the ice ax (or cane, staff, or stick) *provides a third leg.* If a foot slips, weight can be shifted to the ax while recovery is made. To put it another way, the ax is an arm extension that allows use of one or both hands in maintaining stability.

CROSSING STREAMS

A trail is plainly shown on the map, clearly signed at the parking lot, and obviously maintained regularly. Does this not mean that the land-managing agency—U.S. Forest Service, National Park Service, or whatever—officially certifies that every step of the way is certain and safe?

No. Those blue lines on the map always remain the same but not the streams they symbolize. Maps, guidebooks, rangers, cannot provide money-back guarantees that any particular blue line, though usually a peaceful dribble easily stepped across on boulders, may not become, however briefly, a hell-roaring torrent. During a recent several-year period more hikers were killed in the North Cascades by drowning—swept away while fording or after slipping from footlogs—than by falls from cliffs, falling rock, avalanches, hypothermia, and all other wildland hazards combined—and most were on "turnpikes."

The first lesson about stream crossings: a passage simple last week and simple next week may be fatal today. Whenever a solid bridge is lacking—and in backcountry, bridges are often the exception rather than the rule—the trail may be absolutely blocked for hours or days.

In the absence of a bridge, perhaps there is a footlog. Is it wide, dry, and level? Splendid. Or is it narrow, steeply tilted, slippery with spray? Beware. A helping hand may be enough to steady a small child or nervous friend; a rope tied to the waist of the insecure body and anchored from the bank will not prevent a fall but may permit a rescue. The wisest decision may be to give up the trip and try again later in summer, when the log is not water-drenched, the flood has diminished, and the consequences of a tumble are not so drastic, or the trail crew has arrived and felled a bigger tree.

With footlog lacking at the trail crossing and none to be found by searching upstream and down, the trip is not necessarily dead-ended. Quite broad and deep waters can be waded safely if not excessively rapid and cold—but probably not by the beginner, who has yet to learn what "excessively" means. Gently flowing, relatively warm streams of lowlands and deserts are no problem when shallow; even when deep, they are often easily swum, rafting the pack on an air mattress, in the manner Colin Fletcher makes sound such fun. But mountain torrents are something else, and any depth greater than 18 inches or so requires thought. Swift water only knee-deep may boil above the waist, half floating the body; unweighted feet cannot grip the bed, and with the shift of a boulder underfoot, the

hiker becomes a swimmer—except swimming is impossible in tur-
bulent foam composed equally of water and air. Drowning and
battering aside, a person's life expectancy in snowmelt is a matter
of minutes due to instant hypothermia.

Fording big, rough rivers is as complex and hazardous as as-
cending cliffs and traversing glaciers and staring down grizzly bears,
and is far beyond allowable ambitions of the novice. However, by
starting with little creeks, moving to larger ones, studying and prac-
ticing, he can in time handle rather substantial waters. To begin
the education, following are several rules not universally applicable
but often helpful.

Generally cross not at the narrowest point, where kinetic energy
is greatest, but at the widest. Up to a point, choose the slow and
deep water in preference to the shallow and fast. On occasion, pitch
camp by the stream and cross in morning; snowfed rivers are usually
lower after a cool night than at the end of a scorching day; the flash
flood from a cloudburst ordinarily subsides in hours.

Before any crossing not completely worry-free (tricky footlogs as
well as fords), release the hip belt of the pack so the load can be
turned loose instantly; better to splash around to retrieve the pack
than be dragged under by it.

Wear short pants, or in agreeable company, no pants. If the bed is soft sand or rounded boulders and the water not too cold, barefoot wading is good-in-itself; however, wear boots when rocks are sharp, footing treacherous, or water so icy that bare feet might lose sensation. Wet feet on the succeeding trail can be avoided by taking off socks, wading in boots alone, and on the far bank dumping out water and donning the dry socks. Boots can be kept completely dry by wading in heavy socks, adequate for intermediate situations, or in sneakers carried for the purpose.

In rapids, face upstream and move crabwise sideways, using the ice ax—or stout stick—as a third leg. Move each foot separately and place it securely, remembering the tendency of boulders to depart downstream at the slightest excuse.

The point has been belabored sufficiently that a party in doubt must give up the attempt, turn back. However, a ford unquestionably safe for a large adult may surpass the unaided capacity of a smaller one or a child. In such case the big can accompany the little on the crossing to provide support.

Rigging a handline is generally a mistake, since the give of the rope is certain betrayal in time of real need. When more than convoy-type security is wanted, the hiking rope is better tied to the forder's waist, an anchor on shore ensuring against his being swept away—all the way away, that is, the pendulum swing to shore remaining to be endured.

ROCK SCRAMBLING

Another scary subject is raised—to be quickly dropped, and without revealing the formula by which any trail camper can step into a telephone booth and emerge moments later as a human fly. For the sake of family and friends, rangers and rescue groups, and his own tender flesh and brittle bones, a hiker must quit, go back, seek another route, or switch to another destination when confronted by steep rock from which a fall would be damaging. Let him keep in mind that the human body, its hands and eyes at the upper end, its blind and clumsy feet at the lower, is much better designed for going up cliffs than down; a common cause of scrambling tragedies is the daring novice managing to get high on a wall, finding he cannot proceed upward, and then finding he cannot descend what he has climbed; weariness, panic, and gravity do the rest.

However, many trails never improved by blasting powder, and many off-trail routes include brief sections of rock that seem dangerous but really are not, or at least no more so than merging from an on-ramp into freeway traffic. With practice, and always with caution, a hiker can negotiate short rock steps in ease and security by observing the fundamentals of what mountaineers call "balance climbing."

Keep body weight directly over the feet by standing erect. Legs do the work, just as in ordinary hiking. Hands do not pull the body up, as in gymnasium rope climbing, but grip holds that serve as anchors in case a foot slips. Leaning into the slope gives a false sense of security; it actually causes body weight to thrust the feet sideways, slipping off holds or breaking them out.

Support the body always by three points. At every moment, be solidly, surely connected to the slope by two hands and a foot or two feet and a hand. Thus, if a hold fails, two points of connection remain.

Test holds. Before trusting a foothold with body weight, or a hand-

hold as an anchor, make sure it is firmly attached to the mountain.

Move smoothly. Smooth transference of body weight puts minimum stress on holds. A rhythmic pace (the rest step described in Chapter 1) maintains a reserve of strength for surprises and is conducive to mental composure. A jerky pace breaks holds, sets lungs to gasping and heart to pounding, and leads to doubt and thence to fear and panic.

Climb with the eyes. Constantly look ahead to spot the easiest line of progress, to study holds and plan the next sequence of moves, and to avoid climbing into traps.

To repeat with emphasis, these expressions of common sense are words on a piece of paper until they become reflexive in mind and muscle through practice.

Some hikers scramble better than others. In a party of mixed experience or ability, the hiking rope can eliminate terror from short stretches of steep rock (or heather or mud)—a strong and confident scrambler belays from the top, the inexperienced or weary or tiny

companion is protected from a fall by the rope tied around his waist and perhaps on occasion (especially in the case of a child), given a helpful pull to get up a section of thin holds. For reasons stated earlier, the rope should *not* be used as a handline.

Fewer hikers are endangered, injured, and killed by falling from mountains than by being fallen upon, and the most frequent menace is not natural disintegration. Never, ever, should a hiker roll boulders down a slope or throw them into an abyss for the thrill of it—how is he to know who may be below? Never, ever, should a hiker scramble carelessly, blithely loosing barrages. If despite caution he dislodges a rock and there is the slightest possibility that people are below, he must immediately sound the alarm by shouting, "ROCK! ROCK! ROCK!" In steep terrain with a considerable human population, on trails and off, the hiker must at all times be alert for attacks from above, watching and listening, and when appropriate, shouting, cursing, threatening.

SNOW TRAVEL

Snow is tricky. In winter and spring it avalanches. Undermined by streams, it conceals pits. When steep, it provides toboggan runs often ending bloodily in boulders, trees, cliffs. Being cold and wet, it's ideal for hypothermia. All in all, a blanket endorsement of snow play could be interpreted by the courts as homicide. The novice who reads the few words here, rushes off to buy ax and rope, and with no more preparation invades the white wilderness is quite likely to become a statistic. Though *Freedom* offers more background, the subject emphatically should be studied under expert tutelage, as by enrolling in a climbing school offered by an outdoor club, youth group, college, mountain shop, or guide service.

The rewards are worth it. By mastering certain basic techniques, a hiker can enormously enlarge his realm of safe wandering, add months to his high-country hiking season, feel the exhilaration of

walking on top of brush instead of fighting through it, and pretty
much get away from the madding crowds.

As the beginner will be taught in any school, the most important
tools of snow travel are the boots, used to kick platforms, and the
most important technique is standing erect so that boots are not
thrust sideways by body weight, breaking out platforms or slipping
off them. The ice ax, however, serving as a cane—a third leg—is
the tool that gives the stability and thus the confidence necessary
to stand erect, and provides an anchor when a foot skids, stopping
most slides before they start and further reinforcing confidence—
and on snow, confidence is more than half the battle.

Alpenstock, cane, staff, or stick picked up in the woods can also
act as a third leg. The ice ax, though, has a further value in putting
on the brakes once a slide has begun. *Self-arrest*, where a person

digs ax pick into slope, presses chest against shaft to give the pick purchase, and spreads legs and digs in toes, will not be elaborated here. Suffice to say the technique must be learned by anyone intending to do much snow hiking—and cannot be learned from books but only by intensive practice under expert instruction.

The hiking rope has uses in snow when some members of the party are experienced and sure-footed and others are not. For example, a father with a climbing background usually can safely convoy a small child over a snow patch hand in hand. But if he needs both hands for ice-ax control lest he himself slip, he does better to tie the rope to his waist and that of the kid. And if he has any doubts about being able to arrest a joint slide, the mother should stand on safe ground, belaying the child with the rope while the father does convoy duty. (Or mother and father may exchange these roles; climber females have been known to become attached to non-climber males.)

ROUGH ROADS TO FREEDOM

There are hazards in snow travel, rock scrambling, river fording, off-trail wandering generally, rough-country exploring particularly. Many dangers are more apparent than real and vanish like goblins

in the light of experience. While gaining the experience, a hiker discovers unsuspected dangers and how to avoid some, and develops the wisdom and humility to turn back when faced by the others. With patience and caution and imagination he can, if he so wishes, escape the confines of trails, become a cross-country rambler, and to a very considerable extent enjoy what mountaineers call "the freedom of the hills."

18
Suffer the Little Children

We used to go hiking all the time, but then we had the kids."

"We'd like to take the kids hiking with us, but they're too young."

"We'd like to start hiking, and will when the kids are bigger."

Such sentiments are often expressed by parents: experienced backpackers who consider wildlands too brutal for young innocents, or else that coping with children on the trail is too complicated; beginning hikers who still find the backcountry somewhat spooky; car campers who want to venture away from roads but don't quite dare.

Let it be said at the outset that no editorial position is taken on the proper way to run a family. If the father wants to go hiking with friends and leave the wife and kids home, and they don't mind—well and good. Parents with rotten kids may find vacations from them essential to sanity—the rotten kids, parked with grandparents, may enjoy the vacation from rotten parents. In no holy book is it written that a family must always go everywhere together; indeed, if the wife abhors hiking, the marriage is not enhanced by dragging her to agony—which any competent wife can force her husband to share. The reverse, of course, is equally true.

No—this is not a homily on family living. The intent is merely to suggest to beginning hikers, and experienced hikers who are beginning parents, how they may take the children along with fun and games for all.

Certainly many parents so desire. Commonly they wish to raise offspring in their own life pattern. And much of the pleasure of parenthood is watching young ones discover the wide, wide world. Finally, on long backpacks a deprived mother can often be found off in the woods, weeping, and when asked what's wrong, wails, "I miss my baby!"

And what about the children's desires? At a certain age when Mommy is away overnight they fear she has abandoned them forever. Somewhat older, they protest the bitter injustice of their folks going off without them to wonderful secret places, they agitate for Children's Lib, full membership in the family.

No brief is made here for the wisdom or necessity of being totally child-centered; people do not give up all their rights, become third-class citizens, in changing status from "man and woman" to "Daddy and Mama." However, if they *want* to take the kids hiking, they *can*.

Almost invariably, worries are exaggerated. Children are tough little beasts, usually better able than city-pampered adults to withstand trail rigors (except bugs, which eat tender-skinned youngsters alive, requiring special protection). Moreover, ordinarily they are accustomed to a totalitarian regime, to being forced into unfamiliar situations (after all, nearly everything in the world is unfamiliar to them), and stoically put up with a lot of guff. (Not so in extreme cases of the "permissive parent," but brats are a couple of other books.) If introduced to trails early, they probably will grow up to be loyal citizens of the wild country—and better people for it and better Friends of the Earth (editorial opinion).

For many families the question is academic. No free baby-sitters, such as grandparents, are available, and no money for a hired baby-sitter; either the kids go along or nobody goes—or only the father, which is grossly unfair if the mother is a devout wildlander. (The fair alternative is for parents to take turns staying home.)

Hiking with children is a special subdivision of the sport, but not so complicated as some parents and pundits make it. The proper gear solves most problems, as already discussed. That, of course, brings up another problem, which looms especially large in a large family—the cost of equipping children while growing, and growing, and *out*growing. To reemphasize a point previously made, the budget can quickly be busted unless recourse is made to thrift shops and hand-me-downs and hand-arounds among several families of friends.

One bit more about equipment. Poorly fitting boots and badly adjusted packs give a child just cause for complaint and support his paranoid suspicions of an adult plot to destroy him. Protests must be heeded. For example, hurt feet require instant attention, applying Moleskin or the like at the first redness lest a real blister develop and Mommy and Daddy be haled into Children's Court.

So much for prelude. Each family must invent its own formula, write its own history. Following pages offer a mixed bag of hints drawn from the memories of real-life backpacking families—mainly my own and several others we know well, leavened with observations of strangers encountered on the trail and comments by a number of parents and experienced ex-kids.

TAKING IT EASY

The capacity of the average child to endure hardship is incredible. The prime examples are from family annals of Little League parents who brag that Junior carried a 12-pound pack 10 miles when only four, conquered Tiger Tooth at seven, and climbed all the 14,000-foot mountains of the nation before puberty. Aside from being a pain in the neck to other parents, the pace-forcers take a risk; Junior may grow up to be a famous climber but chances are 50–50 that once old enough to escape the lash, he'll turn in boots and pack on a surfboard.

However, Junior's exploits demonstrate that children can perform prodigies of exertion beyond the belief of overprotective parents, and normally with no harm. (Needless to say, strength and hardiness vary widely; doubts should be resolved by consulting the family doctor.)

Nevertheless, a child, just as an adult, gains most pleasure operating below maximum potential. Maybe he *can* do 6 miles in a day but hate it, yet enjoy 3 miles. Trips with kids generally should be shorter than for adults alone, and the pace slower. How much shorter? How much slower? The only way for a family to find out is on the trails; the rule is, take it easy at first, and as muscles and ambitions grow, still keep the effort not only within the *physical* limits but within the *fun* limits.

Applied Child Psychology

Why is it that a child can dash full tilt around a playground for hours, yet collapse on the trail in minutes, whimpering and complaining? Every child is a natural malingerer—it's the only defense against adult tyranny—but the deeper explanation is motivation. The kid is impelled in the playground marathon by a constant succession of immediate goals—racing Patty to the swing, chasing Ira up the monkey bars, Indian-wrestling Tommy, teeter-tottering with Nancy—meaningful goals, kids' goals.

But trail goals are adult goals, incomprehensible or impossibly remote. Describing wonders of the day's destination—the creek to play in, the boulders to climb, the special pudding for dessert—may stir interest, but when they are not instantly attained, the whining questions arise, "Are we almost there? Why do we have

to go there?" What use telling a little child that camp is only an hour away—when he doesn't know what an hour is? Seeing eternal suffering ahead, no fun, he despairs and collapses. At which point Mama may cry, "You poor dear!" and Daddy may find a smug lump perched on his shoulders. Even very tiny kids quickly become adroit at this fraud.

To keep the poor dears happy and off Daddy's back, parents must become equally crafty, and the secret lies in thinking as kids do— from minute to minute, step to step—and seeking or arranging a constant sequence of goals, forgetting the rules for covering ground efficiently. The family group may walk 10 or 15 minutes and rest 15 or 20. Or take a dozen steps and pause, a dozen steps more and pause again. This latter pace, of course, is cruel to burdened adults. The father therefore may pile most of the gear on his back and stagger steadily to camp, leaving lightly loaded Mother to dawdle with the babe. Otherwise, say spokeswomen for Mothers' Lib, the father should alternate in the dawdling duty.

The stops and pauses are occasioned less by needs for rest than by happening upon things that make satisfying kids' goals. Water is an unfailing delight; at an age when gorgeous panoramas mean nothing, a child never tires of tossing pebbles in a pond, floating sticks down a stream, building castles in a sand bar, mucking around in a mud puddle. Perhaps he spots a beetle and is fascinated by watching it creep; parents should then join the watching—perhaps suddenly to remember how once they too loved beetles and ants and ladybugs. And so with flowers and frogs, mushrooms and spider webs, a festoon of moss and a chittering chipmunk. (But drop the pack if the session promises to be long!)

Be alert to point out a hawk circling the sky, a towering cloud that looks like a dog—a knight—a witch—Aunt Prunella. Teach the mysteries and solemnities of the wildland—that the trail lies on the slopes of a volcano and all these rocks were once hot as fire, that the valley below was once full of ice. Answer questions—"Will the volcano blow up while we're here, Daddy? Will the glacier come back and cover us up tonight?"

When nature fails to offer continuity of motivation, stage an impromptu party by bringing from the pack a piece of candy, a favorite toy; chewing a chunk of toffee while playing with cars in trail dust is a worthy goal.

Devices of this sort suffice on leisurely trips. However, with darkness or storm approaching, or for other reasons, sometimes it is necessary to keep a kid purely and steadily walking. Adults then must dip into another bag of tricks to relieve boredom while maintaining motion.

Perhaps promise a party at the very next creek or viewpoint, with animal crackers and root beer, and thus gain ten or so minutes of constant advance. In the interim, a bit of trail candy is usually good for a few more steps.

Try games. Announce that the family is a train and have locomotive Father and caboose Mother and freight-car and mail-car children make appropriate locomotive and caboose and etcetera sounds. (But let kids call their own game—one time a little boy who always before had loved to play train continued glum; that particular day he didn't want to be part of the family train, yet became perfectly happy when permitted to be a Pepsi-Cola truck.)

Tell stories from folk literature, the family past. Or start a story and have each hiker add an episode in turn. Or extract a story by asking a series of questions—one time a boy walked most of a day

without complaint while describing the dinosaurs he was going to invite to his birthday party, and those he was not, and the foods he would serve and the games they would play.

Try singing. One time a father was at the bottom of a nettle patch, awaiting his wife and three-year-old daughter, and was alarmed to hear the girl scream as she was attacked by vicious bushes, and was alarmed further when weird sounds arose from the greenery—until he recognized the child's voice, and the mother's, joined in song: "I'm Popeye the Sailor Man, *toot toot!*"

In such ways do parents outwit offspring. But the wily child fights back. One time a father and mother patiently cajoled their three-year-old daughter three miles upward from a camp beside the Stehekin River nearly to Cascade Pass, turning back in the snow when the girl had a tantrum, apparently from exhaustion. On the descent the poor babe tottered, stumbled, fell, and Daddy carried her the last mile, fearing for the health of the comatose little darling. And immediately on reaching camp, Sleeping Beauty awoke and for hours on into darkness splashed in a river pool, gathered pretty rocks and neat sticks, and when the parents at last sought to stuff her in a sleeping bag, complained, "I'm not tired!"

Similarly, parents have often felt pangs of conscience about pushing the family to a highland camp—and once there the destroyed children have miraculously revived and spent hours running up a snowbank and sliding down. (Snow, incidentally, is even better than mud; any camp with a good supply makes a perfect holiday.)

So goes the psychological warfare, the struggle between long-range goals of adults and short-range goals of children. When the conflict is conducted with love and compromise, both sides win, everybody has fun. In later years the trails and camps may well be remembered as the best of times—the moments when the family was closest.

Obviously, "taking it easy" means one thing with infants and another with teenyboppers, and obviously each family and its trail adventures are unique. However, the following chronological discussion of hiking with children from babyhood through adolescence, though based on the experience of a few families, suggests the possibilities.

BABIES

A babe in arms can be taken on roadside picnics and car camps, and with proper protection from sun and wind and mosquitoes be perfectly comfortable. To be sure, the infant derives little if any pleasure from the outing, but the parents do, and in the process gain confidence for more ambitious ventures.

When the baby is three months or so they can stow him in a child-carrier and on suitably mild days go for short or long walks, hauling the appropriate paraphernalia of diapers and bottles. Babies generally enjoy the lulling bounce and spend most of the time sleeping; in fact, if colicky, they sleep better on the trail than in a crib. Care is required to bundle the baby warmly, shade eyes from sun, protect skin from sunburn and insects. Somewhere around six months a child starts to take a positive interest in wildland attractions, dabbling fingers in sand, picking up pebbles, watching ants.

When does backpacking begin? As far as the baby is concerned, from three or so months on he can be as happy in the backcountry as at home. With one notable exception: Up to about twelve months a baby's respiratory system cannot adjust readily to major changes in elevation. If his home is at sea level, during extended stays at camps above 7,000 feet or so, as in the High Sierras or Wind River Range, he may fuss continuously.

Usually, though, the problem is the parents—more specifically, parents with their first child, still fearful of breaking it. Initial trials should be short, so if something goes wrong—a sudden storm or one of those alarming fevers infants develop without warning for no apparent reason (until Mama's finger runs along babe's gums and finds a new tooth)—a quick retreat can be made to car and home. Though an adult party may consider a camp only a mile or two from the road hardly worth the trouble of backpacking, this much distance reduces the population to a fraction of that in car campgrounds, and on such forgiving trips parents learn how much special gear is needed—bottles, dried milk or formula, strained foods, teething biscuits, baby aspirin, changes of clothing, and the like. Reading Goldie Silverman's *Backpacking With Babies* may save some learning time.

Actually, a child is easier to carry at 1–1½ years and younger than later on, weighing and wiggling less and—being always on the back—not presenting the problems a toddler does on muddy or rocky trails. However, with one parent hauling the babe and thus not much else, the other must pack most of the gear, and this limits the length of a hike.

Still, after a few overnights the family may be ready for deeper probes into wilderness—5 or 7 miles—and longer trips—several days or a week, with a basecamp chosen for immediate attractions and the variety of day hikes and close enough to the car for a parent to fetch more food and diapers in mid-trip.

Thus far the discussion has assumed an only child. In a larger family with children widely spaced, backpacking a baby can be much easier with the older siblings helping. But two children only a year or two apart (or in the extreme case, twins) may be entirely too formidable on the trail until both are well past babyhood; parents probably had best give up extended backpacks the first two or three years and (lacking fond grandparents) take turns baby-sitting.

TODDLERS

The awkward age for backpacking is roughly two to four, when a child is usually too much of a load to be carried any great distance, yet can't walk very fast or far. Also, he has developed definite opinions on how the world should be operated, has a loud wail and

not the slightest sympathy with adult goals. Frequently his attachment to Mama is so firm that more than momentary separation is simply not tolerated, making it hard for Daddy to be an effective baby-sitter or to share dawdling duty on the trail.

Hiking with a toddler demands the utmost patience. A pace of ½ mile an hour may be too swift, and a trip longer than 4 miles too rigorous. Probably he must be carried part of the time, but aside from the fact that parents may find the weight more than they can bear, the lump typically grows bored and wants to get down and walk—or rather stumble. A warning about piggyback rides: They eliminate the child-carrier pack and are thought great fun by little darlings but place such pressure on neck muscles and nerves as literally to cause temporary paralysis. If extended hauling is planned, a child-carrier is essential.

Paradoxically, parents may have to plan shorter trips (and certainly slower) with the toddler than with the infant. As compensation, none of the special gear is required and packs thus are lighter. They are, that is, if Mama doesn't lose her head piling up shirts and pants, skirts and shoes, sweaters and mufflers and pajamas. Daddy must sternly inform her: the toddler is no longer a baby and needs as much clothing as an adult but no more—with the sole major exception of one or two complete changes for when he falls into a creek, and moments later into a second. Oversolicitous, overloading mamas are a major cause of back trouble among daddies.

Many toddlers, though potty-trained, continue to be bed-wetters.

Parents may try such devices as withholding liquids past suppertime and routing the kid out periodically in the night, but nothing works. The best solution is *not* to have the wetter sleep in Mama's bag but in his own—filled with polyester, *not* down.

For all the difficulties of the toddler age, it is a most exciting family era: Fresh young imaginations are stimulated by the richness around them—and their visions can at least be glimpsed by elders. One time a two-and-a-half-year-old boy spent a whole afternoon sitting by himself on a grassy tussock a few feet from the shore of a meadow pond, dabbling a stick in the water, totally absorbed, and when asked what he was doing, said, "Sailing my boat." To what fantastic seas?

And this is the age when trail country puts to shame the playgrounds built by recreation experts. A fallen log wedged between two trees becomes the most exciting teeter-totter ever; on being torn away to go home, the kids ask, "Can we come back again? When? Next week?" Boulders become forts; snowfields, toboggan slides; alpine tarns, the most-fun swimming and wading pools. Beautiful stones are gathered by the pound, and hours spent combing bushes for mountain-goat wool.

If parents do not insist on too-long, too-tough trips, do not force incomprehensible adult destinations such as summits and fishing-

type lakes but learn to accept and enjoy the goals of kids, chances are another generation will be converted for life to the wildland way.

SELF-PROPELLED PACKS

Seen on the trail: a mother and father suffering under huge burdens, their large, loutish kids running about pack-free and happy. Something has gone terribly wrong in this family. The loving daddy doubtless is the same guy who piggybacks his darlings up to the moment they make the high school football team.

Also seen on the trail: a small mountain of gear mysteriously in motion, two legs protruding from the bottom—a self-propelled pack. Tender-hearted adult strangers cry out in horror, packless, drooling louts sneer, but in this family something has gone right.

At a certain age the child must pay the price. He outgrows Mama's sleeping bag and needs his own. Though he doesn't require as many changes of clothing as when he fell in every creek, his body is bigger and clothes heavier. And he eats more, as much as an adult. Unless he starts sharing the burden, the family backpacking becomes too strenuous for parents.

What is that certain age? No absolute rule can be stated; obviously

the size and sturdiness of the child are factors, as well as parental attitude. It is important, however, not to wait too long, but rather to ease the kid into responsibilities gradually—by being saddled when too young to know what's happening, he grows up with the stone and supposes God put it there.

Actually the average toddler, especially if he has older siblings, feels that to lack a pack is to be denied full membership in the family and demands one long before his folks think he's ready. In this case parents should be utterly permissive. Thus, at three or four the kid starts with a little rucksack containing a sweater and a toy. Inevitably the rucksack is taken over by a parent or sibling before the end of any long walk, but the precedent is established.

At four or five a child can proceed beyond tokenism. One time a girl of this age was given strong motivation by being assigned the family's entire candy supply for a whole week and marched as proudly as if carrying Fort Knox.

At around five or eight the self-propelled pack appears, the child carrying sleeping bag, clothing, and perhaps some food, no longer in a rucksack but an internal-frame or external-frame pack; part or all the load is often transferred to bigger backs before camp.

Year by year carrying capacity increases. But parents must not be misled by the youngster's apparently unlimited energy into over-loading his growing, still-soft bones, lest in later years he suffer backpacker's backache.

At around nine or twelve the child carries all his own gear plus a fair share of the food, and parents dream about hiking with steadily lighter packs. However, along about this age independence is declared and Mama and Daddy experience new tribulations.

For one thing, youngsters want to walk faster than the family bunch and discover the country by themselves. The freedom should be encouraged within limits, such as ordering kids to stick strictly to the trail and wait up at forks; stay close to the folks in confusing terrain; give a blast on the emergency whistle if lost or confused; fall only into small rivers and over short cliffs.

For another, children grow bored with parents and seek more exciting tribal relationships. Inviting a pal on a hike adds a new dimension of fun for toddlers; with moody teens a confidant may save the trip. Ideally, compatible families with compatible children should be sought. But when two or more compatible families march

Harvey P. Manning and Trapper Nelson on the Pacific Crest National Scenic Trail. Photo by Harvey H. Manning.

into the wilds with their two or twenty compatible children, they must enforce discipline in order not to render an entire valley uninhabitable. Particular attention must be given to sanitation, since the ordinary human takes a dozen years to learn the manners a cat does while still a kitten.

A few years more, and no matter how closely Mama clutches her baby, he is gone with friends on his own adventures, perhaps to rejoin the old folks on family reunions. The pity is that just as Daddy thought he had it made, a pack mule or two thoroughly seasoned, they leave him in the lurch.

Well, there are always the grandchildren.

19
On Into Winter

Most hikers confine trail trips to summer, and for novices it's just as well, since wildlands are then friendliest and basics of walking and camping can be learned with least discomfort and danger.

Others, who love leaves budding in sudden warmth to green youth and turning in frost to yellow and red death, roam in spring and fall, seasons also offering more solitude.

Fewer think of winter as hiking time, yet the dark months can be bright, and when somber, speak perhaps more profoundly than the months of hot sun. Moreover, in winter the wilderness expands enormously beyond summer boundaries, reclaims large portions of its primeval domains.

The following brief discussion does not amount to even the sketchiest manual on winter travel, but this book cannot conclude without suggesting to the beginner the opportunities that await once he broadens horizons from a "hiking season" to the "hiking year."

BELOW THE SNOWLINE

In parts of America—including the entire South and the Pacific Coast west of the mountains—snow is unknown or infrequent in

Winter hiking at sea level.

lowlands and foothills; trails are open most, if not all, of the winter. A few air hours from the mainland are surfs and volcanoes and subtropical forests of Hawaii, magical over Christmas vacation.

Ocean beaches are never more exciting than in winter, and though the word is getting around, the January population on the sands is still a fraction of that in July.

Winter is the height of the season in some Southwest deserts. The semideserts of the Columbia Plateau and Great Basin often offer delightful walks over rolling ridges and up secret canyons dusted by sun-bright snow while windward slopes of coastal ranges are drenched by rain.

Not to be overlooked are low valleys reaching deep into wild mountains and in a normal winter snow-free (and snowmobile-free) all but several weeks. This is the lonesome time; even the roads, deserted by picnickers of summer and hunters of fall, provide quiet walks. Despite the camper-truck and vacation-trailer revolution, most auto campgrounds are comparatively empty and rarely does a walker feel crowded on trails.

For good reasons. In the latitude of Washington State at the winter solstice the sun is technically up just a bit more than eight hours and is so low in the south that during cloudy weather the entire short day is twilight; on backpacks the camp evenings are almost as much of the trip as actual travel; tent fever may rage. More clothing and other equipment are required to stay warm and dry—safe from hypothermia. From beaches to mountains, the storms are fierce.

The beginner is wisest to sharpen skills in summer, then try spring and fall. But he should not forget winter.

OUT IN THE GRAND WHITE

As winter white expands and contracts, so most hikers retreat and advance. However, more and more of those who value lonesomeness are breaking through the snow frontier, whether on frosted hills near home or in high mountains, where the landscape is totally transformed.

To be sure, North America is suffering a plague of snowmobiles and some time must pass before the patient consents to be cured. Until then, terrain too rough for machines or off limits through administrative ruling or by law (as in the case of National Wildernesses) remains a land of surpassing white peace.

Again there are reasons. Snow country is blizzard country, avalanche country, hypothermia country. Yet with the right equipment and technique any hiker of average strength and determination can experience the vast quiet (of spirit, that is; winds may be loud, very loud).

Booting

The most elementary method of snow travel is booting, identical to trail walking except for the surface differences, which range from minor to considerable.

Into the winter woods at low elevations.

A foot of early-winter fluff or slush impedes passage only slightly. A solid midwinter crust permits a good pace—until destroyed by sunshine, warm wind, or rain. On a late-spring snowpack, feet may sink to the ankles in cool morning—to the shins in hot afternoon.

When legs plunge knee-deep, as they jolly often do after a fresh snowfall, the death of a crust, or the creation by sun, wind, or rain of a snow swamp, the hiker progresses by "post-holing," a technique needing no explanation and deserving no recommendation; a strong party alternating leads may find ½ mile an hour a heroic pace.

Much snow-booting is so easy that a hiker wonders, once he's tried it, why he ever shied away. Even in the extremity of midwinter post-holing, though the effort demanded to get ¼ mile from plowed highway perhaps exceeds that of 4 miles on bare trail, the reward may be 16 times greater, may lead straight to faery. In such ranges as the Cascades, fanatic post-holers begin their travels of high valleys and ridges in April, two to three months earlier than conservatives, who wait for trails to turn from white to brown. Fanaticism pays.

Snowshoeing

When a hiker sinks to the knee, the hip, the waist, the chest, the eyebrows, booting is definitely inferior to webbing. A half century ago snowshoes rather abruptly gave way to skis in the favor of American recreationists, and for decades were virtually extinct. Then, with the general increase in every variety of winter outdoor activity, reflecting the need of urban people for the solace of nature in all

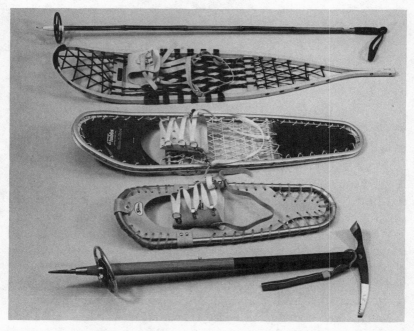

Several popular snowshoe models. The upper one is of an old traditional design, built of wood and rawhide. The lower two are newer, made of aluminum and nylon and plastic. For balance, snowshoers ordinarily use either a ski pole or an ice ax with "basket" attached.

Equipment for cross-country skiing: pole, Nordic ski and boot, spare tip, blowtorch (for waxing), waxing kit, scraper (some skis require no wax). Ordinary hiking gear completes the outfit.

seasons, webs made a comeback, were radically improved, and are now more popular than ever.

Snowshoeing is a go-anywhere sport, at the most advanced becoming winter mountaineering. The main attraction, however, is simplicity. The only significant addition to summer gear is a pair of snowshoes, costing about $125 (rentals available at many backpacking shops) and probably one or two ski poles. Shops with the shoes usually carry manuals on equipment and technique.

No extended training is necessary; with experience a hiker learns refinements, but his very first day he can go for miles, and after a few trial runs is ready to hoist pack and penetrate deep into the heart of winter.

Cross-country Skiing

Until the late 1960s the original form of skiing, cross-country touring, had been so overwhelmed in America by downhill running as to be little more than a memory. Even the few who kept the spark alive mainly used Alpine equipment, which had evolved for towhill conditions and was ill suited to mixed terrain. Then, the old Nordic skis returned to America in force and the cross-country revolution (or reaction) began.

Cross-country skiing is a sport quite different from that of the resorts, lacking the day-long succession of high-speed thrills and/or

balletlike patterns, and of course the effortless ascents and the mass socializing. In compensation? An easy grace all its own. No lift tickets pushing the family toward bankruptcy. The virgin white, and quiet, and wildness.

The technique, though not so elementary as snowshoeing, is far less complex than downhill running or alpine touring. Under expert tutelage a novice can learn enough on his first outing to cover many miles. In contrast to snowshoers, who do well to make 2 miles an hour and 10 miles a day, cross-country skiers of just ordinary strength and competence often slide along at 4 miles an hour on the flat, much faster on slopes, and in proper terrain consider 20 miles merely an average day.

Texts on equipment and techniques are available at shops that sell the gear.

Camping

Booters, snowshoers, cross-country skiers, all may wish to enlarge their knowledge of winter to include nights. Since pure water is all around, by use of a lightweight backpacker's snow shovel, camp can be made anywhere, excavating a flat bed, digging or molding tables and chairs and windbreaks—and in spring the architecture melts, leaving no evidence of the stay, no damage to underlying plants. With "four-season" tent, and sleeping bag, clothing, and other equipment described in earlier chapters, snow camping can be as comfortable as on bare ground, and in much of America offers the only guaranteed opportunity to get absolutely away from mobs.

AN EARTH FOR ALL SEASONS

Many hikers hibernate in winter, doing their share of the work of the world so they may vacation in summer with a clear conscience. But it's too bad for a person who loves trail country to know it in only one season, to miss the full experience of nature from birth to maturity to wearying unto death—the complete cycle of life.

Some wildlanders don't accept the analogy of winter as death, or the connotations of loss and sadness. They say winter is only gloomy viewed through a window from the stupefying interior of an over-heated house. Fly the coop, get out in it, and blood runs fast and spirits rise. For such folk, often of a classical temper as opposed to flower-loving romantics, winter is the uncluttered season, the months of cleanest wildness, the best time of year.

20

The New Ethic

Nature once certified outdoorsmen . . . But now there is such ease of transportation and so much improvement in equipment that anyone can become a wilderness traveler.

— J. V. K. Wagar, *American Forests* (November 1940)

People have scraped the world clean . . . and now they want to run from the dreadful places and find some nice safe country . . . All of them are on the run. They are frightened of the fire.

— V. S. Naipaul, *New York Review of Books* (May 3, 1979)

From cities and suburbs, from coast to coast, Americans are on the run. They run as they live—noisily. As long ago as 1920 Clarence Day, in *This Simian World*, said the din of a modern metropolis is precisely what any person familiar with zoos would expect of monkeys once they'd invented the internal-combustion engine. He hadn't heard nothin' yet. Were Day to revisit this planet and witness the Great American Run—passenger cars and four-wheel-drive pickups and jeeps, camper trucks and motor homes and trailers, motorcycles and snowmobiles and dune buggies and swamp buggies, motorboats and jet boats and Hovercraft, airplanes and helicopters—he'd add his voice to the growing prayer that Someone on high rip open the sky, lean through the hole, and bellow in Commandment, "KNOCK IT OFF DOWN THERE!"

Still, damaging as the racket is to ears and nerves, it's merely a by-product, a symptom. The serious and lasting harm is the squandering of fossil fuels, drowning of rivers, slashing of freeways through jungles and tundras, smelting of mountains, paving of farmlands with suburbs, proliferating of radioactive time bombs.

Only the most depraved real estate speculator could imagine the revels of the past half century continuing another half century—or quarter century. The party is ending, and as is usual with any orgy, in the jangles that are the prelude to crying jags, family quarrels, fistfights, and spitting up. Not nice at all. And so Americans are on the run.

Many—one sometimes feels, most—are evidencing saner instincts by running for the backcountry. However, some are so deranged by the fire, the city, they've lost all notion why they're running. Mounted on ORVs and ATVs, they're not escaping the orgy but simply moving the scene, destroying as they come. Seeing them razz into a wildland, a Disney chipmunk might well chitter, "Saints preserve us!"

And praise be, there truly are saints eager to live clean lives and do good works, and not a lonesome few but a splendid many. A paradox for philosophers: Can there be too much goodness? Apparently. For when the saints shoulder packs and come marching into the backcountry by the platoon, the regiment, the division, the army group, Mr. Chippy amends his chitter to "Saints preserve us from the saints!"

As is often said nowadays, "Formerly the problem was how a small band of travelers could survive in an enormous wilderness. Now it's how a small wilderness can survive an enormous number of people."

The number of people a wilderness can accommodate and survive—that is, remain "wild"—is its "carrying capacity." Everywhere, now, land managers are engaged in studies to determine the capacities of individual wildernesses, valleys, campsites. Again, they are required to be philosophers as well as scientists, to define "wilderness" in a modern context—since, obviously, there is no more wilderness anywhere on earth in the old sense, pre-population explosion, pre-airplane.

One thing they know for certain: A wilderness can "carry" vastly more light-foot walkers and no-trace campers than it can woodcrafters, pack trains, motorcycles, and helicopters. The way to make a wilderness larger is to go slower, quieter.

The U.S. Forest Service blundered in the late 1950s, early 1960s by complacently accepting on trails the first ridiculous little putt-

putt machines. Soon there was nothing to laugh about because the factories in Japan had tooled up and the American backcountry was a-roaring with trailbikers, who by the 1970s were claiming "historic rights." Better call them "wrongs." The mistake must be corrected. Machines must be banned not just from dedicated wildernesses but from all the horse-hiker trails of the nation, from all roadless deserts and prairies and beaches and tundras.

Horses are no noisier than hikers, and in appropriate terrain, in limited numbers, properly handled, little more destructive. Room must be saved for them. Though not for the olden-style thundering herds resembling the U.S. Cavalry headed for the Sand Creek Massacre.

Increasingly the command will be, "Lassie, go home." And Fido, too. Dogs are already excluded from National Park trails and recommended against in popular National Forest wildernesses.

So much for machines and beasts. What about people? When Porky said, "We have met the enemy and he is us," he didn't mean just him and Pogo and Churchy and the rest of the Okefenokee folks. Albert's cigar ain't the only one in the lemonade.

What to do about people? In 1978 the U.S. Forest Service published *Wilderness Management* (a book by John C. Hendee, George H. Stankey, and Robert C. Lucas, with contributions by such other scholars as Roderick Nash and Jerry Franklin), which tells the history of the wilderness concept and discusses the current state of the management art. Not only managers but hikers should study the text so they can participate intelligently in the parliament of wild-landers planning the future.

Plans currently are sketchy. Time since the population deluge has been too short to inventory lands and determine carrying capacities, perfect management techniques through trial and error—or agree on definitions of the "wilderness experience." Debate is unlikely to cease soon. And the end product probably will be plans that differ, as they do now, for National Parks, for dedicated wildernesses in National Forests, National Wildlife Refuges, and other jurisdictions, and for places not formally designated "wilderness" but regulated as "backcountry" or "roadless area" or "scenic area" or such.

The crux of any plan is: How should population be controlled? Everyone agrees that if the carrying capacity of a meadow, say, is determined to be X, when Mr. X + 1 wants to visit he must be denied, lest his boots stomp the flowers to a field of mud only swine could love. But how to handle Mr. X + 1? First, of course, by educating him away from that particular meadow to others equally pretty, or from weekends to midweeks, summers to springs-falls-winters. What if that doesn't work? Must he then be "rationed" in his use of wildlands by issuance of permits? Probably. But then, should the permits be issued at trailhead, ranger station, or headquarters? By mail, months in advance, as firm reservations, or in person, at time of entry, on a first-come first-served basis? In summary, how can a system be designed and fine-tuned to allow maximum visitation and freedom consistent with minimum impact?

The crux of population control is control of camps, where the average hiker spends 60 percent of his wilderness life and focuses more than that of his damage. Some managers, observing that for generations hikers have camped quite happily on bare dirt, argue for "sacrifice areas" where impact is concentrated to spare the surrouding pristinity. (The howls arise when any particular spot is proposed for sacrifice.) Others favor dispersion/minimal impact, accepting the sacrifice inevitable when sleeping bag touches ground but distributing the wear so widely as not to flagrantly mar the

natural appearance of a valley. (The moans arise when tennyrunner friars urge hammocks, sleeping on snow, walking all night.)

Very understandably, in view of the enormity of the task and the shortage of funds and personnel, managers love simple rules, such as no camping in sight of trails, no wood fires above 10,000 feet. The favorite is a ban on camps within a certain distance of water—100, even 200 feet—because waterside camps sometimes foul the water or crush plants, homesteading campers may hog the viewpoints, and such camps are so prominent that their sight and sound over the water is wastefully solitude-consuming.

While granting all this, other managers cite studies made in typical areas that show 90 percent of all campsites—those used by hikers over many generations—have a view of water and 85 percent are within 200 feet of water, nearly half within 50 feet. Can it be that people *like* camping near water, with views of water, and don't really mind bare dirt? Then perhaps it is officious to ruin their fun for the sake of a simple rule. Can it be that in many a valley the geological history has been such that the only campable ground is near water and that a distance of 200 feet would put campers up on cliffs with the goats or out in the swamp with Albert? Then perhaps a manager should walk through his jurisdiction before posting rules at trail-heads. Possibly, simplicity can be impractical, shortcuts that don't work can breed contempt for all regulations, however necessary and wise. The alternative is to judge each campsite on its own merits. Close those with unacceptable physical impacts on land and water or social impacts on the quality of the experience. When closing camps, provide enough others. Beware of personal prejudices, of inflexibility. The manager who breeds contempt for his regulations and himself breeds contempt for the wilderness ideal, endangers proposals to preserve more wilderness.

A policeman's lot is not a 'appy one. But policing there must be, even of wilderness, despite the internal contradiction so hard for old libertarians to stomach. However, management cannot be by simple rules. Rules are words. The language of the land is more complex. Managers must learn it. And not in classrooms and convention halls of the frontcountry. On the trails in the backcountry.

Hikers have a double responsibility. They must read and obey the rules, like them or not. But to debate them coherently when they don't, they must study the land. "An ecosystem includes all the organisms of an area, their environment, and a series of linkages or interactions between them." Ecology, the study of ecosystems, should be the hiker's passion, not merely to enrich his trail pleasure but so he can understand the functioning of the systems and how he can fit in unobtrusively.

The hiker should be a bird watcher and animal watcher and bug watcher. He should be curious about rocks and minerals, and note the slow process by which soil is created. And gain a feel for the dynamic balance of a river, of a glacier, and how they carve valleys. And grow intimate with trees and flowers, mosses and lichens, fungi and molds. And learn the meaning of a progression of clouds, a change in winds, and the relationship of the atmosphere to the mantle of living green and underlying rocks. And at night he should look out to the moon and stars and deeply comprehend this is the only earth we ever will have.

Comprehending that, he may well realize that the light-foot and no-trace camp is barely a start. More, much more "de facto wilderness" (wildlands man hasn't yet got around to plundering) must be statutorily protected as dedicated wilderness by addition to the National Wilderness System. Particularly in the East, and close to

large urban centers everywhere, much more "reconstituted wilderness" (lands now growing wild again, or with the potential to do so) must be set aside for eventual placement in the system.

But wilderness is only a part of a large planet. Or rather, a very small planet. For man to achieve a balance with the ecosystem of earth, whose carrying capacity of superconsumers already is far exceeded, wildland ideals must be transferred to the city. The hiker must work for zero population growth, minimum energy consumption, complete recycling of resources. To quote the old New England adage,

> Eat it up.
> Wear it out.
> Make it do.
> Do without.

Let the purified-in-wildness saints come marching in to city halls, county councils, state capitols, halls of Congress, the White House. In a democracy that operates through pressure groups, this means renouncing anarchism and joining up—adding voice and weight and dollars to one or several groups working to save the frogs in the local pond, forests of the skyline wilderness, whales in the ocean, man on the planet.

By such means Thoreau could be proven right in saying, "In Wildness is the preservation of the World." Let it be so assumed. Let the word go out that the wilderness expects every pedestrian to do his/her duty.

Index

Harvey Manning, wildland backpacker since the 1930s, edited the first two editions of *Mountaineering: The Freedom of the Hills*, contributed chapters to *Wilderness USA*, and is the author of *The Wild Cascades: Forgotten Parkland*, *The North Cascades National Park*, *National Parks of the Northwest*, *Washington Wilderness: The Unfinished Work*, *Walking the Beach to Bellingham*, *On the Trail of the Milky Way*, *Gods, Devils, and Wilderness Pedestrians*, five trail guides to the Cascades and Olympics, and a dozen other books on hiking, climbing, and conservation. For his four-volume series, *Footsore 1–4: Walks and Hikes Around Puget Sound*, he walked 3,000 miles and wore out three pairs of boots surveying trail routes from the cities to the wilderness.

Keith Gunnar, a free-lance photographer, has hiked and climbed from Alaska to Peru, from New Zealand to the Alps, in the Himalayas and throughout the American West. His work has been published in numerous books, magazines, and calendars. He conducts photo classes and workshops and frequently leads seminars and treks involving outdoor adventure activities.

Bob Cram, a free-lance commercial artist, is well known among climbers for his lively cartoons in *Mountaineering: The Freedom of the Hills* and among skiers for his contributions to *Ski* and *Skiing* magazines. He is an avid alpine and cross-country skier but has taken time off from the snows to illustrate a number of books on various subjects—including dictionaries of running and skiing—and to make frequent appearances on television as spokesman for a supermarket chain.